Real Options and Business Strategy
APPLICATIONS TO DECISION-MAKING

Real Options and Business Strategy
APPLICATIONS TO DECISION-MAKING

Edited by Lenos Trigeorgis

Published by Risk Books, a division of Risk Publications.

Haymarket House
28–29 Haymarket
London SW1Y 4RX
Tel: +44 (0)171 484 9700
Fax: +44 (0)171 484 9758
E-mail: books@risk.co.uk
Home Page: http://www.riskpublications.com

Introductory overview © Financial Engineering Ltd, 1999
This compilation © Financial Engineering Ltd, 1999

ISBN 1 899332 47 2

British Library Cataloguing in Publication Data
A catalogue record for this book is available from the British Library

Risk Books Commissioning Editor: Conrad Gardner
Project Editor: Bridie Selley
Pre-press: Lindsey Hofmeister and Martin Llewellyn
Typesetter: Marie Doherty

Printed and bound in Great Britain by Bookcraft (Bath) Ltd, Somerset.

Contents

Authors

P. Balasubramanian is an assistant professor of management information systems in the department of information systems, Boston University. His current research interests include designing knowledge management systems using concepts from systems design; hypertext design and workflow management; exploring the role of IT architectures in delivering business capabilities; querying complex dynamic systems; hypermedia design and development; and model management systems. Professor Balasubramanian received his PhD from New York University with a minor in computer science.

Yann Bonduelle is a partner at PricewaterhouseCoopers' financial advisory services. He leads the European practice of the applied decision analysis group of corporate value consulting. In the life sciences, high tech, and automotive industries, Dr Bonduelle is involved with developing business, market, and product strategies using ADA's real option valuation process and models of customer purchase decisions and market dynamics. His expertise has focused on delivering operational strategies in the areas of product design and development, pricing, introduction of new products into new markets, product portfolio planning, adoption of new technologies, customer satisfaction, and customer segmentation. In addition, Dr Bonduelle is also working in the area of R&D project valuation and portfolio strategy, concentrating on technology strategy portfolio issues. He received a BA in electrical engineering from the Institut National des Sciences Appliquées (INSA) and his MA and PhD in engineering-economic systems from Stanford University.

Peter Carr is a principal at Banc of America Securities LLC. He is the head of equity derivatives research and is also a visiting assistant professor at Columbia University. He is currently an associate editor for six academic journals and is the practitioner director for the Financial Management Association. Prior to his current position at Banc of America, he spent three years in equity derivatives research at Morgan Stanley and eight years as a professor of finance at Cornell University. He has published articles in numerous finance journals. His research interests are primarily in the field of derivative securities, especially American-style and exotic derivatives. He has consulted for several firms and has given numerous talks at both practitioner and academic conferences. He received his PhD in finance from UCLA in 1989.

Prasad Chalasani is currently a quantitative research analyst at HBK Investments, a hedge fund in New York City. He received his BTech (1987) in Computer Science from the Indian Institute of Technology, and his PhD (1994) in Computer Science from Carnegie Mellon University. Prasad has published journal articles on combinatorial optimisation and approximation algorithms, on-line algorithms, and the pricing of path-dependent derivatives. His current interests include the analysis of models for pricing derivatives in the presence of transaction costs and in the application of optimisation techniques to derivatives analysis.

Richard Chatwin is an assistant director of the applied decision analysis group of corporate value at PricewaterhouseCoopers in London. He has nearly ten years of experience in developing and implementing mathematical models to address business decisions. At the applied decision analysis group of PWC, Richard developed a real options methodology for asset valuation in the oil and gas industry, quantitative models of planning processes for electric utilities and statistical analyses and optimisation models to support market analysis in the computer and automobile industries. Dr Chatwin received a BA and a MA in mathematics from Cambridge University and a PhD in operations research from Stanford University.

Larry Chorn has applied real options analysis to complex capital budgeting issues for more than five years. His experience includes more than fifty real options analyses involving more than US$25 billion in capital. He has presented seminars worldwide and written five articles on real options. He is a visiting faculty member at The American Graduate School of International Management. Previously, Dr Chorn was Mobil Oil Corporation's valuation advisor for exploration and production. His career also includes positions as R&D planning manager and senior research advisor. He received his PhD in chemical engineering from the University of Illinois. More recently, he received his MBA from Southern Methodist University.

Gonzalo Cortazar is a professor at the Pontificia Universidad Católica de Chile. He is also president of Cortazar & Schwartz Financial Research and Consulting where he works extensively on real option valuation for natural resource companies. Prior to his current academic position he has served as an executive for several companies. Professor Cortazar has published many research papers in academic journals such as *The Journal of Business* and *Management Science* and lectured extensively to practitioners in Latin America. He holds a MBA, a MA in economics and a PhD in management (finance) from UCLA, with an undergraduate degree in industrial engineering from PUC-Chile.

Marco Antônio Guimarães Dias has been a Petroleum Engineer with Petrobras since 1983, working with the economic analysis of Exploration & Production (E&P) projects since 1989. He is the External Financial Relations Coordinator of E&P. Marco holds a Master of Science in Production Engineering, Finance and Investment Analysis, by PUC-Rio, with a thesis on real options applied to E&P investment. He teaches regular courses on real options in Petrobras and eventual courses in Brazilian universities. He has been developing real options analysis in Petrobras, and is also a member of the Real Options Group (ROG) on the Corporate Advisory Board.

David Epstein is a founding director of DH1 Software. His most recent publications include *A Nonlinear Non-probabilistic Spot Interest Rate Model* and the instructors' manual for *Derivatives: The Theory and Practice of Financial Engineering*. He is currently pursuing the possibility of a move from academia to the city. He has just completed a DPhil in uncertain interest rate theory at Oxford University during which he engaged in consulting work and course tuition for a number of financial institutions.

Anne Goodchild is a manager at PricewaterhouseCoopers' applied decision analysis group of corporate value, consulting in London. Her experience is in applying mathematical modelling to product planning and development. Her project experience includes market strategy analysis projects involving quantitative modelling, conjoint analysis and software system development for high tech, automotive, and health care companies. Ms Goodchild specialises in mathematical modelling of consumer behaviour and market forecasting and has researched mathematical models of natural systems. She received a BA degree in mathematics from the University of California at Davis.

Franchee Harmon is a director at PricewaterhouseCoopers in London. She directs the technology, information and communications team of corporate value consulting, including the internet sector. She has worked for more than five years on economic and strategic issues relating to project assessment and valuation, serving as the lead consultant or strategist on engagements. Her team developed the high-tech Toolkit product as a means to assist understanding the value potential of early-stage businesses. She received a BA in construction engineering from Bradley University and a MA in business administration from the Graduate School of Business at the University of Chicago, with specialisation in finance.

Somesh Jha is a post-doctoral fellow in the computer science department at the Carnegie Mellon University. His main areas of interest are in formal methods with applications to communication protocols, software engineering, computational finance, and developing financial software. He is also interested in applications of economics to software engineering decision making and electronic commerce.

Nalin Kulatilaka is a professor of finance at the School of Management at Boston University. Professor Kulatilaka's current research examines the strategic use of real options and risk management tools. He is the co-author of *Real Options: Managing Strategic Investments in an Uncertain World* (1999). He received his degrees from Imperial College London, Harvard University and the MIT.

Onno Lint is affiliated as a senior research fellow with the Erasmus University Rotterdam and the Eindhoven University of Technology. His research program mainly focuses on option pricing techniques for R&D decision making. He has had many articles published in the European Journal of Operational Research, Long Range Planning, and R&D Management. He set up his own consulting company and served over a hundred small and medium-sized enterprises on new product development. He recently sold his stock in order to concentrate more on academic work and to serve major R&D-driven companies in the evaluation and selection of R&D projects. In particular, he has served the research departments of Philips Electronics, BSC/Hoogovens, Thomson-CSF/HSA, and KPN.

Nick Mayor is a pan-European, e-commerce and retail analyst at ABN AMRO. Having since joined the bank in 1997 he has worked extensively in the field of real option valuation, publishing both in academic literature and in ABN AMRO publications to the investment community. His current research includes the evaluation of internet market opportunities and start-up companies as real options. Nick has a BA in PPE and a MPhil in economics both from Oxford University.

João Mazzuco is an executive of the applied decision analysis group of corporate value at PricewaterhouseCoopers in London. At PWC Mr Mazzuco has undertaken strategy analysis and real option valuation work in the high tech, biotech and oil and gas industries. He has over ten years experience working in the oil and gas industry, where he has extensively used statistical models for the design of sub sea production facilities, as well as developed and implemented probabilistic models for the evaluation of offshore construction operations. He received a BA and a MA in naval architecture and ocean engineering from the University of São Paulo and a MA in decision sciences from the London School of Economics.

Alberto Micalizzi is professor of finance at Bocconi University and at Bocconi Business School (SDA). He also teaches in the PhD programme at

Imperial College London and the Centre for Quantitative Finance. He is a partner and director of the Real Options Group (ROG). He specialises in capital budgeting, financial markets, derivatives and risk management. He has previously consulted in the pharmaceutical sector, media and telecommunication, automotive, banking and other industries. He has been employed by such multinational firms as Glaxo Wellcome, Ernst & Young, Eli Lilly, Nomura International, Danone Group and Schering Plough. He has published books and articles on real options and valuation under uncertainty.

Arun S. Muralidhar is vice president and head of currency research at JP Morgan Investment Management. Prior to joining JPMIM he was a member of the Investment Management Committee and head of research at the World Bank. He has taught in the MIT Sloan Fellows Executive program and has been a guest lecturer at MIT for Professor Modigliani. Dr Muralidhar holds a PhD in managerial economics from the MIT Sloan School of Management. His dissertation explored the impact of volatility of tax regimes, currencies and input costs on the valuation and real location decision of multinational enterprise.

Enrico Pennings is a visiting professor at University Pompeu Fabre. His research mainly focuses on real options and managerial decision making. He has been a visiting scholar at MIT, and has held research fellow positions at the Erasmus University Rotterdam and the Catholic University of Leuven. He has had articles published in Economics Letters, European Economic Review, European Journal of Operational Research, and Journal of Futures Markets. He is also a consultant to the European Commission and Philips Corporate Research.

Justin Pettit is a partner of Stern Stewart & Co. He has worked in many industries including banking, insurance and financial services, manufacturing, marketing and distribution, retailing, mining, cargo and liner shipping, cellular communications and hotels and gaming. His previous experience includes Citibank's global structured finance group and several years in a variety of engineering positions with a global automotive supplier. Publications include case studies in derivatives and structured finance and articles for *The Journal of Applied Corporate Finance*, *Corporate Finance Review*, *Canadian Investment Review*, *Business Quarterly*, *The National Post* and *The Globe & Mail*. Justin is a referee for the *Journal of Financial Practice and Education* and holds a MBA (Western) and a BASc in mechanical engineering.

Vibha Sazawal received her BS in systems engineering from the University of Virginia. She is now a PhD candidate in the department of computer science and engineering at the University of Washington. Her research interests include the design and development of large-scale software systems, particularly the tradeoffs made in design and development decisions.

Philipp Schönbucher is a researcher at the department of statistics, Bonn University. His main area of interest is credit risk modelling and credit derivatives pricing on which he has written several papers and led professional training courses. He has also published papers on stochastic volatility models, market illiquidity, real options and exotic option pricing. He holds an MSc in mathematics from Oxford University, a Diploma in economics from Bonn University and is close to completion of his PhD in economics at Bonn University.

Han T.J. Smit is associate professor of finance at Erasmus University. He has been a visiting scholar at Boston University and Columbia University. Dr Smit has experience in researching corporate finance, strategy and uses a combination of real options and game theory to model competitive strategies. He has published several articles on financial management. He received a MBA from Erasmus University and his Phd from the University of Amsterdam.

John E. Stonier is an Airline Marketing Director for Airbus Industrie. During the last few years he has been involved in many sales campaigns with major international airlines around the world, and is currently located at the company's North American headquarters in Herndon Virginia. He has published articles on the aircraft acquisition process, and specialises in the latest investment appraisal techniques and their application to the airline and aircraft manufacturing industries. John is a graduate of Manchester University England, with a BS in Aeronautical Engineering and an MBA from Manchester Business School.

John Storck is an assistant professor of management information systems at the Boston University School of Management and is director of the Master of Science programme in management information systems. Professor Storck joined the Boston University faculty after an extensive career in industry, which included several years working in Europe as a vice president of the Chase Manhattan Bank.

Kevin Sullivan is now assistant professor in the department of computer science at the University of Virginia. His research in software engineering focuses on design modularity and evolution. He has projects in component software, software economics, reliability and the dependability of software for critical infrastructures. He publishes in the IEEE Transactions on

Software Engineering, IEEE Transactions on Reliability, and ACM Transactions on Software Engineering and Methodology. He has also written articles, chapters and software on nuclear arms control and radiotherapy planning for cancer. He received a BA in mathematics and computer science from Tufts University in 1987 and his MS and PhD in computer science and engineering from the University of Washington.

Alexander J. Triantis is an associate professor of finance at the Robert H. Smith School of Business at the University of Maryland. Previously he was a faculty member at the MIT Sloan School of Management (as a visiting scholar) and the University of Wisconsin. He has published over a dozen articles in the area of real options in academic journals including *Journal of Finance*, *Journal of International Economics*, *Journal of Law and Economics* and *Management Science* and in practitioner journals such as *Risk* and *Mergers and Acquisitions*. He is an editor of *Financial Management*. He has consulted and provided executive training in the areas of real options analysis, risk management, derivatives pricing, capital budgeting, and project finance for numerous multinational corporations and organisations. He received his PhD from Stanford University.

Lenos Trigeorgis is professor of finance at the University of Cyprus and until recently, was a visiting professor of finance at the University of Chicago, Columbia University and Bocconi University. He previously taught at Boston University and the University of Massachusetts. He has been published in numerous journals on corporate finance, competition and strategy and capital budgeting; he serves on the editorial boards of several journals. He has edited several volumes and is the author of *Real Options* (1996). Dr Trigeorgis is the president of the Real Options Group (ROG) and he holds a PhD (DBA) from Harvard University.

Elizabeth Whalley is currently a lecturer in finance at Warwick Business School. Previously she was Research Fellow in the department of economics at the University of Surrey. She has also taught at Oxford University and is an editor of *Applied Mathematical Finance*. Her research interests include the modelling of investment decisions using real options, in particular incorporating time to build, the impact of market imperfections, in particular transaction costs, on the valuation and hedging of derivative securities and the effect of liquidity constraints on firms and households.

Paul Wilmott is a quantitative financial consultant and trainer with Wilmott Associates. He is the author of many research articles, books and models in finance. His book *Derivatives* was for many months the top-selling quantitative finance textbook.

Introduction

Lenos Trigeorgis

University of Cyprus and Real Options Group

Real options is currently revolutionising decision making across corporate America and among leading corporations around the world. Real options is a new valuation, project management and strategic decision-making paradigm that allows for making flexible or staged decisions under uncertainty. It captures the value of managerial flexibility to adapt and revise decisions at a future time under the right conditions with the benefit of better information.

Real options is moving from early applications in natural resources/energy and real estate, to new product development in pharmaceuticals and valuation in high tech industries. Applications are now seen in the transportation (cars, airlines), infrastructure (eg, power, telecommunications, information technology), investment banking (IPOs, M&As, corporate restructuring), and the multimedia/intellectual property sectors. Indeed, real options is coming to be seen not only as a valuation tool, but as a management process. Once its link to broader risk management, performance measurement and the incentives/compensation system becomes a reality, it will provide a holistic, enterprise package solution that will allow it to also serve as a change process and an organisational model.

We are in the midst of a revolution in managerial thinking and practice that may eventually touch all industries and most major corporations. Improvements are being made incrementally, but at an accelerating pace. The chapters in this book provide a taste of this incremental progress and excitement. The first chapters discuss the links of real options with shareholder value, business strategy, and value-based management. The next group of chapters present actual applications in various contexts and industries, from pharmaceutical R&D, to airline purchase options, to evaluation of e-business start ups, to information technology (infrastructure) justification, and software design insights. A number of chapters follow, dealing with the value of learning and acquiring information in natural resources and other contexts, as well as the flexibility acquired from a network of multi-national operations.

In the first part, Alberto Micalizzi and Lenos Trigeorgis (Chapter 1), of the Real Options Group, provide a comprehensive overview of corporate project evaluation and strategy through the real options perspective. After reviewing the basic determinants of risk and the notion of the cost of capital under uncertainty in light of shareholder value maximisation, they discuss investment opportunities as a source of generating corporate real options, the various types of such options, and their occurrence in different industry sectors over various development phases of a project. Following a project classification scheme, they discuss some benefits or real options analysis as well as future directions and applications.

Han Smit and Lenos Trigeorgis (Chapter 2), also of the Real Options Group, consider a firm's growth opportunities as a package of corporate real options that is actively managed by the firm and that may be affected by competitive actions, such that various strategic considerations of importance to practising managers can be finally brought into the analysis in a rigorous fashion, that is consistent with the tenets of both industrial organisation and modern finance. They suggest that a combination of real options analysis and game theory can help answer many strategic questions that are important for corporate success in dynamic and volatile industries, such as: what is the value of the growth opportunities in the business? When is it appropriate to speed up investment in order to capture a larger market share or pre-empt competitive entry altogether, and when is it better to maintain the flexibility of a "wait-and-see" approach? Should the firm compete in R&D or is it more beneficial to take an accommodating stance vis-à-vis competition (eg, via a joint research venture that may allow not only sharing of costs but also implicit coordination and appropriation of the option value of waiting, in light of demand uncertainty)? They also suggest that real options thinking can help explain (at least part of) the seemingly high market valuations observed nowadays in a number of dynamic industries, by properly accounting for the strategic option characteristics of a firm's growth opportunities.

Alexander Triantis (Chapter 3), of the University of Maryland, provides an interesting discussion about creating and managing shareholder value through a real options perspective. The option analogy is examined in detail and examples of strategic investment opportunities in different industries are provided. Triantis focuses the chapter on understanding how to create options within a firm, how to protect and enhance the value of these options, and how best to exercise these options. He goes on to explore how real options analysis can help a firm better plan its financing, portfolio optimisation, risk management, and compensation strategies in relation to shareholder value creation.

Justin Pettit (Chapter 4), of Stern Stewart & Co., revisits value-based management and economic value added (EVA) not merely as a metrics and measurement tool, but also attuning it with management processes, such as planning, portfolio management and strategy, as well as the compensation and incentive systems. After motivating the need to focus on shareowner value and pointing out pitfalls of traditional performance measurement (overinvestment, overproduction, "starve the stars" and "feed the dogs") he discusses a framework for linking performance measurement, value and strategy and he illustrates his points by discussing cases from various sectors (such as brewing and pharmaceuticals). The role and importance of real options thinking in the overall process is crucial, particularly in dynamic and volatile industries. He finally discusses various aspects of financial policy and the need to match it with business strategy.

In the second part, Alberto Micalizzi (Chapter 5), of the Real Options Group, discusses an actual application of real options analysis in evaluating product development and expansion opportunities for a new pharmaceutical (antibiotic) product at Glaxo Wellcome. He provides not only an interesting discussion of classic issues and questions faced by management in the new product development area, but also an evaluation of the various options and their interactions: the option to discontinue development (at the third stage of clinical trials), and the option to expand the market by later launching a solid version following the oral product version. Capturing the non-additivity of option values is important for proper evaluation and decision making.

Onno Lint and Enrico Pennings (Chapter 6) describe an option model capturing business shifts or jumps in market, competitive or technology conditions and discuss a set of qualitative managerial support tools (scoring models etc), to help evaluate and manage a portfolio of R&D options based on experiences of utilising real options insights at Philips Electronics. The desired R&D portfolio attempts to balance short-term projects having rather sure payoffs with the long-shots or blockbusters (having low arrival frequency but high impact). A classification based on arrival (frequency) and impact is presented, and related strategic and organisational issues are discussed.

John Stonier (Chapter 7), of Airbus Industrie, discusses the value of the option to purchase aircraft by an airline who must adapt to changes related to its overall fleet capacity and aircraft mix as well as corresponding issues for the manufacturer. He particularly focuses on the flexibility created by reducing manufacturer lead time in aircraft delivery and by product standardisation (operational, design and manufacturing commonality, eg, via identical aircraft of different sizes). Interesting questions in the airline business include: what is the value of aircraft purchase options to an airline (and the cost to the manufacturer)? How should manufacturers allocate options to maximise value added? What is the value of shortened lead times? What is the optimal contractual design of orders?

Richard Chatwin and his co-authors (Chapter 8), of PricewaterhouseCoopers, discuss a case study of valuing an e-business start up to demonstrate an ROV process, based on standard decision tree analysis rather than option pricing. High-tech companies face major uncertainties, such as the acceptance of new technology and the pace of technological change, competitive threat and short product cycles, making real options valuation very useful. They examine a structured discussion process with management to help identify key uncertainties, decisions and options, a market model for identifying different scenarios in the broader environment, a learning model of the company's decision process and a consumer choice model for forecasting sales under various scenarios. Finally, they interpret the key information that results when the decision tree output is used to value the company under various scenarios.

Nalin Kulatilaka and his co-authors (Chapter 9), of Boston University, discuss a framework using real options to evaluate investments in information technology (IT) infrastructure. IT (and general infrastructure) investments are inherently difficult to value because, although the costs are easily identifiable, many of the benefits are elusive and contingent on future events. They address a number of related interesting questions: how should IT investments be evaluated and managed consistent with corporate strategy? How can they be justified prospectively, and their success measured retrospectively? What other investments are needed to realise their full potential and how can they be managed over time? The authors recognise that the design and justification of technology investments begins with the set of desired capabilities that derive from the business goals and that such investments help transform today's capabilities into those desired for the future. They discuss the linkage of capabilities to value and illustrate their approach in the case of National Mortgage Trust's acquisition of a large IT investment.

Kevin Sullivan and his co-authors (Chapter 10) identify problems in software design due to the lack of an underlying theory, for example, in making tradeoffs in design involving flexibility in the face of uncertainty or in understanding the connections among basic design concepts such as information hiding or spiral process, and draft Real Options theory to help bridge the gap. To help provide a more reasoned and unified account of software design concepts, they view software design as an investment process under uncertainty (eg, in market or technology trends or changes in requirements) and try to assess the value of flexibility that software design unlocks. Information hiding is seen as creating flexibility to change systems at a modular level, while a spiral process is now seen as a value-enhancing (rather than merely risk-reducing) practice that creates flexibility to change the development path as uncertainties become resolved. Sensitivity to real options parameters leads to a set of qualitative design principles largely consistent with accepted good practice, but now grounded in theory and supported with options insight. For example, the flexibility to wait provides a basis for refining the commonly used heuristic calling for delay of design decisions until they are forced.

Gonzalo Cortazar (Chapter 11), of Pontificia Universidad Católica de Chile, provides an overview of the use of real options in the valuation of natural resources. He discusses the pitfalls of traditional NPV and shows why a real options approach, based on arbitrage valuation and taking account of market information contained in futures prices, is better suited for valuing natural resource investments by more properly handling the estimation of relevant cash flows, optimal operating decisions during the life of the project, and properly adjusting for risk. He then discusses some recent advances that can enhance the value and applicability of real options for practitioners, for example in the area of modelling commodity price uncertainty or extending Monte Carlo simulation to handle American-type option problems with early exercise features.

Larry Chorn and Peter Carr (Chapter 12) use real options techniques to value information and learning in natural resource or energy projects. Management manages risks in such projects by making staged or incremental investments as new information reduces underlying uncertainties to acceptable levels. The authors view acquiring information (eg, via seismic tests, well testing or appraisal drilling) as purchasing an option on the project, and apply their ideas to value the information surrounding a production capacity decision for an offshore gas field development project. Thus, they value not only the basic field development alternatives but also the option to acquire incremental information along the way and use that information to realise additional value over the project's life.

David Epstein and his co-authors (Chapter 13) model the value added to a firm of undertaking market research into a particular product opportunity. The authors investigate the way in which information regarding the potential of the project arrives and how, during its life, the evolving knowledge is modelled using the theory of optimal filtering. The value of the project and optimal entrance decision rule is then derived as the solution to a partial differential equation, using boundary conditions that reflect the structure of the project.

Arun Muralidhar (Chapter 14), of JP Morgan, discusses strategic decisions facing multinational enterprises (MNEs) to gain competitive advantages in the global marketplace by responding flexibly to changing market conditions and taking advantage of cost and other disparities across markets. Such disparities may relate to uncertainties in product demand, relative input factors, exchange rate differentials etc. MNEs can be seen as having a switching option across countries allowing flexibility to optimally manage a network of economic activities. Such switching flexibility has an impact on strategic decisions relating to the location of the MNE's global economic activities, maintenance of excess capacity, and possibly investment timing choices. Empirical wage data across countries are provided to support the presented model with flexibility to switch production across countries. The analysis and sensitivity results provide interesting insights, eg, concerning the impact of European integration (and the resulting reduction of cross-country correlations) on the MNE's flexibility value.

Finally, Marco A.G. Dias, of Petrobas, provides a note with a perspective to the bibliographical evolution of real options and a related bibliography.

It is hoped that the chapters in this book, by illustrating a variety of real options applications in a spectrum of industries, and by providing conceptual linkages to important issues in strategy, value-based management, capabilities, learning and other important value drivers, will help advance the practice and stimulate further developments in the theory of the real options valuation and management paradigm.

Project Evaluation, Strategy and Real Options

Alberto Micalizzi*‡ and Lenos Trigeorgis†‡

*Bocconi University; †University of Cyprus and ‡Real Options Group

In the on-going debate over risk management in investment decision-making, many of the assumptions underlying traditional methods of capital budgeting must be reconsidered in light of real options theory. Under traditional analysis, including net present value (NPV) and other techniques based on discounted cashflow (DCF) analysis, the impact of risk is one-directional: risk presumably depresses the value of the investment. By contrast, real options show that risk can be influenced through managerial flexibility, which becomes a central instrument for value creation. Under such circumstances, uncertainty may amplify the value of an investment opportunity.

If the role of risk is revised in this way, it also becomes necessary to reconsider the concept of the opportunity cost of capital, and all the traditional theories of value creation based on the opportunity cost concept. For example, the notion of opportunity cost must be adjusted to take into account the value of strategic opportunities arising from a project.

Under uncertainty, it is also important to consider the issue of investment timing. This now involves the cost (or value) of renouncing the option to defer a project's implementation until an optimal future moment, and of conditioning the investment decision on a favourable evolution of the state (or reference) variables.

From this basic concept of value determination, one can proceed to incorporate other types of corporate real options that capture the inherent value of active management of the risk factor.

BASIC RISK DETERMINANTS: AN OVERVIEW

Before initiating a discussion on risk and uncertainty, it is first necessary to define the determinants of risk, ie, the factors responsible for the volatility of business results. For this purpose, a "map" of risk areas is presented below, in which each risk area is examined in relation to its role in managerial flexibility. Generally, risk can be broken down into the following categories.

Operational and financial risk

This refers to the variability of business results deriving from the operational structure of a firm, ie, from the nature of a firm's business activities. This risk becomes more evident upon breaking down a firm's costs into fixed and variable costs.[1] The mix, or balance, of fixed versus variable costs is an important indicator of operating risk. Both industry analysts and investors recognise the usefulness of this ratio. All other factors being equal, an operating structure characterised by a prevalence of fixed costs is rigid and difficult to modify when production levels or market conditions change. The degree of a cost structure's rigidity significantly conditions the effects that changes in volume may have on operating results; the effect that sales variations can have on operating results is a direct consequence of the weighting of fixed costs, a concept known as "operating leverage."[2]

Operational risk

The concept of operational risk is of immense importance in understanding the role of managerial flexibility – and the problem of irreversible investment decisions. High fixed costs tend to render many corporate decisions difficult to reverse, and often require significant "reconversion costs". Given such irreversible costs, there is value to the possibility of delaying a project's implementation under uncertainty, and conditioning such decisions on a favourable evolution of the state (or reference) variables. This conditioning is particularly important in the case of sequential investments or compound options, in which each investment stage becomes the basis for an option to acquire the next stage of investment.

Interest rate and exchange rate risk

Beyond operational risk, it is possible for a business operation to be affected by two types of financial risk: interest rate and exchange rate risk. Interest rate risk originates from the possibility that, with a given term structure, a variation of market interest rates can cause an unforeseen opportunity cost for the firm due to a discrepancy between active and passive rates – ie, the mismatching risk. Moreover, a variation in interest rates may cause a variation in the prices of financial activities. This is the case in which a fixed-rate bond's price and value decreases when rates increase, and vice versa.

Similarly, the problem of exchange rate risk arises when there are changes in the active and passive values of the currency in question. In this case, the risk can have a purely transactional effect if the fluctuations in exchange rates affect commercial operations. Alternatively, exchange rate risk could have a translation effect if currency values are transformed in the process of preparing a holding company's consolidated financial statements. The problem arises when reconciling the statements of affiliates that operate in currencies other than the currency of the holding company.

The interest rate and exchange rate risk may of course be interrelated, being central to strategic choices, especially for firms wishing to relocate their production to emerging economies. Under such circumstances, a clear understanding of financial risks allows a proper strategic analysis, and therefore the identification of relevant strategic options. One such option might be to shift production between two countries whose exchange rates fluctuate, with the objective of dynamically minimising production costs. In this case, the option to switch among alternative operation modes constitutes an important source of managerial flexibility. Such flexibility allows a reconsideration of the total investment value.

Firm-specific versus systematic risk

A second cut of analysis identifies a distinction between firm-specific versus systematic risk.[3] Aware of the diverse nature of risk, investors seek to diversify their investments by selecting particular combinations of securities to offset the part of risk that may be diversified. Such a portfolio composition is then presumably subject only to factors arising from systematic risks. The risk of a specific activity can then be measured on the basis of its marginal contribution to the riskiness of a well-diversified market portfolio. The measurement of such risk is represented by the covariance between the returns of the individual investment and the market portfolio.

Industry risk

Coming to industry risk, it is useful to identify two additional determinants of risk: competitor and technology risk.

Competitor risk

Competitor risk originates from the possibility that the tactical–strategic choices by principal competitors will have consequences on the industry structure and the cost-earnings of a firm. For example, aggressive attack strategies based on price-competition; the introduction of innovative products to the market; mergers and acquisitions that create vertical integration; and bold cost-cutting investments that shift the production efficiency curves of an industry. The topic of competitive interaction offers some of the most promising opportunities to apply and further develop Real Options theory for two reasons. First, the abandonment of deterministic types of valuation allows the formulation of strategic decisions that otherwise could not be taken into consideration in an organic analysis scheme. Second, many of the most important industry sectors – ie, pharmaceutical, oil and transportation – are assuming an oligopolistic structure, and this makes the evaluation of strategic decisions that impact on competition even more critical.

Technological risk

Technological risk is partially related to competitor risk, and can be thought of as the combination of the factors that can cause a firm's loss of competitiveness. This applies especially to those sectors characterised by continuous technological innovation (eg, internet/e-commerce, biotech). Specific sources of risk can be tied to both the well-known phenomenon of technological obsolescence and the loss of competitiveness, in terms of costs as well as quality. Uncertainty and managerial flexibility in the case of technology unlock new horizons for valuation. The process of innovation is by definition uncertain, and a critical challenge arises in defining the most advantageous time to invest in innovation. Theoretically, the best moment to invest is when the expected benefits – broadly defined to include any option value – exceed the opportunity cost of invested capital. One important application is in the pharmaceutical sector, where enabling technologies such as genomics and combinatorial chemistry have been playing an increasingly important role in improving the R&D efficiency, thus allowing companies to optimise the stop–go decisions related to their pipeline. From this perspective, Real Options theory offers notable advantages over traditional valuation methods, especially when considering the strategic timing to either invest in the next stage of the project, or defer.

Market-demand risk

Market-demand risk provides another angle from which to analyse the determinants of volatility. This type of risk can be easily identified in the area of customer satisfaction, due to the volatility in consumer needs and preferences that may leave the firm unprepared. Such risk crosses over into other categories that have already been mentioned. For instance, the risk arising from a firm's inability to quickly adapt to changing consumer tastes is related to competitor risk. There are, of course, sectors in which market-demand risk is prevalent, such as the tourism and automotive sectors. Market-demand risk underlines the important role that managerial flexibility can have in the formulation of strategic positions and product choices. Product families or simple combinations of complementary products can be evaluated in the broader context of the client-market relationship. It is in this context that many of the more noteworthy opportunities for market expansion create value. An example is the option to expand.

Country risk

Finally, there may be country risk stemming from the commercial and industrial relationship between firms and the country's governmental organs. Country risk is particularly important in relation to South American and East Asian countries, the two most important commercial areas outside Western economies. The individual sources of risk may vary. One example might be the risk represented by the possibility of local authorities revoking a firm's authorisation to operate inside a particular country. Another example could be non-recognition of foreign credit due to economic fluctuations in that country, such as changes in the inflation rate, interest rate or GDP.

Even at the level of country risk, there is a role for managerial flexibility as a source of value creation under uncertainty. Firms often evaluate the level of attractiveness or risk profile of a country by applying a mix of economic-financial variables based on the concept of country competitiveness. These variables are typically financial, such as the exchange rate. There are also economic variables, such as the inflation of the country under evaluation. In particular, the binomial exchange rate–inflation is often a significant factor in the decision to allocate resources among various countries.

SHAREHOLDER VALUE AND THE COST OF CAPITAL UNDER UNCERTAINTY

The underlying principle of value creation is that the return of an investment must remunerate the opportunity cost of invested capital. The most common application of this principle is the Discounted Cashflow (DCF) approach. In conjunction with the theory of capital markets, the DCF approach identifies an investment project's opportunity cost as the expected yield of similar investments with the same level of risk. Consequently, the capital asset pricing model (CAPM) has been thought to offer a relatively agile instrument through which to understand and utilise the project's systematic risk.

Although appealing due to its simplicity, the standard opportunity cost concept is in many cases inadequate because it does not fully consider the timing flexibility of investments, or other follow-on options of strategic importance. To simplify the problem, imagine a world in which competitive games have no relevance. Under such circumstances, when a firm decides to invest in a given project it is in effect renouncing two important alternatives:

1. investing immediately in a "twin" security or similar assets of equivalent risk; and
2. investing in the same project at the best future moment.

The first aspect is meant to be captured by the concept of opportunity cost. Under conditions of uncertainty, the second aspect is not fully captured by traditional NPV analysis. This makes uncertainty very important in evaluating an investment, for it establishes a link between information acquisition over time and financial value. NPV implicitly assumes that all information needed in order to maximise the allocation of capital is available at time zero – this can be done because it is possible to define the degree of economic desirability of the project conclusively from the start. But in the actual world of uncertainty, this is not so.

Real Options theory takes this dimension of risk, which is linked to the acquisition of useful information supporting better future contingent decisions, into account. In this way, Real Options theory profoundly distances itself from the standard NPV approach. The output of a valuation based on Real Options theory considers that although an investment might not be economically advantageous today, if the underlying stochastic variables evolve favourably, the investment might become advantageous down the road. According to this rationale, the decision-maker must incorporate the option to postpone an up-front decision. Conversely, even though a project has a positive NPV if taken immediately, an appropriate delay may result in even more value.

These factors argue in favour of extending the concept of opportunity cost, at least by considering the value of the option to postpone an investment project. This "extended" concept of opportunity cost becomes the revised "minimum yield" that a project should offer in order to be economically advantageous in terms of value creation.

A useful by-product of the Real Options approach is the ability to simultaneously determine the optimal timing of an investment and determination of the investment project's value. This means that two kinds of relevant information must be taken into account:

❑ the value of the project, including the value of managerial flexibility (in this case the option to postpone); and
❑ the optimal timing at which to exercise the option (the critical exercise price schedule).

These two kinds of information are different, but when used together they offer managers a very powerful tool for creating value. Determination of the project's value allows determination of the best strategies for the project's development, and a policy for its active management over time. These considerations underline another key aspect: assuming that the decision maker will act rationally (ie, optimally), an option that provides flexibility has value under conditions of uncertainty. This means that the option has full value only if it is exercised in an optimal way (ie, at the right time).

The above analysis does not take into account the important problem of competitive strategies. In a context of competitive interaction, postponing an investment decision may result in a loss of value to competitors, which may in turn offset the value of waiting under uncertainty. Under such broader circumstances, the concept of opportunity cost must be reconsidered, with the value of investing earlier included. Such an adjustment must also consider potential interactions among various options, including the option to expand, abandon or postpone. These considerations underline the structural limitations of deterministic investment valuation methodologies.

INVESTMENT AS A SOURCE OF CORPORATE REAL OPTIONS

Both theoretical analysis and empirical evidence lead to the conclusion that NPV does not properly evaluate the strategic impact of investment decisions. The reason for this lies principally in the fact that NPV cannot take into account the interaction between present alternatives and future opportunities for investment. When a firm decides to launch a new product in a new market, or invests in research and development, the results of that investment cannot be measured merely in terms of the cashflows that are directly connected with the project. Often, such investments have a value that is linked to the future opportunities brought about by the investments themselves.

In general, the goal of many strategic investments is partially to gather information about a given product or market (as well as to influence the behaviour of other agents in the market). Just as a firm might decide to pay for market research to obtain a better estimate of the probability of a given product's acceptance by consumers, another firm might likewise decide to tentatively launch a product, or fund a research and development project, or acquire patents or copyrights. For these types of activities, the costs are relatively known, but the benefits are highly uncertain. But even if the NPV is negative, the firm could well decide to proceed with the investment if its managers estimate that the value of future opportunities justifies the initial cost.

In practice, most firms decide to overrule straight NPV and undertake certain types of investments that have negative NPVs. The concept of flexibility value and strategic adaptability is very clear in managers' strategic analyses. This flexibility value can be seen as a source of corporate real options that can be optimally exercised over time. Real Options theory seeks to value an investment project considering that a firm has various possible future courses of action. These courses of action are intertwined with the broader concept of managerial flexibility/adaptability.

There are two key assumptions underlying the new theory:

❑ investment decisions are characterised by uncertainty; and
❑ decision makers can benefit from managerial flexibility to adapt to uncertain developments.

Figure 1 underscores that investment uncertainty and managerial adaptability are the two fundamental factors behind the Real Option approach. Research and development projects, acquisitions of copyrights and patents, investments in flexible automation, entering new

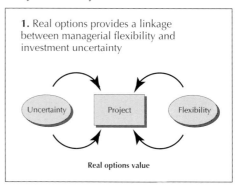

1. Real options provides a linkage between managerial flexibility and investment uncertainty

Uncertainty — Project — Flexibility

Real options value

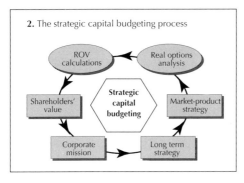

2. The strategic capital budgeting process

markets, alliance formation (joint ventures), and the launching of new products are all examples of highly "risky" projects. Here, the degree of managerial flexibility becomes a necessary competitive instrument in achieving the goal of value creation.

By helping to evaluate a project in light of the strategic opportunities it offers, real options becomes a source of value. Real Options theory allows the breaking of the wall dividing strategic analysis and financial theory. Therefore, the following two important objectives can be achieved.

1. It guides managers in focusing on the different strategic alternatives that can open up after the launch of an investment, eg, that a global vision of the investment process can be maintained.
2. It provides a more accurate means of incorporating the impact of uncertainty inherent to the project, thus allowing the evaluation of strategic opportunities.

With Real Options theory, the analysis of a given project's economic desirability and strategic considerations become a unified objective. In this way, real options allow a reconciliation of strategy and finance under what may be called "strategic capital budgeting". Strategic capital budgeting is not a top-down approach, but it is an interactive decision-making process. When properly implemented, it entails a contextual and optimal involvement of all the capital and human resources and techniques in the entire decision-making process. Each element contributes, at different levels, to the implementation of the project. The strategic orientation becomes an element that interacts with other aspects that together define a firm's optimum strategy. As summarised in Figure 2, it unifies the decision-making process, highlighting the role of managerial flexibility in a context of uncertainty.

DIFFERENT TYPES OF REAL OPTIONS
An investment project may involve different types of corporate real options. Table 1 summarises these options and provides specific applications and related references.

The option to postpone
The option to postpone concerns the decision of when to begin a project. For instance, such an option can arise from contractual rights to explore for mineral reserves, from the patenting of a new product, or more generally from any situation in which the start of a project can be delayed without

Table 1. Real options categories and major authors

Real option	Description	Specific applications	References
Deferment or temporary suspension	Option to postpone the investment outlay or to temporarily suspend production while preserving the technical feasibility of the project	Natural resources and oil, real estate and vacant land, launch of new products	Mcdonald & Siegel (1986), Paddock-Siegel-Smith (1988), Ingersoll-Ross (1992), Trigeorgis (1990)
Expansion	Option to expand the scale of the project by investing an additional amount of capital as exercise price	Launch of new products or new versions of the base product, targeting new market niches, entering new geographical markets, strategic alliances	Kester (1984), Mcdonald & Siegel (1985), Trigeorgis (1988)
Switching	Option to switch among alternative operating modes according to the relative fluctuation of some reference variables	Research and development, geographical diversification, global cost reduction strategy	Kensinger (1988), Kulatilaka (1988), Kulatilaka and Trigeorgis (1993), Margrabe (1978)
Contraction and/ or abandonment	Option to reduce the scale of the project, or to abandon it to realise its scrap value	Altering the R&D process, withdrawing from a market niche, reducing the capital invested in a business unit	Myers & Majd (1990)

jeopardising its technical feasibility or market position. As noted earlier, the option to postpone is a useful starting point for introducing an extended notion of the opportunity cost of capital. This extended concept of opportunity cost emphasises that the decision to invest immediately entails renouncing the undertaking a similar investment and postponing the implementation of this particular investment. Therefore, it "kills" the option to wait and see. These considerations become especially important under conditions of uncertainty where the evolution of time reveals valuable information.

The option to expand
The option to expand allows increase in the scale and/or scope of a project by investing more follow-on capital. For instance, when launching a new product, the decision to extend distribution to new markets is often best taken after the success of the initial launch has been established. For example, suppose that a pharmaceutical product has been launched for the treatment of disease "X". After further tests, the results achieved from initial trials reveal that there is a possibility that the product can also be

prescribed for disease "Y". This, evidently, would have major effects on the size of the market, and therefore on the initial project's current total value.

The option to contract
The option to contract is the opposite of the option to expand. The decision to reduce the size of a production facility can be taken in case of unforeseen unfavourable market developments. This option allows limiting downside losses. The precise and possible courses of action would have to be determined well in advance.

The option to switch
The option to switch refers to the feasibility of choosing among alternative operating modes – for example, switching among alternative energy sources in the case of a chemical plant, or switching production among various locations internationally for a multinational.

The option to temporarily suspend operations
This option rests between the choice to abandon and the option to postpone. This option exists when it is technically feasible and economically desirable to temporarily stop the production of a certain good or process for a given period of time when awaiting a more positive market development. The benefits of this option are due mostly to the savings in variable costs. This option is particularly relevant for productive optimisation strategies.

The option to abandon
The option to abandon a project altogether highlights the importance of developing a dynamic management attitude. Management must be able to exercise all elements of flexibility presented by a given project's structure and characteristics. During the project's preliminary evaluation phase, it is necessary to recognise and evaluate the value represented by the opportunity to recuperate part of the investment, in case the project should be abandoned for scrap value.

According to Real Options theory, the principal elements characterising a project's value are:

❑ initial investment, linked to the implementation of the project;
❑ one or more uncertain variables, upon which future decisions regarding the project depend;
❑ the gross value of the opportunity (the underlying asset) characterised by the benefits deriving from exercising the option – ie, the project's final value upon exercising the option;
❑ the additional investment necessary in order to exercise the option (ie, the strike price);
❑ the volatility attributed to the uncertain variables;

❑ the expiration of the option (ie, time to maturity); and
❑ the risk-free rate.

REAL OPTIONS BY INDUSTRY SECTOR AND DEVELOPMENT PHASE

Identification and specification of corporate real options can be facilitated by creating a conceptual map of the principal areas of managerial flexibility. There are two main categories:

1. real options determined by the characteristics of specific industrial sectors; and
2. real options for each development phase of a project, ie, process-specific real options.

The first category of real options stems from the specific structural characteristics of a given industry. Examples of such options are the option to develop, which is crucial for the pharmaceutical industry, or the option to temporarily suspend, which may be relevant in certain mineral extraction industries. The second type of options arises from the particular product phase, which of course also depends on the industry sector. The option to abandon is usually present in the research and development phase of new products. Likewise, the option to expand commercially arises from the product-launch phase of a new product or the penetration of a new market.

Table 2 illustrates the two-dimensional specification of options by industrial sector and product phase. Knowledge of specific industry sectors in addition to the respective product development phases enables management to better define the types of real options present in the cycle.

The Internet/e-commerce sector
This is one of the most challenging sectors where ROV can add significant value because the high uncertainty over Internet traffic development in coming years makes dynamic management's role critical in switching strategies to exploit alternative portal configurations, revenue models and resulting nested expansion options. Many current e-commerce IPOs are strongly underpriced since the (linear) multiples used for relative pricing underestimate the non-linear relationship between traffic and business value (ROV). In effect, they misestimate dynamic management's ability to creatively manage the portal to exploit expansion opportunities and adapt to the rapidly changing environment.

The film and publishing sector
Regarding industry sector-specific real option applications, in the film and publishing sectors there is a significant development phase related to the marketing of products. This is typical of the acquisition contracts in the

Table 2. Real options in different industry sectors over various development phases

Sector	R&D	Manufacturing	Marketing
Internet/e-commerce			Switch/expansion
Telecommunications	Deferment Abandonment Switching	Optimisation	Expansion
Pharmaceuticals	Deferment Abandonment Switching	Optimisation Abandonment	Expansion
Oil development	Deferment Abandonment	Deferment	Expansion Deferment
Publishing	Switching		Expansion
Trading			Expansion
Big orders		Optimisation	
Real estate development	Deferment	Expansion Switch	
Transportation (eg, auto and air)	Abandonment Switching	Optimisation	Expansion
Utilities (eg, electricity and water)	Deferment Abandonment	Substitution	Expansion

film industry that incorporate the rights to acquire future sequels in the event of a successful debut. Publishing companies, on the other hand, may purchase publishing rights based on the assumption that, for instance, the launch of new magazines will be successful. The exercise cost of such an operation is the royalties that must be paid. The benefits are uncertain and, naturally, are linked to the possible success of the launched project.

The pharmaceutical sector
This sector is often characterised by abandonment options, typically after a long research and development cycle in the face of newly-uncertain market conditions. At the same time, different market conditions may provide opportunities to expand; this is another frequent type of real option in this industry. A pharmaceutical company might choose to expand into new markets with an existing product, if research and development reveal the product's effectiveness for different applications.

In the mineral extraction sectors, one can easily identify valuable options to abandon or temporarily shut down or postpone operations. The decision to exploit new resources depends on the market price of such minerals and the cost of extraction. These factors are uncertain and typically subject to fluctuation, which is a source of option value.

The transportation sector

In this sector – ie, the auto and airline industries – the option to optimise production by cutting production costs is particularly significant. Similarly, the option to switch production facilities or design contracts with options to purchase or lease transportation vehicles – eg, aircraft – can also be a potential source of value creation.

AN OPTION-BASED PROJECT CLASSIFICATION: COMPETITION, DEFERABILITY, AND COMPOUNDNESS

The first "cut" in any strategic analysis is to take account of any competitive interactive implications. A fundamental question to be addressed is the degree of exclusivity to expropriate the value of a particular real option. Exclusive rights – ie, those secured through a patent, lease or license – provide a "proprietary" real option. For example, if a new, patented product is introduced to the market, the patent impedes competitors' strategic actions. Proprietary real options may also arise from the possession of specialised business know-how, or may arise in businesses protected by high barriers to competitive entry. Other situations may involve non-exclusive rights shared by many competitors in the industry, ie, "shared" real options. For instance, the option to enter into a certain market niche may be available to all – or almost all – competitors in a certain industry.

The distinction between shared and proprietary options is not always that clear. Among the firms that possess a potentially shared real option, a leading firm may take such actions, or acquire such market power, that the option is effectively, or almost, exclusive. This may be true if this particular firm enjoys considerable cost advantage, which may be due to either economies of scale or that firm's lead over its competitors with respect to the learning curve. In such a case, the virtual "exclusivity" of the option does not stem from a patent-regulating contractual situation, but instead arises from an economic situation concerning relative costs and revenues.

In the case of shared options, it is essential to consider the nature of the firms' competitive interactions, which are generated by potential exercise or abandonment of the option. Two cases can be identified. If there is a low degree of competitive interaction among firms operating in the same industry, the actions of one firm may not have a direct consequence on the actions of competitors. For example, in the beverage industry, the introduction of a new beverage to a market already filled with different products might not be perceived by competitors as a direct threat meriting a strategic response. By contrast, if a firm operating in the airline, fast food or the oil industry decides to significantly lower its prices, it is likely that competitors will follow a similar course of action. If they fail to take strategic action, such competitors will likely suffer a loss in their relative competitive position.

In the context of intense competition, the firm who first exercises a shared option – the "first mover" – does not always necessarily generate losses in the competitive position of rivals. Consider an advertising campaign by a firm in which the advert promotes the generic product instead of a specific brand – for example, publicity campaigns for national products such as wine or olive oil. Another case is the penetration of a new market under conditions of high uncertainty. The first mover in such cases is acting as a trailblazer. Rivals may want to "wait and see" – and learn – and may or may not follow, depending on the success of the first mover. Such rival firms can avoid the costs and risks undertaken by the first mover. In general, when a real option is shared in a context of elevated competition, it is essential to introduce strategic-competitive analysis to understand the circumstances under which it may be optimal to follow an early or delayed entry strategy. Game theory analysis can be particularly useful in such situations.

A second significant strategic question regards the duration and expiration of the investment opportunity. It is useful to distinguish between deferrable and expiring real options, which are immediately exercisable.

❑ An expiring real option diminishes the decision-making capacity of the manager, and consequently the value of the investment opportunity. Such situations are typically found in highly competitive situations, in which competitive considerations overtake the value of any wait-and-see option.

❑ A deferrable real option is distinguished by the possibility of postponing the decision to exercise the option to a future moment without much expected damage. For example, an oil company may postpone their decision to begin exploitation of a new oil reserve. The decision regarding when to exercise the option will be partially based on the uncertain fluctuation in oil prices that could render the postponement of the exploitation desirable.

The degree to which an option is deferrable depends of course on whether the option itself is shared or exclusive. A determined circumstance that would transform an exclusive option to a shared one could similarly transform a deferrable option into an option that expires immediately. As before, under such circumstances, the particular economic and strategic-competitive situation would define the degree of an option's deferability. In general, managers must carefully value the costs and benefits associated with the deferment of an option. The threat of entry by new competitors – due to the presence of a deferrable and shared option – might motivate a firm to invest sooner than planned for strategic reasons, or it might motivate a firm to increase existing investments, thus creating barriers to entry and pre-empt competition. The three principal strategic considerations discussed above are summarised in Figure 3.

3. Project classification based on the characteristics of real options[4]

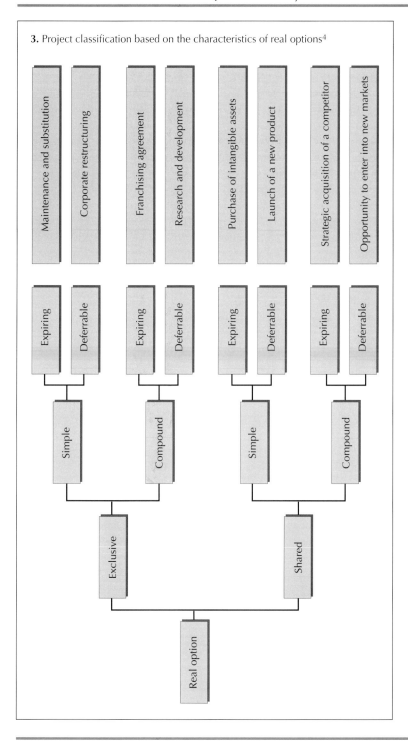

The series of investments outlined in the last column of Figure 3 provides examples for the different categories of options discussed above. An investment in maintenance or replacement of existing plants could be classified as a proprietary, simple and expiring option. It could also be deferrable depending on the degree of obsolescence of the existing plant. An industrial restructuring process, when it is not launched as an emergency measure, can typically be classified as a proprietary, simple and deferrable opportunity. In cases in which the project can generate additional future opportunities for the firm, the option should be configured as a compound – ie, multistage – real option.

The offer to participate in a franchising operation can generally be defined as a proprietary, compound and expiring option. The exclusivity in such cases is notably mitigated by a situation of urgency in which a firm has a relatively short period of time in which to either reject or accept a franchising offer. In this and other cases, the manager must consider the degree of exclusivity of the option in his evaluation and decision. Often, in spite of verbal and written contracts, an option's exclusivity cannot be clearly established.

Research and development activity for a new product is in a sense proprietary, compound and deferrable. The exclusivity and partial deferability depends largely on the patent coverage that usually characterises sectors with high technological reliance. Usually, the research and development activities in such industries lead to the acquisition of numerous patents.

The buying and selling of company assets, whether tangible or intangible, is an example of a shared, simple and expiring option. The degree to which the option is shared depends on whether or not the firm is interested in acquiring a competitor's brand.

The case of a product launch is slightly different: it can be classified as a shared, simple and deferrable option. The fact that it is shared is not to be taken for granted. The reason why it is shared is because the launch does not depend on research and development activities that are covered by patents. If the launch depended on research and development, it might be proprietary. Since a product launch can be considered independently from R&D, it is usually shared. The shared option refers typically to sectors in which widely available goods are produced and traded. Food and non-exclusive clothing are examples of such sectors because they are open to numerous competing firms.

Merger and acquisition operations typically fall into the category of shared, compound and – frequently – expiring options. There are naturally exceptions to the classification as shared. Consider the case of a firm that is an acquisition target, while the purchaser's goal is the firm's know-how. In such a case, the acquisition activity is proprietary and deferrable, as long as the acquisition offer remains valid for a specified period of time. Moreover, in spite of contractual arrangements, the option might not be deferrable. It could also happen that the know-how is not transferable, despite written contracts and verbal agreements. In such cases, the take-over target would effectively be a monopolist.

The area of strategic acquisitions holds rich potential for application of Real Options theory. This is because many acquisitions are motivated by the necessity to acquire intangible assets, such as copyrights, patents, trademarks and know-how. The value of such acquisitions is directly connected to the opportunities that can be derived from owning these assets.

The opportunity to enter new markets represents a shared, compound and deferrable option. It is difficult to imagine a case in which entry to a new market would be an exclusive right. Generally, the penetration of new markets is undertaken as an exploratory and experimental measure. Abandonment, expansion or postponement can follow. The penetration of a new market is usually deferrable, except when strategic-competitive conditions necessitate immediate entry.

The above considerations are crucial in order to properly incorporate real options considerations within the strategic evaluation framework. (The cases that follow in this volume elaborate on these ideas.)

THE FUTURE IS NOW

Real Options theory is already displacing the traditional investment valuation techniques used by multinationals operating in various industries around the globe. After several years of experimentation in the field, there now exists a significant base of knowledge that can be used for valuation purposes.

At the international level, areas where real options experimentation has been concentrated include the fields of natural resources (especially the oil sector), pharmaceuticals, and research and development projects in general. Notable examples can also be found in the transportation and multimedia industries. There have also been important applications in the real estate sector. The natural resource industry offered the first important references for options pricing, mainly because the commodity market is very similar to the financial markets. Both markets make clear reference to an uncertain observed variable (the commodity price) and both make available historical price series (or forward data), which facilitate the estimation of option valuation parameters. But Real Options theory is currently fruitfully applied also to sectors in which the identification of the underlying asset is less clear.

In the 1990s, there have been notable applications based on specific corporate challenges. Some examples are the evaluation of strategic acquisitions, the valuation of options with uncertain expiration dates, and the valuation of the flexibility of productive processes.

Recently, a prominent area that has emerged is the valuation of corporate decisions in the context of competitive interactions. Many of the traditional issues in business strategy are being revisited from the point of view of Real Options theory, combining the underlying options logic with principles from industrial organisation and game theory. This work has numerous empirical implications and is destined to attract more interest, due to the changes in the industry structure of sectors that are becoming increasingly competitive or oligopolistic in nature.

Moreover, developments arising from applications of Real Options theory themselves promise to expand the role that Real Options theory may have on corporate decision-making processes. Real Options theory is rapidly expanding in several interrelated ways, namely as:

❑ a valuation model;
❑ a decision-making process;
❑ a way of thinking; and
❑ an organisational model.

The first applications of the early 1980s were primarily focused on the modelling aspect. They started as simple replicas of financial option-pricing models applied to real assets. Many papers published during this early period paid less attention to the specific corporate realities, focusing more on theoretical modelling issues.

Later, emphasis shifted to decision-making processes, following an approach between finance and strategy. This led to the development of a managerial theory about the valuation process based on real options. It was recognised that every time an investment project, corporate acquisition or restructuring process requires an immediate or future decision based on the evolution of uncertain state variables, the decision itself is an opportunity that can be evaluated using real options theory.

Within the classic field of valuation, there are two directions: theoretical/quantitative versus application-oriented. From the theoretical/quantitative side, significant attention has been given to the uncertainty of the option's expiration, the investment decision's dependence on numerous related variables, the modelling of shocks that affect critical variables, and the application of exotic options to corporate decisions. On the application side, real options theory is being extended to numerous new sectors and decision-making situations. At the industry sector level, there are interesting applications in a number of areas:

❑ Internet/e-commerce/IPOs;
❑ publishing;
❑ telecommunications;
❑ transportation (automotive, aerospace); and
❑ building and real estate.

With respect to decision-making processes, the following areas are currently under examination:

❑ firm valuation;
❑ corporate restructuring processes;
❑ valuation of intellectual property rights and intangible assets;
❑ financial structure decisions; and
❑ competitive strategies.

The third phase will involve the marriage of real options theory with global organisational models. From this point of view, promising directions include:

❑ developing incentive systems that properly incorporate managerial flexibility;
❑ defining appropriate control mechanisms based on option theory;
❑ revising strategic planning procedures in light of strategic opportunities as options;
❑ revising learning theories under conditions of uncertainty;
❑ developing new organisational assets capable of optimising the allocation of capital and human resources with the objective of enhancing managerial adaptability; and
❑ diffusing a new business culture oriented towards enlarged perceptions of the role of risk and uncertainty in the resource allocation process.

The concepts underlying real options have already entered the daily language of many managers, and are quickly becoming part of the decision-making processes in large organisations around the globe. Real options is an innovation with no equal in the last decades of capital budgeting and business strategy. We venture to predict that it will not take long for the concepts to expand beyond the area of capital-budgeting decisions, as a way of thinking about and framing any type of decision-making process under uncertainty, from personal choices to managing international conflicts.

1 Fixed costs are those costs that are effectively uncorrelated with the volume of production and sales. Fixed costs are, therefore, a result of a firm's operating structure. On the other hand, variable costs are directly related to production volumes, and so are directly determined by the purchasing-transformation-sales process.
2 The measurement of the effect of sales variation on operating results is quantifiable by considering the contribution margin – ie, the difference between sales and variable costs compared to the operating income.
3 Systematic risk pertains to general events that impact on the economy as a whole. Some examples are unexpected fluctuations in oil prices, armed conflict, interest rate fluctuations, and the declaration of bankruptcy by a state. Firm-specific risk is peculiar to a specific firm's business environment, eg, the failure of a product launch, death of the firms' chief executive, illiquidity of a firm's treasury, or the entry of an important competitor.
4 Trigeorgis, L., 1996, *Real Options*, MIT Press, p. 145.

2

Growth Options, Competition and Strategy: An Answer to the Market Valuation Puzzle?

Han T.J. Smit and Lenos Trigeorgis

Erasmus University Rotterdam; University of Cyprus and Real Options Group

GROWTH OPTIONS, COMPETITION AND STRATEGY

In volatile markets, the strategic position of a firm can be vulnerable not just to the actions of known competitors, but also to the unanticipated entry of new competitors, substitute products or entirely new technologies, all of which can modify the very competitive landscape it operates under. The new conceptual approach presented here considers a firm's growth opportunities as a package of corporate real options actively managed by the firm. These opportunities may be affected by competitive actions to the extent that various strategic considerations, important to practising managers, can finally be brought into the analysis in a rigorous fashion consistent with the tenets of both industrial organisation and modern finance.

A combination of Real Options analysis and game theory can help answer many strategic questions vital to corporate success in dynamic and volatile industries. For instance, what is the value of the growth opportunities in the business? When is it appropriate to speed up investment to capture a larger market share (or to pre-empt competitive entry altogether) and when is it better to maintain the flexibility of a "wait-and-see" approach? And should the firm compete in R&D, or is it more beneficial to take an accommodating stance with regards to competition – for instance, via a joint research venture or another form of strategic alliance?

A firm's growth opportunities and its strategic position in the industry are presumably reflected in stock market prices. Of course, not all stocks generate the same earnings stream or have the same growth potential. Growth stocks (eg, in bio-tech, pharmaceuticals or information technology) typically yield high price-earnings and market-to-book ratios. In fact, it is precisely the intangible and strategic value of their growth opportunities that most determines the market value of high-tech firms in a constantly changing environment. A proper analysis of this strategic growth value is more difficult to grasp than price earnings ratios, book-to-market or other

INDUSTRY (AVERAGE) VOLATILITY (MARKET AND FIRM-SPECIFIC UNCERTAINTY) AND PROPORTION OF PVGO TO PRICE FOR A NUMBER OF REPRESENTATIVE INDUSTRIES, AS OF JUNE 30, 1998

Table A, based on the authors' preliminary findings, shows that industries such as information technology, pharmaceuticals and consumer electronics, which experience higher volatility, higher risk (market, firm-specific, or total) and greater option value, tend to have more valuable growth opportunities and a higher proportion of present value of growth opportunities (PVGO) to price on average, than industries such as transportation, chemicals and electric power. The first group of industries experience more unexpected technological changes and competitive moves; as the firm's (or the industry's) dynamic path unfolds, management must be better prepared to learn, adapt, and revise future investment decisions. The market appropriately rewards those firms better able to cope with change, capitalising on the upside potential while mitigating downside risk, with higher market valuations.

Averages per industry are equally weighted (to avoid excessive influence of large firms), based on monthly returns over the period 1988–98. Total risk (volatility), σ_T^2, is estimated as the variance of monthly returns,: market (or systematic) risk, $\sigma_{M,i,t}^2$, is estimated from $\sigma_{M,i,t}^2 = \beta_{i,t}^2 \sigma_{m,t}^2$, where $\sigma_{m,t}^2$ is the volatility of the S&P 500 market index at time t, and $\beta_{i,t}$ is the beta or sensitivity of monthly returns of firm i to monthly market returns of the S&P500 estimated over a period of ten years. The present value of growth opportunities (PVGO) for firm i is estimated by subtracting the discounted value (with the discount rate estimated from the market model, or from the risk-free rate plus a 6% risk premium) of its perpetual stream of earnings (under a no-growth policy) from its market price.

Table A

| | Uncertainty (σ_T^2) | | | Average PVGO/P | |
Industry	Market (σ_M^2)	Firm-specific (σ_S^2)	Total ($\sigma_T^2 = \sigma_S^2 + \sigma_M^2$)	Market model	Risk free rate + 6% premium
Information technology (%)	3	20	23	84	83
Pharmaceuticals (%)	2	12	14	92	83
Consumer electronics (%)	5	21	26	83	70
Food (%)	1	5	6	81	72
Banking (%)	2	4	6	81	55
Transportation (%)	2	7	9	62	38
Chemicals (%)	2	4	6	46	47
Electric power (%)	1	3	4	60	48

multiples might suggest, although an underlying theory that can explain this market valuation is available if we consider the strategic option characteristics of a firm's growth opportunities.[1] There is indeed a clear appreciation in the market for a firm's bundle of corporate real options (present value of growth opportunities, or PVGO).

The new insights and valuation tools from modern, real options-based corporate finance, which we discuss here, married with basic principles from industrial organisation and game theory, can help management more fully appreciate the value of corporate capabilities to enhance the firm's adaptability and strategic positioning in a competitive and volatile environment.

GROWTH OPPORTUNITIES AS CORPORATE REAL OPTIONS

The Real Options approach has been embraced by corporate strategists who recognised at an early stage the importance of active managerial flexibility in adapting to a changing market environment. It has been motivated by the substantial premiums paid in take-overs, oil leasing bids, and the high prices commanded by high-tech and other growth stocks. For example, in April 1997, Hewlett-Packard agreed to buy Verifone, the leading maker of credit card authorisation devices, for US$1.15 billion. Hewlett-Packard were attracted by Verifone's potential to dominate the emerging electronic commerce business, despite the fact that its 1996 earnings of just US$39.3 million gave a "negative NPV" (net present value). In the same month, Microsoft bought WebTV Networks, maker of set-top boxes bringing the Internet to televisions, at a price of US$425 million, despite its previous year's loss of over US$30 million. Again, this negative NPV acquisition can be justified for its growth option value as part of Microsoft's strategy for dominating the Internet.

In an increasingly uncertain and dynamic global market place, strategic adaptability has become essential if firms are to successfully take advantage of favorable future investment opportunities, respond appropriately to threatening competitive moves, or otherwise limit losses from adverse market developments. Thinking of future investment opportunities in terms of real options has provided powerful new insights and has already enabled substantial progress in modern corporate resource allocation. For example, real options stresses the importance of "wait-and-see" flexibility, suggesting that managers should wait until the project is more clearly successful, requiring a premium over the zero-NPV critical value. During postponement, new information can be revealed that might affect the desirability of the project; if the future prospects turn sober, the firm has implicit insurance cushioning it against downside losses by choosing not to proceed with the project. Real options also introduces an insight with respect to the effect of uncertainty on investment opportunity value that runs counter to traditional thinking about the role of risk. Because management is asymmetrically positioned to capitalise on upside opportunities while cutting losses on the downside, more uncertainty is actually benefi-cial when it comes to option value. Hence, more can be gained from oppor-tunities in highly uncertain or volatile markets as they offer an exceptional upside potential combined with limited downside losses, since manage-ment can default on planned investment instalments or simply decide not to proceed to the next stage.

However, from a strategic perspective, it is not always advisable to wait and see. For instance, by making an early strategic R&D investment, a firm may develop more cost-efficient or higher quality products or processes, and this can result in a sustainable cost or other competitive advantage, and a higher market share down the road. Or, a firm anticipating competi-tive entry may commit to excess production capacity at an early stage to pre-empt competition altogether. Therefore, optimal investment timing often involves a trade-off between wait-and-see flexibility and the "strate-gic value" of early commitment. A valuable extension proposed herein is embedding competitive game considerations within a dynamic strategic investment analysis based on real options. We therefore suggest moving to an expanded – or strategic – NPV criterion, which allows us to capture the strategic value of competitive interactions as well as management's flexi-bility regards altering planned investment decisions in the face of future changes in market conditions.

To help focus managerial attention on both the strategic and flexibility value of investment decisions, we suggest using the project classification scheme based on real options for analysing growth opportunities (Figure 1). Managers must first define the value characteristics of the project, which may be categorised from amongst the following option types.

Simple options
Investment opportunities that realise their benefits primarily through an expected stream of earnings, or operating cash inflows, are classified as simple options, requiring a relatively simpler analysis.

Compound options
Compound, or multi-stage, real options involve more pure growth-option (or strategic) value. They are better seen as a first link in a sequence of interrelated investment opportunities, the earlier of which are options to proceed to the next stage (and thereby acquire follow-on options), but only if it appears beneficial to do so. Strategic investments, such as R&D, exploration drilling for oil, or a pilot project, derive most of their value from the creation of follow-on investment opportunities. Actually, the dis-tinction between simple and compound corporate real options is closely related to the Wall Street classification of stocks into income versus growth stocks.

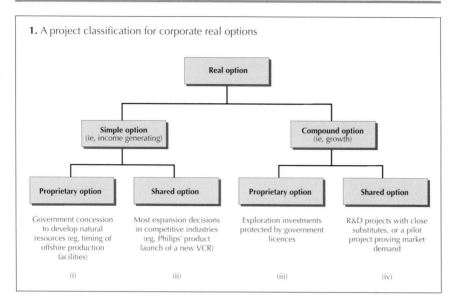

1. A project classification for corporate real options

- **Real option**
  - **Simple option** (ie, income generating)
    - **Proprietary option**

      Government concession to develop natural resources (eg, timing of offshore production facilities)

      (i)
    - **Shared option**

      Most expansion decisions in competitive industries (eg, Philips' product launch of a new VCR)

      (ii)
  - **Compound option** (ie, growth)
    - **Proprietary option**

      Exploration investments protected by government licences

      (iii)
    - **Shared option**

      R&D projects with close substitutes, or a pilot project proving market demand

      (iv)

Proprietary options

Another important aspect in the valuation of corporate real options involves defining whether the firm would fully appropriate the benefits created by its investment or whether it would share them with its competitors. Proprietary options may result from license or patent protection, high barriers to entry, or a unique knowledge that cannot be duplicated by competitors. Such proprietary options allow management to focus on optimisation problems against nature under conditions of demand uncertainty.

Shared options

Shared options are opportunities held by more than one competitor in the industry, possibly requiring a more involved, game-theoretic analysis. Examples of shared real options include the opportunity to introduce a new product that is not protected from the possible introduction of copies, or the opportunity to penetrate a new geographic market without any barriers to competitive entry.

Using the above classification scheme, we can now position some examples within the framework shown in Figure 1.

i.   A production license that gives the right for a specified period to invest in production facilities and produce proven reserves can be classified as a *simple proprietary* option.

ii. An exploration license that allows an oil company to invest in exploration wells can be viewed as a *compound proprietary* option. The investment in test and appraisal wells in a petroleum development programme, while typically yielding a low return, actually creates an option to invest in subsequent production facilities.

iii. Most expansion decisions in competitive industries can be seen as *simple shared* options. Examples of such options include the opportunity to introduce a new product impacted upon by the introduction of close substitutes, or the opportunity to penetrate a new geographic market without barriers to competitive entry. For instance, the introduction of the multimedia compact disk developed by Sony (and Philips) in 1995 faced exogenous competitive erosion from companies like Toshiba, Time-Warner and Matsushita (with the Super-Density Disk). Similarly, Texas Instruments' entry into the digital TV with its digital light processing technology for high quality, big screen television, developed over a decade for over US$500 million, faced anticipated competitive erosion with substitute products by Sony, Fujitsu and Sharp.

iv. Investment in R&D for the production of a new product with close substitutes can be classified as a *compound shared* option. Research success may lead to commercialisation, and potentially follow-on generations of the product (a compound option), all of which may be impacted upon by introduction of competing products. In consumer electronics, firms like Philips and Sony competed in the development of technologically innovative products, such as video and CD technology, the development of which resulted in various new product introductions.

Growth firms – eg, leading firms in information technology, pharmaceuticals, and consumer electronics – tend to have a higher option value component (PVGO) than income stocks, for two reasons. First, they tend to operate in more volatile and rapidly evolving industries, characterised by more frequent technological innovations and a more intensely competitive environment, with the higher underlying volatility being translated into higher option value. Second, they tend to have a higher mix of compound than simple real options, which, being options on options, further amplifies their option value. This higher growth option value is in turn translated into higher market valuations for high-tech or growth stocks; this increase in value may appear excessive from the perspective of standard DCF valuation methods. Hence, the future is uncertain and in an uncertain environment, having flexibility definitely has option value.

SIMPLE COMPETITIVE STRATEGY GAMES

An important step in closing the gap between traditional corporate finance theory and strategic planning is combining the real options approach with game theory, taking into account competitive counteractions. For instance, the commercialisation decision of Digital's Alpha chip was in fact greatly influenced by Intel's decisions regarding its Pentium processor; similarly, Philips' and Sony's strategy to commercialise the Digital Video Disk was affected by competitive decisions by Toshiba and Time-Warner, and vice-versa. These decisions are often seen as strategic games that are against both nature and competition. Management's investment decisions are made with the explicit recognition that they may invite competitive reaction, which in turn impacts the value of the firm's investment opportunity. In such cases, the strategic value of early commitment must be offset against the option value of waiting; potentially, it justifies early investment.

As noted, in some circumstances, strategic considerations would make it imperative for a firm to make an early investment, giving up the "option premium" of a wait-and-see approach. This allows the firm to gain a cost or other advantage, thus being in a position to either capture a larger market share or pre-empt entry by competitors – for example, the classic innovation or patent race among two like players where "the winner takes all." As shown in Panel 2, the competitive pressure to be the first to win the innovation race and capture the whole "pie" induces competitors to invest prematurely (a variation on the classic "prisoners' dilemma" problem), thus "killing" the option value from a "wait-and-see" approach under technological or demand uncertainty.

Indeed, in many high-tech industries, we often see firms rushing into innovation races, even forming strategic partnerships to acquire a first-mover or time-to-market advantage.[2] Yet sometimes, under competitive pressure to be first, several competitors may simultaneously rush to make similar innovation investments, with one or more parties potentially getting hurt badly. For example, Novell became hurt due to the intense competition in networking products; Apple lost its lead as a user-friendly computer with the development of Microsoft's Windows; and in the 1980s, Philips was hurt by losing the race against Matsushita over the VCR standard.

Both sides in such an innovation race would in fact fare better if they could wait and condition their investment decisions on the future development of market demand. It would be preferable for them to coordinate their investment strategy to more fully appropriate the flexibility benefits of the "wait-and-see" option; besides, they would be saving costs by sharing the investment expenditures, while avoiding the inferior "panic equilibrium" situation resulting from competitive pressure under which everybody is forced to rush and invest prematurely.

Of course, in many cases the players may not be similar and in like positions, as one of them may enjoy a more dominant market power position. The value of each firm's organisational capabilities, the bundle of corporate real options and uncertainty itself, may be idiosyncratic. Similarly, the exercise price of a corporate real option may be idiosyncratic, depending on what other resources and assets the firm already has. For instance, exercising the option to launch a new Windows-based software package is going to be less expensive for Microsoft than for another player, by virtue of its earlier strategic investments and the complementary assets that enable dominance in the desktop market. In some cases, a firm may pre-empt competition and capture a significant share of the market by

INNOVATION RACE: COMPETITIVE PRESSURE TO BE THE FIRST INDUCES FIRMS TO INVEST PREMATURELY (A "PRISONERS' DILEMMA"), EVEN THOUGH BOTH MIGHT BE BETTER OFF WAITING.

Suppose that the total market value (NPV – pie) from immediate investment (whether by a single firm or shared equally among two firms) is US$4 billion. The additional value of the flexibility to wait and see under demand uncertainty (without adverse competitive interaction) is US$2 billion. This results in a total (shared) growth option value (option pie or expanded-NPV) of US$6 billion, if the two firms could fully appropriate the flexibility value of waiting. This is summarised in Figure A.

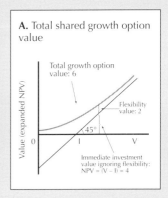

A. Total shared growth option value

Table A presents the payoffs for Firm A and B in four investment-timing scenarios:

i.   When both firms invest immediately and simultaneously, they share in equal parts the total NPV ($^{1}/_{2} \times 4$), resulting in a (2, 2) value payoff for each firm;

setting the product standard at an early stage. For instance, Intel pre-empted 80% of the microprocessor market with its Pentium microchip. This then became the product standard, forcing competitors like Digital to retreat from the market, even though Digital's Alpha chip was three to four times as powerful as the Pentium chip at a fraction of the cost.

If the competitors' relative market power and asset base differ, we can distinguish different investment timing strategies, as shown in Figure 2.

Characteristics of the four different investment timing strategies shown in Figure 2 are as follows.

i.   Projects that have relatively low NPV from immediate investment, but which operate in uncertain markets, have relatively larger flexibility (option) value, and it may be preferable to postpone these projects. If a company already has a dominant position in its industry, there is little threat of complete pre-emption by a competitor. The company can safely postpone the project and decide to invest at a later date if the ii–iii. When Firm A or B invests first while the other waits, it pre-empts its competitor and captures the full NPV value (4) for itself, resulting in a payoff of (4, 0) or (0, 4) respectively; and

iv. When both firms decide to wait they share in equal parts the value of the investment option ($1/2 \times 6$), resulting in a (3, 3) payoff.

Table A. Competitive pressure to be first induces firms to invest prematurely

		Firm B	
		Wait	Wait
Firm A	Wait	iv (3, 3)	iii (0, 4)
	Invest	ii (4, 0)	i (2, 2)*

The above value-payoff structure results in a Nash-equilibrium outcome of invest-invest (2, 2). Firm A's payoff from immediate investment (which can be seen on the lower row) exceeds its payoff from a wait-and-see strategy (upper row), regardless of which strategy firm B chooses (4 > 3 in left "wait" column, 2 > 0 in right "invest" column) – ie, firm A has a dominant strategy to invest, regardless of the timing decision of its competitor. Firm B also has a dominant strategy to invest regardless of A's decision, resulting in a Nash equilibrium outcome (*) in the lower right cell, from which neither firm can improve by making a unilateral move; here, both firms receive their second-worst payoff of (2, 2), an example of the well-known "prisoners' dilemma". (In the classic prisoners' dilemma, two prisoners accused of a crime would be worse off if they both confess (2, 2) than if they do not (3, 3), but the fear of the other prisoner confessing (0, 4) puts pressure for both to do so even though not confessing would have been preferable for both.) Here, both firms would be better off to co-ordinate and fully appropriate the option value of waiting (3, 3).

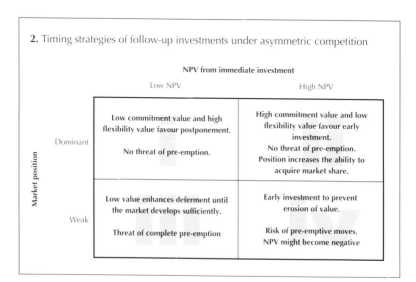

2. Timing strategies of follow-up investments under asymmetric competition

		NPV from immediate investment	
		Low NPV	High NPV
Market position	Dominant	Low commitment value and high flexibility value favour postponement. No threat of pre-emption.	High commitment value and low flexibility value favour early investment. No threat of pre-emption. Position increases the ability to acquire market share.
	Weak	Low value enhances deferment until the market develops sufficiently. Threat of complete pre-emption	Early investment to prevent erosion of value. Risk of pre-emptive moves. NPV might become negative

market develops favourably, or if the weaker competitor invests. It may sometimes even make sense for a dominant company to delay investing even when a weaker competitor does invest, but especially if the weaker competitor can "prove" the market without gaining a significant market share.

ii. Projects with relatively high NPV (from immediate investment) are likely to have a high opportunity cost of deferment (in the form of either missed cash inflows during the deferment period or potential competitive damage), inducing a dominant firm to invest early.

iii. If the company has a weak position in the market, undertaking the project immediately is not likely to sustain a large NPV, due to competitive vulnerability. Only later, if the market develops sufficiently, will it be appealing to start the project.

iv. If the firm has a weak market position and its project does appear to have a positive net present value, the company may consider investing immediately, if such early investment can pre-empt the competitor or create a sustainable cost advantage. However, because of its weak position, the firm must be mindful that a stronger competitor might come in and erode its project value.

When there are many competitors in the industry, each with negligible market power, their combined impact can erode the value of a project. When there are only a few competitors with substantial individual market power, there can be a threat of competitive pre-emption that may justify an early investment commitment.

TOUGH VERSUS ACCOMMODATING STRATEGIES, AND VALUE-CAPTURING VERSUS VALUE-ALTERING COMPETITION

We will now consider the question of when a tough or an accommodating stance in relation to a competitor should be adopted in the first stage of a multi-stage game (a compound option) such as R&D. For example, a high-tech company must decide if it should make an early strategic R&D investment in order to acquire an option to proceed at a later stage with the commercialisation of a more cost-efficient version of a given product. A related question is whether the firm should make such a strategic investment commitment immediately, or whether it should instead follow a "wait-and-see" approach, conditioned on the future evolution of market demand.

A key issue in determining an appropriate competitive strategy is whether an early strategic investment (eg, R&D to develop a more cost-efficient product or technological process) would make the pioneering firm more "tough" or "accommodating" – ie, "tough" in the sense of appropriating the resulting benefits for itself and hurting its competitors, or "accommodating" through a willingness to share the benefits of the resulting advantage with rivals.

A second important issue is the competitor's anticipated reaction to such a tough or accommodating stance by the pioneer firm. This may depend on the type of industry, and specifically on whether competitive actions are reciprocal or contrarian – ie, whether the firm and its competitors act in a similarly accommodating way towards one another, or whether they take advantage of the other's accommodating stance. Frequently, quantity-type competition, when a larger quantity produced by one firm results in a lower quantity for its competitor in equilibrium, is regarded as contrarian – eg, when a firm captures a larger market share via economies of scale or a learning cost advantage. Competitive reactions are typically reciprocal or complementary under price competition. Here, one firm matches the low price set by a competing firm, with the result that both experience lower profit margins. Such price wars have often been disastrous in the food, tobacco and airline industries. In such situations, firms may be better off if the leading firm instead sets a higher price that competitors would follow, allowing implicit co-ordination benefits. Contrarian reactions are typically associated with quantity competition in a value-capturing game; while the total growth option "pie" is roughly constant, an an aggressive investment can appropriate a larger market share if competitors retreat due to a tough stance. To put it simply, in a win-lose situation, the total pie is fixed and one player's gain is the other's loss. By contrast, the reciprocating reactions that typically characterise price competition may alter the size of the total pie. Firms can increase the total size of the pie if they are accommodating to each other (eg, through joint R&D ventures, standardisation agreements, price collusion), resulting in a win-win situation. On the other hand, the size of the pie can decrease if a firm plays tough – for instance, by making an early investment that would give it a threatening competitive advantage – and therefore encourages an intensified price competition, or a "war of attrition" in gaining larger market shares, leading to a lose-lose situation.

We can thus distinguish various competitive investment strategies, depending on whether a competitor is reciprocating through a complementary stance, or whether they are being contrarian, and whether the resulting benefits are proprietary or shared. This analysis is summarised in Figure 3.

The four different competitive strategies shown in Figure 3 are as follows.

i.   Firms in this category become offensive by making an early investment commitment and playing tough if the competitor is likely to back down under contrarian competition. In a value-capturing game (characterised by contrarian quantity competition when the size of the market pie is fixed), an earlier or heavier investment commitment enables the firm to obtain a first-mover proprietary advantage, expanding its market share at the expense of its competitors. Competition will retreat and the pioneering firm can gain leadership as the industry grows. For example,

3. Different competitive strategies following a tough or accommodating position under contrarian (value-capturing) or reciprocating (value-altering) competition

		Competition	
		Contrarian (value-capturing) *eg, quantity competition*	Reciprocating (value-enhancing) *eg, price competition*
Pioneer	Tough position *eg, proprietary investment* *(hurt competition)*	**Committing and offensive** Invest early	**Flexible and inoffensive** Don't invest/wait
	Accommodating *eg, shared investment* *(benefit competition)*	**Flexible and offensive** Don't invest/wait	**Committing and inoffensive** Invest early

Intel captured the micro-processor market selling 65 million chips in 1996, compared to Digital's 0.2 million Alpha chips, despite the latter being three times faster and cheaper.

ii. Firms in this category become offensive by staying lean and flexible, thus avoiding a vulnerable competitive position in a value-capturing game. A contrarian-type competitor may take advantage of the pioneer's accommodating position and capture most of the shared benefits of its strategic investment. The firm may be advised not to invest in the strategic project straightaway, as in doing so it may be paying the bill for the creation of valuable shared opportunities. Technological innovation diffused throughout the industry may result in a lose-win situation if a competitor takes advantage of the pioneer's accommodating stance and shared knowledge.[3] By contrast, in a value-altering game, a firm's strategic investments and their impact on competition, whether damaging or beneficial, are likely to invite a similar retaliatory or accommodating competitive response. This may significantly shrink or expand the size of the total market pie, ending up in a lose-lose cut-throat price competition or a "win-win" implicit collusion situation.

iii. If so, the firm in this category may wish to stay flexible and inoffensive if their strategic investment is likely to be under threat from aggressive, retaliatory competition. In a reciprocating-type industry, a firm should be reserved and careful with proprietary strategic investments, if these investments are likely to threaten competitors and invite a retaliating response.[4]

iv. For firms in this category, taking an accommodating stance via a shared strategic investment can be mutually beneficial if competition is expected to reciprocate, thereby allowing both to maintain high industry prices and enjoy higher profit margins. By investing in goodwill

COMPETITION VS. COORDINATION GAMES

In the late 1970s, the introduction of three types of video recorder illustrated that tough positions and reciprocating reactions can result in intense competition which impacts on everyone's bottom line. Philips launched the V2000 system to compete with Sony's Betamax and JVC's VHS system. Instead of following a single shared standard, these companies took positions that resulted in an intense battle for market share. In retrospect, it should have been clear from the beginning that only one of these systems could become the product standard in the market, to which other firms would eventually have to switch. In a "war of attrition" game such as this, the winner can take all – ie, acquire the standard – while the losers can be left wishing they had never entered the fight.

However, a decade later, the same players followed a wiser strategy, choosing to enter into agreement to adopt a common, industry-wide standard for the high-density CD. These same players now realised that under reciprocating competition it may be better to follow an accommodating strategy and share opportunities with competitors, increasing the total value for the entire industry. Philips, recognising that the CD player would only be a success if technology were shared other firms were allowed to produce CDs and CD players, exchanged licenses for a CD standard. The joint development of the CD turned out to be a success, resulting in a range of subsequent growth opportunities.

The standardisation game of the new-generation high-density CD further illustrates when it may be best to co-operate in R&D instead of competing. By 1995, it became feasible to increase the storage capacity of the CD with new compression techniques, with the new technology expected to result in valuable future growth opportunities. Initially, one might expect that the development of the high-density disk would end up in a technological war. Instead, it ended up in a co-ordination game. On one side of this game was an alliance between Toshiba and Time Warner, who had jointly developed the super density disk. On the other side were Philips and Sony with their multimedia compact disk. The two sides recognised that the launch of more than one system would result in confusion and major capital waste, and that an accommodating standardisation strategy might lead to a preferable outcome for both. The computer industry itself encouraged the two sides to negotiate and co-ordinate, and subsequently, the strategic moves of these firms changed from tough to accommodating.[1]

Besides collaboration at the R&D stage, we have recently witnessed a co-operative trend in other areas. For instance, it has emerged in production and services among many leading Japanese and US firms: IBM and

Toshiba jointly manufacturing liquid-crystal display panels; GE supplying components to Toyota, while Toyota helps distribute GM's Cavalier through its dealership network in Japan; Mitsubishi and Dupont launching a joint polyethylene manufacturing venture; and Sumitomo and Exxon cooperating in oil and gas development in China.

1 However, these firms could not agree on the number of patents for each firm that joined in the standard, which resulted in subsequently taking tough positions. Firms do have an incentive to cooperate and follow accommodating positions with standardization agreements via joint research ventures that would increase the size the pie, but otherwise will compete more heavily for a larger share.

that will be inoffensive, the firm may actually benefit the entire industry – ie, if the firm promotes the entire product category rather than its own particular brand. For example, Mobil placed an advert in the New York Times aimed at educating the public about the benefits of oil refining for society in general.

The above analysis can provide a useful roadmap, helping managers to consider under what circumstances it may be beneficial to make an early strategic investment or follow a wait-and-see strategy, and when to take an accommodating or a tough position, depending on the type of industry and nature of competitive reaction, as well as the proprietary or shared nature of the resulting innovation.

CONCLUSION: EVOLUTION, LEARNING AND COOPERATION

The evolution of an industry's market structure may be the result of strategic investment behaviour under uncertainty. Actions and best competitive strategies of individual firms may themselves be evolving over time, as firms constantly reassess their strategies, adapt to changes in their environment, and learn form their own and competitors' actions. Firms can observe their own payoff and the payoff and actions of their competitors, and may decide to switch their decision to play tough or accommodating next time around. As noted, a proprietary R&D investment may become a strategic disadvantage if it provokes a retaliating competitive response and intense rivalry.

The combined real options and industrial organisation framework can help guide managerial judgement and intuition in deciding whether, when and under what conditions it may be appropriate to make a strategic investment, as well as whether to go at it alone or in collaboration with other players, all consistent with market valuation. The insights from real options and game theory help bridge the gap between business strategy and finance, as they recognise the importance of active managerial flexibility in both adapting to a changing market environment and reacting to competitive moves; help us understand the potentially beneficial role of uncertainty; and explain the substantial premiums paid in take-overs as well as the high growth option values reflected in high-tech and other growth stocks.

1   This is covered in the articles "How Do you Read this Crazy Market?" in *Business Week* (March 29, 1999) and "Valuation Puzzle for Tech Stocks" *International Herald Tribune* (April 22, 1999).
2   The race in memory chip development is a case in point. In February 1997, Hitachi, Mitsubishi Electric and Texas Instruments announced they would jointly develop a one-gigabyte DRAM. NEC, which has been co-operating loosely with ATT spin-off Lucent Technologies and Samsung, announced in June 1997 that it had developed a 4Gb DRAM, the largest-capacity memory chip ever developed, putting NEC in the lead in the intensely competitive memory chip technology race.
3   Examples of competitors taking advantage of one's goodwill and vulnerability are abundant. In May 1997, one week after Intel announced its next-generation microprocessor, the Pentium II, Digital sued Intel claiming remarkable similarities with its Alpha chip; Digital had revealed the Alpha design to Intel during their failed negotiations on licensing Alpha technology for Intel's next-generation chip in 1990–1. In an independent suit in 1997, Fujitsu agreed to pay compensation to IBM in a decade-old suit for allegedly copying IBM products.
4   In May 1997 Microsoft announced an all-out attack on the lucrative heavy-duty corporate computing market, traditionally a mainframe task performed by IBM, Sun Microsystems and Oracle. This is a high-risk strategy for Microsoft: if successful, it may have a sweeping impact on business computing, just as its Windows software has had on PCs. But the competition, already having made heavy investment commitments, does not seem ready to retreat; instead it is poised to reciprocate and fight to the end: "Every major corporation needs its Vietnam, and this will be Microsoft's", responded an IBM executive (New York Times, May 19, 1997).

BIBLIOGRAPHY

Baldwin, C., 1982, "Optimal Sequential Investment When Capital is not Readily Reversible", *Journal of Finance*, 37(3), June, pp. 763–82.

Baldwin, C., 1987, "Preemption vs. Flexibility in New Product Introduction", working paper, Harvard Business School.

Bowman, E.H. and D. Hurry, 1993, "Strategy through the Option Lens: An Integrated View of Resource Investments and Incremental-choice Process", *Academy of Management Review*, 18, pp. 760–82.

Brandenburger, A.M. and B.J. Nalebuff, 1995, "The Right Game: Use Game Theory to Shape Strategy", *Harvard Business Review*, 73, July–August, pp. 57–71.

Brennan, M. and E. Schwartz, 1985, "Evaluating Natural Resource Investments", *Journal of Business*, 58(2), April, pp. 135–57.

Cox, J.C., S.A. Ross and M. Rubinstein, 1979, "Option Pricing: A Simplified Approach", *Journal of Financial Economics*, 7, September, pp. 229–63.

Dixit, A., 1980, "The Role of Investment in Entry Deterrence," *Economic Journal*, 90, March, pp. 95–106.

Dixit, A. and B.J. Nalebuff, 1991, Thinking Strategically, New York: Norton Press.

Dixit, A. and R. Pindyck, 1994, *Investment under Uncertainty*, Princeton, NJ: Princeton University Press.

Fudenberg, D. and J. Tirole, 1994, "The Fat-Cat Effect, The Puppy-Dog Ploy, and the Lean and Hungry Look", *American Economic Review*, 74, pp. 361–66.

Grenadier, S.R. and A.M. Weiss, 1995, "Investment in Technological Innovations: An Options Pricing Approach", *Journal of Financial Economics*, 44, pp. 397–416.

Kemna, A., 1993, "Case Studies on Real Options", *Financial Management*, 22(3), Autumn, pp. 259–70.

Kester, W.C., 1984, "Today's Options for Tomorrow's Growth", *Harvard Business Review*, 62(2), March–April, pp. 153–60.

Kolbe, A.L., P.A. Morris and E.O. Teisberg, 1991, "When Choosing R & D Projects, Go with Long Shots", *Research-Technology Management*, 34, January–February, pp. 35–40.

Kulatilaka, N. and E. Perotti, 1998, "Strategic Growth Options", *Management Science*, 44(8), pp. 1021–31.

Luehrman, T., 1998, "Strategy as a Portfolio of Real Options", *Harvard Business Review*, 76, September–October, pp. 89–99.

Mason, S. and R. Merton, 1985, "The Role of Contingent Claims Analysis in Corporate Finance", in *Recent Advances in Corporate Finance*, Altman, E. and M. Subrahmanyam, Richard D Irwin, Homewood, Illinois.

McDonald, R. and D. Siegel, 1986, "The Value of Waiting to Invest", *Quarterly Journal of Economics*, 101(4), November, pp. 707–27.

McGahan, A., 1994, "The Incentive not to Invest: Capacity Commitments in the Compact Disc Introduction", in Rosenbloom and Burgelman (eds.), *Research on Technical Innovation, Management and Policy*, Greenwich, CT: JAI Press.

Myers, S.C., 1987, "Finance Theory and Financial Strategy", *Midland Corporate Finance Journal*, 5(1), Spring, pp. 6–13.

Nichols, N.A., 1994, "Scientific Management at Merck", *Harvard Business Review*, 72, January–February, pp. 88–99.

Porter, M.E., 1980, *Competitive Strategy*, London: Collier Macmillan.

Reinganum, J., 1983, "Uncertain Innovation and the Persistence of Monopoly", *American Economic Review*, 73(4), September, pp. 741–48.

Sick, G., 1989, *Capital Budgeting With Real Options*, Salomon Brothers Center, New York University.

Smit, J.T.J. and L.A. Ankum, 1993, "A Real Options and Game-Theoretic Approach to Corporate Investment Strategy Under Competition", *Financial Management*, 22(3), Autumn, pp. 241–50.

Smit, J.T.J. and L.Trigeorgis, 1993, "Flexibility and Commitment in Strategic Investment", Working Paper TI 95-74, Boston University and Tinbergen Institute.

Smit, J.T.J. and L. Trigeorgis, 1995, "R&D Option Strategies", Working Paper, Erasmus University.

Smit, J.T.J. and L. Trigeorgis, 1995, "Flexibility, Strategic Options and Dynamic Competition in Technology Investments", Working Paper, Erasmus University.

Smit, J.T.J., 1996, "The Valuation of Offshore Concessions in the Netherlands," *Financial Management*, 26(2), pp. 5–17.

Smit, J.T.J., 1996, "Growth Options and Strategy Analysis", Ph.D. dissertation, University of Amsterdam.

Smith, K.W. and A. Triantis, 1994, "The Value of Options in Strategic Acquisitions", in Trigeorgis, L. (ed.), *Real Options in Capital Investment: Models, Strategies, and Applications*, Westport, Conn.: Praeger.

Smith, M.J., 1974, "The Theory of Games and the Evolution of Animal Conflicts", *Journal of Theoretical Biology*, 47, pp. 209–21.

Spatt, C.S. and F.P. Sterbenz, 1985, "Learning, Preemption, and the Degree of Rivalry", *Rand Journal of Economics*, 16(1), Spring, pp. 84–92.

Spence, M., 1979, "Investment Strategy and Growth in a New Market", *Bell Journal of Economics*, 10, Spring, pp. 1–19.

Tirole, J., 1990, *The Theory of Industrial Organization*, Cambridge, MA: MIT Press.

Trigeorgis, L., 1988, "A Conceptual Options Framework for Capital Budgeting", *Advances in Futures and Options Research*, 3, pp. 145–67.

Trigeorgis, L., 1991, "Anticipated Competitive Entry and Early Preemptive Investment in Deferrable Projects", *Journal of Economics and Business*, 43(2), May, pp. 143–56.

Trigeorgis, L., 1993(a), "The Nature of Option Interactions and the Valuation of Investments with Multiple Real Options", *Journal of Financial and Quantitative Analysis*, 28(1), March, pp. 1–20.

Trigeorgis, L., 1993(b). "Real Options and Interactions with Financial Flexibility", *Financial Management*, 22(3), Autumn, pp. 202–24.

Trigeorgis, L., 1995, *Real Options in Capital Investment: Models, Strategies, and Applications*, Westport, Conn.: Praeger.

Trigeorgis, L., 1996, *Real Options: Managerial Flexibility and Strategy in Resource Allocation*, Cambridge, MA: MIT Press.

Trigeorgis, L. and S.P. Mason, 1987, "Valuing Managerial Flexibility", *Midland Corporate Finance Journal*, 5(1), Spring, pp. 14–21.

3

Creating and Managing Shareholder Value: A View Through a Real Options Lens

Alexander J. Triantis

University of Maryland

It is now widely accepted that corporate decisions should be made consistent with the maximisation of shareholder wealth. Value based management has been emphasised as a disciplined approach for making strategic and operating decisions. Value based metrics such as Economic Value Added (EVA), Return on Invested Capital (ROIC), and Cashflow Return on Investment (CFROI) have been developed as quantitative tools to help firms formally evaluate the impact of their decisions on shareholder value.

However, the discipline that comes from using value based metrics is often set aside when managers feel that these metrics fail to capture the true value of long-term investments. In such cases, there is often an appeal to the "strategic value" of the investment – implicitly saying that there is some significant strategic benefit that can't easily be quantified. These benefits may be associated with future growth opportunities arising from a project, or perhaps from some flexibility that the investment brings to the firm. While these "intangible" benefits are argued and often appreciated, they are not properly compared against the costs associated with the strategic investment, let alone against the benefits associated with alternative strategic investments.

This rift between strategic decision making and value based management is particularly troubling given that a considerable, perhaps an overwhelming, fraction of shareholder value rests on the outcome of key corporate strategic decisions. This is magnified by the importance of large investments being made in the New Economy targeted at growth, innovation and agility. Are we really better off using our intuition when making these decisions, rather than applying appropriate valuation techniques in a systematic manner?

Rather than completely abandon the use of traditional value based metrics, it is more appropriate to understand the shortcomings of these metrics, and to adopt techniques that respond to these inadequacies. Of greatest concern is that conventional calculations of EVA, ROIC and even DCF tend to take a rather myopic and inflexible view of an investment opportunity.

For example, typical DCF valuations ignore the ability that managers have to revise and delay decisions over time in response to the resolution of uncertainty. This decision flexibility alters a project's cashflows – the firm can take actions to cut losses or to better capitalise on future growth opportunities, and it can also acquire information that will lead to better future decisions. Moreover, managerial decision flexibility can significantly affect the risk profile of the firm's investments, and thus the appropriate adjustments in the valuation procedure to account for risk. By ignoring these effects, incorrect valuations could lead to erroneous recommendations. It is not surprising that when recommendations seem counterintuitive, managers tend to fall back on their gut intuition to guide strategic planning.

However, by recognising that a firm's ability to delay and revise its investment and operating decisions over time is analogous to the discretionary exercise of financial options, we can appeal to option pricing techniques to help capture the value of flexibility and growth options. These techniques can properly account for the altered cashflow and risk profiles inherent in firms' investment opportunities. Moreover, by thinking of a firm's investment opportunities as "real options", and leveraging the intuition we have concerning financial options, a firm's investments can be examined from a different perspective, yielding new insights regarding investment strategy.

The option analogy is examined in greater detail below by discussing examples of strategic investment opportunities from different industries. The focus of this chapter is on understanding how to create options within a firm, how to protect and enhance the value of these options, and how best to exercise these options (Figure 1). The intuition behind option valuation techniques is also briefly discussed, since these techniques provide a valuation anchor for the real options paradigm, in that they can help quantify the impact of a firm's decisions on shareholder value. Finally, this chapter will also explore how real options analysis can help a firm better plan its financing, portfolio optimisation, risk management, and compensation strategies with an eye towards shareholder value creation.

ENHANCING SHAREHOLDER VALUE BY IDENTIFYING, CREATING AND ACQUIRING REAL OPTIONS

Typically, real options represent over half of a company's value, and in the case of companies operating in emerging product markets, virtually all of it. This option value can be attributed to two main sources. First, firms can position themselves to potentially exercise profitable "growth options" in the future by investing in research and development, IT expertise, brand name recognition and other sources of competitive advantage. While

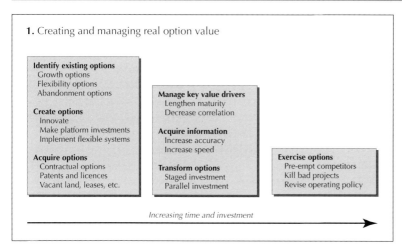

1. Creating and managing real option value

Identify existing options
  Growth options
  Flexibility options
  Abandonment options

Create options
  Innovate
  Make platform investments
  Implement flexible systems

Acquire options
  Contractual options
  Patents and licences
  Vacant land, leases, etc.

Manage key value drivers
  Lengthen maturity
  Decrease correlation

Acquire information
  Increase accuracy
  Increase speed

Transform options
  Staged investment
  Parallel investment

Exercise options
  Pre-empt competitors
  Kill bad projects
  Revise operating policy

Increasing time and investment

growth may seem to be an imperative, rather than an option, there are potentially different directions for growth, some of which will turn out to be profitable, and others that will not. Commitments to grow in a particular direction can be delayed until sufficient information can justify making a significant, and possibly irreversible, investment.

Second, firms typically have the ability to revise their investment and operating decisions over time as uncertainty is resolved. These "flexibility options" may include the ability to expand or contract a manufacturing operation, to switch the mix of outputs produced at a plant, to re-deploy assets, to outsource at peak times or to shut down or abandon operations. The costs associated with making and implementing these managerial decisions will determine the degree of flexibility available to the firm.

Table 1 lists examples of growth and flexibility options from a variety of different industries. These are discussed in more detail below to illustrate how these opportunities can be created or acquired through strategic investment. While these investments can be thought of in traditionally

Table 1. Examples of growth and flexibility options in different industries

Industry	Growth option	Flexibility option
Pharmaceuticals	Research and development	Outsource production or sales
Oil & gas	Lease blocks	Delay production
Power	Global expansion	Peak generating plants
Computer hardware	New model under brand name	Assembly configuration
Financial services	IT infrastructure	Abandon service or divest
Airline	Aircraft delivery options	Contingency rights
Real estate	Undeveloped land	Redevelop with adjusted mix
Telecommunications	Mergers and acquisitions	Re-deploy assets
Internet	Marketing investments	Outsource services

strategic terms (eg, creating barriers to entry), the option analogy empha-sises that these investments have unique risk and return characteristics, similar to financial options. Furthermore, we can leverage our intuition regarding financial options to understand why variables such as volatility and time can actually have a positive impact on the value of these invest-ment opportunities. This is particularly important in appreciating how to manage real options and how to communicate the value of these invest-ments to senior executives as well as to analysts and investors.

Growth options
Companies may have different opportunities to grow, for example, by try-ing to increase market share, by introducing new products, or by entering new global markets. To position themselves for growth, significant up-front investments are typically required – in R&D, marketing, IT infra-structure, or foreign production capacity, to name but a few. How can a company justify such expenditures?

Pharmaceutical companies spend billions of dollars on R&D each year. These companies are effectively purchasing call options on future profits from selling new drugs. Ignore for the moment that there are various stages involved in the R&D process (this will be discussed later in this chapter). If the research program fails, the outcome is quite clear – no addi-tional investment is made. However, if a compound is developed that proves to be an effective and safe treatment for some illness, and there is a significant market for the drug, then the present value of all future profits may exceed the up-front costs associated with marketing, producing and distributing the drug. In option terms, at some point in the future (often five to ten years out), if the present value of the underlying opportunity exceeds the "exercise price", then the option to invest should be exercised. While many of a firm's R&D options will become "out-of-the-money", the returns on options that end up "deep-in-the-money" can be extremely high.

Firms in other industries also recognise that future growth is often con-tingent on creating a portfolio of risky options through investing in R&D. Failure is to be expected on some R&D investments. In fact, if failure never occurs, it is often a signal that a firm is not actively investing in creating growth options through R&D. In the oil and gas business, firms actively bid for lease blocks. These leases allow for exploration, with the potential for future production if sufficient reserves are found which can be extracted at reasonable cost. Investment in the lease, costing perhaps in the millions of dollars, is analogous to the purchase of call options. These options will be exercised if the present value of future production income is found to be higher than the costs of setting up the extraction infrastruc-ture. This decision will depend on the outcome of various uncertainties including the cost of extraction, the size of reserves and the price of oil.

Perhaps the most compelling example these days of a growth option is the investment in Information Technology (IT).[1] These platform investments do not directly lead to cashflows, but enable a firm to offer new services in a highly efficient manner. Consider, for example, the significant investments that financial services firms have recently made to enable their clients to trade securities on-line and to have ready access to large amounts of information about their own accounts, as well as about the financial markets at large.

In addition to investing in IT infrastructure and the development of new services, internet firms specialising in e-commerce have invested heavily in marketing and brand name recognition. As advertising draws in new customers, a wider array of products may be offered at a single site, providing an engine for revenue growth. Early investments in marketing are often seen as a positive signal of the value of a firm's future growth options.

While growth options can be created through investment, acquired from other firms, or become naturally available as a result of a firm's competitive position in the industry, they can also be purchased outright in the form of contracts, directly analogous to financial options. Consider, for example, that airlines must expand their fleet capacity in order to realise an increased market share or growth into new domestic and international markets. This capacity expansion takes place by putting in orders with aircraft manufacturers over time.

An airline has a natural option to delay investment, whereby it simply waits until it has a better gauge of market conditions and its capacity needs. However, in a peak market, if the airline decides it wants to expand capacity, its orders could be in a queue for three years or longer, and the aircraft price may have significantly increased. Alternatively, the airline can negotiate today to get option delivery contracts from the manufacturers. These contracts lock in the lead-time for delivery once the exercise decision is made, and also specify a firm price for aircraft delivery (the exercise price). These types of contractual real options also exist in other industries (eg, options to purchase power), and have recently been integrated into merger and acquisition transactions and joint venture deals.[2]

Flexibility options

Growth options are valuable because they allow firms to capture potentially profitable opportunities on the "upside", while limiting future investment on the "downside", ie, when the combined outcome of the uncertainties underlying the project is unfavorable. Investments in flexibility can have a similar impact on the firm's risk profile. They enable the firm to limit the impact of negative outcomes by changing course – producing new products, shrinking capacity, etc. At the same time, they allow firms to take advantage of favourable situations – by increasing production, refocusing on new opportunities, etc.

Consider an automobile manufacturer that recognises that one of its product lines is lagging in sales. While the product line is still marginally profitable, it is recognised that the firm's production capacity and labour force could perhaps be better deployed by producing a more popular line of vehicles, in particular one that is currently facing constraints in meeting customer demand.[3] Whether this redeployment is feasible and, moreover, profitable, depends on the ability of the firm to reconfigure its existing manufacturing plants, to train its employees to assemble a different style of vehicle, and to alter its distribution strategy. Such flexibility can be extremely valuable when there is considerable uncertainty regarding the future demand for a company's products, and when the demand for the company's different product lines are not too closely correlated.

The option to adjust a firm's mix of products or services, ie, output flexibility, can be found in virtually any industry. In the computer hardware and peripherals industry, plants are designed such that the assembly mix of different computers or printers can be altered over time. In the oil industry, flexible refiners allow for frequent readjustment of the mix of outputs. Real estate properties are increasingly being designed for mixed uses, and can be redeveloped over time in response to changes in the relative demand for different uses (such as office, retail, condominium, etc.).

Output flexibility may require that the mix of inputs can also be readjusted relatively easily. However, output flexibility is not a necessary driver for input flexibility. For example, in the power industry, there may be a variety of alternatives available for generating electricity. Depending on the relative prices of, for instance, oil and gas, a firm that has invested in plants that can be fired by either input can take advantage of diverging prices of these inputs.

A special case that necessarily combines both input and output flexibility is the ability to scale production volume up or down (or to adjust the scale of a business in general) in response to demand and/or price uncertainty. The ability to reduce the scale of a business – eg, by shutting down a plant – may be largely driven by the relative size of fixed versus variable costs. If the firm cannot easily downsize its labour force, sell off its excess capacity, or avoid significant fixed costs associated with maintenance, then it has little flexibility, and may be forced to sustain losses for extended periods of time. In contrast, power companies find significant flexibility in plants that have low costs to switch on and off and negligible fixed costs while idle, even if they have high variable costs of operation. With the recent high volatility in electricity prices, these flexible "peaking" plants have turned out to be very profitable.

In some cases, scaling down may require an all-or-nothing decision, such as the mothballing of a plant, or the abandonment of a product or service line. Rather than abandon an entire product or service, a firm may simply decide to stop performing specific parts of the value chain in-house and instead outsource these functions. For example, a smaller pharmaceutical company that finds it too costly to maintain its own sales force may decide to abandon that function internally and outsource sales. However, if the firm knows that demand tends to be somewhat cyclical, or varies through time depending on the timing of introduction of new drugs and the demand decay over time for older drugs, it may retain flexibility to keep some of this function in-house and selectively outsource during peak demand periods.

Whether associated more with growth or with flexibility, the array of real options that exist within firms is clearly extensive. In fact, one could argue that virtually all investments have real options embedded in them. In many cases, these real options already exist as a result of prior strategic investments. A firm must simply uncover their existence and carefully manage these opportunities to extract maximum value from them, an issue that will be addressed later in this chapter.

Deciding which real options to purchase or create

When specific real options do not already exist in a firm, opportunities to create or purchase these options should be considered. While the idea of having the ability to selectively capitalise on growth opportunities in the future, and the flexibility to adapt a firm's operating and investment decisions over time seems inherently appealing, there are often significant up-front costs associated with positioning the firm in such a manner. Furthermore, these investments may be extremely risky – these options may never pay off. Thus, the decision to purchase or create real options is not an obvious one, despite the inherent appeal of these options. The following three examples relating to growth, flexibility and contractual options further explore how to consider value and risk when making strategic investments in real options.

Growth options in real estate development

A real estate developer's business essentially involves converting growth options, in the form of vacant land, into developed properties. The price of each growth (call) option is the cost of the land, the exercise price is the cost of development, and the underlying asset is the present value of the future income stream from the developed property. Successful developers carefully manage their portfolios of growth options, deciding which parcels of land to purchase, which to keep undeveloped, and which to develop into income-generating properties. Developers could purchase speculative land parcels – growth options that are out-of-the-money, where the properties are unlikely to be developed soon, if ever. Alternatively, they could avoid the risk and holding costs associated with these speculative options, and purchase land that can be immediately and profitably developed (ie, deep-in-the-money options).

When deciding between these two alternatives, one must take into account that the more promising parcels of land are likely to be considerably more expensive than the speculative ones. However, it is possible that, given the uniqueness of the asset and the search costs involved, one of the parcels may be undervalued relative to what its true market price should be, presenting an attractive buying opportunity. Furthermore, if the developer has some comparative advantage in one location due to superior information about potential home buyers, or economies of scale due to other projects in the area, the private value to the developer of one of the parcels may be significantly higher than its market value. The ability to bear risk will also figure into the developer's purchase decision given that the out-of-the-money options are much riskier. Thus, just as when an investor creates a portfolio of securities, a firm must carefully select options to purchase, and must keep in mind the overall risk profile of the portfolio.

While it may be possible to appraise the value of a parcel of land, which provides a (noisy) estimate of its market value, most real options do not have a readily observable market value. However, it is often possible to implicitly calculate such a value based on the relationship of the real option to underlying variables that have known market values. The technique for doing this relative valuation was originally developed to price financial options, and is currently extensively employed to value real options.

Flexibility options in equipment manufacturing
This valuation approach can be illustrated with an example of a flexibility option.[4] An equipment manufacturer based in the US recognises that foreign-based competitors periodically obtain a competitive advantage when their currencies depreciate relative to the dollar, since their operating costs become lower than those of the American manufacturer. The American firm could neutralise this advantage if it were to locate production abroad. Furthermore, if its domestic and foreign plants were built with excess capacity, the company could shift production between countries in response to currency fluctuations, increasing production in countries that have a relative cost advantage.[5] In this manner, the firm is not simply hedging its competitive risk exposure, but is also creating value by decreasing its cost basis through time.

However, it is clearly costly to build new production plants, to allow for excess capacity in these plants, and to shift production between locations. In fact, it is quite possible that the investments made to build additional plants will never pay off, eg, if the volatility in exchange rates subsides. Thus, the firm must carefully evaluate whether the flexibility option it could create has sufficient value to offset the costs. To do this, it is important to consider an alternative mechanism for achieving the same cost savings, namely using foreign exchange derivatives. What is needed is a carefully crafted derivatives portfolio strategy that yields profits when the value of foreign currencies depreciate relative to the US dollar, that are equivalent to the cost savings that would be achieved through the real investment in the global plants.

This financial derivatives investment strategy is somewhat complex and requires frequent re-balancing through time. But, it is in fact possible to produce cashflows that match the savings that would be achieved through locating production abroad and switching locations over time.[6]

Assuming that financial markets are efficient, the cost of this derivatives portfolio is equal to its value, and should be taken as a proxy of the value of the flexibility option, since they both yield the same payoffs. Thus, to justify creation of the flexibility option, this value must exceed the cost of investing in the real option.

Note that this is like saying that since the same cashflows can be achieved either through investment in real assets or financial assets, one should decide to create the real option only if this is the least expensive way of achieving the desired contingent cashflow. This concept is the economic underpinning of capital budgeting, where a company's goal should be to create shareholder value through investing in projects that yield higher returns relative to financial investments that have similar risk.

Contractual options in aircraft manufacturing

As mentioned earlier, a firm may acquire growth and flexibility options through contracts with other parties. In some cases, these options can be embedded as part of complex supply or purchase contracts. While a firm may desire to build in options into its contracts, it is important for the firm to understand what it is giving up in the process. It may have to make other concessions in the contract, such as paying a higher price for goods purchased.

It is interesting that with a contractual real option, one party purchases the option and the other party sells it, or, to use financial option parlance, "writes" it. The option feature can (and hopefully does) create value for both parties. For instance, in the case of aircraft delivery options, aircraft manufacturers are willing to grant options to airlines because the value of these options to the airlines presumably exceeds the cost to the manufacturer. This additional value is implicitly split between the two parties through negotiation.

The value creation comes from at least two sources. First, aircraft manufacturers have invested in flexible aircraft designs (commonality within a family of aircraft) and flexible manufacturing facilities that allow for shorter lead times and the ability to assemble different aircraft types at the same facility. This flexibility is best exploited by allowing airlines to postpone their purchase decisions under favourable terms. Second, aircraft manufacturers are able to diversify some of the risks that airlines face. Since not every airline will ultimately be able to increase its market share, some of the options granted to airlines may not be exercised. Thus, while selling options is often characterised as being quite risky, certain firms have a comparative advantage at bearing and managing the risks associated with contractual real options (similar to the role of investment banks in the financial options market), and thus can create shareholder value in this manner.

MANAGING REAL OPTION VALUE

Characterising a firm's growth opportunities and managerial flexibility as real options provides a different perspective from which to examine how management can enhance shareholder value. By understanding the drivers of option value, and using insights gained from financial option pricing, stronger intuition can be applied to making value enhancing strategic and operating decisions. Furthermore, the value added from these decisions can be quantified based on option pricing techniques, and thus appropriately reflected in the company's share price and in the compensation of managers who make these decisions. While the analogy to financial options is intuitively appealing and useful in understanding the characteristics of real options, there are many limitations to this analogy, as will be shown below, requiring that we develop some insights that are unique to real options alone.

The key value drivers for options

The following six key factors determine the value of a call or put option:

1. the current value of the underlying asset (or, equivalently, the present value of cashflows from the investment under consideration);
2. the exercise price (the investment cost paid when the option is exercised);
3. the time to maturity of the option (how long the opportunity exists to delay the investment decision);
4. the risk or "volatility" of the underlying investment (which is measured as the standard deviation of the rate of return on the underlying investment);
5. the risk-free interest rate (roughly speaking the rate of return on a US Treasury security whose maturity matches that of the option); and
6. the payout (eg, dividend rate) on the underlying asset.[7]

The directions in which these factors affect call and put option values – eg, an increase in exercise price decreases the value of a call option and increases the value of a put option – are shown in Table 2.

With a financial option, it is reasonably assumed that the holder of the option can do nothing to influence the value of the option, other than to ensure that it is exercised optimally. After all, the exercise price and time to maturity are specified in the option contract, and the holder cannot (legally) affect the price path of the underlying asset.[8] In contrast, there are many ways to affect real option, and thus shareholder, value.

The six value drivers listed above will be examined in greater detail to determine how each may be used as a lever to control option value. The optimal exercise of real options and opportunities to transform the nature of these options will then be explored.

Table 2. Effect of an increase in six key value drivers on call and put option values

Option value driver	Call option	Put option
Underlying asset value	Increase	Decrease
Exercise price	Decrease	Increase
Time to maturity	Increase	Increase
Volatility	Increase	Increase
Risk-free interest rate	Increase	Decrease
Payout rate	Decrease	Increase

Controlling the value drivers

To enhance the value of a growth option, the present value of the underlying investment opportunity needs to be increased through better product design, marketing, etc. The investment cost (or exercise price) should be decreased, for instance, by employing less expensive technology, taking advantage of economies of scale, etc. This is hardly surprising and would also apply to an investment opportunity that was being considered for immediate implementation. Similarly, it is clear that a put option's value increases with its exercise price. For example, the value of an abandonment option can be enhanced by increasing the salvage value of a project's assets.

The time to maturity of an option and the volatility of the underlying asset jointly affect the value of an option in a very important way.[9] Relative to deciding today whether or not to invest, an option provides the ability to wait for additional information before making the investment decision. The more informed this decision can be, the better, as the probability of making a decision that would ultimately prove to be a costly mistake is reduced. Thus, what makes an option valuable is the amount of relevant information that can be obtained during the life of the option. Clearly, the longer the maturity of an option, the more time there is to obtain information. But, just as important is the level of volatility – the greater the volatility, the more uncertainty will be resolved over a given period of time.

With financial options, the naturally evolving value of some underlying variable, such as a stock price, is the process by which the option holder becomes better informed over time. In contrast, with a real option, a conscious, and typically costly, effort must often be applied to resolve uncertainty. The way in which information is acquired can have a significant effect on the value of the option to the firm. To increase the amount of information available to make a future decision, a firm could try to lengthen the maturity of its option, speed up the rate of acquiring information, or increase the precision of its estimation process. These methods of acquiring additional information are illustrated below.

How can a firm increase the duration of its options? In some cases it may be as straightforward as renegotiating (at a cost) the maturity of a contractual real option, such as the option to purchase power. However, it often involves redesigning a process so as to give the firm more time before it must commit to making a decision regarding production, delivery, etc. Coy (1999) reports that Hewlett-Packard (HP) used real options analysis to justify a reconfigured assembly system. Rather than perform final assembly of printers destined for foreign markets at the factory, the company introduced the flexibility to only partially assemble printers at the factory and then to complete customised assembly at foreign warehouses once it had firm orders in specific countries. Though local customisation is more costly, this change to the assembly process enables HP to delay the final customisation, and avoid over or under-supply of printers in various foreign markets.[10]

One of the defining elements of the New Economy is the facility by which information can be gathered quickly and accurately, and then applied to optimise strategic and operating decisions. Technology has had an impact not only on new Internet-based companies, but also on some of the pillars of the traditional economy. For instance, elaborate 3-D simulations are now being employed in the upstream oil business. This technology allows firms to better evaluate potential drill sites, and thus to reduce the likelihood of spending significant money to drill a hole that turns out empty.

The speed and accuracy with which firms can now acquire information means that they can make informed decisions much more quickly. This underscores the importance of investing in these information acquisition technologies as a competitive tool to allow earlier exercise of a firm's growth options. Of course, some growth options still require long periods of time before sufficient information can be obtained on which to base a decision – R&D being a case-in-point. Here too, though, there has been increased pressure on scientists and engineers to resolve initial uncertainty as quickly as possible – to "fail fast" if that is the likely ultimate outcome.

Optimal exercise of real options

The case of vacant land as a growth option is an interesting one in that there is no fixed exercise date for this option. In other words, the option has an infinite horizon. A real estate developer that has strategically acquired land in an urban area showing signs of revitalisation could begin development of an office complex immediately. However, there are a number of uncertainties to be considered. A subway extension to the area is being evaluated by the county, but it may not materialise. There is uncertainty surrounding the interest rate at which the project can be financed – a decrease in the interest rate could make the project much more profitable than it would be if it were financed today. Furthermore, other developers are considering similar projects and should they all choose to develop, there may be oversupply in the market.

By delaying construction, the developer can benefit from (at least partial) resolution of these and other project and market uncertainties. For instance, should demand soften or construction costs increase, the firm would further delay development. However, the developer does have some of his capital tied up in the land and is forgoing potential income from a developed property. Furthermore, there may be a first-mover advantage to securing key long term leases if the future demand may not be sufficient to fill all the office space that will be available over the next few years.

Another important but difficult strategic decision that firms face is the decision to kill a project. Should a project be abandoned as soon as it becomes unprofitable? Not necessarily, if it is difficult to reverse this decision once abandonment occurs. The intuition is similar to the rationale for waiting to invest. By delaying abandonment, even though the firm incurs some losses in the short run, it is leaving open the option to have resumed profitability if favorable conditions return. If losses instead continue over time and the project shows no promise of a turnaround, the firm can always abandon the project at some later date.

While it may be easy to identify the pros and cons of delaying the exercise of a real option, a more rigorous framework is needed to carefully identify the optimal time to exercise the option. The optimal exercise decision is intertwined with the pricing of the option itself, since the option value is contingent on the exercise policy. In practice, this problem is formulated using a binomial option pricing model, where a binomial (ie, up-down) tree of possible scenarios is first generated, and then the decision to exercise is evaluated periodically throughout the time horizon.[11] More frequent and accurate reviews of the tradeoff between immediate exercise versus delayed exercise are thus a critical way in which the firm can fully capitalise on its option value.[12]

Enhancing option value by transforming the nature of real options

Most call options traded in financial markets have a simple payment structure – there is an initial payment to purchase the option, and a second payment when and if the option is exercised. However, a special type of call option called a compound (or sequential-pay) option has the attractive feature that, rather than pay for the option all at once, the option holder pays periodically through time to keep the option alive. Each time a payment is made, the option holder is essentially deciding to purchase an option to exercise the next stage of the option, and so on. The option holder has the right to stop payment at any time, and thus can avoid paying for the full cost of the option if it seems that the option will not ultimately be profitable.

Not surprisingly, this privilege to stop paying for the option at any time means that the compound call is likely to be more expensive than the standard call. In fact, in the highly efficient financial option markets, the total payments made by the holder of a compound call option – assuming the option is held to maturity – is indeed higher than the single initial payment of an otherwise equivalent standard call option. The more stages there are, the higher the differential between the costs of the two options.

However, in the case of real options, this is not necessarily the case. Many strategic investments can be staged over time, rather than requiring all investment to be made up front. While in some cases it may be more expensive to split a project into phases (eg, due to lost economies of scale), the additional cost is often minimal. A firm may even be able to cut costs by managing a project in this manner, since the demand for labour and other scarce resources is spread out through time.

By transforming a growth option from a simple call option to a compound call option at a relatively low cost, a firm may significantly enhance the value of its options. Investments made at each stage will be more informed than if they were all made at once. Knowledge is gained from implementing the previous project stages, as well as simply from the passage of time. For example, more will be known about financial market variables such as the level of interest or exchange rates, the price of oil, etc.

The idea of staging is pervasive in the Internet industry, despite the widely cited imperative of speed in implementing an idea. For instance, Amazon.com focused first on creating a successful on-line retail market for books before making a sequence of investments to expand its menu of Internet services. Staging is also the *modus operandi* when funding R&D projects. R&D projects are frequently reevaluated as they proceed through a series of gates. It is also not surprising that venture capitalists fund start-up companies in a series of rounds, allowing the VCs to periodically reevaluate the likely success of each company in their portfolio.

Another way for a firm to transform the nature of its real options is to employ a *parallel investment* strategy.[13] Consider an automobile manufacturer that invests in an R&D program in order to potentially develop a new convertible sports car. This call option may pay off if a technically sound and aesthetically appealing car can be developed. However, even though it requires additional investment in the R&D stage of the project, the company may be better off by trying to develop three new designs instead of one. With three designs available, a better car is more likely to be developed, and more likely to be worth producing.

Thus, despite the increase in cost, it may be worthwhile to transform a simple call option into an "option on the max", namely an option to take the most profitable design from the choices available, and to sell this product if its discounted cashflow exceeds the costs of setting up production, marketing and distribution. An option that has several underlying variables is particularly valuable if the correlation between these different variables is low, or negative. Thus, the more distinct the designs coming out of the lab are (and the greater the number of them), the higher the value of the option to choose the best design. This suggests that separate teams should develop the competing designs.

Real options may also be transformed when firms enter into transactions such as mergers and acquisitions (M&As) or joint ventures. There may be value added from combining real options within a single firm. For instance, information could be shared that would allow either more informed, or equally informed but more rapid, decisions to be made. With horizontal mergers, the option to wait to invest becomes more valuable since some of the competitive pressures that trigger early exercise are relieved (this could be viewed as extending the time to maturity of the option). Also, there may be various synergies that could reduce the cost of future exercise decisions, and increase the value of the underlying opportunities.

Generally, when contemplating transactions with other firms, one must examine whether there are real option opportunities that are better exploited by one firm versus the other, or by the merged firms. The recent M&A activity in the Internet industry points to the benefits of combining options. Since most real option opportunities are not easily separated from the firm as a whole, an acquiring firm would have to make an assessment about the overall portfolio of options that could be acquired, recognising that some of these options may be less attractive than others.

These transformations of simple real options into compound options, options on the max and option portfolios illustrate that the very nature of real options can be altered in order to increase their value. Of course, variations of these transformations could be combined to further enhance shareholder value. For example, a biotech firm could stage its R&D process, pursuing several possible products during the early stages, and allowing for the possibility of entering into a joint venture with another firm at later stages where research knowledge can be shared and development costs can be reduced.

APPLYING REAL OPTIONS ANALYSIS TO OTHER CORPORATE DECISIONS

Real options analysis is typically prescribed as a way of evaluating or justifying specific strategic investments in the firm. While it certainly provides a financially disciplined approach to making strategic investment decisions, the conceptual and valuation benefits of this analysis technique can be applied to other corporate decisions, including financing strategy, project portfolio optimisation, enterprise risk management, and compensation policies. Some of the issues to consider regarding the connections between these important decisions and real options analysis are outlined below.

The term "real options" first appeared in a chapter by Stewart Myers (1977) that focused more on the effect of a firm's financing strategy on the investment decisions of the firm, than on the evaluation of the firm's investments. Myers pointed out that a highly levered firm may not optimally exercise its growth options if the exercise price must be paid entirely by the shareholders, while the benefits are shared with the bondholders. This "underinvestment" or "debt overhang" problem illustrates the importance of designing a firm's financing strategy to be consistent with extracting the maximum value out of a firm's portfolio of real options.

The "portfolio" aspect of a firm's investments in real options needs to be highlighted. While the typical application of real options analysis is geared towards maximising the value of a particular investment, it is important to note that this is not necessarily consistent with shareholder value maximisation. While this may seem puzzling, a project could potentially negatively impact a firm's other projects or future opportunities, thus negating any value that the project would create on its own.

To illustrate, consider a computer manufacturer that decides to take a big bet by investing significant resources into developing and selling a hand-held computer. Should the product fail in the market, the company may not only face significant losses from this project, but may also suffer lower profitability in its other projects. This could occur if the firm is highly levered and the losses from the new product push the firm to the brink of insolvency, causing disruptions due to nervous customers, suppliers and employees. Even if leverage is not the problem, the losses may mean that new opportunities may not get funded if the firm is short of cash and wishes to avoid the costs associated with accessing external financial markets. Thus, by pursuing one growth option, the firm may forgo the creation and/or exercise of other, potentially more profitable, growth options.

To maximise total shareholder wealth, rather than simply the value of a single real option, firms should engage in a portfolio optimisation exercise that takes the firm's financing (and any other) constraints into account. Since a real options analysis can calculate not only the value of individual projects, but also the riskiness of those projects, it can provide all the key inputs to the optimisation, even the correlation between the values or returns across projects.

The portfolio optimisation can be extended even further to include the firm's risk management activities – the use of option and forward contracts for delivery of products, insurance contracts and derivatives trading. This enterprise risk management (ERM) analysis is likely to reveal the following intuition. Flexibility options allow a firm to truncate its downside risk – in fact, this explains part or all of the value of these options. Growth options, on the other hand, tend to introduce risk into the firm (consider the impact of introducing call options into one's stock portfolio). After all, these options have the possibility of delivering a huge return, but may also return nothing at all. The flexibility options, together with the other risk management strategies that a firm pursues, allow the firm to increase its capacity to bear risk, and thus to invest in profitable growth options.[14] Thus, value creation through investing in and exercising real options requires a holistic view of the enterprise and its risk capacity.

The ability to create a valuable portfolio of real options and to nurture and exercise these options with an eye towards maximising enterprise value, rests within the control of a firm's managers. Will they allocate significant parts of their budget toward projects that may never pay off, or may start paying off only years into the future? Will they advocate killing unprofitable projects in their divisions? Will they be patient to wait before exercising options in order to acquire additional information? Perhaps, but these actions are more likely if managerial compensation packages include incentives that align managers' interests with the objective of creating and enhancing option value.

Structuring compensation that reflects real option value is not easy. Of course, in smaller organisations, equity-based compensation may provide the appropriate incentives if the value of a firm's real options are properly reflected in the market price of the firm's shares. But otherwise, firms need to try to quantify the value of newly created options as well as the value added from skilled management of existing options, and tie compensation to these metrics.

THE EQUITY MARKET'S VIEW OF REAL OPTIONS VALUE

Viewing a firm's growth and flexibility opportunities as real options provides a new framework for examining corporate strategy. Furthermore, using the tools of real options analysis, alternative strategies can be more carefully compared from the perspective of shareholder value maximisation. If managers' incentives are appropriately aligned, they will actively create real options, take steps to enhance the value of existing options through controlling key value drivers and transforming the nature of the options, and select the appropriate time to exercise the options.

While a firm's managers may be confident that their actions increase the fundamental value of the enterprise, it is not a given that the market value of the firm's shares will reflect this value. Though managers presumably try to focus on increasing firm value without worrying about the daily variations in the market price of a firm's shares, the market value may in fact be relevant for legitimate reasons. The firm may need to raise additional equity, it may want to use its stock to acquire other firms, or it may wish to use equity-based compensation to motivate its employees.

Thus, it is important that equity analysts and investors recognise the value added from increased option value. Is this currently true? Internet companies seem to be educating investors very quickly about the value of real options. Hopefully this understanding will continue to spread to shareholders of other companies, without requiring that companies have negative earnings for real option value to be appreciated.

1   See Kulatilaka, Balasubramaniam and Storck, 1999, for a discussion on the use of real options analysis to justify investment in IT.

2   See Paul-Choudhury, 1999, for an example involving F. Hoffman – La Roche and Genentech.

3   General Motors recently shelved its plan to introduce an entirely new design for the Chevrolet Cavalier line, and redirected its resources towards getting several other product lines to market faster (see White, 1999).

4   The purpose here is to explain the intuition behind the valuation of real options, stressing in particular the relationship between the value of a real option and a portfolio of market securities that could yield the same payoff as the option (this is discussed at greater length in Amram and Kulatilaka, 1999). The exact valuation mechanics are carefully developed in numerous academic articles on real options, including Mello, Parsons and Triantis (1985), who deal directly with the case of valuing global production flexibility, as well as in books by Dixit and Pindyck (1995) and Trigeorgis (1996).

5   There may also be logistical advantages associated with creating a global production configuration, but we leave those aside here to focus on the cost savings from being able to capitalise on exchange rate fluctuations.

6   To truly produce identical cashflows, it is necessary that foreign exchange derivatives exist on each currency in question, and with maturities that go out as far into the future as the production plants would continue operating. Since these conditions may not hold in practice, the value of the financial derivatives strategy may only approximate the true opportunity cost of investing in the global production network.

7   These are the six parameters that appear in, for example, the Black-Scholes formula. See Hull (1999) for more details about this formula and other option pricing approaches.

8   The notable exception to this statement is that corporate insiders can, and hopefully should, affect the value of their executive stock options by adding value to the firm, and thus its equity. They could also conceivably increase option value by controlling the firm's dividend payout, the volatility of the stock, and the stock price path (through timing information releases), none of which is consistent with the underlying rationale for granting these options.

9   Independent of volatility, the time to maturity can also affect option value in two other ways. First, if the exercise price is fixed (as it is in the case of a financial option), the longer the time until that cost is incurred, the lower its present value would be. This would increase the present value of a call option and decrease the value of a put option. However, if the exercise price is expected to rise at the risk-free interest rate, which might well be expected for many investment projects, this benefit of a longer time to maturity is neutralised. Second, if there is an expected "leakage" in the present value of the underlying asset or opportunity (eg, due to a dividend payout), then the longer the time to maturity, the more pronounced an effect this will have on decreasing the value of a call option and increasing the value of a put option.

10 Modularity of design and assembly allows a firm to design and produce new products more quickly. This can be viewed as giving a firm the advantage of getting products to market more quickly than its competitors, or, alternatively, the advantage of being able to delay launch decisions (lengthen option maturity) until more information is acquired, without losing market share due to a delayed product launch. Baldwin and Clark (1997) explore the many advantages of modularity.

11 Formally, this decision problem is called a dynamic programming problem. Decisions are made starting at the end of a horizon under all possible scenarios at that point in time. Then, working systematically back through time, decisions to be made at any point in time take as given the set of optimal decisions, and thus outcomes, in all future scenarios. A detailed analysis of the value of waiting to invest that uses this procedure can be found in McDonald and Siegel (1986) and, in the context of real estate development, in Titman (1985). The option to abandon is examined in Brennan and Schwartz (1985) and Myers and Majd (1990).

12 Corman (1997) suggests that, back in the early 1970s, New England Electric exercised its option to construct the Seabrook nuclear power plant too early, and should have waited for

additional resolution of uncertainty surrounding gas prices and capital costs. Now, the company is timing its investment decisions more carefully by making use of real options analysis. With the benefit of perfect hindsight, a poor exercise decision based on information that was available when the decision was made may be confused with a poor investment decision based on the knowledge of actual outcomes after the decision was made. Nevertheless, in some cases there does appear to be a tendency for firms to exercise their options too early even when they don't face competitive pressures to do so.

13 Childs, Ott and Triantis (1998) analyse the advantages of parallel and sequential investment using a real options model.

14 Triantis (1999) discusses these issues at greater length. In an interview conducted by Nichols (1994), Merck's CFO Judy Lewent states that Merck hedges its foreign exchange risk in order to be able to ensure that it can continue to invest in R&D, a real option that has been highly profitable for the firm.

BIBLIOGRAPHY

Amram, M. and N. Kulatilaka, 1999, *Real Options: Managing Strategic Investment in an Uncertain World*, Harvard Business School Press, Boston, Massachusetts.

Baldwin, C. and K. Clark, 1997, "Managing in an Age of Modularity", *Harvard Business Review*, September–October, pp. 84–93.

Brennan, M. and E. Schwartz, 1985, "Evaluating Natural Resource Investments", *Journal of Business*, 58, pp. 135–57.

Carman, L., 1997, "To Wait or Not To Wait", *CFO Magazine*, May.

Childs, P.D., S.H. Ott and A.J. Triantis, 1998, "Capital Budgeting for Interrelated Projects: A Real Options Approach", *Journal of Financial and Quantitative Analysis*, 33(3), pp. 305–34.

Coy, P., 1999, "Exploiting Uncertainty: The real options revolution in decision-making", *Business Week*, June, pp. 118–24.

Dixit, A. and R. Pindyck, 1995, *Investment Under Uncertainty*, Princeton University Press, New Jersey.

Hull, J.C., 1999, *Options, Futures and Other Derivative Securities*, Fourth Edition, Prentice Hall, Englewood Cliffs, New Jersey.

Kulatilaka, N., P. Balasubramanian, and J. Storck, 1999, "Using Real Options to Frame the IT Investment Problem," in *Real Options*, Risk Publications, London.

McDonald, R. and D. Siegel, 1986, "The Value of Waiting to Invest", *Quarterly Journal of Economics*, 101, pp. 707–27.

Mello, A., J. Parsons and A. J. Triantis, 1995, "An Integrated Model of Multinational Flexibility and Financial Hedging", *Journal of International Economics*, 39, pp. 27–51.

Myers, S., 1977, "Determinants of Corporate Borrowing", *Journal of Financial Economics*, 5, pp. 146–75.

Myers, S., and S. Majd, 1990, "Abandonment Value and Project Life", *Advances in Futures and Options Research*, 4, pp. 1–21.

Nichols, N., 1994, "Scientific Management at Merck", *Harvard Business Review*, January–February, pp. 89–99.

Paul-Choudhury, S., 1999, "Reaping Real Rewards," *CFO Europe*, July–August, pp. 48–52.

Titman, S., 1985, "Urban Land Prices Under Uncertainty", *American Economic Review*, 75, pp. 505–14.

Triantis, A.J., 1999, "Real Options and Corporate Risk Management", in *Corporate Risk: Strategies and Management*, ed. Brown, G.W. and D.H. Chew, Risk Books, London.

Trigeorgis, L., 1996, *Real Options – Managerial Flexibility and Strategy in Resource Allocation*, MIT Press, Cambridge, Massachusetts.

White, G.L., 1999, "Why GM Rewound Its Product Strategy, Delaying New Cavalier", *Wall Street Journal*, July 30, pp. A1–6.

4

Applications in Real Options and Value-based Strategy

Justin Pettit

Stern Stewart & Co.

VALUE-BASED MANAGEMENT

Managing for value has become the mantra of today's executive in the US and, increasingly, in other parts of the world, such as Germany and Japan. Companies as diverse as Siemens, Sony and Molson have publicly announced the formal implementation of economic value added (EVA)[1] management systems in their quest for the value-maximisation proposition.

Many academic writers, mainstream journalists and even analyst community members have interpreted these initiatives merely as an advance in metrics and measurement. But such a narrow interpretation would seem to imply little fundamental change to the behaviour of the many people responsible for the decisions and actions that create value. To function as a more robust measure of financial performance and related financial management tools to create value, EVA must be coupled with a powerful change to management processes, including planning, portfolio management, strategic and tactical decision making, and total compensation strategy.

Pitfalls of traditional performance measurement

The maxim "what gets measured gets managed" does not only refer to shareowner value. A review of businesses' favourite financial performance measures – and their pitfalls – shows that managers and executives should be very careful. While business schools have been preaching valuation concepts for decades, earnings per share and other traditional financial measures continue to rule supreme. However, these metrics have many risks.

Over-investment

Profit and profit margin measures often drive over-investment and vertical integration because they overlook capital and its cost. Increasingly, different businesses and business models consume varying levels of capital at

WHY SHAREOWNER VALUE?

Shareowner value is all the buzz in business – move over total quality management. Activity-based costing and business process re-engineering too have been eclipsed by the value-bandwagon. "Valuespeak" now permeates annual reports, mission statements, etc. Why all the fuss? What are companies saying when they climb aboard the value bandwagon? What about stakeholders? Who are these demanding shareholders and what's in it for us?

Asia's recent economic crisis illustrates the risk to social and economic stability and standards of living created by a poor corporate governance climate – the measures, incentives, tools and controls that support decision making must be consistent with strategies to maximise shareowner value. Prolonged periods of pervasive capital misallocation and mismanagement destroy massive amounts of wealth and undermine the economy.

One of the most basic and fundamental tenets of capitalism is the obligation to maximise shareowner value. This is nothing new. An expectation of a return is created with every dollar raised and invested. A tacit promise to maximise value is also made to shareowners with each dollar of profit that is retained rather than distributed. Thus, the litmus test behind any decision to raise, invest, or retain a dollar must be to create more value than the investor might have achieved with an alternative investment opportunity of similar risk. This is, of course, all motherhood and apple pie.

A simple home-front example shows the importance for managers and employees of keeping sight of the need to manage for value. What would happen if "Brick Bank" paid only a 5% rate of interest on savings accounts, while "E-Bank" offered 15% on money market accounts of virtually equal risk? Obviously, a 15% rate of return is much better than 5%, when all else is equal. Consequently, many people will storm into Brick Bank, withdraw their life's savings, and march down the street to E-Bank.

This example illustrates that capital is a scarce resource that all businesses, and even government agencies, must compete for and efficiently manage. This means that they must provide customer-valued products and services effectively and efficiently to maximise the utility of their invested capital. The limited supply of, and liquid markets for, capital require that its users maximise its value – maximise shareowner value, or face the flight of capital to more attractive opportunities.

If managing for value is embracing the interests of owners, what then of the interests of other stakeholders? Let's start with a look at who these owners are, for they are not rich young professionals on Wall Street. Our mutual funds, pension plans, life insurance policies and many small investor holdings represent the vast majority of stock ownership. Our largest institutional investors represent the savings of everyday citizens. We invest our savings and bear risk, in the hope of the best return possible.

But this need not imply a conflict between the interests of customers, employees, owners and the managers, executives and directors who act as stewards of our savings. Fashionable shareowner- stakeholder discussions belie a confusion of means and ends. Value maximisation, the heart of economic growth, is a long-term proposition that delivers higher economic output and prosperity through productivity gains, employment growth and higher wages. The interests of stakeholders and of society are best served when our scarce resources are put to their most productive uses. Management's most important mission is to maximise shareowner wealth; managing for value directs our scarce resources to their most promising uses and most productive users. The societal benefits of managing for value are clear. The more effectively our scarce resources can be deployed and managed, the more robust will be our economic growth and the rate of improvement in our collective standard of living. It is no secret that weak systems of corporate governance, inhibited market discipline, and a general apathy toward the value maximisation imperative have played an important role in the Asian economic crisis.

The challenge facing investors is to place their savings with stewards of capital who will manage to the value-maximising proposition. This ensures an efficient allocation of our limited supply of capital. But distinguishing the value-maximisers from the value-destroyers has always been at best an art form. A look beyond the glossy pages to the proxy can be a good start. How much do your stewards – the Board and management – have at stake? What tangible factors drive their personal returns? Is there any mention of accountability for past goals?

Another risk that our investments in many companies face is the exaggerated reliance on signals from accounting information. Traditional accounting based performance measures and incentives not only encourage rampant short termism among managers, but also lead to other forms of dysfunctional behaviour. The systematic underpricing of capital by accounting has also driven broad capital misallocation and mismanagement.

Globalism presents investors with both an opportunity and a challenge. As historically insular product, labour and capital markets become increasingly global, companies will continue to face increasing competitive pressures. Under pressure to perform, institutional investors are warming to the notions of shareowner activism and heightened corporate governance. Market liquidity and the emergence of more sophisticated and demanding institutional investors have made the consequences of destroying shareowner value much more material to today's employees, executives and directors.

varying costs. Managers are often drawn to higher margin businesses that, on the surface, may seem more attractive. For example, profits are often improved with newer production technology – but they must be, to compensate for the higher levels of investment. Because traditional financial measures ignore the returns that shareholders expect, any corporate project with a positive – but not necessarily adequate – return above zero can improve a manager's margins, unit cost, profit and productivity measures. However, such a project can also destroy value.

Over-production
Traditional measure of unit cost, utilisation and income frequently promote troublesome over-production, particularly at the end of a year or quarter. Producing to capacity rather than to demand often appears to reduce costs, yet doing so can also raise the cost of invested capital. The bias towards over-production, despite demand, is exacerbated by absorption accounting practices, which convert operating costs into inventory. This practice gives the illusion of lower costs from the distorted perspective of a cost per part, while creating operating burdens (eg, uneven and inflexible production) and vast quantities of unnecessary inventory. Foregone revenue is endemic to this vicious circle, because heavy discounting and trade promotion are needed to unload the extra product, often at the end of each quarter.

Feed the dogs, starve the stars
Many managers have a strong affinity for percentages because of their intuitive appeal. Unfortunately, a focus on percentage margins and rates of return starves the "stars" and feeds the "dogs" (see Table 1). A low-return "dog" business might be motivated to pursue return-expanding growth that, if below the cost of capital, would destroy value. A high-return "star" business might overlook or reject return-diluting growth that, although above its cost of capital and therefore additive to value and EVA, will decrease returns.

Table 1. Traditional performance measures "starve the stars" and "feed the dogs"

	"Feed the dogs"			"Starve the stars"		
	Bus. "A"	Bus. "B"	Sum	Bus. "A"	Bus. "B"	Sum
Sales	US$250	US$133	US$383	US$1250	US$1000	US$2250
Margin	20%	30%	23%	20%	10%	16%
Income	US$50	US$40	US$90	US$250	US$100	US$350
Capital	US$1,000	US$500	US$1,500	US$1,000	US$500	US$1,500
Return	5%	8%	6%	25%	20%	23%
Capital cost at 10%	US$100	US$50	US$150	US$100	US$50	US$150
EVA	(US$50)	(US$10)	(US$60)	US$150	US$50	US$200

Service economy

Traditional financial measures, being based on traditional business models, have not kept up with the pace of change. New business models are often based on services, outsourcing, partnerships and other innovative ways of doing business. Therefore, traditional financial measures are inherently biased against the new service economy. Their blunt nature is too simplistic, creating impediments to profitable growth in a world where more and more service-oriented businesses are being designed around razor-thin margins, but with low capital investment. Similarly, a bias against viable, long-term investments and economic growth can result from a simplistic, near-term income focus.

Poor decisions

Traditional financial measures exclude the shareholders' investment in the business; an incomplete measure that ignores capital is entirely inappropriate to handle the many business decisions that trade-off between profit margin and capital utilisation. Traditional financial measures confuse accounting anomalies with the underlying economics of business. When tied to incentive compensation, this can lead to dysfunctional behaviour among managers and top executives alike. A cellular company delayed the rollout of its digital network conversion by several months to avoid depreciation, despite the fact that the cash was already spent and competition was stealing customers with digital service. One company executive once explained that, "in business, you must often make decisions that you would never make if you actually owned the company." A lesson overlooked by business schools is that accounting often drives major business decisions despite – and not because of – the economics.

What is EVA?

Peter Drucker writes, "There is no profit unless you earn the cost of capital. Alfred Marshall said that in 1896, Peter Drucker said that in 1954 and in 1973, and now EVA has systematised this idea, thank God." (Drucker, 1998.)

Economic value added, or EVA, is a measure that enables managers to see whether they are earning an adequate return. Where returns are lower than might reasonably be expected for investments of similar risk (ie, they are below the cost of capital), EVA is negative, and the firm faces the flight of capital and a lower stock price.

Quite simply, EVA is a measure of profit less the cost of all capital employed. It is the one measure that properly accounts for all the complex trade-offs, often between the income statement and balance sheet, involved in creating value. EVA is also the spread between a company's return on and cost of capital, multiplied by the invested capital:

$$EVA = (\text{rate of return} - \text{cost of capital}) \times \text{capital}$$

For example, a US$1000 investment in a hot-dog stand produces a 5% return, where investments of similar risk elsewhere can earn 15%. The EVA from this case would be:

$$EVA = (5\% - 15\%) \times US\$1000 = -US\$100$$

An accountant measures profit earned, whereas an economist looks at what could have been earned. Although the accounting profit in this example is US$50 (5% × US$1000), there was an opportunity to earn US$150 (15% × US$1000).

Under EVA, each business is effectively charged by investors for the use of capital through a "line of credit" that bears interest at a rate equal to the cost of capital. Therefore, shareowner accountability is effectively decentralised into the operating units. EVA simultaneously focuses on both the profit and loss statement and the balance sheet, and can be tailored to remedy accounting anomalies that fail to reflect economic value. Finally, EVA sets a required rate of return – the cost of capital – as a hurdle rate below which performance is unacceptable.[2]

Therefore, a perhaps more meaningful way for operating managers to think of EVA comes from multiplying through by capital:

$$EVA = \text{operating profit} - \text{a capital charge}$$

where,

$$\text{capital charge} = \text{cost of capital} \times \text{capital}$$

For example, if a US$1000 investment in a hot-dog stand yields a US$50 annual profit, compared to a US$150 opportunity elsewhere, EVA can be expressed as:

$$EVA = US\$50 - US\$150 = -US\$100$$

To summarise, EVA is the only operating measure to account for the many income statement-balance sheet trade-offs involved in creating value because of its simultaneous focus on profit and capital. Under EVA, every business unit is, in effect, explicitly charged for the use of capital through a "line of credit" that bears interest at a rate equal to the cost of capital. This effectively decentralises shareowner value accountability well into the operations. EVA also sets the expected return, the cost of capital, as a hurdle rate below which performance is unacceptable. This clearly identifies the benchmark to create shareowner value.

Donaldson Brown, Chief Financial Officer of General Motors, wrote in 1924,"The objective of management is not necessarily the highest rate of return on capital, but … to assure profit with each increment of volume that will at least equal the economic cost of additional capital required."[3]

Although in any given business there are countless individual operating actions that can create value, eventually they must all fall into one of four categories measured by an increase in EVA. Specifically, EVA can be increased through the following four means.

1. *Improving the Returns on Existing Capital.* This might be achieved through higher prices or margins, more volume or lower costs.
2. *Profitable Growth.* This might be achieved through investing capital where increased profits will adequately cover the cost of additional capital. Investments in working capital and production capacity may be required to facilitate increased sales, new products or new markets.
3. *Harvest.* This might be achieved through rationalising, liquidating or curtailing investments in operations that cannot generate returns greater than the cost of capital. This might be through divestitures or through withdrawing from unprofitable markets.
4. *Optimise Cost of Capital.* This might be achieved by reducing the cost of capital but maintaining the financial flexibility necessary to support the business strategy through the prudent use of debt, risk management and other financial products.

EVA is not just a performance measure. Properly implemented, EVA is much more: it is an integrated performance measurement, management and reward system, encompassing the full range of business decision-making and moving shareowner accountability to the same level as decision-rights. Above all, it is the centerpiece of business literacy and for this reason, corporations throughout the world now use EVA to remake governance from within.

EVA management system

An increasingly popular topic among institutional investors, managers, legislators, regulators and academics is that of corporate governance. While a hot issue such as this is typically interpreted differently by different people, a broad definition formulated by Kenneth Scott of the Stanford University Law School asserts that, "Modern corporations, to take advantage of technological progress and scale economies, are large organisations requiring heavy investment. The amounts of capital required often can be raised only by pooling the savings of a multitude of investors, who rely on others to manage their investments and run the enterprise. The institutions – the particular set of legal rules, incentives, and behaviors – that support and underlie that reliance by investors constitute the system of corporate governance in a given society."[4]

A corporate management system is the governance framework that defines the measures, incentives, tools and controls supporting decision-making consistent with a company's strategies to maximise shareowner value. Many management systems, based on archaic metrics and accounting conventions, are quite adept at discouraging, if not destroying, value. These systems were designed primarily as reporting and control systems for lenders and subsequently adopted by managers as variance measurement tools in the centralised command-and-control organisations more suited to less turbulent times.

Despite the best of intentions, many managers fail to create value for many of the following reasons.

❏ The performance measures are too blunt and not systematically tied to value.
❏ There are too many performance measures, often giving conflicting signals and failing to prioritise or reveal connections, therefore hindering efforts to focus and cut through the complexity.
❏ Targets are often set through a counter-productive negotiation process that encourages managers to understate and under-perform their business's true potential.
❏ There is no integration of the incentive, planning, capital budgeting and reporting processes, or the operating and strategic levers that drive the business.
❏ Bonus plans are short term oriented and offer too little risk and reward.
❏ Inadequate attention has been given to employee education and business literacy.

Companies use a variety of conflicting measures such as earnings growth, earnings per share, return on equity, internal rate of return, market share, margin and revenue. Being less correlated to shareowner wealth, these measures are therefore more likely to lead to incongruent decision-making. Conflicting messages from different measures set the stage for internal conflict, dysfunctional behaviour and the sub-optimisation of total enterprise value.

An EVA management system aligns the interests of employees with shareowner value to promote and reward high performance. With a focus on organisational and behavioral change, this "rewires" the brain of companies to:

❏ decentralise ownership accountability;
❏ develop strong business literacy throughout the workforce;
❏ confer economic discipline at all decision-making levels of the company; and
❏ institutionalise a culture of high performance.

In 1998, Paul Romer of Stanford University, an expert on economic growth, reported that, "I was talking … with Mike Volkema … they (Herman Miller) have had great success with EVA. It's a good illustration of how abstract ideas, codified formulas, can create value in a company."[5]

An EVA management system must establish clear, accountable links between strategic thinking, budgeting and capital planning, daily operating decisions, incentive compensation, and shareowner wealth. The power of such a system rests in the fact that it creates commonalty across processes, ultimately leading to employees who think and act like owners.

So, why not just turn employees into owners? The broad use of stock and stock options throughout the workforce has increased dramatically in recent years, and yet, contrary to the myopic view often espoused, real success has been elusive. Direct ownership may give employees a share in the enterprise value, but this is well beyond the sight lines of most employees. It also fails to provide the necessary linkage between action and results ie, the operational levers and firm value. Finally, while everyone wants to share in a bull market, the syndication of market risk by under-diversified employees in a bear market can be quite discouraging.

Strategically, enterprise value is not maximised solely through the maximisation of current operations value (COV), but through the simultaneous maximisation of the sum of *both* COV *and* future growth value (FGV), including the value of real options.

While the valuation of internet stocks might be interpreted as proof of a forward-looking stock market, leading business strategists are concerned that many of today's corporations remain overly fixated on the near term.[6] The implications for business strategy, and for the supporting financial policy, financial management and compensation strategies, are far-reaching.

VALUE-BASED STRATEGY

The importance of Value-Based Management to strategy is perhaps best understood by examining three "real-world" cases in fallacious strategic analysis and decision-making.

The first case is a global automotive supplier that ran into trouble in the first half of the 1990s, having made a decision to embark away from its roots on a bold new strategy. The Company had enjoyed success in the original equipment (OE) side of the business, primarily supplying the "Big 3" assemblers, making it a "Tier 1" supplier. It enjoyed a reputation as a good manufacturer, having successfully implemented lean production concepts in some of its plants. However, it is common knowledge that the aftermarket side of the automotive parts business is a much higher margin business than manufacturing, offering 10–20% as opposed to 5–10% margins. Conventional wisdom also has it that this business is at least countercyclical, if not even less cyclical than the OE business. The Company decided to focus on the aftermarket business; the OE guys became the poor cousins. Yet analysis then determined that margins were better still even further down the "value chain". Indeed, aftermarket distribution channels are a myriad, with multiple steps, buffers and handling points in the system all offering much higher margins. Therefore, the Company embarked

WHEN A PENNY MATTERS:
A FRAMEWORK TO LINK PERFORMANCE
MEASUREMENT, VALUE AND STRATEGY

Our pockets have been increasingly laden with change in recent years – and far too many pennies. Many complain that pennies are simply not worth the effort. Why then, when a company announces that it will miss quarterly earnings estimates by a mere penny, does the stock plummet? When does a penny matter?

Simplistically, one can express a company's value as the present value of all future cashflow.[1] While net present value concepts are more easily and therefore commonly applied to fixed income valuation (eg, the value of bonds), the same concept also holds for stocks, albeit with much less certainty in the forward numbers. Therefore, a business generating US$100 per year, every year, can be valued into perpetuity as US$1000, assuming a 10% cost of capital, or time value of money (US$100 ÷ 10% = US$1000). This base, or zero-growth, case implies a "multiplier" of 10 times operating cashflow, and is the current operations value (COV).

Now, let's try a growth case where operating cashflow grows at a rate of 5% per year, forever. While many of us might think that forever is a long time, it may not be long enough to justify some of the recent internet stock prices! This business can be simply valued on a present value basis at US$100 ÷ (10% – 5%), or US$2000. This growth case implies a multiplier of 20 times and happens to illustrate a price level common to today's marketplace where many stock prices imply a multiplier of 20 times or more. In this case, the market has based one half of the stock price on the present value of current operating cashflows, forever, and the other half on growth expectations above this level – ie, fifty percent of the value is COV, while the remainder is future growth value (FGV). The FGV term subsumes not only *expected* growth, but also implicitly values any *real options*. For example, the 5% growth assumption might really be a proxy for a 90%

A. Enterprise value as the sum of current options value (COV) and future growth value (FGV), including real options value

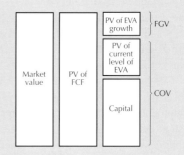

likelihood of no growth, and a 10% chance of 50% growth. Figure A illustrates the general form of this valuation framework.

When a company misses its earnings number, what are the implications for its net present value? If the miss has absolutely no implications for the future, the value of the stock is reduced by only one cent. If the miss is expected to persist for each of the four quarters, the value of the stock is reduced by four cents. If the four cent annual reduction is expected to be permanent, then we can apply our multiplier of 10 times to show that the stock value is now reduced by 40 cents.

However, if the shortfall has implications for growth opportunities, we might expect a much larger impact, like our example with a 20 times multiplier. A one penny shortfall on the quarter, or a four cent shortfall for the year, can cause not only a 40 cent reduction in the perpetuity value, but another 40 cent reduction in the growth value – a penny with an 80 cent impact![2]

A healthy dose of prudence on the part of analysts and investors can lead to an even larger stock price impact than what we have developed thus far. This is what many on Wall-Street will refer to as the "where there's smoke, there's fire" investment hypothesis. Managers within many public companies have significant financial incentives to do just about anything to shore up disappointing operating cashflows to avoid falling short. Public results often understate how bad things really are. For example, pharmaceutical companies have been known to cut their research and development budgets in poor times to boost their earnings, despite the fact that such "spending" is really "investing". Other tactics can include asset dispositions, and heavy-handed cuts to advertising or other marketing costs.

The final reason why even a one penny shortfall can have such a profound and seemingly exaggerated impact is that aggressive, albeit legal, accounting practices have been employed to salvage earnings numbers. Several cases have received considerable press in recent years. Just a few examples of the games of which investors must be wary are changes in revenue recognition; netting offsetting gains and losses; and reversals in acquisition, restructuring, warranty, bad debt, inventory and actuarial reserves. Therefore, when a company does miss by a penny, what we see is often only the tip of the iceberg, potentially warranting a dramatic, downward revision of future cashflow expectations, and dramatically lowering future growth values and stock prices.

---

1   This can also be expressed as the mathematically equivalent sum of capital and the present value of all future Economic Value Added (EVA).

2   The current operations value can be also expressed as the sum of capital invested, plus the present value of current EVA into perpetuity, with no growth. The nominal zero-growth assumption implies decay in real terms.

on an international retail strategy which ultimately failed, leading it to replace its executive team a few years later.

The second case is a national brewer that found market share stalling and profitability waning under the weight of a proliferation of brands. A consultant was promptly called upon to examine the portfolio and refocus the Company's strategy. It took no time at all to determine that several big-name import brands were only marginally profitable. Apparently, the margins on non-owned, non-brewed brands were far lower than the margins on brewed, owned and brewed, non-owned brands. Also, partly because they were growth brands, the non-brewed brands were a distraction on scarce management resources. A recommendation to trim these brands from the portfolio was made, but luckily, not followed.

The final example is a high growth manufacturing company with blanking, stamping and assembly operations. Two new plants were added to the business – one as part of a much larger acquisition and one through direct investment – and these shared a similar product and customer. The greenfield "South" plant was quite a success – investments in automation and state-of-the-art technology led to a very low cost per unit, high efficiencies and high margins of 10–15%. Yet, the acquired "North" plant seemed barely profitable, with margins of only 1%! Company management heavily weighed the fate of the North plant within their portfolio.

A Value-Based Management analysis sheds new light on these examples. In the case of the manufacturing company, it was observed that the unique supply agreements of the North plant were such that it enjoyed *negative* capital employed. While its margins were only about 1%, return on capital employed was *indeterminate* and its economics were very good! The brewery's only growth was in its highly economic, non-brewed imports, where very little capital were needed (no breweries being necessary). The automotive supplier stumbled under the load of the massive capital expenditures, inventories and receivables required for its new international retail strategy. The higher margins were more than offset by the capital intensity of the business, making its economics attractive only to the "category-killers" well-versed in retail distribution strategies and tactics.

An appreciation of fundamental valuation concepts and value-based measures of performance (EVA) avoids such strategic missteps. With little appreciation or understanding for valuation or decision analytics, it is not surprising that people work from intuition. Unfortunately, strategy often seems a vocation for innumerates who lack the disciplined methodology or analytic rigour practised in the sciences. In business circles, the term "strategic" seems to be a synonym for negative net present value. However, *analysis paralysis* – when the analysis starts to resemble an end rather than the means and indecision sets in – is just as deadly. Therefore, Value-Based Strategy and Real Options must be employed to bring discipline and rigour to support, but not encumber, strategic thinking and decision-making.

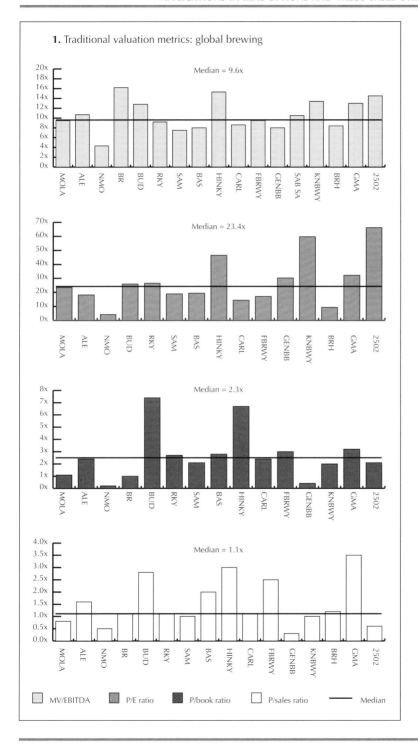

1. Traditional valuation metrics: global brewing

MV/EBITDA P/E ratio P/book ratio P/sales ratio —— Median

Limitations of traditional valuation frameworks: global brewing

The workings of the markets are a mystery to many. Several of the market stories that get picked up and interpreted by the media do not help: market volatility and the contradiction in values between those in and out of favour add to the notion of general market irrationality. All this noise leaves executives and strategists looking to investment bankers to identify the actionable value-drivers upon which to build and gauge alternative strategies and plans.

But the traditional valuation metrics are clearly flawed. As discussed earlier, the income statement measures fall short in many regards and are therefore not ideal indicators with which to gauge the best laid plans.

Not only are the measures themselves flawed – being incomplete, they are more likely to lead to incorrect signals and actions – but they are also highly subject to error. Table 2 illustrates these metrics for the global brewing industry, showing a high standard deviation in results for each approach. The EBITDA multiple is a ratio of enterprise market value (MV) to earnings before interest, taxes, depreciation and amortisation (EBITDA). As a rough proxy for operating cashflow, it works the best, while the sales multiple works the worst. However, each shows wide dispersion.

Finally, the strategic implications of the multiples themselves are not always clear. For example, many executives struggle with whether they're looking for highly accretive strategies and investments, that typically reduce multiples, or a higher multiple which typically comes with weaker, or even dilutive, earnings. This conundrum can apparently lead to a perpetual deal-machine for investment bankers. For example, one Michigan manufacturer spun off, then reacquired and then again sold one of its largest business units within a five year period.

Organisational software strategies: pharmaceuticals

In recent years, the market run-up has been partially fuelled by a run-up in current operations values. This has been evident in the broad EVA growth of the market, several industries and a majority of companies. However, the current operations value of the market has not kept up with the market in total, as future growth values have increased overall. A larger proportion of the market's value is now predicated on profitable growth (both linear and real options value). For example, America Online's value is roughly 96% future growth value, with only 4% of its market value explained by the present value of its current operating cashflow, ie its current operations value.

Primary resource industries and basic durable goods producers have not fared as well in the marketplace, with little increase in Market-to-Capital ratios, and little, if any, appreciation in future growth values. These industries are ones that often fail to earn their cost of capital on capital that is very tangible rather than flexible. They are characterised by heavy

Table 2. Market value-to-capital ratios for a sample of industries

	Market value per capital US$	Future growth as % market value	EVA per capital US$
Computer software and services	US$8.20	80%	6.7%
Pharmaceuticals	US$6.60	71%	9.1%
Personal care	US$4.40	66%	5.1%
Beverages	US$4.30	70%	3.1%
Mean	**US$3.20**	**63%**	**0.2%**
Other non-ferrous metals	US$1.20	63%	−5.6%
Cars and trucks	US$1.20	33%	−1.9%
Forest products	US$1.10	53%	−4.8%
Aluminium	US$1.00	78%	−7.8%
Steel	US$0.90	17%	−2.5%

investments in "rigid" capital, ie, investments that are sunk or irreversible, offering few real options through growth, flexibility or deferral.

Table 2 shows that much of the advance has been across industries where "flexible" capital prevails, and where investments are intangible. For example, Research and Development (R&D) is a large percentage of sales for biotechnology (41%), software (18%), pharmaceuticals (11%), and electronics (6%) industries. Brand and franchise values, and organisational "software" (covering capabilities, processes and competencies) can also be considered flexible capital.

General Electric (GE) and Wal-Mart utilise organisational "software", ie, a platform option to expand and replicate proven success on a broader scale. Pharmaceutical companies invest in a pipeline of new drugs, constituting a portfolio of new product options. Beverage companies have growth options to carry strong brands into new markets. A host of studies have shown that R&D returns are significant, and that the stock market recognises and rewards R&D investment.[7] The pharmaceuticals therefore carry a significant premium in their values (see Table 3). Nearly three-quarters of the industry's value is premised on the present value of profitable growth ie, positive NPV (Net Present Value) projects that do not yet exist – the industry pipeline. Unlike the aluminium industry, this result is not a skewed result due to any lack of current profitability – the industry exceeds its cost of capital by 11%. In fact, the result appears related to the R&D intensity (11%) of the industry.

A sampling from the pharmaceutical industry clearly shows that even within the industry, R&D intensity drives valuations. Four of the five premium-valued companies also invest more heavily in R&D, with the smaller Warner-Lambert (now merging with American Home Products) being an obvious exception. Schering-Plough and Eli Lilly seem to be the best examples of executing strategies to maximise *both* current operations values (evidenced by their high returns above the cost of capital) *and* future growth

Table 3. Pharmaceutical valuations, performance & R&D intensity

Company	Market value (US$MMs)	% COV	% FGV	EVA per US$ capital	R&D as % sales
Pfizer	162,876	15%	85%	7%	17%
Schering-Plough	81,778	21%	79%	26%	12%
Warner Lambert	64,418	24%	76%	7%	9%
Eli Lilly	100,167	27%	73%	13%	19%
Pharmacia & Upjohn	29,858	27%	73%	–2%	17%
Median	**90,972**	**27%**	**73%**	**11%**	**11%**
Bristol Myers Squibb	135,233	27%	73%	16%	9%
Abbott Labs	77,925	33%	67%	13%	10%
Johnson & Johnson	116,963	34%	66%	9%	10%
Merck	182,720	35%	65%	18%	11%
American Home Prod.	81,462	43%	57%	7%	12%

values (a high percentage of total value stems from future growth expectations, partly due to high R&D intensity and effectiveness).

Value-based strategy application: global brewing

The valuation (market value per dollar of capital) and performance (EVA per dollar of capital) of the major players in the industry is depicted in Figure 2. Brahma (BRH) and South African Breweries (SAB) each enjoy monopolistic market shares and earn 10–15% more than their costs of capital – SAB also has the highest asset turns in the industry. Bass, Heineken (HINKY) and Busch (BUD) are the next highest performers in terms of

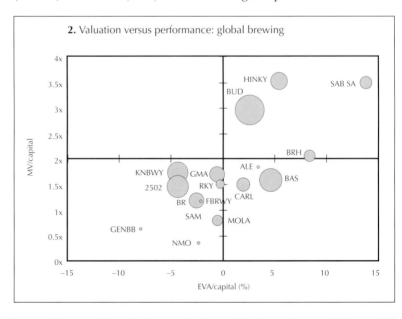

2. Valuation versus performance: global brewing

3. Future growth values versus performance: global brewing

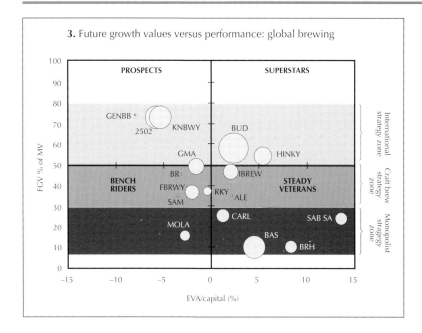

EVA per dollar of capital, with a 5% return premium over their cost of capital. While Bass and Busch accomplish this through margins, Heineken employs a very different export strategy. Premium pricing is offset by higher costs, but asset turns is very high, leading to exceptional performance. In general, the positive EVA companies trade above twice book, while the others trade at one to two times book.

Figure 3 recasts the industry with a new vertical axis and the current operations values removed from each of the market values, leaving only the future growth values. The top left quadrant are "Prospects"; performance is poor (ie, negative EVA) but expectations for improvement are high.

In the bottom left quadrant are the "Bench Riders", where performance is poor and valuations are low ie, future growth values are low. The bottom right quadrant has good EVA, but values remain low, there being little upside opportunity. The real options afforded to others are lacking, so this quadrant is therefore labelled "Steady Veterans". Finally, in the top right quadrant are the "Superstars", exhibiting high performance (EVA) and high valuations, ie, future growth value.

Despite, or perhaps because of, their high returns, Brahma and SAB market values imply very modest expectations for future growth values. Alternatively, the extremely poor all-round performance of Asahi (2502) and Kirin (KNBY) drives high expectations for improvement, rather than growth. Busch and Heineken dominate the "Superstar" quadrant, with Interbrew (IBREW), a private concern with public debt and interpolated market value likely to be in the same league.

Three valuation zones that transcend the performance effect on valuations emerge from the picture. In general, the monopolists are valued as being market constrained, with few growth options available. In reality, most of them have been creating international growth options, but at this point they are both small in size and reasonably well out-of-the-money – market entry prices have been steep and these companies have no proven ability to penetrate emerging or mature foreign markets. In fact, given their domestic situations, their core competencies are more likely be in operational excellence rather than marketing.

The top valuation band applies to the global strategies of those players who, like Busch and Heineken, manage a portfolio of in-the-money international growth options, although each execution differs between Busch's direct investment and Heineken's export strategy.

Finally, the glamorous world of "craft brewing", typified by Sam Adams (SAM) and Sleemans (ALE), lies in the middle, having been accorded some future growth value, but far less than either the more scalable global brewers or the equity markets in general.

So, what prescriptive insight does this study provide? Should each of the brewers run out and buy into the Indian, Polish or Chinese markets? As we have seen, the price of these options combined with a lack of expertise has not made this a good get-rich-quick bet. Additionally, Noble China (NMO) appears to have made a disastrous enough foray into the Chinese market to give others cause for caution. Until brewer/marketers can show true success at home, they might be best deferring their international growth options.

Real options application: automotive platform bidding

Let's move from big-picture value-based strategy to the micro-level – a real-world application in new business quoting. For example, in an automotive platform bidding opportunity, a large US assembler planned the launch of the "GMT666" truck platform, and solicited bids for a structural system. The assembler anticipated a volume of about 5 million units over a 5 year life, and expected to pay its supplier about US$600 per unit. A structural systems supplier put a team together to look at this opportunity, and, determining that a US$400 million capital investment was required to support the bid, developed the EVA and NPV analysis of Table 4. Due to the large investment and low margins, the projected volume was not sufficient to provide a positive NPV, as EVA only reached the cost of capital by about year three.

However, the lead platform engineer knew that volume projections are fraught with uncertainty – launch dates may be delayed, demand may be unexpectedly high, etc. Remembering something she had read about uncertainty analysis, she re-ran the analysis with the same expected volumes, but used a Monte Carlo simulation to make the volume assumption a "live" variable. She looked at relevant historical platform volumes and

Table 4. Initial GMT666 platform EVA & NPV analysis

	0	1	2	3	4	5
Volume (MMs)		1	1	1	1	1
Revenue (US$)	600	600	600	600	600	600
Costs		577	577	577	577	577
NOPAT		23	23	23	23	23
Capital	400	320	240	160	80	0
Capital charge		40	32	24	16	80
EVA		−17	−9	−1	7	15
PV(EVA)		−16	−8	−1	5	9
NPV	−10					

determined the data fitted a lognormal distribution with a standard deviation of about 30%. While the NPV did not change, she determined that the investment had a 50% probability of being positive, within a potential range of negative US$25 million to positive US$75 million.

However, the engineer also realised that in many cases, a platform is "freshened up" and re-launched at the end of its initially-planned life. As the supplier to the original platform, they could easily be best positioned for a successful follow-on supply contract for a successor chassis. She identified a second opportunity embedded within this supply contract opportunity in that many of the more successful truck platforms have spin-off models eg, extended cab, 4×4 and sister models. Finally, she identified a third embedded opportunity in the assembler's overseas affiliates, which was rather a long shot: if GMT666 derivatives were ever launched by the assembler's European and Japanese companies, again, they could be best positioned for the new business.

After attending a two-day conference in New York, the platform engineer realised that the opportunities embedded within the original supply contract represented real options which could be quantified for their contribution to value within the economic analysis of the platform bid.

Therefore, she increased the initial investment by a further US$100 million to add sufficient flexibility to the investment for the original bid (to support the platform life extension real option). She also determined that an approximate volatility of 60% was reasonable to capture the volatility, and a volume of 2.5 million units over five years at US$550.

While a static NPV analysis assigns a value of –US$10 million, the option value appropriately captures the value of flexibility: +US$24 million, bringing the NPV of the bid to a positive US$14 million, even without capturing the value of the real options that were more of a long-shot. Therefore, while the initial analysis required an uncompetitive price, the extended NPV analysis, incorporating even only the most likely real option, showed the business to be attractive.[8]

FINANCIAL STRATEGY

To meet the relentless escalation of shareholder expectations arising from a decade-long bull market, many companies are turning to share buybacks.[9] Is this tactic part of a shareowner value strategy, or just another chapter from the earnings-per-share manipulation playbook? While earnings-per-share growth "window dressing" has nothing to do with value, there may be a sound economic rationale to share buybacks. However, this tactic may not serve all equally well.

Share repurchases are a more tax efficient form of cash distribution than any form of dividend. They can also enhance shareowner value through a combination of improved capital structure, reduced agency costs and signalling effects.[10] While financial strategy is often narrowly interpreted as an exercise in the cost of capital *minimisation*, in practice, the determinants of financial policy must support enterprise value *maximisation*. Certainly, the firm's cost of capital and any resulting impact on firm value is one important element, but financial strategy must also support the company's business strategy and consider financial flexibility, agency issues, flotation costs, signalling and clientele considerations.[11]

Target capital structure

Repurchases can quickly and decisively move a company closer to its target capital structure, potentially creating value through the benefit of the tax shield of debt. The after-tax cost of debt is well below the expected return on equity, reducing the weighted average cost of capital and increasing value. However, debt reduces financial flexibility, especially in turbulent times, and this may lead to foregone opportunity. While debt increases *current operations value*, *future growth value* can be constrained, risking a sub-optimisation of total enterprise value.

While one supplier might achieve their lowest cost of capital, and highest current operations value, at a level of debt consistent with a B or BB rating, the option value of one-time investment opportunities with positive NPV in either growing or consolidating industries might dictate a near investment-grade financial policy. Indeed, this is the prevailing strategy among many automotive suppliers, for although cost of capital and current operations value may suffer, this can be more than offset by increased opportunity for future growth value. Therefore, optimal capital structure is partially dependent on the financial flexibility required to execute their strategy.

For example, current thinking among OE automotive suppliers, especially the leading Tier One suppliers, is that an active role within the industry consolidation will facilitate the extraction of further economic profits – partly due to increased bargaining power, partly to leveraging specific knowledge, and partly to process capabilities and a move to modular supply. Anticipated benefits include better design-for-manufacture; modular product integration and sequencing; supply-chain integration and logistical coordination; and the improved utilisation of fixed costs and capital by leveraging across common suppliers.

While no rigorous literature empirically supports these expectations, they are intuitive; the frequently cited "pilot" is the success of Lear, JCI and Magna with the modular supply of seating and interior systems. However, even Tier Two players in this segment may have economic out-performance – is it a function of the segment, or of operational excellence, bargaining power or exogenous factors?

Agency costs

Agency issues are a determinant in both the target capital structure and the distribution policy decision. Mature companies often generate significant levels of free cashflow, leading to excess capital, with a tendency to retain and then waste capital through over-investment and diversification schemes. The need to either service debt or pay dividends can alleviate a company's inherent propensity for reinvestment in any project, business or acquisition with a positive return. The greater good of debt is its discipline in forcing capital efficiency and reducing agency costs.[12]

Some have adopted a more elegant solution to the agency issue, institutionalising fiscal discipline and capital efficiency. EVA brings the discipline of debt, without the pain of covenants, by charging for all capital employed. An EVA management system can provide not only the discipline of debt, but also tools, skills and correct incentives. While EVA is no substitute for a sound business strategy, it can be used to evaluate and identify the best strategy, and, more importantly, to support strategy execution and operational excellence.[13]

Signalling

There are secondary issues that are not constraints so much as effects to be managed within the corporate financial strategy framework. The object of the most academic study has been that of the signalling effect said to arise from the information asymmetries between managers and investors. Distribution policy is construed as information laden, creating a self-reinforcing pattern that then signals the profitability expectations of insiders to outsiders. In a world of asymmetrical information, where insiders are believed to have superior knowledge with respect to the future prospects of the business, this signalling provides a market in knowledge regarding expectations for future performance.

"Bargain prices"

Beyond any effects of capital structure, agency issues and signalling, a share repurchase is an economic non-event *until* the share price stops trading at a discount to its intrinsic value. Total enterprise value and total equity value are each diminished by the amount of cash disgorged –

Table 5. "Bargain" impact to intrinsic value per share as a function of market discount and buyback size

Market/ intrinsic value ratio	% share buyback				
	5%	10%	15%	20%	25%
90%	1	1	2	3	4
85%	1	2	3	4	6
80%	1	3	4	6	8
75%	2	4	6	8	11
70%	2	5	8	11	14
65%	3	6	10	13	18
60%	4	7	12	17	22
55%	4	9	14	20	27
50%	5	11	18	25	33

shrinking the business, as if it has gone ex dividend. For every share-owner, the sum of the values of cash in hand plus the new ownership stake is *equal* to the value of the pre-deal ownership stake, net of taxes. This outcome is similar to the case where no repurchase is undertaken, and each shareowner participates fully in the upside appreciation of their ownership stake when the stock stops trading at a discount – but for one difference.

Because a business is smaller after a repurchase, its eventual appreciation in *percentage* terms is magnified if and when the stock approaches its "true" intrinsic value. The larger the repurchase, the larger the percentage gain. Therefore, the math-ematics of percentages might provide a motive for repurchase. The general case as a function of both market/intrinsic value ratio and repurchase size is shown in Table 5.

The analysis in Table 5 provides the following practical observations.

❑ The gains from such an undertaking are not as substantive as one might expect, if none of the more traditional "theoretical" benefits of a repur-chase is to be recognised.
❑ The "Bargain Price" motive for share repurchases is only material where the market price is at least 20% below the intrinsic value.
❑ A "Bargain Price" driven repurchase requires at least a 10% buyback for material impact.

Matching financial policy to business strategy

Financial policy can be considered to be largely driven by the enterprise's business strategy and operating plans, and this is well illustrated by the global beer industry example of Figure 1. In an otherwise low FGV indus-try, Anheuser-Busch (BUD) and Heineken (HINKY) stand out for their FGV premiums, implied in the 1998 year-end values. This is reinforced by their above-average price-to-earnings ratios.[14] Conversely, South African Breweries (SAB), Bass, and Brahma typify the industry's low future growth values and price-to-earnings ratios.

If the "today map" (Figure 4) is any indication of the strategies and expectations for future performance, then we can see a strong relationship between financial policy – in terms of financial leverage and dividend poli-cies – and future growth value premiums. Valuation premiums are accorded to BUD, HINKY and Groupo Modello (GMOD), who earn

SHARE REPURCHASE ALTERNATIVES

While open market repurchases are easiest to initiate, their greater flexibility and control comes at the cost of speed and commitment, weakening the signalling effect and slowing execution. Safe harbor provisions ensure a longer period to effect a recapitalisation. Fixed Price self-tender offers provide a more timely mechanism to recapitalise, and a stronger form of signalling than other forms of repurchase.[1] However, studies have also shown that higher premiums are typically paid in fixed price offers.[2] The "Dutch Auction" self-tender offer is an increasingly common method of quickly repurchasing a large portion of the company's stock, with a more efficient pricing mechanism. A significant premium must be offered to effect a successful tender, and insiders must commit not to participate in the tender.

1   In a comparison of three forms of common share repurchases, fixed price self-tender offers were found to be the strongest signal of stock undervaluation, followed by the Dutch Auction. Open market share repurchases were found to be a relatively weak signal. The signal was found to be strongest when insider wealth was at risk – where management did not tender. Comment, R. and Jarrell, G.A., "The Relative Signalling Power of Dutch Auction and Fixed Price Self-Tender Offers and Open-Market Share Repurchases" *The Journal of Finance* XLVI(4), September 1991.
2   Self-tenders pay a substantial premium for tendered shares, Peterson, D.R. and Peterson, P.P., "Dutch Auction Versus Fixed-Price Self-Tender Offers: Do Firms Overpay in Fixed Price Offers?" *The Journal of Financial Research*, XVI(1), 1993.

healthy returns in excess of their cost of capital (driving COV, but carrying significant expectations for profitable growth) driving FGV. Presumably, the greater opportunities afforded require the financial flexibility derived from generally lower financial leverage and dividend yields. It would also seem that the risk of agency issues is lower for these proven industry leaders, reducing the need for higher leverage or higher dividends as a safeguard mechanism for shareholders.

There can be sound economic rationale to share buybacks, though these are not typically expressed in the case of many companies announcing such tactics. With so many firms employing or considering share buybacks, a value-based framework for relating financial strategy and tactics to economic performance and business strategy becomes increasingly important. Share repurchases can be a more tax efficient form of cash distribution than dividends. They can also enhance shareowner value through a combination of improved capital structure, reduced agency costs and signalling effects. While financial strategy is often interpreted narrowly as an exercise

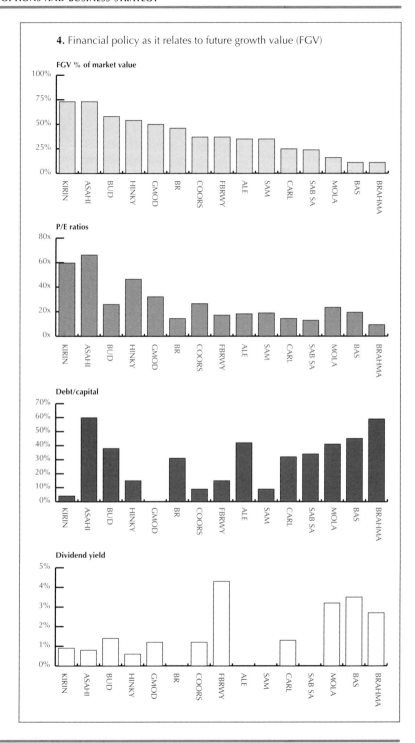

4. Financial policy as it relates to future growth value (FGV)

in cost of capital minimisation, in practice, the determinants of financial policy must support enterprise value maximisation. While the firm's cost of capital and the resulting impact on firm value is an important element, financial strategy must also support the company's business strategy and consider financial flexibility, agency issues, flotation costs, signalling and clientele considerations.

CONCLUSION

The measurement and management of corporate (or enterprise) perfor-mance has received a glut of attention over this past decade – on the heels of the restructuring of the 1980s. But the 1990s has been a decade of remak-ing the public corporation from within – reforming governance and restructuring businesses, largely without the hostile external impetuses.

In the late 1990s, under the pressure of rising market expectations implicit in any long bull-market, companies face unprecedented demands for profitable, long-term growth. In most industries, and the market as a whole, market capitalisation is largely premised on profitable growth beyond the present value of all current operations – positive NPV invest-ments that have yet to be discovered. In this environment, the value of intangible investments into organisational software – brands, processes, patents and intellectual capital – have become the most strategic invest-ments an enterprise can contemplate. Financial policy must be updated and framed within the context of this new world – a financial policy con-sistent with, and supportive of, growth needs of business strategy, and the expectations of the market.

Growth options, flexibility and options to defer, have all become neces-sary tools to manage and exploit the value of uncertainty and volatility. The financial measures, tools and management systems of the modern cor-poration have had to keep pace with the more complex and rapidly chang-ing business environment. Whether managing global growth options, or the options implicit in a new business bid, executives apply much more rigorous and sophisticated analytics. The key to their successful use will be the extent to which they can be simply applied and communicated.

1   The EVA framework is presented in more detail in *The Quest for Value*, Harper Collins, 1991 by Bennett Stewart. EVA© is a registered trademark of Stern Stewart & Co.
2   EVA thus attempts to resolve the agency issues identified by Michael C. Jensen in "The Agency Costs Of Free Cash Flow: Corporate Finance and Takeovers", *American Economic Review* (1986), 76(2), (May), who observed that "mature" companies often generate significant levels of free cash flow with a tendency to retain and waste this capital through over-investment and diversification schemes. Under EVA, the need to "service" the capital charge might partially alleviate a company's inherent propensity for reinvestment in any project, business or acquisition that may have a positive return, and is thus earnings accretive, but does not earn its cost of capita.
3   Sloan, A.P., 1996, *My Years with General Motors*, ed. McDonald, J. with Stevens, C. and P.F. Drucker (Introduction).

4   Scott, K., "The Role Of Corporate Governance In South Korean Economic Reform", *Journal of Applied Corporate Finance*, 10(4) Winter 1998. This entire issue highlights topics in international corporate governance. For a broader introduction to the subject, see also Monks, A.G., and Minow, N., *Corporate Governance*, 1995, Blackwell Business, or Chew, D.H., *Studies in International Corporate Finance & Governance Systems*, 1997 Oxford.

5   Romer, P., "Bank of America Roundtable – The Soft Revolution: Achieving Growth by Managing Intangibles", *Journal of Applied Corporate Finance*, Summer 1998.

6   See, for example, the roundtable discussion led by C.K. Prahlad of the University of Michigan, *Journal of Applied Corporate Finance*, Volume 12, Number 2 (Summer 1999).

7   See, for example, Baruch Lev and Theodore Sougiannis (1993), Bronwyn Hall (1994), Su Chan, John Martin & John Kensinger (1990, 1992), and George Pinches, V.K. Narayanan and Kathryn Kelm (1996).

8   To ensure that the initial investment did not dilute the business unit's EVA, the supplier adjusted the straight-line depreciation charge of US$100 MM (of the initial US$500 MM investment) and the associated EVA capital charge to a sinking fund depreciation (a mortgage payment function) approach.

9   See, for example, "Buyback Myopia", *Treasury and Risk Management*, July 1999.

10   See, for example, a discussion of the reasons for dividends in Bagwell, L.S. and Shoven, J.B., "Cash Distribution to Shareholders", *Journal of Economic Perspectives*, 3(3), Summer 1989.

11   For further discussion of practical issues in corporate financial strategy, see for example, the case of the first self-inflicted dividend cut by a healthy, major US utility in D. Soter, Brigham E. and Evanson P., "The Dividend Cut Heard Round The World: The Case Of FPL", *Journal of Applied Corporate Finance*, Spring 1996.

12   Debt creation, without retention of the proceeds of the issue, enables managers to effectively bond their promise to pay out future cash flows. Debt can therefore be an effective substitute for dividends, a fact not generally unrecognized in the literature. Jensen, M., "Agency Costs of Free Cash Flow, Corporate Finance, and Takeovers", *American Economic Review*, 76(2), (May 1986).

13   A Stern Stewart & Co study of our own EVA clients found that they outperformed their industries by an average of 8.5%, compounded annually, for five years post-implementation, with outperformance in every year.

14   While Japanese beers Kirin and Asahi also exhibit higher premiums, their case is one of more a function of poor operating results than a premium valuation – essentially a smaller denominator, rather than a larger numerator. Thus, the future growth value implies a significant expectation of "improvement" due to the valuation floor.

BIBLIOGRAPHY

Drucker, P., 1998, "Peter Drucker Takes the Long View", *Fortune*, September.

5

The Flexibility for Discontinuing Product Development and Market Expansion: The Glaxo Wellcome Case

Alberto Micalizzi

Bocconi University and Real Options Group

This case investigates the research and development (R&D) investment valuation of a pharmaceutical product belonging to a new class of antibiotics, based on a tricyclic-structure compound. This product is mainly aimed at solving the problem of the formation of antibacterial resistance, which causes a reduction in the efficacy of cures based on long-term treatments.

Two important aspects characterise this analysis. First, the high degree of innovation implied in this project poses a problem of uncertainty over the market impact of the new product, in terms of units sold. As a consequence, the entire project's value is uncertain. Second, the strategic analysis of the project identifies two important flexibility options embedded in the decision-making process. The first option allows the company to default on the third (and last) stage of clinical trials, thus saving the cost of additional investment. The second option gives the opportunity to expand the market share by launching the solid version of the product, one year after the base launch of the oral version. The interaction between the two options should also be considered. If the project were defaulted, the expansion options would be killed, and there would be a negative interaction among options.

Therefore, the final purpose of the case is twofold:

❏ to calculate the value of the opportunity to invest in the last stage of clinical trials, which must take into account the following option to expand the market share; and
❏ to analyse the interaction among options and compare the combined value of options with their algebraic sum, which leads to determine the combined Real Options Value (ROV) ie, the value of expanding the market after completing the project development, as a specific output of the model.

The final result shows how each option positively affects the project's value, and therefore how the project's structure can be optimally modelled according to the task of maximising the managerial flexibility and enhancing shareholders' value under uncertainty. In more detail, the sensitivity analysis helps to indicate that the two options play a different role according to the underlying project's value. In addition, the analysis of option interaction shows that the combined ROV is less than the algebraic sum of the two separate options.

The real options valuation is based on the binomial model. It assumes that in each discrete time interval, the underlying project's value goes up or down by an amount that also depends on the volatility of the underlying variable. The up and down movements follow a binomial probability distribution.

The chapter will begin by introducing the pharmaceutical sector, the company profile, and the management corporate attitude towards valuation under uncertainty and R&D investment valuation. It focuses on the therapeutic problem, thus providing the general features of the product in object, and illustrates the patent process. The four main phases in which the entire research and development process is divided are: primary research stage; exploratory development stage; full development; and marketing/expansion options. The next section provides a clear picture of the project's structure and a preliminary analysis of the characteristics of the two major areas of flexibility. Therefore, it is of fundamental importance for analysing the whole decision-making process, and the relative embedded options. The chapter then illustrates the valuation procedure and analyses the option interaction. The major valuation results are presented and discussed in the final sections.

PROFILE: GLAXO WELLCOME

Glaxo Wellcome[1] (GW) is a pharmaceutical firm active worldwide in the research, development and marketing of drugs for human consumption. In the past, the GW group's activities have covered diverse business areas including baby products, drugs and products for veterinary use, surgical equipment, and pharmaceutical preparations for human use. Since 1980, GW has concentrated its activities on prescription drugs, focusing its resources, skills and efforts on the development of increasingly safer and more effective drugs. (A distinction is made between so-called ethical products, which are sold only under prescription and patent medicines or over-the-counter – OTC – drugs, which can be purchased without a prescription.)

Within the framework of its product portfolio (see Table 1), the drugs are divided into categories distinguished essentially by the varying degrees of *marketing risk* and *technical difficulty* encountered in creating the product. In particular, pharmaceutical products fall into four groups:

❏ *Innovative products.* These are products based on a new biological mechanism. Their launch calls for a conspicuous marketing effort. An example is Imigran, used in the treatment of migraines.

❏ *Early entrants.* These products are launched immediately after the innovative ones. Sometimes this strategy permits the manufacturer to exploit a favourable environment for the diffusion of the drug, despite the limitations of entering the market as a follower.

❏ *New compounds in well-established therapeutic classes.* These compounds are similar to other pre-existing drugs in that they target the same therapeutic area; however, they are more innovative in terms of the chemical composition of the molecule.

Table 1. Portfolio of Glaxo products and date of initial launch

Launch date	Drug	Therapeutic class
1993	Flixotide	Respiratory
1993	Zofran	Antiemetic
1991	Imigran	Antimigraine
1991	Lacipil	Antihypertensive
1991	Cutuvate	Dermatological
1990	Serevent	Respiratory
1990	Flixonase	Antirhinitic
1987	Zinnat	Oral antibiotic
1987	Volmax	Respiratory
1983	Fortum	Injectable antibiotic
1981	Zantac	Antiulcerant
1978	Zinacef	Injectable antibiotic
1977	Trandate	Antihypertensive
1975	Beconase	Antirhinitic
1973	Dermovate	Dermatological
1972	Becotide	Respiratory
1969	Ventolin	Respiratory
1964	Betnovate	Dermatological

❏ *Me-too products.* These are copies of drugs that have already been marketed. They present an extremely low technical risk, but a high marketing risk; compared to existing drugs they involve the risk of not obtaining the administrative authorisation required to be included in the National Health Service dispensary.

THE CHANGING PHARMACEUTICAL SECTOR AND GLAXO WELLCOME'S RESPONSE

Considerable upheaval characterises the whole pharmaceutical industry these days. Market growth has been only 6% in 1993 compared with 10% in previous years (for a total value of about 160 billion euros). The decline is particularly evident in the industrialised countries (Europe, the US, Japan), which together represent 84% of the market.

Several factors influence the ongoing evolution of the sector. The amount spent on all-round healthcare contribution is increasing, both in the industrially developed countries and in emerging markets. On the other hand, *public* spending on health and price-setting mechanisms for pharmaceutical products in many countries are undergoing drastic reductions on account of tighter budgets. Moreover, the reviewing of processes for patenting (of compounds) and registration (of drugs) has also lengthened the time required to develop and launch new drugs.

As a result, the market has become increasingly more competitive, "hostile", and more selective. In such a context, the ability to innovate by launching new drugs is undoubtedly a critical factor for long-term success. One must also consider the constant commitment to speed up development cycles and the need for *the development of new applications* from the existing portfolio. In particular, the search for new indications from existing drugs can expand the target market and significantly increase economic value added. In fact, a new research project is often started from line extensions seized after the successful initial launch of a product. Rapid and widespread access to the market is a further competitive factor that is becoming increasingly critical. This is effectively the only way to withstand the challenges of rival products by increasing the profitability of research activities and reducing risk.

In the second half of the 1980s, GW's top management, conscious of the sector's evolution and growing dynamism, decided to give a strong boost to the company's research and development activities. This aim was achieved by substantial progressive increases in the financial resources made available for research. Glaxo Wellcome's research and development expenditure jumped from £32 million in 1980 to £858 million in 1994, the equivalent of 16% of its total turnover. In addition, GW made investments for the creation of research centres in the US, Japan and the UK (Stevenage – Medicines Research Centre). Since 1986, the focus on research and development activities has enabled the launch of 11 of the major products that are the pride of GW's current portfolio.

This expansion was accompanied by an ambitious *internationalisation*, aiming to strengthen GW's presence on major world markets by a more effective, penetrating and appropriate organisation and marketing strategy. Geographically, the group has increased its penetration, boasting marketing companies in 59 countries and products sold in 150 countries around the world. The group's international organisation envisages one business area specialisation per country.

THE CHALLENGE: VALUING A RESEARCH AND DEVELOPMENT PROGRAMME

The high degree of uncertainty inherent in research and development makes the evaluation of such investments particularly difficult. The strong impulse given by GW to its primary research activities was in the spirit of the traditional methodologies (net present value) for the assessment of the economic feasibility of research and development projects. It underscored the need to overcome the natural but detrimental friction often created between the administrative and financial functions responsible for the allocation of financial resources, and the people in charge of research, development and planning, who produce the ideas/projects that require financing (see Panel 1).

A PHARMACEUTICAL DEVELOPMENT MEETING

The scene is Verona, 1999. A meeting has been called, with all the GW managers working on the 3BAC project, to discuss its progress. This is one of the precious occasions when they find themselves sitting around the same table discussing one of the most interesting projects ever developed by GW Italia Research. Following the reorganisation carried out in 1994–5, and following plans developed for the centralisation of research and development activities, GW UK (the parent company) has put pressure on the Verona centre to limit its research initiatives. Some of the research programmes have been drastically cut back or postponed. On the other hand, the 3BAC project has been considered worthy of continued research. The product in question is an antibiotic with microbiological characteristics that make it highly innovative. It is currently at the beginning of the second stage of development and clinical trials are about to be carried out on healthy volunteers. In fact, one of the main items on the agenda is a report on the results of the first clinical trials. In spite of the positive results obtained so far, the survival of the project is open to dispute.

At corporate level, the intention is to bring a significant reduction in the level of resources made available for the continuation of the 3BAC development program. Verona is strongly opposed to abandoning 3BAC and the meeting is expected to produce all the evidence needed to convince the parent company of the feasibility and strategic importance of the project. In the course of discussion, various points of view emerge and, as always, the remarks reveal the different approaches of the participants, particularly relating to the *uncertainty factors*.

"After all, dear Dr Thomson," – Dr Thomson is the Finance Director – *"the problem can be solved if you succeed in persuading your colleagues in London that the project is worthwhile!"* says the project manager, Dr Gott. *"We'll give you all the information we have and show you all the opportunities this project will provide if it is commercialized … but at the end of the day, it is you who has to produce the numbers that convince them! The only thing they understand is numbers!"*

"… pharmaceutical investments are always highly subject to uncertainty, particularly in the initial stages of research and development," observes Dr Benton, the CEO, *"It is often the case that the project has to be abandoned because the associated risks do not justify its continuation. On the other hand, if we want to go on competing with the other giants in the sector, Merck, Eli Lilly, etc., we need*

new products that are innovative, efficacious, and indisputably safe. So we must accept the risks involved and the associated costs!"

"They don't all seem to be convinced of that in London," retorts Dr Gott. *"On the contrary, it seems to me that London HQ is more concerned with the costs of development, that are financed by them as a consequence of the transfer of patent. I'd like to remind you that on primary research we alone have already spent about £43 million!"*

"At any rate," the CEO adds, *"we are faced with fundamental questions that affect the whole project's structure. For instance, we have not yet solved the issue of the timing and sequence of launches. Someone argues that we should simultaneously launch both versions of the product, giving a strong signal to the market, whereas others believe that we should stay flexible, waiting to launch the solid version."*

"That's precisely where my problem lies," declares Dr Thomson. *"I'm asked to provide an evaluation of the economic feasibility of the project, to reduce it to numbers, so that I can state that, above and beyond the faith we all have in the project, it can be demonstrated that Glaxo will see it as worthwhile! As is often the case, however, I find myself having to evaluate a project with an uncertain outcome, with a purely indicative time horizon, for which a variety of alternative development and marketing scenarios could be conjectured; don't forget the number of variables on which the overall value of the project depends."*

"What you're saying basically, if I've understood correctly," puts in the CEO, *"is that the very broad time horizon and the inevitable need to reassess the development of the project after every important milestone achieved, modifies pre-established plans and prevents you from providing reliable estimates of the project's value!"*

"Yes, but that's only part of the story. As with all investment projects, the definition of a time horizon and possible reference scenarios is necessary to be able to estimate costs and returns directly attributable to the investment. For example, from the experience gained on other research and development projects similar to this one, we can draw useful information for (approximate) estimates of the amount and timing of cashflows relating to the clinical research stage. As far as expected returns are concerned, estimates formulated in the marketing plan are even more uncertain, because the reference horizon is even longer, but above all, because the different scenarios are conditioned on the results obtained in the early development phases. To put it plainly, I often find myself having to make conditioned forecasts: for example, if the drug were also developed in an injectable dosage form, we could exploit the hospital channel as well, thus expanding our target market. As you can imagine, the project's value would increase enormously! So, which evaluation should I submit to our friends in London?"

"I imagine that it is possible to obtain valuations on the basis of various fundamental hypotheses which can then be 'weighed' according to the probability that certain events will occur," suggests the Planning Manager, Dr Nakam. *"We could revise the underlying assumptions whenever we felt that events had*

modified the underlying scenario or important variables, and recalculate the value to assure ourselves of the economic feasibility of the investment we are making! This way, we can adjust our valuations contingent on the scenario as it unfolds!"

"Certainly, this has been the aim of the valuation methods put in place so far. What I have doubts about, though, is the validity of this kind of approach. In the end, the fundamental finance rule states that 'the higher the risks the lower the value', and this seems to threaten the project desirability because of the many sources of uncertainty we have been talking about."

"But how can you attribute to all the uncertainty a negative factor?" asks the CEO. *"I assume that we will not be asleep during the project development; personally, I think that optimizing the project value along the way is one of our most critical tasks. Take the destiny of the injectable dosage form, for example: if we decide to postpone it, we'll need to make up our minds whether to launch it or not only after analysing the initial sales results of the oral version. That's a tremendous source of flexibility in our hands!"*

"And this is precisely the limitation of the evaluations we have always made! I fully agree with your observation ... what we need is to account for flexibility! It is simplistic to reduce a project with a complex, uncertain and contingent structure to a series of annual cash flow estimates. I would like, already at this stage, to be able to evaluate both the risks to which the project is exposed and the opportunities it could afford over time and summarise them in a single numerical value!"

"In addition to that," puts in Dr Gott, *"let's keep in mind that in 2002, at the end of the second stage of clinical trials, London's decision makers will again wonder whether the third and most critical investment stage is worthwhile, and will remind us that we could also decide to stop the project and sell it to one of our competitors, that may only pay for it as much as approximately 60% of the capital invested in the second stage of development."*

"So, in the end," asks the CEO, *"is there any way to see part of the uncertainty in a favourable light?"*

The meeting raised more doubts and left the participants somewhat bewildered, and an in-depth investigation of the problem was put off until the following session. The meeting continued with a detailed report on the activities already carried out and those still to be conducted according to the project plan. Knowing that the documents were to be sent to London, the participants made an effort to present all the possible alternatives. Critical factors were taken into consideration (eg, the cost of raw material, yield of the synthesis process, the possibility of abandoning development, as well as various launch and positioning alternatives) and an attempt was made to understand how the same could be managed. The wide array of alternatives that emerged made it more difficult for the participants to find their bearings, but the structure of the project became clearer.

The strategic value of research and development activities sometimes comes into conflict with the need to contain expenditures within rigid budgets. Moreover, the complex and contingent nature of research and development, its aleatory elements and its lengthy cycles often make it difficult to assess all the opportunities and spinoff applications appropriately. This explains the continuation of certain research programmes that, on the basis of pure NPV of expected cashflows, should be abandoned, but which conserve enormous potential in terms of future growth opportunities.

ANTIBACTERIAL RESEARCH: THE 3BAC STORY

Antibacterial research began at GW in 1989 when, following an international reorganisation of the GW group's research activities, the research themes assigned to the Verona subsidiary were those concerning antibacterial agents and the central nervous system.

GW is one of the leading manufacturers in the market for *cephalosporins* (β-lactam antibiotics), which represent a substantial share of the antibiotics market. Nowadays, a great number of antibiotics can be found that are well tolerated and have complementary antibacterial spectrums, thanks to which almost all bacterial infections can be successfully treated.

The antibiotics currently produced and marketed by GW are: Zinnat (cefuroxime axetil) which is an orally administered cephalosporin, Fortum (ceftazidime) and Zinacef (cefuroxime), which are injectable products used for the treatment of bacterial infections. With this portfolio, GW ranks fifth in the antibiotics market, with a world market share of 6%.

The therapeutic problem

A serious therapeutic problem in connection with the formation of antibacterial resistance, which causes a reduction in the efficacy of cures based on treatment with antibiotics, remains unsolved.

After an antibiotic has been introduced in therapy and is used efficaciously on a wide scale, an increasingly large number of bacteria mutate in a way that enables them to produce enzymes that chemically render the drug inactive, reducing its therapeutic value (a process called "β-lactamase").

This resistance problem forces pharmaceutical manufacturers to continue innovating the chemico-molecular structure of antibiotics and to constantly dedicate themselves to the search for new classes/families of antibiotics that can gradually substitute for the existing ones, as bacterial resistance reduces their level of efficiency.

The attempt to overcome this problem once and for all was therefore a crucial topic of research. Glaxo Wellcome research efforts were launched with the specific aim of isolating an antibiotic with an efficacy profile that remained *constant over time*. The availability of such a drug would constitute a differentiating competitive advantage in terms of both accumulated scientific know-how and portfolio strategy. The intention was to offer a unique product to meet the needs of *protracted therapeutic treatment*.

Research began in 1990 with the attempt to associate β-lactamase inhibitors with GW cephalosporins, compounds that were already known and towards which resistant bacterial strains had already developed, in order to isolate drugs that were both well tolerated and more resistant. Research continued with the synthesising of compounds with more complex chemical structures. Initially the only substantial innovation with regard to well-known compounds was attempted by means of molecular modification, ie, creating tricyclic structures instead of bicyclic ones. This change in chemical structure increased the "shield" against the effects of β-lactamase. Research in this field continued from 1990 to 1992 *without* producing the desired results.

However, the chemical synthesis knowhow that had steadily accumulated made it possible to switch relatively rapidly from one line of research to another. In fact, the chemical laboratories acquired knowledge of chemico-synthetic processes that could be applied to *other classes of antibiotics*. The attempt to "potentiate" the chemico-molecular structure of known compounds thus led to the discovery of authentic *new classes* of antibiotics. Attention was initially concentrated on the development of the *penems*, which already possessed a higher resistance profile than the cephalosporins. The synthesis of new penems was attempted, but the modifications made did not lead to compounds that were more resistant than the known ones.

The appearance of new structures of β-lactam antibiotics with antibacterial profiles that were even better than those of the penems – the *carbapenems* – led GW researchers to attempt chemical substitutions in order to isolate potential antibiotics. The objective they pursued was to produce carbapenems that were completely original chemically in order to overcome the chemical and metabolic stability problems presented by carbapenems and to isolate a structure that would permit numerous subsequent chemical variations so as to inhibit bacterial resistance as it developed.

The first tricyclic-structure compounds were synthesised in 1994: the basic research laboratories could claim to have effectively isolated a new compound of totally synthetic origin, called *3BAC*. A few months later (1995), the chemists isolated a few milligrams of GG 326 (the codename for the oral compound), which proved to have an important microbiological profile and greater metabolic stability than the known carbapenems. The microbiological profile of this compound was considered exceptional for an oral compound. It was thus decided to apply immediately for a patent.

THE PATENT PROCESS

The substance to be patented was the drug molecule 3BAC, from which GW intended to develop the antibiotic. Once a compound possessing the structural characteristics and microbiological profile corresponding to research objectives has been isolated, a patent application is immediately filed, even though research for the development of the antibiotic continues.

There are certain features that a compound must have before the patent process can be initiated. The compound must be:

❑ new (newly synthesised);
❑ never previously reported in medical literature;
❑ innovative (not obvious); and
❑ useful.

In the pharmaceutical industry, the patentability of the base compound is an indispensable condition for continuing research on the drug molecule.

There are various types of patents, on:

❑ products;
❑ processes; and
❑ new uses.

The choice of country in which to file a patent application is extremely important. Even though the 3BAC research and development project is being carried out by GW Italia, the patent will be filed in many countries (foreign files) in view of the intention to market the product worldwide and the consequent need to protect it in various markets. Furthermore, the patent process, its duration and the guarantees offered by patents are not identical in all countries. In the US, for example, the patent is valid for 20 years, while in many European countries, up until 1978, it was not even possible to register pharmaceutical discoveries.

With the lapse of a patent, the price of the drug usually collapses as a result of the entry of general followers. The various phases of the patenting of the 3BAC compound are illustrated schematically in Table 2.

Table 2. The patent process

1992	1993		1995	1996+
Filing of patent application in the UK.	Completion of ascertainment of the compound's prerequisites and deadline for presentation of claims, if any.	Filing of patent application in principal foreign countries (foreign filings).	Publication of patent application: within 18 months competitors must file counter-applications, if any.	18 months after publication of the patent application, the patent is granted. After this, the newly discovered compound becomes technical, ie, is produced by ordinary commercial processes.	Granting of patent.

RESEARCH AND LAUNCH STAGES

The characteristics of the new compound gave GW's management reason for confidence in the continuation of the project. At this point, it was a matter of proceeding with the long series of toxicological and therapeutic efficacy studies that accompany the development of a drug. In 1993, the development process formally started. At GW, this process is divided into four broad phases, characterised by a gradually increasing commitment of financial resources and risk capital:

❑ primary research stage;
❑ exploratory development stage;
❑ full development stage (with flexibility option to abandon the project); and
❑ launch stage (with marketing and flexibility options to expand).

The primary research stage (1994–6)

The aim of this initial stage is to isolate a compound possessing the desired characteristics, which can be patented. This stage requires the greatest effort, which focuses on the *chemical synthesis* process. The primary research stage generally takes two years, but in the case of particularly innovative products it can be preceded by a preliminary phase of four or five years, which is needed to test the validity of the idea and to perfect the drug molecule. During the primary research stage, the risk of having to abandon the initial research goal is very high. At the same time, however, there is a possibility of useful methodological implications for other products – ie, there is a certain amount of flexibility in passing from one line of research to another, thanks to which a partial failure in one line can open up the way for another.

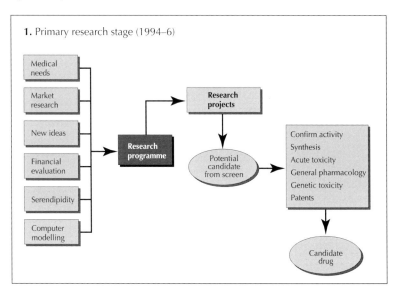

1. Primary research stage (1994–6)

The first tricyclic-structured compound (3BAC) was synthesised in 1993, but it took another 18 months to gain a full understanding of its microbiological activity and to find an ester, Exetil, which would permit an acceptable oral absorption of its active component.

By 1996, primary research on the drug molecule had been completed and the patent application was filed.

The process for obtaining 3BAC, a synthetically derived antibiotic, is rather complicated. The "raw material" of the chemical synthesis is represented by a basic compound, acetoxi-azetidone, used by all pharmaceutical manufacturers to produce antibiotics. This compound, which has a proven ability to ward off the effects of β-lactamase, is obtained by means of chemical chain reactions, as described below: progress made during research brought, among other things, the reduction of the number of reactions from 11 to 6.

$$A \Rightarrow B \Rightarrow C \Rightarrow D \Rightarrow E \Rightarrow F$$

| starting | synthesis | 3BAC |
| material | intermediates | |

The chemical process above is rather complicated as it envisages a high number of chain reactions between compounds and "reagent" substances. The essential aspect is the *yield* of each chain reaction, which cumulatively determines the total yield in the transformation. In practice, the chemical "efficiency" of the process is measured by the quantity of output (3BAC) obtainable as a percentage of a given quantity of the starting material (acetoxi-azetidone) used.

Evaluation of the economic feasibility of a research and development project is meaningful only after the basic compound has been developed, or at the end of the primary research stage.

Exploratory development stage (1997–9)

During the primary research stage, the synthesised compound must undergo a painstaking series of short and long-term *toxicity tests*. This is a very critical phase and is therefore subject to strict control. Glaxo Wellcome started its first toxicity tests on oral 3BAC (GG819) in November 1997, immediately after being granted the patent for the compound.

Initially, toxicity tests are carried out on laboratory rats to verify the immediate reactions of the animal body. The laboratories continue to improve the compound as regards stability and microbiological characteristics. At the same time experiments are conducted to find the dosage form that ensures the maximum biochemical absorption of the drug.

The efficacy of the *dosage form* is of considerable economic importance in the development of the antibiotic in question because it can enhance the

2. Exploratory development stage (1997–9)

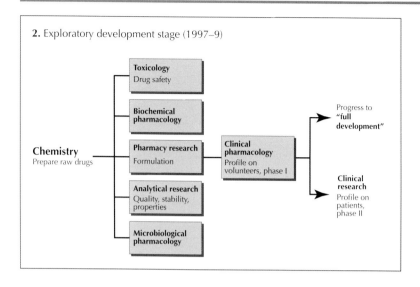

economic feasibility of the drug. In fact, owing to the high cost of the raw material for synthesis, efficient utilisation represents a particularly critical factor in determining the production cost of the compound. It is possible to increase the *yield factor*, both through improvements in the chemical synthesis process and by means of a dosage form that accelerates and facilitates absorption of the drug's main active component by the organism. Therefore, for a given quantity administered, the greater the *biochemical absorption* of the drug the greater its yield.

Tests are subsequently carried out on humans (phases I, II, III). In order to verify how well it is tolerated by the human body, it is at first administered in tiny doses ($^1/_{100}$ of a dose) to 20–30 *healthy* individuals (phase I, March 1998). Once the *exploratory development stage* has been completed, the full development stage begins in which clinical trials are carried out – the compound is no longer administered to healthy subjects but to patients affected by the diseases the antibiotic is destined to treat.

Full development (2000–3)

Once the tolerability of the product has been ascertained, experimentation proceeds with the setting up of clinical trials: the substance is administered to patients (phase II, January 2000) in order to verify its therapeutic efficacy.

This is when the present case is dated. Thus, the second stage of clinical trials is the first *incremental* investment needed to carry out the product development.

The aim of these tests is not only to see whether the human body tolerates the compound well, but also to demonstrate its real benefits compared with drugs already available.

3. Full development stage (2000–3)

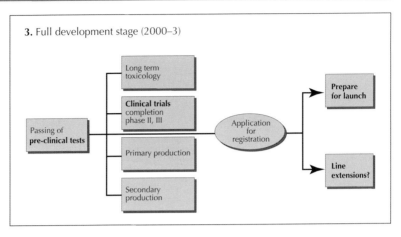

Once this is over, the most costly and demanding part of the research (phase III, 2002) is entered. Long-term toxicity testing (eight to 12 months) is continued and carried out on 3,000 patients. At the same time, at this stage of the drug's development, there is a so-called *technology transfer*, the readying of productive capacity for the large-scale manufacturing of the drug. Two kinds of investments need to be made:

❑ a *primary* production plant (development of the active component); and
❑ a *secondary* production plant (encapsulation of the compound and production).

The full development stage lasts on average three to four years, although in the case of drug molecules relating to the central nervous system it can last as long as six to seven years. This phase ends with the preparation of the documents to be submitted with the application for registration and approval, or inclusion in the dispensary (presumably in 2003). The utilisation of pharmaceutical products is strictly specified by their *indications* – by the acknowledged suitability of the product for use in specific therapies. The documents must include the results of the research studies carried out and the trials conducted in phases I, II, and III, and demonstrate the drug's greater efficacy compared with analogous drugs already on the market. It appears evident that the number of approved indications is a strategically important element, because the size of the reference market depends on this.

Marketing/expansion options (2004–5)
The product's introduction on the market generally takes place immediately after the date of registration. The objective of marketing is its inclusion in the National Health Service dispensary.

The initial launch is planned for 2004. At first, only dosage for oral administration (tablets and suspension) of 3BAC will be launched.

Subsequently (after 12 months), on the basis of market data available on the launch of the oral forms (sales, market share, efficacy), GW will decide whether to launch the injectable form as well.

Although the drug is the same, there are at least two important differences between the two dosage versions. The oral form has a far larger market, as it is destined both for sale in chemist shops (under prescription) and hospital use. The injectable form, on the other hand, is primarily destined for hospital use, which means a much smaller and more competitive target market. In addition, the *injectable form is often considered "complementary" to the oral form* – it is assumed that the two routes of administration can be used contemporaneously. Because of this, GW expects a certain "carry-over" effect from the success of the oral form to the injectable version.

Another factor concerns a *distorted perception* of oral antibiotics by the market. Generally, injectable drugs are considered more potent and more effective than their oral equivalents. Often it is the patient who asks for intramuscular rather than oral administration. Actually, the two forms contain exactly the same main active component and the effect is therefore identical. It is simply that when drugs are administered orally, their absorption is a little slower.

The fact that the market considers an injectable drug more potent, to be used in particularly serious cases, opens up two possibilities for the positioning of the injectable version of 3BAC:

❏ hospital; and
❏ hospital niche.

In the first case, injectable 3BAC would have a broad target market represented by hospital patients and all those who prefer administration by intramuscular injection. The size of the target market depends on the possibility of differentiating the drug from those already in use, thus expanding as much as possible its adoption alongside the oral form. The success of the oral drug is undoubtedly a precondition for setting the price of the injectable form in a medium-high price range, thus making it remunerative.

By contrast, the impossibility of differentiating the drug from others already in use prevents the possibility of remunerative pricing. A second strategy, therefore, is to try to position injectable 3BAC amongst the (niche) antibiotics specifically aimed at patients in serious conditions or with infections that require particularly potent treatments. In this way, by exploiting the distorted perceptions of the market (which generally consider injectable drugs more efficacious) it would be possible to set a very high price.

Price setting is further complicated by the fact that the sector is subject to public regulations. In the past, the authorities set the highest possible price, given that the National Health Service paid for most drugs; currently, the

4. The total project development

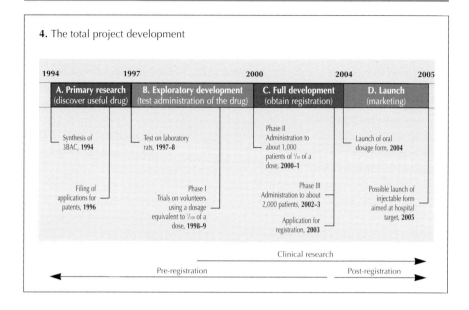

price is anchored to a group average, on condition that the Health Ministry approves it.

The overall structure of the project is summarised in Figure 4.

MILESTONES IN THE DECISION-MAKING PROCESS

Three features peculiar to research and development activities, and especially to the 3BAC project, are evident. Firstly, the development of the new drug extends over a broad *time period*, from 1992 to 2004, and is characterised by areas of complexity deriving from the *risks/opportunities* inherent in the project (for instance, the option to "discontinue" the research).

Secondly, the project is structured in a series of sequential and interconnected phases – ie, it is a *sequential investment*. Basically, a number of attributes of the project can be defined only in light of the results of preceding phases so that management is often called upon to make decisions for the directing or redirecting of research efforts as opportunities and problems present themselves.

In particular, the project involves the following investment stages:

❑ investment in the second stage of clinical trials in 2000;
❑ investment in the third stage in 2003 in order to complete development;
❑ development plan to launch 3BAC in the oral form in 2004; and
❑ market expansion in 2005 and new development plan for the solid (injection) version.

The project entails a continual decision-making process, in the course of which management is in a position to make decisions redefining the course of the project. Thus, managerial flexibility can be represented by a collection of "real options" to defer, abandon, launch, and so forth.

Lastly, one needs to chart the course of a project and identify all the incidents that represent decision nodes (whenever alternatives are presented, the value of which is dependent on the result of a previous event or on the existence of a certain state of nature.) This is very important in order to identify "options", their nature, and the extent to which they are interdependent. The result is a kind of mapping of the project out of a *decision tree*.

Decision tree analysis is quite a useful instrument when dealing with multistage decision problems, where the choice of a certain option depends on future decisions to be made. As a consequence, the decisions made at different stages of the project development interact with each other.

For the purpose of this case, the decision tree serves two purposes. It helps clarify the structure of the problem and the different scenarios that occur when certain decisions are made and it serves as a reference for developing a binomial model of option pricing.

Based on such an analysis, in this case we have identified two kinds of project options:

❏ the option to default on development costs (a put-type option); and
❏ the option to expand the market share (a call-type option).

A call option gives the right to buy an asset at a fixed price whereas a put option gives the right to sell it. Real options can belong to either category depending on the characteristics of the decision problem.

In addition, call and put options can be American or European kind of options. The American kind of option can be exercised any time up to a certain maturity date, whereas the European option can be exercised only at maturity.

The option to default on development

According to the project development plan, in 2002 GW is faced with the question of whether to complete the full development stage started in 2000.

In particular, in 2002 the third stage of clinical trials would be entered, which represents the most costly and partly irreversible capital investment. As a matter of fact, the total investment required for completing the second half of development consists of two parts:

❏ the toxicity testing process, carried out on a large number of patients for approximately one year; and
❏ the transfer of technology and the beginning of process industrialisation.

The principal task of process industrialisation is to transfer the drug production methods developed by pharmaceutical technical research management to an industrial scale, and to verify their compatibility with the existing plant facilities. Further, only after process industrialisation has begun is it possible to make fairly reliable estimates of expected production costs, depending on the amount of starting material required and the methods employed for its use.

At a first glance, assuming that the present value of expected cash inflows (PV) is uncertain, one might conclude that in 2002 the project would be abandoned if this PV were less than the total incremental investment required to complete full development. The uncertainty over this PV is assumed to depend on the volatility of units sold, given that the output price will remain constant as well as most of other costs.

In other words, this flexibility allows management to default on planned investment related to the second half of the full development stage thus saving any further capital expenditure required to complete the project. Such an option arises as a result of the *sequential nature* of the total investment programme, which is divided into different instalments each of which can be seen as the exercise price to pay in order to acquire the next stage of the project. In this case, the exercise price is the investment needed for the period 2002–3 in order to complete the full development and enter the marketing stage.

Another important aspect is that of interaction among options. The correct analysis of the option to default requires the simultaneous consideration of both options, including the option to expand market share. The possibility of expanding affects the optimal exercise conditions of the abandonment, whereas exercising the abandonment option would kill the option to expand (see Trigeorgis, 1993).

By abandoning the project, the company benefits from the salvage value due to the possibility of selling the asset on the second-hand market. In this case this is mainly represented by biotech firms and other pharmaceutical firms quite keen on acquiring the patent and related knowhow, represented by the results of previous stages of trials conducted on the molecule. Thus, part of the investment already sustained can be recovered. On the other hand, the incremental investment for the second part of the development stage is considered substantially irreversible in that it is extremely focused on the specific indication for which the company plans to enter the filing stage and get the approval from the drug administration.

That is why the possibility of abandoning the project makes more sense in 2002, when the third stage of trials and the transfer of technology represent quite a specialised and irreversible investment decision.

The option to expand the market

The launch of the oral form of the 3BAC has been planned for 2004. Competitive reasons and the problem of patent expiry suggest that, once approval has been obtained, the company should enter the market as soon as possible with the safest version of the product. The oral version allows the broadest spectrum of use. In fact, not only can physicians prescribe it, but it can also be destined for hospital use in conjunction with the injectable form.

Launching the oral version is also of great importance for forecasting the market potential of the solid one. The marketing manager points out that from a pure market perspective, it is not advisable to boost 3BAC's market presence unless the "basic" dosage form meets with a certain amount of interest, measurable, for example, in terms of market share. Moreover, the success of the oral form would spread the company's image as a leader in this new class of antibiotics, also increasing the probability of the success of the solid version and its positioning in the hospital market niche.

However, the market results of the oral version are uncertain; in particular, sales of the oral version are subject to a certain volatility, dependent on both the innovative chemical composition of the drug and the specific market target represented by patients subject to protracted therapeutic treatment.

Therefore, GW's management finds it intuitively sensible to postpone the launch of the solid version, in order to have the possibility of revising its decision to expand later. It thus prefers to focus all its research efforts on the oral form, which appears to have a larger market and which will, in any event, stimulate the use of the injectable dosage form as well.

It is worth noticing that each new indication/version of the product requires a new plan of development and a new filing process. Thus, the opportunity to expand the market through the launch of the solid version can be exercised by incurring a certain strike price consisting of the following elements:

❏ the cost of completing the trials with specific reference to the solid version;
❏ the cost for filing for the new indications; and
❏ the investment needed for re-setting of the production facilities.

The total structure of the project is shown in Figure 5.

OPTION INTERACTIONS AND VALUATION PROCEDURE

The project's structure clearly shows that the above two options are subject to a certain degree of interaction. In particular, the option to default on the planned third-stage investment must be carefully evaluated in light of the following option to expand; in other words, given the uncertainty over the present value of cash inflows due to the oral version at the abandonment maturity in 1997, there is a cutoff value above which the project should be developed in order to acquire the next option to expand.

These are interacting options, where the first option depends on the potential value due to the second option.

The purpose of the next part of the case is twofold:

---

5. The project's overall structure – the options to default on development and expand market share

---

❏ to calculate the expanded value of the opportunity to invest in the second stage of clinical trials, as of 1999, considering the combined Real Options Value (ROV);[2] and

❏ to analyse the degree of interaction among options by comparing the combined option value with the algebraic summation of the two options evaluated as being independent.

In terms of valuation procedure, we use risk-neutral valuation, assuming that the PV of the cash inflows due to the oral version follows a binomial process.

To start accounting for the interaction among the two options, we initially calculate the value of the option to expand at maturity. We will use the rolling-back method and find the underlying values in 2002, when the option to abandon expires. Once the exercise conditions have been applied, we then calculate the expanded present value of the project capturing the combined ROV.

Separately, we can also calculate the value of the option to abandon without considering the possibility of further expansion, to determine the degree sign of interaction between the two options.

The exercise conditions for the option to expand are expressed by the following:

$$\text{Max}(eV - I_e \, ; 0)$$

where:
V = present value of cash inflows due to the base-scale, oral version;
e = expansion factor, expressing the market potential of the solid version relative to the oral one;

Ie = additional investment required to execute the new plan of development for the solid version (including the last phase of trials and filing costs).

The exercise condition for the option to expand can also be expressed as follows:

$$V + Max(eV - I_e ; 0)$$

In this case, it represents the project value plus the option to expand.

As far as the option to default is concerned, the exercise conditions as of 1997 are:

$$Max(V' - I_3; S)$$

where:

V' = present value of cash inflows due to both oral and solid versions;[3]
I_3 = additional investment required to conclude the third stage investment and proceed to the marketing stage;
S = scrap value represented by the value of recoverable investments.

THE PROJECT'S DATA

Tables 3–6 summarise the data used for the calculation of the present value of cash inflows from the launch of the oral form and for the analysis of the two options.

Given the data presented in the tables and considering an estimated opportunity cost of capital of 12%, one can calculate the PV and the (passive) NPV of the total investment, assuming no flexibility options.

Table 3. Marketing plan (2004–9)[1]

	2004	2005	2006	2007	2008	2009
Oral version						
Price (factory unit)	1.90	1.90	1.90	1.90	2.00	2.00
Quantity sold (unit)	50	97	110	115	130	130
Revenues	95	184	209	219	260	260
Cogs	22	58	74	81	86	90
Injectable version						
Price (factory unit)	4.5	4.5	4.5	4.5	4.5	4.5
Quantity sold (unit)	2	5	9	13	19	25
Revenues	9	23	41	59	86	113
Cogs	3	7	13	19	27	36
Total sales	104	207	250	277	346	373

[1]In 2009 the product is withdrawn. Therefore, the terminal value is assumed to be zero.

Table 4. Marketing and distribution costs (2004–9)

	2004	2005	2006	2007	2008	2009
Total sales	104	207	250	277	346	373
Oral	95	184	209	219	260	260
Percentage	91%	89%	84%	79%	75%	70%
Injectable	9	23	41	59	86	113
Percentage	9%	11%	16%	21%	25%	30%
Marketing support	104	155	125	69	86	93
% sales	100%	75%	50%	25%	25%	25%
Oral	95	138	105	55	65	65
Injectable	9	17	20	15	21	28

Table 5. Research and development plan (1999–2004)

	1999	2000	2001	2002	2003	2004
Historical costs	27					
				1	1	1
Glaxochem	8	8	1			
Glaxochem	1	1				
Verona	6	6	6	5	4	3
Verona	1	1	1	3	2	2
GRD staff	2	3	4	4	2	1
GRD staff				2	1	1
Trials		1	1	5	4	
Trials		6	10	10	7	

Table 6. Investment plan (1999–2008)

	1999	2000	2001	2002	2003	2004	2005	2006	2007	2008
Transfer of technology										
Production: primary		10								
Production: secondary				7						
Depreciation (10 years) (%)	10					1.7	1.7	1.7	1.7	1.7

The calculations below are based on the market forecast for the oral version. All the investment costs required are discounted at the risk-free interest rate, since they are relatively certain (and uncorrelated with market movements).

The NPV determination is shown in Table 7. From the analysis, we can also obtain some important data for valuing the option to abandon. The option to default allows the company to save the investment needed for

Table 7. NPV calculation

	1999	2000	2001	2002	2003	2004	2005	2006	2007	2008	2009	2010
Revenues						95	184	209	219	260	260	
Cogs						22	58	74	81	86	90	
Gross margin						**73**	**126**	**135**	**138**	**174**	**170**	
Marketing and distribution						95	138	105	55	65	65	
Operating margin						**-22**	**-12**	**31**	**83**	**109**	**105**	
Depreciation						1.7	1.7	1.7	1.7	1.7	1.7	
Tax						-7	-4	9	26	34	32	
Working capital (variation)						20	21	7	3	8	1	
Working capital (level)						20	40	47	50	58	58	-58
Stocks						7	19	25	27	29	30	
A/R						16	31	35	36	43	43	
A/P						4	10	12	14	14	15	
Operating cashflow						**-33**	**-27**	**16**	**56**	**69**	**74**	**58**
V	62.8											
R&D plan	0.1	0.1	0.1	0.5	0.5	0.5		0.3	0.3	0.3	0.3	
R&D cost (Verona)	-1	-1	-1	-3	-2	-2						
Ground staff				-2	-1	-1						
Trials		-1	-1	-5	-4							
Glaxochem	-1	-1										
Total	-1.6	-2.3	-2.1	-9.5	-6.5	-2						
Production inv.												
Primary production		-2										
Secondary production				-12	-15	-20						
Total cash outflows	**-1.6**	**-4**	**-2**	**-22**	**-22**	**-22**						
I_0	-65.5											
$Npv = I_0 + V$	-2.7											

executing the second-half stage of the full development process. From this perspective, the total investment (I_0) of 65.5 million can be divided as follows:

❑ £7.8 million, representing the present value of the development costs from 2000 to 2001, ie, the capital required for executing the second stage on clinical trials; and

❑ £57.8 million, which is the present value of the investment due to the third stage of development; this amount can be thought of as being in escrow for three years, corresponding to the £63.1 million that the company can save in 2002 by defaulting on the third investment stage.

The inputs for calculating the option values are:

Option to expand (gross) project
V = underlying value following a binomial process, where V_0 = 62.8;
e = 1.6, determined by the marketing department;
I_e = 32, based on the development plan required for obtaining the new approval.

Option to abandon
V′ = underlying value. It results as a consequence of the exercise conditions of the option to expand when calculating the combined option value;
I_3 = 63.1, third stage development costs that can be abandoned;
S = 5, resale value guaranteed by a biotech firm interested in acquiring the scientific results.

Other estimates required for the risk-neutral valuation are:

Annual volatility (σ) = 35%, based on historical data of units sold of similar antibiotic products
Continuously compound risk-free interest rate (Rf) = 3%.[4]

VALUATION RESULTS

Table 8 reports the valuation results obtained based on the above data.

It can be seen that the combined ROV makes the project more valuable and worth investing in. The expanded net present value (E-NPV), which incorporates the combined options and represents the total value of the opportunity to invest in the second stage of clinical trials in 2000, is positive (10.7).

Therefore, GW should invest in the full development stage and proceed with the second phase of clinical trials.

It is also worth pointing out that the combined ROV (value of both options together) is 13.5 and is less than the algebraic sum of the two separate options (11.2 + 4.2 = 15.4); the difference (1.9) represents the negative interaction. Intuitively, if management defaulted on investment, the expansion would not take place in any case, thus exercising the first option would kill the second.

This negative interaction is the result of the monodirectional relationship among these options, where the expansion affects the opportunity to default, but the latter can only kill the project or leave it as it was before. By defaulting on the investment for the third stage of clinical trials, GW renounces (kills) part of the value due to the possibility to expand the project later. The amount of expansion value "destroyed" by abandoning the project midstream helps explain the negative interaction among these options.

Table 8. Valuation results

	NPV or E-NPV	Real options value
Base project	–2.7	
Project with combined options	10.7	13.5
Project with option to expand	8.5	11.2
Project with option to default	1.4	4.2
Option interaction		–1.9

SENSITIVITY ANALYSIS

In this section we analyse the value of both options and the combined value as the underlying project value changes.

The resulting graphic results can help optimise the project management given the current inputs.

Figure 6 shows how the value of the option to expand alone changes as the underlying project value changes. The option to expand allows the company to choose the best between the expanded value of the project net of the incremental investment required and zero. As Figure 6 confirms, this is the traditional value of a call option, where the option will be in-the-money (worth exercising it) if the underlying value is higher than approximately 48.

Figure 7 shows the option to abandon as being the only option on the project. The figure shows the typical payoff of a put option. This helps understand the role of the opportunity to default on planned investment in the current project. Such an opportunity makes more sense (ie, is more valuable) for lower values of the underlying, when the possibility to default and save a certain part of the investment enables the company to limit downside fluctuations.

In 1999 the option to abandon is out-of-the money (not worth exercising) but its value depends significantly on the time to maturity (three years) and the volatility of the underlying project value.

Figure 8 shows how the combined ROV behaves as the underlying value changes. The two options affect the total value of the project with different intensity, according to the specific range of the underlying values. In particular, for small values of the underlying assets the option to abandon plays the role of "insurance" that allows the company to recover part of the

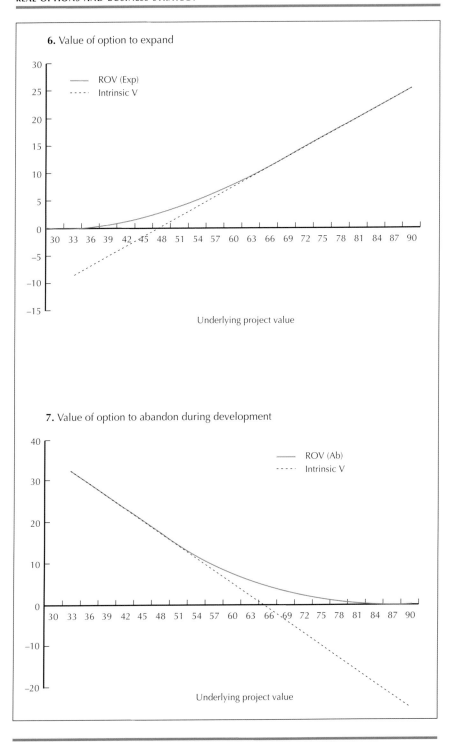

6. Value of option to expand

— ROV (Exp)
---- Intrinsic V

Underlying project value

7. Value of option to abandon during development

— ROV (Ab)
---- Intrinsic V

Underlying project value

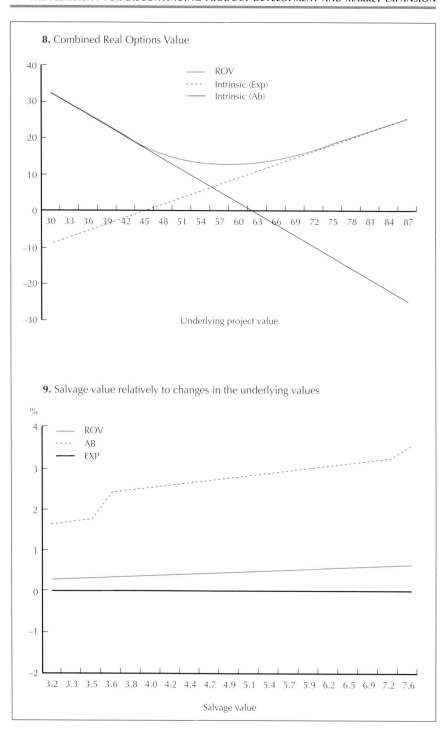

8. Combined Real Options Value

Underlying project value

9. Salvage value relatively to changes in the underlying values

Salvage value

value or limit the total loss; for large values of the underlying variable, the option to expand boosts the project value and increase its expected return. The probability distribution of expected return is skewed in such cases.

Figure 8 also shows the relative importance of each option. For those values of the underlying assets in the range 0–55 the option to abandon adds the most important value to the project; in the range 55–60 the combined ROV remains roughly steady, due to the decreasing importance of the option to abandon and the increasing role of the option to expand. For underlying values above 60, the option to expand far offsets the value of abandonment, thus increasing the combined ROV as the underlying value increases.

Figure 10a shows the non-linearity of the intrinsic value of the option to abandon when considering the effect of the option to expand (Intrinsic (Ab')). This curve lies below the normal intrinsic value (Intrinsic (Ab)), and the difference represents the contribution of the option to expand to the combined option value.

Figure 10b shows this situation in more detail. Two arguments appear to be relevant in the analysis of the combined ROV. First, lets look at the segment A–B. If the underlying value is 51, the option to abandon is clearly in-the-money (regardless of whether we consider the option to abandon alone or as part of the combined option). As a consequence, the company should exercise it. Point A indicates the intrinsic value of the abandonment option as if it were the only option on the project – ie, it is the option payoff which considers the benefit of the defaulted investment plus the scrap value, net of the underlying value (which is abandoned). Point A is equal to 11.2. Point B (equal to 8.3) has a similar meaning, but it also considers the *differential value lost due to the option to expand*. In other words, if at maturity V is 51, GW will find it convenient to exercise the abandonment option; in which case, *it will also destroy the value of the option to expand*, which is shown by the segment A–B (equal to 2.9).

Let us focus on the segment C–D. Point D (approximately 62) represents the underlying value at which the option to abandon, as a single option on the project, is at-the-money. At maturity (ie, in 2002) GW should default on the third investment stage if the underlying value were less than 62. Actually, this is not the case. As a matter of fact, if V were 61 (or any value between C and D), by abandoning the project the company would also lose the value of the option to expand. As a consequence, the combined ROV becomes in-the-money for lower values of V, and in particular, for values lower than 60, given by point C.

Point C sets the cutoff level below which the project should actually be abandoned because the option to abandon is in-the-money or, alternatively, the strike price (investment saved plus scrap value) is higher than the underlying project value (V) by an amount that offsets the loss of

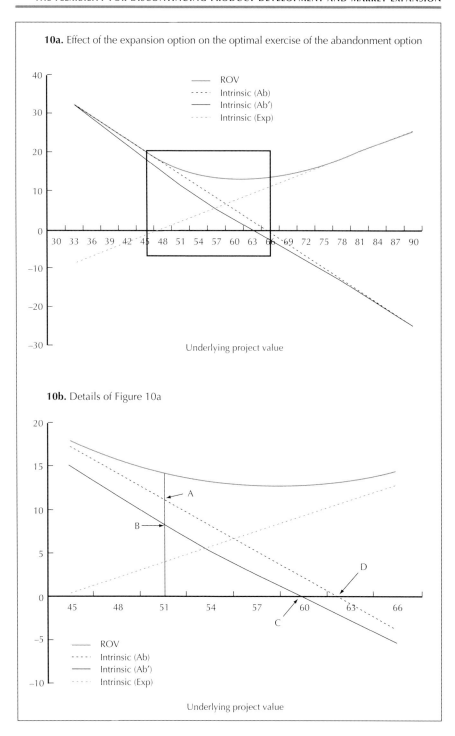

10a. Effect of the expansion option on the optimal exercise of the abandonment option

10b. Details of Figure 10a

expansion value. This also suggests that *for all underlying values between C and D, Glaxo will invest in the third stage of clinical trials only to "acquire" the opportunity of expanding the project later.*

Such an analysis reinforces the concept that the combined ROV is based on a different mix of the two options depending on the specific underlying value.

Other sensitivity results can be seen with regards to some other specific project inputs, one of which is the scrap value. One possibility is for this value to be determined by contract, where both parties agree to give one the right to sell the research output to the other for a predetermined price and at a certain maturity.

The "writer" of such an option is usually a biotech firm or another pharmaceutical firm that is interested in pursuing research activity or acquiring the scientific results achieved.

Option analysis proves to be a valuable instrument for the assessment of such specific contractual aspects. In this regard, there are at least two elements worth noticing.

Firstly, Figure 8 clearly shows that the impact of both the scrap value and the investment default option partly depend on the initial underlying value (V_0); when the underlying value is far above the threshold of 60, the importance of getting better conditions in terms of scrap value and delaying capital investment is weaker. The project's expanded value is highly sensitive to these values for lower underlying values (ie, less than 40).

Figure 9 shows how the ROV changes as the scrap value increases by 5% (the horizontal axis represents increments of the scrap value by 5% per step). For example, starting from the case of S = 4.9, if it increases by 5%, or £0.24 million, the combined option value increases by 0.02% or £0.06 million.

This gives a measure of the relative weight of the scrap value as one of the two major benefits of defaulting the project and allows us to conclude that the most critical role in the value of abandonment is played by the ability to postpone and default capital investment during the third stage of trials.

Another important variable is the coefficient α that represents the impact of the new indication of the product in terms of market size. Figure 11 indicates that, assuming V = 62.8, for α less than 1.3, the option to expand is almost worthless and the E-NPV mainly depends on the option to abandon. Alpha starts playing a critical role in terms of total project value when it is higher than 1.3. Thus, this represents the minimum expected market expansion due to the solid drug version (relative to the oral one) below which there would not be value for expanding the project.

Similar sensitivity analysis can be applied on the volatility parameter and its interaction with the option to expand. Figure 12 shows that the value of the option to expand is more sensitive to the volatility for lower values of the strike price (which is the total investment needed to obtain

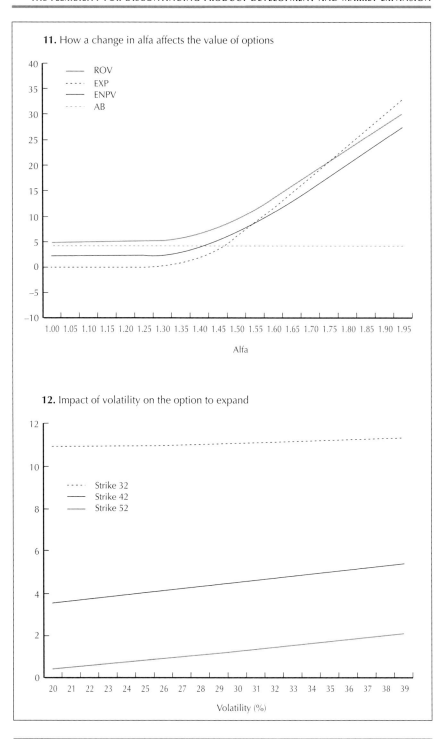

11. How a change in alfa affects the value of options

12. Impact of volatility on the option to expand

the solid indication). This result is important because it indicates that for $V = 62.8$ and $I_3 = 32$ (the project's input) the change in the volatility of the underlying value only slightly affects the value of expansion.

1   The present case is based on a real project developed by GW in recent years. However, for pedagogical purposes the author has revised (and partly changed) terms and situations that refer to the real case history.

2   In the following part of the case we use the term "combined Real Options Value" to denote the value of the option to abandon which includes the value of the opportunity to expand the project.

3   It is worth noticing that the valuation of the option to abandon as a separate option on the project will require to assume that V is the present value of cash inflows only due to the oral version.

4   From the above we derive: # interval per year (n) = 12, length of each interval: $h = t/n = {}^1/_{12}$ of year, upward movement (u) = 1.0293, downward movement (d) = 0.971, risk-neutral probability (p) = 0.54.

6

A Business Shift Approach to R&D Option Valuation*

Onno Lint and Enrico Pennings

Erasmus University Rotterdam and Eindhoven University of Technology;
University Pompeu Fabra

Conventional capital budgeting methods cannot properly capture the option value in Research & Development (R&D) – since market and technology uncertainties change expectations about the viability of many new products, the value of a project is frequently adjusted during the R&D stages. Also, capturing the adjustment in expectations has an option value that may significantly differ from the net present value (NPV) of R&D projects. However, there are no historic time series for estimating the uncertainty of the value of R&D projects, which means that the standard Black–Scholes model for financial option valuation does not apply in a straightforward way.

The aim of this chapter is to provide an analysis of a managerial tool that captures a particular option pricing model which helps set the budget for R&D projects. The option value of this model captures jumps or business shifts in market or technology conditions, and therefore enables one to build a consistent and transparent portfolio of R&D options. Since conventional valuation methods such as NPV truncate long-term R&D, such a portfolio makes an objective comparison between short-term projects with a relatively certain payout and long-term projects with uncertain payouts possible. In this manner, management can maintain the potential for strategic opportunities in future growth. The framework for our analysis originates from work undertaken at Philips Corporate Research, in applying option insights to the R&D pipeline.

Major international companies with large research departments continually face the problem of selecting an optimal portfolio of research projects. The NPV rule and other discounted cashflow (DCF) techniques for capital

*This research was supported by the Technology Foundation (STW) in the Netherlands. The chapter originated from co-operation with Philips Corporate Research and Philips Corporate Strategy. We are grateful to Conrad Gardner for fruitful suggestions.

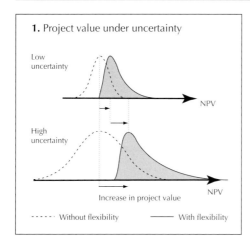

1. Project value under uncertainty

Low
uncertainty

NPV

High
uncertainty

NPV

Increase in project value

----- Without flexibility ——— With flexibility

budgeting may distort the process of building a balanced portfolio of research projects. They favour short-term projects in relatively certain markets over long-term, and relatively uncertain, projects. Figure 1 illustrates how uncertainty affects the value of a project when management has the option to abandon the project. By acknowledging the value of managerial flexibility under uncertainty, a real option portfolio does not, *a priori*, kill all projects with a negative NPV.

Without turning the risks of developing products with uncertain future payouts into opportunities to gain competitive advantage, companies cannot survive in the long run. The costs of developing new products are low in comparison to the investment costs necessary for a global market introduction; therefore, if management holds the option to abandon a project, the cost of R&D investments can be thought of as the price of an option on major follow-on investments. Accordingly, the theory of real options can be applied to R&D investments – up to the moment of market introduction, management has the flexibility to react to unexpected events that can change the value of the research project. Hence, management can revise the decision to continue research for the new product and to eventually market it.

It maybe worthwhile to undertake R&D investments with a negative project value[1] when early investment provides information about future benefits or losses of a project (Roberts and Weitzman, 1981). Since R&D projects are characterised by a long planning horizon and uncertainty, the value of this managerial flexibility may be substantial (Trigeorgis, 1996; Amram and Kulatilaka, 1998). According to Dixit and Pindyck (1995), the conventional NPV rule for capital budgeting only yields the same results as real option analysis when market and technology uncertainty tend to zero and the investment that is required for market introduction of the newly developed product is reversible. This means that the investment can be undone at no cost and expenditures can be fully recovered.

In Pennings and Lint (1997) and Lint and Pennings (1998) it was found that managers do not continuously adjust the value of an R&D project, but may do so when information with a strategic impact arrives. This is due to reasons of efficiency, as senior managers only respond to new information and rebalance current activities when they think that the impact of the information reaches a certain threshold. This threshold is subjective and based on managerial experience.

Strebel (1992), among others, provides insight into these business discontinuities or business shifts, which lead to changes in the perception of project values by management due to the arrival of new information. Strebel analyses mainly shifts in performance trends of products that already exist, arguing that industry breakpoints are often accompanied by sharp shifts in competitive behaviour. Competitive shifts consist of both standardisation and rejuvenation shifts. Successive examples of these shifts include the standardisation of technology and the introduction of differentiated products, designed to increase perceived value. With the shrinking product and technology life cycles in today's markets, Strebel asserts that standardisation shifts often follow closely on rejuvenation shifts. These competitive breakpoints frequently occur in the product development process and have a large impact on the decision whether or not to industrialise the new product at the end of the R&D stage.

As mentioned, we intend to use this chapter to discuss a managerial software tool that captures a particular option pricing model for setting the budget of R&D projects. We developed and implemented a software package to value the contingent character of research projects. The approach we take is firstly to explain the software tool and demonstrate how our option pricing model captures jumps or business shifts in market or technology conditions. Uncertainty is decomposed in the impact of such shifts and the frequency of the shifts, with the software enabling more consistent decision making and more effective communication between the R&D, finance, marketing, and strategy departments. Secondly, we open the black box of uncertainty to managers and illustrate the impact-arrival portfolio. Through this portfolio, we show how the characteristics of five industry sectors differ with respect to the impact and arrival of business events.

The remainder of this chapter is structured as follows:

❏ in order to develop an appropriate framework, there will be a brief discussion of the major issues in real option assessment in practice;
❏ we then present our "Primary Assessment Tool" (PAT), the extended scoring method which has been developed;
❏ we follow this with a look at the impact-arrival portfolio; and finally
❏ we present our conclusions.

PITFALLS OF OPTION ANALYSIS IN R&D PORTFOLIO MANAGEMENT

The analogy between real and financial options has already been well documented (eg, Trigeorgis, 1996), and is summarised in Table 1.

In literature, most applications of real options investment analysis use the Black and Scholes (1973) formula for pricing European options. These options cannot be exercised prior to maturity, in contrast to American options, which can be exercised at any moment up to maturity. R&D options can be considered as European when two conditions hold:

Table 1. Analogy between real and financial options

Financial options	Real options
Time to maturity	Time until the investment opportunity disappears
Exercise price	Costs of irreversible follow-on investment
Volatility of stock return	Variability of growth in project value
Share price	Present value of expected cashflows
Risk-free rate of return	Risk-free rate of return
Dividend	Value lost by waiting to invest

❏ market introduction before successful completion of the R&D stages has severe implications on future market share; and
❏ waiting to introduce a new product leads to a loss of first-mover or pioneering advantages.

Especially in markets which are characterised by decreasing product-life cycles and growing competition, competitive advantage primarily exists in the early stages of the product-life cycle. Hence, in markets where strong first-mover advantages exist (see Lieberman and Montgomery, 1988), firms with superior R&D competencies typically exercise R&D options just at the industrialisation moment (ie, the moment of market introduction) when the NPV is positive at that moment. Since waiting is useless due to evaporating first-mover advantages, these R&D options are European.

A striking problem, that arises from the observation that the underlying asset of a real option is non-traded, concerns estimating the volatility of the underlying asset. In contrast with financial options, there are no historic time series that can be used for estimating the uncertainty of the underlying asset. However, it is a well-established fact that the option value is very sensitive to the uncertainty of the underlying asset. Reasonable estimates of the volatility are therefore required. Often, the value of the underlying asset depends on price movements of natural resources. Brennan and Schwartz (1985), for example, value the option of mothballing and later reactivating a copper mine. With a time series of copper prices, an estimate of the variance can be obtained. Another example is given in Quigg (1993), who values the option of waiting to develop land, using data on land transactions to get an estimate of the variance.

Options in R&D require an alternative approach to estimate volatility. At Merck, for example, they take stock volatility in order to approximate the volatility of the NPV of future cashflows resulting from pharmaceutical R&D (see Nichols, 1994). This may be a viable approach when the risk characteristics of a single R&D project match the risk characteristics of the stock. As intuitively clear, it may be difficult for R&D management to find a matching stock. If so, this method has the advantage that existing models

Table 2. Approaches to estimating volatility regarding R&D

Stock volatility of ventures	Pharmaceutical industry (Nichols, 1994)
Managerial judgment	IT (Benaroch and Kauffman, 1999); consumer electronics (Lint and Pennings, 2000)
Volatility of realised projects with similar risk characteristics	Consumer electronics (Pennings and Lint, 2000)

for financial option pricing can easily be applied. Using the judgements of senior management to attain reasonable values for the uncertainty provides another approach. Unfortunately, no convincing heuristics have been proposed so far. Table 2 summarises approaches to estimating volatility regarding R&D.

Any approach using the Black–Scholes formula implies a continuous arrival of information that changes the underlying variable. In finance theory, the underlying assets are traded and new information will directly be reflected in the prices of the assets. Considering R&D options, information that leads to adjustments in the project value will only arrive at discrete points in time. From interviews with senior management we find that the financial status of research projects – once undertaken – will only be sporadically revised in the case of arrival of new information. Nevertheless, our first intention at Philips was to implement a kind of Black–Scholes option model to value the contingent character of research projects. The advantage of the seminal Black–Scholes formula is its widespread use in the financial world and the fact that the scope of the model is easily communicated. However, determining the standard deviation of the underlying value appeared to be arduous within R&D practice, and future use of this approach should therefore be limited.

Pennings and Lint (1997) propose a model that opens the black box and appears to provide a closer match with reality. The approach developed is based on a discontinuous arrival of new information affecting the present value of future cashflows (see Panel 1 for examples).

Changes in the underlying variable (ie, the project value) occur at a random number of times during the R&D period. We often observe clusters of information arrivals in a certain time period instead of regularly, which may be the result of competitive reactions. These upward or downward changes have a different impact on the underlying variable and are therefore assumed to be stochastic.

When a major shift in market or technological conditions occurs, management can revise the business plan, recalculate the option value and rebalance the R&D portfolio. Positive shifts may result in a higher budget and more R&D efforts, while negative shifts will have the opposite effect. Figure 2 illustrates the organisational process of adjustments in R&D project value.

EXAMPLES OF ADJUSTMENTS IN R&D PROJECT VALUE

Examples of adjustments in the present value of future net cashflows include the discovery of new production technologies, resulting in cost reduction, or the fast entrance of competitors with a market penetrating strategy that entails future price erosion. In the first example, cash outflow drops while, accordingly, the present value of future cashflows increases. The second example induces a reduction in cash inflow, and hence in the net present value of future cashflow. Other examples of events include the outcome of negotiations on standardisation, unexpected strategic alliances or take-overs, and changes in patent positions. A Poisson (jump) process would be able to describe these movements in the underlying variable. This way, the variance of the underlying asset can be deconstructed into the expected number of information arrivals and the expected jump sizes of both upward and downward shifts.

Investment decisions with a positive probability that the present value of future cashflows jumps to zero have been examined by McDonald and Siegel (1986). If the jump occurs, the investment opportunity becomes worthless: it is as if the investment opportunity expires. In their model, the distribution of the waiting time until the jump occurs is exponential. Jumps in financial assets in general were first introduced by Cox and Ross (1975) and Merton (1976), in whose models the underlying value can jump to any value. Moreover, since the project value does not jump to zero *per se*, their models allow for more than one jump during the lifetime of the option. The distribution of the number of jumps is Poisson.

From our experience that information arrives discontinuously in time, we present a model in which the present value of future cashflows follows

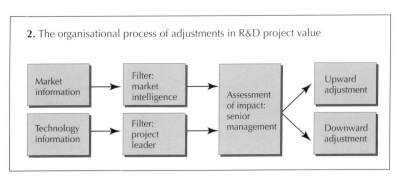

2. The organisational process of adjustments in R&D project value

a deterministic movement, upon which are superimposed stochastic jumps. This model builds further on the approaches already mentioned; for a detailed description of the model, see Pennings and Lint (1997); for a detailed treatise on the process of data gathering for a multimedia R&D project at Philips Electronics, see Lint and Pennings (1998).

OPTION VALUATION WITH THE PRIMARY ASSESSMENT TOOL AT PHILIPS ELECTRONICS

Scoring model

In order to assure an integrative use of the developed model, it must be incorporated into the new product development (NPD) process; it must also be transparent and enhance communication among the different functional areas involved.

Given the transparency and broad applicability of scoring methods, it was decided at Philips Electronics to develop an extended scoring method to support technology management (The use and applicability of scoring methods are explained in Panel 2). The approach developed, namely the Primary Assessment Tool (PAT) for new business creation, specifies the minimum set of data that is required to make an initial assessment of the relative attractiveness of proposals and to determine their option value. Besides financial elements, the tool also incorporates a preliminary set of marketing and organisational elements to capture organisational risk. A high level of consistency of proposals is accomplished by accurately defined questions and scoring methods. PAT was customised for potential use by corporate research, corporate strategy, and product divisions, and has since been adopted as a "concise and powerful tool".

Illustration

We illustrate PAT with an example of a current research project at Philips Electronics. At Philips Corporate Research an innovative technology has been developed: optical recording with the use of tape. This combines the best of both worlds: an optical system (hence no decay), and an enormous storage capacity, on tape, of currently 75Gbyte. This is a 100 times the capacity of the present CD, and seven times more than the double-layered Digital Versatile Disc (DVD).

Optical tape is a true research opportunity. From a technological standpoint the project is in the research stage and, therefore, important uncertainties still exist concerning its feasibility as a consumer product. According to the researchers involved, it takes five years before the technology will be available for marketing. Market uncertainty is even larger in high-tech markets, being determined by uncertainties with relation to cost price, sales volume, standardisation opportunities and support by software industry. Even applications such as video, PC and multimedia are not

> ### PANEL 2
>
> # SCORING MODELS
>
> Most scoring models apply to situations where there is a low degree of quantification, a low degree of interdependency among projects, and where multiple objectives exist. While checklists and project profiles can be applied in situations involving several objectives, scoring models are widely used since multi-dimensional comparisons are difficult to convert into a ranking without any aggregation procedure. Different methods for scoring and aggregating selection criteria exist in order to obtain a single criterion. A general scoring model is structured as a number of independent decision alternatives compared by means of quantitative and qualitative criteria. These criteria represent relevant and preferably mutually exclusive objectives and are usually assigned different weights according to their relative importance. A five-point scale generally measures the characteristics of a project with respect to one criterion. The project is scored on each criterion, and the score is multiplied by the weight of that criterion. The project value is calculated by adding the weighted scores over all criteria. The ranking of the projects according to their values guides the selection decision. The cut-off point may be determined by a value threshold or by resource limitations.
>
> A variety of scoring models has been proposed (for a recent survey, see Liberatore and Stylianou, 1995). Proponents argue that scoring models are perhaps the best screening tool available at the early stages of new project development (NPD), and that such models have utility for the following reasons (Cooper, 1985):
>
> ❑ they make highly judgmental decisions somewhat more objective, and they systematise the review process;
> ❑ they force management to subject projects to a consistent set of review criteria, meanwhile focusing attention on the most relevant issues;
> ❑ they require management to state goals and objectives clearly – moreover, scoring methods are easy to understand and use; and
> ❑ they are generally applicable and can be used company-wide for R&D and NPD project selection and initial evaluation.

precisely clear. However, Philips could expect large gains in the multimedia market if such a technology breaks through on a global scale after standardisation, bringing them the benefits of first-mover advantages. If the software industry uniformly chose optical tape as a worldwide standard, such a technology could be a gold mine, because of the many product possibilities and worldwide market opportunities.

Additional technological developments and new market information (business shifts) during research stages strongly influence the (un)attractiveness of an eventual market introduction. The opportunity to adjust the strategy for market in the meantime adds important flexibility or option value to the optical tape recording project. The full investment trajectory is not committed to at once, only the initial investments in R&D. The option value of these investments is largely determined by the opportunity to make the final decision on market introduction with substantially more technological and market information. This option value must compensate the R&D costs necessary to create this option; the option approach provides a practical instrument for this purpose.

Parameterisation

PAT is illustrated in Figure 3. The financial information from PAT (sales potential, probability of success, capital and marketing expenditures, cost of capital, level of operational cashflow (as a percentage of annual sales) and time-to-market information) are used to calculate the option value of a project. The economic evaluation of R&D options incorporates seven basic variables:

❏ underlying value;
❏ average impact of business events;
❏ frequency of business events;
❏ exercise price;
❏ option price;
❏ risk-free rate; and
❏ exercise time.

The underlying value (S) is the present value on the exercise date of future expected net cashflows from operation, generated by market introduction during the economic life of the investment. The level of operational cashflow resulting from sales is expressed as a percentage (b) that will vary across the product divisions of a company as a result of different market circumstances. The sales potential (P) is asked for the fifth year after market introduction, assuming that sales resulting from the new technology or product reach their peak level in that year. From the fifth year after market introduction, no revenues from the new technology or product are considered, since product and technology life cycles in high-technology markets tend to be very short, and product prices drop fast after market introduction.

By means of a dialogue box, PAT asks the user whether the development of sales in time for the first five years after market introduction is known. If so, these numbers are requested and used for calculations. If not, it is satis-factory if the user gives an estimate of the sales in the fifth year after market introduction. PAT makes subsequent calculations on the assumption

3. Primary assessment tool

TITLE: Optical tape recording   **DATE:**   Jan 1995

Proposed by	Affiliation
Business owner	Affiliation
PDs involved	Source R&D
External partners	Source strategy

Vision (scope, strategic fit)

To be a dominant player in the field of mass data storage (75GByte) for consumer electronics and PC applications, and to set optical tape as a uniform global standard. Optical tape extends Philips' patent and technology position in CD and DVD.

Ambition: Sales potential (Mfl) | 3000 | P
(5 years after market intro)

Investments: Capital exp. (Mfl) | 400 | I_1
Marketing exp. (Mfl) | 1000 | I_2

Uncertainty: Annual number of shifts | 3.35 | λ
Business shift size | 0.11 | γ

Financial parameters: Riskfree rate | 7% | r
Cost of capital | 12% | μ
Operational cashflow | 20% | b

Attractiveness: 0 1 2

Market profitability:
Market growth:
Industry concentration:
Value chain complexity:

Uncertainty   20% σ *(Calculated by PAT)*
Option value   33 F   *(Calculated by PAT)*

R&D exp. (Mfl)   15 C   (Cost of the option)

Timing: Philips time to market | 2000 | T

rating   *(calculated by PAT)* | 75

Competencies/challenge: 0 1 2

Technology:
Production/sourcing/operations:
Distribution/customer base:
Entrepreneurial team:

Business development graph:
Stage

Business plan
3
2
1
Technology ———————●——————— Project champion
Budget

rating   *(calculated by PAT)* | 63

Issues
– Product standardisation
– Market take-off

that sales grow linearly to this peak level. Present values are calculated by discounting the cashflows against the firm's cost of capital (μ). Formally, the underlying value at the exercise time is automatically calculated by PAT:

$$S = b \cdot P \cdot \{0.2/(1 + \mu) + 0.4/(1 + \mu)^2 + 0.6/(1 + \mu)^3 + 0.8/(1 + \mu)^4 + 1/(1 + \mu)^5\}$$

Since in our example P = Fls3,000 million, b = 20%, and i = 12%, PAT calculates S(T) = Fls1,200 million.[2]

The exercise price (I) consists of the present value on the exercise date of investments that are necessary for market introduction. These are investments in new production processes (I1) and marketing expenditures, which cohere with the market introduction (I2). This is put as I = I1 + I2. In our case, I = Fls1,400 million.

The cost of the option (C) consists of the present value of R&D costs, which are necessary to create the option (the decision on market introduction). In our case, the research cost amounts to Fls15 million.

The risk-free rate of interest (r) is set equal to the annual return on government bonds with the same maturity as the R&D stages of the project. In our case example, this appears as 7.0%.

Another variable is the exercise time (T). The necessary duration of experiments and various tests on material suitability and the durability of prototypes determine T. In our example T = the year 2000.

The last two variables are λ (the number of annual expected business shifts) and γ (a yardstick for the expected absolute change in the underlying value at every business shift). The variance of the underlying value (σ^2) can be written as $\sigma^2 = \lambda\gamma^2$. The parameter λ can be estimated as the ratio of the number of business shifts in the entire period and the number of years the period lasts. An estimate of γ^2 can be obtained by taking the mean of all quadratic changes in the underlying value at each business shift. Both are maximum likelihood estimators.

We studied events that happened between January 1990 and February 1995. Within these five years, 17 events were observed[3] to have strategic impact on the underlying value of R&D on optical tape recording. Hence, λ is estimated at 17/5.08 = 3.35. It appears that γ equals 0.107, so the standard deviation is 0.2. This calculation is based on the assumption that business shifts in past multimedia research projects are comparative with the shifts during the optical tape recording research project.

Applying asymptotic theory, the option value, F(t) can be approximated with the Black–Scholes formula where the variance is replaced by $\lambda\gamma^2$ (Pennings and Lint, 1997). Thus,

$$F(t) = S(t)\Phi(d + \sqrt{\lambda(T - t)}\gamma) - I\Phi(d)\exp(-r(T - t))$$

with

$$d = \frac{\ln(S(t)/I) + (r - \frac{1}{2}\lambda\gamma^2)(T - t)}{\sqrt{\lambda(T - t)}\gamma}$$

With these parameters the option value of the optical tape recording project is calculated by PAT at Fls33 million.

Since the present value of future cashflows from the market introduction of optical tape recording discounted to the moment of market introduction of optical tape is Fls1,200 million and the necessary cost of the investment is Fls1,400 million, the NPV is negative. The NPV calculation, however, denies the flexibility of abandoning the optical tape technology at the moment of market introduction. Contrary to conventional analysis, the option approach supports embarking on R&D, since the value of the option exceeds the cost of the option.

Strategic management with PAT

PAT not only provides financial information, but also incorporates the strategic setting of an R&D project, where the explicit criteria scored are attractiveness and competencies. These criteria are used to link marketing and strategic information in the business environment to financial information about the project.

Market attractiveness is an exogenous factor that generally cannot be influenced by proactive management. To determine the market attractiveness of a particular project, scores are asked for the following key market dimensions:

❑ market profitability;
❑ market growth;
❑ industry concentration; and
❑ value chain complexity.

Porter's model (1985) is used to estimate market profitability by determining the weakness or strength of each of the following five forces:

❑ bargaining power of suppliers;
❑ bargaining power of customers;
❑ threat of new entrants;
❑ threat of potential substitutes; and
❑ rivalry.

Finally, the total score of the market profitability is determined according to the number of unfavourable forces. Market growth is classified according to the expected annual growth percentage of the targeted market. The industry concentration determines the competitive structure of the targeted market, and is related to the current aggregated market share of the four main players in the industry. To assess value chain complexity, the main underlying question is which elements in the value chain have to be altered, and are new to the business. By determining the number of elements that are affected or have to be put in place before the new product or service can be launched, value chain complexity can be set. Finally, the programme determines the overall rating of attractiveness by calculating the scores of:

❑ market profitability;
❑ market growth;
❑ industry concentration; and
❑ value chain complexity.

As a second step, in a similar way to determining market attractiveness, the relative position of the core competencies of the company in relation to the targeted market is assessed. Scores are asked for:

❑ technology/patent position;
❑ production/sourcing/operations
❑ distribution/customer base; and
❑ entrepreneurial team.

For these items, the scoring is more subjective and expresses the opinion of the project team, whether the item is absent, partly in place, or fully in place. By determining the scores, an overall rating on the company's competencies in accordance with the targeted business is established. The missing competencies can be viewed as challenges and targets to secure a successful market introduction after R&D completion.

A complementary way to monitor the development of competencies through time is illustrated by the business development graph (see Figure 4), a checklist based upon the Bell–Mason diagnostic (Bell and McNamara, 1991). A major benefit of this polar graph is that the number of spokes, and the rules, are time varying due to the questions evolving that become more detailed with each stage of development. The polar graph is automatically generated by PAT based upon interactive input from the project team.

IMPACT-ARRIVAL PORTFOLIO

Industry sectors differ in their characteristics of the arrival rate and the impact of business events. Figure 5 shows the impact-arrival portfolio for five industry sectors.

The financial sector typically exhibits a continuous arrival of information with a relatively low impact. In this case there are time series available that serve to estimate volatility. The business shift approach has relatively little value for management and the classic Black–Scholes approach to option pricing therefore suffices. On the other hand, the pharmaceutical sector is

4. Business development graphs from concept to market development

Business plan

Stage 1: Concept

Business plan

Stage 2: Technology development

Business plan

Stage 3: Market development

5. Illustration of expected number of business shifts per annum (λ) and yardstick for the expected size of the business shift (γ) for different industry sectors

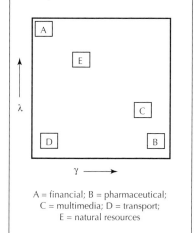

A = financial; B = pharmaceutical;
C = multimedia; D = transport;
E = natural resources

confronted with a low frequency, but a substantial impact of business shifts. Taken to the extreme, Schwartz and Moon (1999) provide a model for the pharmaceutical industry in which the value of the project may jump to zero at any moment. Of course, breakthroughs are rare but imply considerable upward shifts, as recently exemplified by Pfizer's Viagra.

The multimedia sector (electronics and information technology) closely resembles the pharmaceutical industry, although the sector faces relatively more business shifts with a relatively lower impact. Since the pharmaceutical industry is transparent in the R&D process (briefly summarised as pre-clinical testing, clinical testing, FDA approval), projects in the R&D pipeline are much more public. Given transparency, companies in this sector may adjust their R&D and alliance strategies to avoid the risk of developing competitive drugs. As a consequence, pharmaceutical companies have a monopoly over drugs that are proven to be better than standard after the R&D stages. In the multimedia sector, different product or technology standards may coexist after R&D completion. A typical example is the battle over the DVD in which Sony and Philips competed against Toshiba and Time Warner (see Lint and Pennings, 1999). Firms try to avoid product homogeneity by producing differentiated goods. Therefore the arrival of strategic information affecting project values of multimedia companies is more frequent than in the pharmaceutical industry, although the impact is slightly lower.

The transport industry is a typical example of an industry where the frequency and impact of events is relatively low. Business is mature, competition is based on price, and there are little opportunities for innovation (exceptions are just-in-time delivery and value-added logistics). The market value of companies in this sector primarily consists of the assets in place, while the present value of growth opportunities (PVGO) is relatively small. In a recent empirical paper, Smit (1999) analysed the PVGO as a percentage of market value for different industries. His results confirm our hypothesis that PVGO is relatively small in the transport sector.

Finally, we consider industries extracting natural resources (oil and mining). Since natural resources are continuously traded, the frequency of events comes closer to the frequency perceived in the financial sector, although the impact is slightly larger. For this reason, the first steps in the application of real option pricing have been taken in this field (Brennan and Schwartz, 1985).

CONCLUSIONS

The option approach based on jumps or business shifts in technological or market circumstances contributes to real option analysis in R&D practice, and the option value serves as a practical instrument to research management. The value calculated indicates the maximum size of the R&D budget from an economic point of view. For our case study, for example, the present value of the budget for researching optical tape recording should not exceed Fls33 million. This way, in terms of the capabilities and allocation of researchers, guidelines for the optimal total number of researchers working on this project for different R&D phases can be derived. Moreover, a balanced and optimised R&D portfolio that is consistent with current financial thinking can be created. Also, the option value of the potential benefits of marketing new products based on advanced R&D is estimated in an appropriate way (note that this goes far beyond conventional myopic use of methods like Payback, NPV, ROI or percentage methods).

1 Project value is defined here as the present value of net cashflows resulting from sales to customers.
2 By discounting at the firm's cost of capital, S(t) = Fls660 million where t is current year (1995).
3 For example the formation of a joint venture with Apple, Eastman Kodak, Corning and two regional telephone companies in 1992, bringing interactive multimedia services to homes and schools.

BIBLIOGRAPHY

Amram, M. and N. Kulatilaka, 1998, *Real Options: Managing Strategic Investment in an Uncertain World,* Harvard Business School Press, Boston.

Bell, C.G. and J.E. McNamara, 1991, *High-Tech Ventures: The Guide for Entrepreneurial Success,* Amsterdam, Addison-Wesley.

Benaroch, M. and R.J. Kauffman, 1999, "A Case for Using Real Options Pricing Analysis to Evaluate Information Technology Project Investments", *Information Systems Research,* 10, pp. 70–86.

Black, F. and M. Scholes, 1973, "The Pricing of Options and Corporate Liabilities", *Journal of Political Economy,* 81, pp. 637–59.

Brennan, M.J. and E.S. Schwartz, 1985, "Evaluating Natural Resource Investments", *Journal of Business,* 58, pp. 135–57.

Cooper, R.G., 1985, "Selecting Winning New Product Projects: Using the NewProd System", *Journal of Product Innovation Management,* 2, pp. 34–44.

Cox, J.C. and S.A. Ross, 1975, "The Pricing of Options for Jump Processes", Working paper, Rodney L. White Center for Financial Research, University of Pennsylvania.

Dixit, A.K. and R.S. Pindyck, 1995, "The Option Approach to Capital Investment", *Harvard Business Review,* 73, pp. 105–15.

Liberatore, M.J. and A.C. Stylianou, 1995, "New Product Development Decision Making", *Management Science,* 41, pp. 1296–316.

Lieberman, M.B. and D.B. Montgomery, 1988, "First-Mover Advantages", *Strategic Management Journal,* 9, pp. 41–58.

Lint, O. and E. Pennings, 1998, "R&D as an Option on Market Introduction", *R&D Management,* 28, pp. 279–87.

Lint, O. and E. Pennings, 1999, "The Recently Chosen Digital Video Standard. Playing the Game within the Game', Working paper, Erasmus University Rotterdam.

Lint, O. and E. Pennings, 2000, "The Option Value of Developing Two Products Simultaneously When the Final Standard Is Uncertain", in Lenos Trigeorgis (ed), *Real Options: New Developments and Applications,* Oxford University Press, forthcoming.

McDonald, R. and D. Siegel, 1986, "The Value of Waiting to Invest", *Quarterly Journal of Economics,* 101, pp. 707–28.

Merton, R.C., 1976, "Option Pricing when Underlying Stock Returns are Discontinuous", *Journal of Financial Economics,* 3, pp. 125–44.

Nichols, N.A., 1994, "The New Pharmaceutical Paradigm", *Harvard Business Review,* 72, pp. 88–105.

Pennings, E. and O. Lint, 1997, "The Option Value of Advanced R&D", *European Journal of Operational Research*, 103, pp. 83–95.

Pennings, E. and O. Lint, 2000, "Market Entry, Phased Rollout or Abandonment", *European Journal of Operational Research*, forthcoming.

Porter, M.E., 1985, *Competitive Advantage: Creating and Sustaining Superior Advantage*, New York, The Free Press.

Quigg, L., 1993, "Empirical Testing of Real Option-Pricing Models", *Journal of Finance*, 48, pp. 621–39.

Roberts, K. and M.L. Weitzman, 1981, "Funding Criteria for Research, Development, and Exploration Projects", *Econometrica*, 49, pp. 1261–88.

Schwartz, E. and M. Moon, 1999, "Evaluating Research and Development Investments", Working paper, Anderson Graduate School of Management, UCLA.

Smit, H., 1999, "Empirical Characteristics of Growth Options", Working paper, Erasmus University Rotterdam.

Strebel, P., 1992, *Breakpoints: How Managers Exploit Radical Business Change*, Harvard Business School Press, Boston.

Trigeorgis, L., 1996, *Real Options: Managerial Flexibility and Strategy in Resource Allocation*, MIT Press, Cambridge.

7

Airline Long-Term Planning Under Uncertainty: The Benefits of Asset Flexibility Created Through Product Commonality and Manufacturer Lead Time Reductions

John Stonier

Airbus Industrie of North America, Inc.

INTRODUCTION

With the economic life of a large commercial aircraft exceeding twenty-five years and a minimum scale to which an airline can economically commit in terms of fleet type, an airline's decision to purchase a new aircraft type is often a multi billion-dollar bet. The significant sunk costs associated with training, spares inventory and route development, and the difficulty for airlines to economically re-market customised aircraft in large numbers, make the purchasing decision essentially irreversible.

In general airlines use relatively sophisticated but conventional capital budgeting techniques in their long term fleet planning. For example in order to quantify the various attributes of aircraft over their projected life-time such as fuel burn and maintenance on the costs side and passenger and cargo loads on the revenue side, airlines use discounted cashflow analysis (DCF) projecting twenty years or more into the future.

This form of long term strategic planning in the airline industry offers some interesting challenges. Not least of these is the lag between making a fleet planning decision and seeing the effects of that decision in the composition of an airline's fleet of aircraft. Airlines typically have had to wait up to three years to take delivery, which then often spans several years. The uncertainty created by this time lag renders conventional DCF techniques somewhat obsolete. Even airlines than use scenario planning are "stabbing in the dark". Exogenous shocks such as fuel price spikes, economic recession and the threat of war, along with endogenous shocks due to competitive moves within the industry go together to create a very uncertain future.

Robert Crandall, the ex CEO of American Airlines, was quoted as saying that the company had never purchased an aircraft and used it in the role it was originally envisaged for. Airlines have learnt that asset flexibility is a very important attribute. Asset flexibility has many dimensions. The historical reliance on debt financing or long-term tax leases with their high cost to unwind has for some time now been diminishing, and Operating Lessors are playing an increasing roll in the make-up of an airline's fleet. Airlines often maintain a number of older fully amortised aircraft, which they would otherwise retire for reasons of high cash operating costs. These low fixed cost aircraft can be grounded relatively economically in case of an industry downturn. All these assist the airlines in managing the uncertainty they face today with respect to future capacity needs.

Aircraft delivery flexibility is another type of asset flexibility, and an area that manufacturers have recently made significant improvements in. Historically, one of the elements that has contributed to the industry's cyclical nature are long manufacturing lead times. Airlines have ordered aircraft during a cyclical upturn but taken delivery of them in less than ideal conditions. In order to satisfy customers and also to reduce manufacturing costs, both Airbus and Boeing have for some time now been working towards reduced manufacturing and configuration lead times – consequently, significant progress has already been made. The flexibility that this offers can be greatly enhanced for airlines operating a family of aircraft from the same production line, eg, the A320 family and the A333/340 family. Airlines can now choose to take delivery from a range of capacities and capabilities with lead times as low as 15 months. Airlines fix schedules in their computer reservation system (CRS) and sell seats 330 days in advance. Additionally, lead times on buyer furnished equipment (BFE), such as seats and galleys, are approximately 12 months. Crew training can also take several months. Therefore, airlines now have the flexibility to commit to an aircraft delivery only three months prior to a firm schedule commitment.

This reduction in delivery lead times binds the fortunes of the aircraft manufacturer and the airline even tighter. In the past, manufacturers with a short memory, who indiscriminately increased production during cyclical upturns, contributed to the over-capacity induced downturn. This is easily done when the post-manufacturing asset risk is totally in the hands of the airline. By reducing manufacturing lead times, airlines can better control capacity and therefore yields, resulting in more sustained profitability. This in turn allows airlines to retire older aircraft sooner, creating a younger and more efficient fleet of aircraft.

Airlines tend to believe that they carry a disproportionate amount of the overall asset risk associated with the industry value chain. However, the risks are just as great in the manufacturing side of the business. Manufacturers commit several billion dollars over a period of five to six years to design and build an aircraft for which the market is uncertain. Technological risk is also very present. Profitability is only assured if a significant production volume is reached, and launching a product during a downturn can significantly affect the chance of this. Therefore, a more stable market is in the interest of both the manufacturer and the airlines.

While some airlines now intuitively realise the value of delivery flexibility, especially within a family of aircraft, the explicit value quantification of this has, to my knowledge, eluded them. Additionally, airlines have tended to underestimate this value, as manufacturers, in order to bolster their order books, have given away delivery option positions at very little real cost to the airlines. A small fee is often required, yet the fee is applied to the price of the aircraft if the option is exercised. This is unlike the pricing of stock options, where the price of the option is significantly larger in a proportional sense, and becomes a sunk cost regardless of whether the option is exercised or not.

OPTION PRICING THEORY AND ITS APPLICATION TO REAL OPTIONS

New applications of existing financial theory are now allowing practitioners to quantify real options – as opposed to financial option – in many capital-intensive industries. There is, in fact, a very good analogy between the value of a traded stock option and an aircraft delivery option. Two American economists, Myron Scholes and Robert Merton, recently won the Nobel Prize for economics for their pioneering work in financial options, conducted some 25 years ago. The well known Black–Scholes option pricing model – as developed by Fischer Black and Myron Scholes (1973) and extended by Robert Merton (1973) – is the foundation of all option and other derivative pricing analysis used by traders today. This novel equation is able to address what academics call *exogenous uncertainty*, ie, uncertainty caused through external shocks which are (at least partially) resolved with the passage of time. Discounted cashflow (DCF) techniques, the workhorse of all financial analysis, is able to capture the concept of risk yet remains unable to model uncertainty. As a result, real options are currently a hot topic at Business Schools around the world.

Option pricing 101
The Black–Scholes formula for a European Call option is:

$$\text{Option value} = SN(d) - Xe^{-rt} N(d - \sigma\sqrt{t})$$

where S is the share price today, σ is the volatility of the share price over time, $N(d)$ is the proportion of shares (in a levered position) required to replicate the option, $N(d - \sigma\sqrt{t})$ is the risk-neutral probability that the call option will be exercised, t is the time to exercise or maturity, X is the strike or exercise price, and r is the risk free discount rate.

The methodology uses the fact that taking a levered position in the underlying stock and re-balancing this position over time in a self-financing manner can duplicate the return on an option. If we value the loan and the stock, we can value the option. The first term in the formula is the value of the stock in the levered position, the share price today multiplied by the proportion of shares required (this will later be termed *delta*). The second term is the value of the loan, which turns out to be the expected cost associated with the exercise, ie, the exercise price multiplied by the probability that the call will be exercised discounted back to today. The market price of the stock is assumed to be stochastic (following a random walk), where the past share price movement is irrelevant. It can be seen that the value of the stock option increases with both the time to exercise and the volatility of the underlying share price. This is because the longer the time to exercise and the higher the volatility, the more likely the share price is to rise above the exercise (or strike) price. If the share price falls below the exercise price, then the option expires unexercised, and the only cost is the price paid for the option. Thus, options create value by truncating downside risk while still allowing the holder to take advantage of upside potential.

In order to apply this model to valuing aircraft delivery purchase options, we assume that the value of an aircraft is the discounted present value of all its cashflows in operation over its economic life, ie, its present value (PV). In the long run, airlines will only be able to afford aircraft whose value exceeds the capital cost. Thus, S becomes the present value of the underlying asset (the aircraft), while X becomes the aircraft price. t is the time from when an airline obtains an option delivery position until it must exercise the option and confirm delivery.

The Black–Scholes analogy immediately tells us that real options are valuable in capital intensive industries where returns on assets are highly variable – this is certainly a characteristic of the airline industry. Continuing this analogy, Figure 1 shows an airline that makes an economic justification to purchase new aircraft at point "0" in time (ie, today), which will yield it a return of 12% based on a DCF analysis of future expected cashflows. Let's assume its WACC (weighted average cost of capital) is 10%. As the investment provides a positive return today, it obtains two delivery options which mature at points 1 and 2 in time. When point 1 is reached, it exercises its right to take delivery, and earns an even greater return until the next

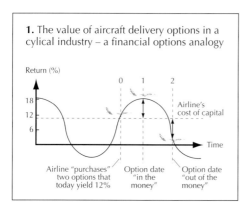

1. The value of aircraft delivery options in a cylical industry – a financial options analogy

cyclical downturn. The option is "in the money". When point 2 is reached, the industry is in recession, and the option is "out of the money". It does not exercise the purchase option and avoids the loss associated with operating that aircraft during a recession. The aircraft delivery option position gives the airline the right, but not the obligation, to take delivery of an aircraft at a specific point in time. Thus, the option allows the airline to take advantage of upside potential that may arise, but protects it from downside risk.

A key input, the volatility σ, is the variability of the value of the underlying asset – the aircraft. We will discuss how to measure this in more detail later. However an estimate can be made from the movement of an airline's share price, which can be used as a proxy for the volatility of the aircraft investment. If we believe in the efficient market theory, then the value of an airline (its market capitalisation) is an accurate reflection of the discounted present value of all its individual investments. In the airline industry these are overwhelmingly aircraft. However, just like in the capital asset pricing model (CAPM), the volatility, and therefore required return, is a function of both the specific industry risk and individual company's leverage. It is therefore necessary to make adjustments based on individual airline leverage. This is analogous to the measurement of stock *beta*. Thus, as volatility increases option value, highly levered airlines with highly variable returns should assign greater value to aircraft delivery flexibility than their industry peers. Figure 2 compares the volatility of two US airline stocks, one with a relatively strong balance sheet and the other with significantly higher leverage. The lower graph shows the variation in the share price of the more volatile stock as a percentage of the less volatile stock's price.

DISCOUNTED CASHFLOWS AND DECISION TREE ANALYSIS

Another useful framework for real options is decision tree analysis. Firstly, let's demonstrate the fallacy of static DCF techniques for justifying new investments. Referring to Figure 3, let's assume we can invest today in an aircraft which gives an implicit return of 12% in perpetuity – net present value (NPV) equals 0, with 12% discount rate – and our WACC is 10%. Let's further assume stochastic variability for the return on an asset. The probability of the return increasing to, say, 14% is the same as it decreasing to 10% at some future point in time, such that the expected value of the outcome is still 12%. Traditional DCF analysis says it is optimum to accept the investment today, as the expected return of 12% is greater than the cost of capital. However, if we wait until tomorrow to make a decision, then we can get a 14% return in perpetuity, and, if the return falls to 10% instead of rising to 14%, we reject the investment. In this and the above example, we have made quite a few simplifying assumptions to make a point, yet as we proceed, we can relax these.

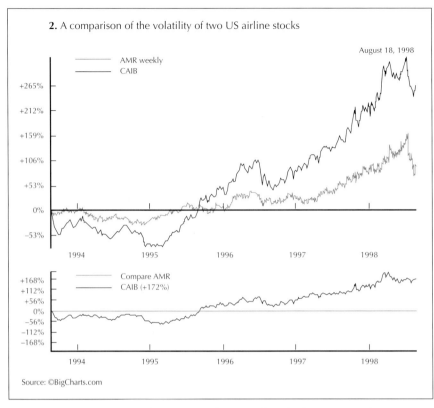

2. A comparison of the volatility of two US airline stocks

August 18, 1998

AMR weekly
CAIB

Compare AMR
CAIB (+172%)

Source: ©BigCharts.com

Let's now use a decision tree framework to look at an aircraft investment decision in a little more detail. Again, suppose that we analyse the investment today, but have the option to wait till tomorrow to decide to invest by virtue of an aircraft delivery option, which fixes the investment price (or strike price) in real terms. Referring to Figure 4, the aircraft costs US$40 million today and the Airline Planning department expects the aircraft to provide a stream of future contributions when it is delivered in one year's time. The contribution is valued at US$51 million with a probability of two-thirds (0.67) if the market

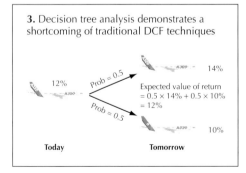

3. Decision tree analysis demonstrates a shortcoming of traditional DCF techniques

12%

Prob = 0.5

Prob = 0.5

14%

Expected value of return
= 0.5 × 14% + 0.5 × 10%
= 12%

10%

Today   Tomorrow

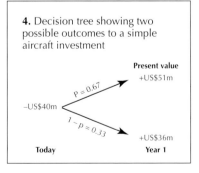

4. Decision tree showing two possible outcomes to a simple aircraft investment

Present value

+US$51m

P = 0.67

−US$40m

1 − p = 0.33

+US$36m

Today   Year 1

remains favourable, and a contribution of US$36 million with a probability of one-third (0.33) if the market deteriorates. This uncertainty is resolved in a year's time. If the airline's required hurdle rate for new investments is 20%, then traditional DCF values the investment as:

$$NPV = -US\$40m + \frac{(0.66)(US\$51m)}{1.2} + \frac{(0.33)(US\$36m)}{1.2}$$
$$= -US\$40m + US\$28.4m + US\$10m$$
$$= -US\$1.6m$$

and therefore should not be implemented.

Now suppose that the delivery of the aircraft could be delayed subject to managerial discretion by virtue of acquiring a delivery option. For simplicity, we assume that the airline puts down a refundable deposit of 10% (US$4 million) today and acquires the right, but not obligation, to take delivery of the plane in two years' time subject to confirmation of delivery one year prior (a one year lead time). We also assume that the aircraft price escalated at the risk free rate of 10%, while the project value grows at the required hurdle rate, so that the airline is indifferent to simply delaying the purchase. The investment now looks like Figure 5, showing the PV of the investment at year 1. The present value today of the two scenarios are then:

$$PV\,(good) = \frac{-(US\$36m)(1.1)}{1.1} + \frac{(US\$51m)(1.2)}{1.2^2} = +US\$6.5m$$

$$PV\,(poor) = \frac{-(US\$36m)(1.1)}{1.1} + \frac{(US\$36m)(1.2)}{1.2^2} = -US\$6.0m$$

Allowing for the ability of management to decline delivery in one year's time the value of the delivery option today is:

$$NPV = (-US\$4m + US\$6.5m)(0.67) + (-US\$4m - US\$6.0m)(0) = +US\$1.7m$$

Thus, the investment becomes profitable and the value of the flexibility created by the option is:

US$1.7m − −US$1.6m = +US$3.3m

Even if the 10% deposit had been non-refundable, the value of the delivery option would still be:

$$NPV = -(US\$4m) + (US\$6.5m)(0.67)$$
$$= +US\$0.4m$$

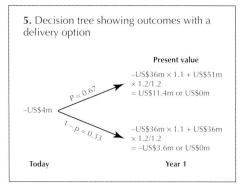

5. Decision tree showing outcomes with a delivery option

Present value

−US$4m

$p = 0.67$

−US$36m × 1.1 + US$51m
× 1.2/1.2
= US$11.4m or US$0m

$1 - p = 0.33$

−US$36m × 1.1 + US$36m
× 1.2/1.2
= −US$3.6m or US$0m

Today   Year 1

Risk-adjusted decision trees

In the previous example, we made an estimate of what the correct discount rate should be – ie, 20%. In any capital budgeting exercise, we know that whenever the payoff characteristic changes, so does the appropriate discount rate to use. Building options into the decision tree changes the payoff characteristics. As the payoff changes at each node in the decision tree, so should the discount rate used to discount that payoff back to today. So, in order to correctly value the delivery option, we need to know the correct discount rate in each node of the tree.

We know from option theory in financial markets that options are more risky than the underlying stock (but less risky than a levered position in the stock). The discount rate increases for call options, decreases for puts, and can "net out" for a combination of calls and puts. So, we suspect that the 20% discount rate is too low to value the option. Even if we were certain about the appropriate rate to discount the cashflows in the first example (firm delivery date one year from today), it would not be correct for the delivery option.

Rather than trying to risk-adjust discount rates at each node, we can perform a *risk neutral* valuation of the option by discounting at the *risk free rate* and accounting for the relative riskiness of the possible outcomes by modifying the probability of each outcome in the tree. This probability is known as the *risk neutral* probability. In order to do this, we take a leap of faith and assume that there is a *twin security*, or portfolio of securities that exists, which is traded in financial markets and has the same risk characteristics (ie, is perfectly correlated with) the underlying asset. We are effectively saying that the risk and return characteristics of an aircraft asset in operation with an airline (ie, its cashflow stream) can be perfectly replicated by the cashflow stream of a portfolio of traded assets. As aircraft assets are not freely traded, it may be difficult to identify the twin security or securities, but the valuation procedure still holds in principal.

In order to determine the risk-adjusted probabilities, we can use the no riskless profitable arbitrage condition. This simply says that the outcome of a long call position can be replicated with a levered position in the underlying stock, and that the value of the option must be consistent with this, or profitable riskless arbitrage could be achieved. For example, if the option is priced too high, a market participant could take a levered position in the underlying stock, write the option (ie, take a short position) and make a riskless profit. Building on our existing example, the possible present values of the cashflow from aircraft investment are shown in Figure 6. Working backwards, the present value of the cashflow today must be:

$$V = \frac{(0.67)(US\$51m)}{1.2} + \frac{(0.33)(US\$36m)}{1.2} = US\$38.34m$$

6. Decision tree showing present value today of the two possible outcomes (the discounted expected value)

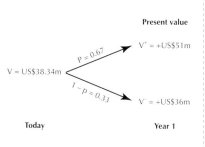

7. Decision tree showing "twin security" with the same payoff distribution

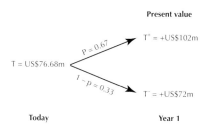

8. Decision tree showing the present values of the two outcomes (option only exercised for the upper branch)

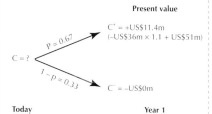

9. Decision tree showing the replicating portfolio

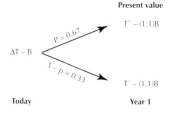

We define the twin security T as having the identical payoff as the investment – this is shown in Figure 7 (we have just multiplied all the outcomes by a factor of two to demonstrate that we are using the twin security and not the present values of the investment itself). Now looking at the option case, the outcomes are as in Figure 8. However, we can no longer use the 20% discount rate to work backwards to today. We now create a portfolio that exactly replicates the option payoffs by purchasing Δ (*delta*) shares in the twin security and financing the purchase, in part by borrowing D dollars at the risk free rate, which we define as 10%. The replicating portfolio is shown in Figure 9. We now have two equations and two unknowns:

$$C^+ = (\Delta T^+ - (1.10) D = US\$11.4m$$
$$C^- = (\Delta T^- - (1.10) D = US\$0m$$

The hedge ratio

$$\Delta = (C^+ - C^-)/(T^+ - T^-)$$

$$= (US\$11.4m - 0)/(US\$102m - US\$72m)$$
$$= 0.38$$
$$D = C^+T^- - C^-T^+)/(T^+ - T^-)(1.10)$$
$$= \frac{(US\$11.4m \times US\$72m - 0 \times US\$102m)}{(US\$102m - US\$72m)(1.1)}$$
$$= US\$24.87m$$

and

$$C = \Delta T - D$$
$$= 0.38 \times US\$76.68m - US\$24.87m$$
$$= +US\$4.27m$$

So when we account for the correct discount rate the value of the call option is +US\$4.27m, and the net present value of the investment today is:

$$NPV = -US\$4m\ (0.67) + US\$4.27m = +US\$1.60m$$

This compares to +US\$1.7 million previously calculated.

Finally we may ask, what is the correct discount rate, for the option:

$$+US\$1.6m = -US\$4m\ (0.67) + (US\$11.4m\ (0.67) + 0\ (0.33))/(1 + r^c)$$
$$r^c = 78\%$$

Stepping back from the details of the option valuation methodology, we can characterise the value of the option as the difference between the value of an investment that can be postponed and one that cannot. The value of the option can be seen in Figure 10. If the investment is a "now or never" choice, then the value of the investment is the solid line. If the investment can be postponed, by virtue of delivery options, it is valuable, even if the project NPV is zero or negative.

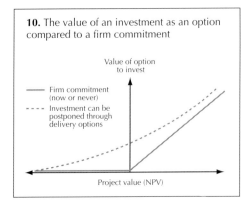

10. The value of an investment as an option compared to a firm commitment

Value of option to invest

Firm commitment (now or never)

---- Investment can be postponed through delivery options

Project value (NPV)

A European option like a simple aircraft delivery option can only be exercised at a specific future point in time. Each option represents a manufacturing slot on the production line. It is easier to think of the ability to delay an investment in terms of an American option, which can be exercised at any point up to the expiration date for the option. However, a series of European options can also allow postponement. Additionally, aircraft manufacturers are now offering "rolling options", which give an airline the right but not the obligation to take delivery of a specified number of aircraft in each of a consecutive number of years.

THE DIVIDEND EFFECT AND FOREGONE EARNING

So far, we have assumed that the value of a project is the discounted present value of its future cashflow stream. As shown, in conventional capital budgeting exercises the choice is between accepting the project today or cancelling indefinitely, a "do-or-die" decision. There is no mention of a delay. With options, we can explore this ability to delay. We can examine the value of waiting for more perfect information, and calculate the cost of waiting. With real assets, this cost may relate to revenues lost in the period before the project is initiated, or it may be incurred because a competitor pre-empts the market and the opportunity no longer looks so favourable. These lost revenues must be traded off against the value of waiting. With financial options for a non-dividend paying stock, we implicitly assume in the Black–Scholes formulation that the value of the stock increases at the same rate as the cost of capital. This results in the well known implication that it is never optimal to exercise an American call option on a non-dividend paying stock before its expiration. In the context of real options, this could wrongly be interpreted as implying that investments should never be undertaken until the last possible chance to invest.

Robert Merton[2], to account for dividends, later modified the Black–Scholes formula. Most traded assets and securities have a dividend-like effect, which is simply the value of holding onto the asset. For securities, it is the foregone interest or dividend payments, and for commodities it is the convenience yield. This value can be seen in the difference between spot and discounted future prices of traded securities and commodities.

For a security:

$$\text{Future price}/(1 + r_f)^t = \text{spot price} - \text{PV(forgone interest or dividend payment)}$$

and for commodities:

$$\text{Future price}/(1 + r_f)^t = \text{spot price} - \text{PV(net convenience yield)}$$

Early work on real options concentrated on commodities because they are traded assets for which a lot of data is available. For example, in calculating the value of an option to develop an oil or gas field, forward prices for oil and gas are readily available. In the case of sunk development costs and production costs below the price of oil, it is optimal to produce if the convenience yield is less than the inflation rate. Otherwise, it is optimal to wait.

There are no futures markets for large commercial aircraft, so there is no easy way to determine a convenience yield. There are many companies in the industry that track the historic value of aircraft by their specific type –

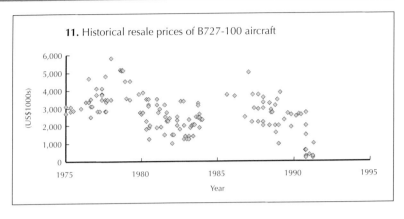

11. Historical resale prices of B727-100 aircraft

for example, Halerstrom and Melgaard (1998). Figure 11 shows the historical price (or value) for the B727-100. Aircraft, unlike commodities, depreciate with age, an indication than an aircraft has a finite economic life. Aircraft appraisers categorise aircraft price changes as being due to either depreciation of their base value or supply-demand driven changes around the base value. Figure 12 shows historical price changes in the same aircraft when the trend in base price is eliminated. This is the closest we can get to real market data for spot prices over time, but we cannot really infer anything from this regarding the convenience yield of aircraft. This type of data could be used to calculate aircraft PV volatility, but we have not done this for a few reasons. The data of prices for aircraft in the secondary market may be somewhat inaccurate, the market is small and relatively inefficient, and there are significant reconfiguration costs involved for airlines purchasing used equipment. Additionally, only in an *efficient market* would the PV of the aircraft equal its price. There may be many airlines where the

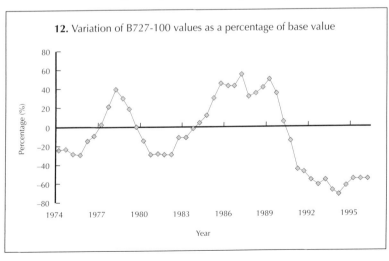

12. Variation of B727-100 values as a percentage of base value

PV considerably exceeds the price: only for the marginal airline would the PV and price be equal.

Returning to the dividend or foregone earnings issue, we have built into the model a lost revenue factor. This accounts for the fact that in a rising market, when it is quite likely that new aircraft would be profitably utilised, a long lead-time would prevent this. Of course, the delayed delivery results in losses in the short run, but yields profits on the far end of the aircraft's life. However, due to the time value of money, these are not equal. Another benefit to earlier delivery is the ability to begin operating aircraft before the effect of mean reversion pulls down high profitability towards the mean. Consistent with the Black–Scholes model, we still assume that that the rate of change (ie, increase) in the mean reverting value of the aircraft (its PV) is the same as the market cost of capital. Mean reversion will be discussed in detail in the following section.

AIRCRAFT DELIVERY OPTIONS IN A REAL OPTIONS FRAMEWORK

The Black–Scholes model and risk-adjusted decision trees can be used to demonstrate the analogy between financial and real options, and to model simple scenarios. However, the application of real option techniques to the aircraft delivery option is, in reality, somewhat more complex. With a financial option, the purchaser of the option transfers the asset value risk to the option writer (the seller) from the time the option is purchased until the option is exercised. With an aircraft purchase option, the airline transfers the aircraft asset value risk to the manufacturer up to the point in time when the option must be "firmed-up" – from this point on the asset value risk is transferred back to the airline (Figure 13). The shorter the manufacturing lead-time (L_d), the less risk the airline is exposed to, as risk increases with the time horizon.

In order to capture this and other complications, a *discrete time* rather than a *continuous time closed form solution* such as the Black–Scholes is used. In the above example (Figures 4 and 5), we have used a binomial decision tree, ie, one period, two-outcome. However, the decision tree can be enlarged, and the time step reduced to the extent that the distribution of PVs in the tree approximates a lognormal distribution. Thus, we

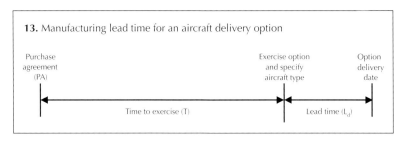

13. Manufacturing lead time for an aircraft delivery option

Purchase agreement (PA)

Exercise option and specify aircraft type

Option delivery date

Time to exercise (T)

Lead time (L_d)

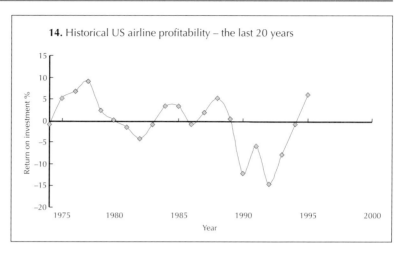

14. Historical US airline profitability – the last 20 years

approximate a continuum of possible outcomes using a discrete time process. In the late 1970s, three economists – John Cox, Stephen Ross and Mark Rubinstein (1979) – developed their well know Binomial approach to option valuation, which in a limiting case collapses to the Black–Scholes formulation. This methodology is based on a very large decision tree, which is *risk-adjusted* at every node. The discount rate used is the risk free rate and the range of possible outcomes in the matrix characterises the uncertainty. The *no profitable arbitrage* condition is used to determine the possible outcomes and solved using backward recursion, from the boundary condition. The boundary condition is the point the option is either exercised or not, and the value of the option at this point can be simply expressed as the maximum of PV − X, or 0.

Another complication is the stochastic assumption inherent in Black–Scholes. History has shown that airline industry profitability is cyclical and not a random walk. Industry practitioners constantly discuss the current stage of the cycle, and when the expected downturn – or upturn – will come. Thus, the industry can be better characterised using a mean reverting model. In this model, the more the airlines' profitability strays from equilibrium value, the greater the probability of it returning. Figure 14 shows historic US airline profitability over the last twenty years; the returns certainly appear to be cyclical.

Mean reversion is often used by economists to model interest rates and currency exchange rate variability. Mean reversion has been modelled (Figure 15), and is consistent with that used by Hull and White (1990) to model interest rate movements. The linear model creates a strong pull to the mean when the PV is far from the mean, and a gentler pull when the PV is closer to the mean. A mean reverting tendency can significantly reduce the value of options on the underlying asset. With a simple random walk, the probability of a future upward or downward motion is independent of all previous movements. Thus, the asset value can stray very significantly from its long-term trend line. With mean reversion this wandering is halted: volatility can still be high but the extent to which the value strays over a set period of time is much smaller.

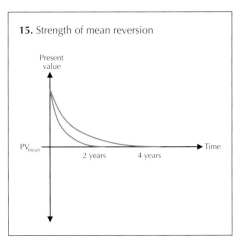

15. Strength of mean reversion

Yet another complication is that airlines have a *naturally occurring option* available to them with regard to purchasing aircraft. As we have discussed above, there is value in waiting as time resolves uncertainty regarding an airline's future aircraft needs. This *natural* option is the option to wait and commit to purchasing aircraft at a later date, rather than commit today to a long stream of (firm and) option aircraft. However, rightly or wrongly, airlines perceive that in order to maximise their buyer power, they should both place large orders,and negotiate at a particular time in the economic cycle of the industry. While airlines holding a stream of option delivery positions need only to suffer the lead-time wait (L_d), other airlines, depending upon the point in the industry cycle, may face three to four year waits until aircraft become available. This is reinforced by the strong correlation between the industry cycle and the airframe order backlog (Figure 16).

The value of aircraft delivery options is in fact the difference between the naturally occurring option to wait and the aircraft delivery option

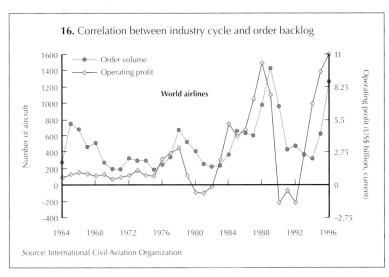

16. Correlation between industry cycle and order backlog

Source: International Civil Aviation Organization

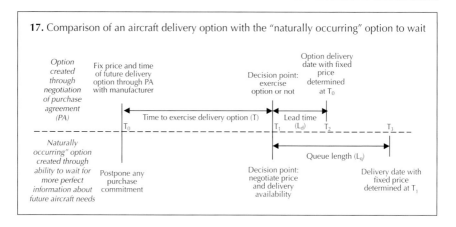

17. Comparison of an aircraft delivery option with the "naturally occurring" option to wait

(Figure 17). The choice is between negotiating today for future delivery option positions with the price and delivery dates determined today, or waiting. If the airline waits, it submits itself to whatever delivery queue length (L_q) and market pricing (X) is in force at the future point in time when it does commit to deliveries. Therefore, there are two degrees of uncertainty, resolved by the option positions: price and queue length. However, in the model, as will be explained, both price and queue length are deterministic. The "naturally occurring" option to wait cannot be more valuable than committing to the delivery option. Even in a severe recession scenario, where pricing between T_0 and T_1 drops and the queue length becomes its minimum (L_d – the lead time), the airline is not committed to that higher pricing, as it can always decide not to exercise the option in favour of renegotiating purchases at a later date.

Another type of option offered by manufacturers are *rolling options*. These options are purchase rights at a given price condition, to be exercised within a given time frame subject to production availability. Rolling options only resolve price uncertainty but not queue length uncertainty. They are valuable to airlines when prices increase in future years. However, queue length (L_q) and aircraft price (X) are in reality likely to rise together, limiting the availability of production slots for the rolling option holders when they become valuable.

The queue length is another important input to the model. Queue length (L_q) we assume to be correlated with the economic cycle,

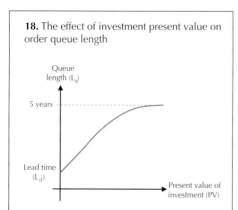

18. The effect of investment present value on order queue length

and is therefore modelled as a function of the PV of the aircraft investment. The queue length will rise and fall as the PV rises and falls in the decision tree (Figure 18); however, the lower bound is fixed at the lead-time (L_d). As can be seen, there is also an upper bound on the queue length by using logarithmic scaling.

Aircraft pricing (X) is also modelled as a function of aircraft value (PV). As the amount of profit an air-line can produce with an aircraft increases, so does the price it is willing to pay for that aircraft. However, there are however bounds to this – Figure 19 shows how it has been modelled. As the aircraft value increases, the price also increases, but at a slower rate. The additional profitability is shared, but predominately captured by the airline. There is an upper limit to price movements. This limit can be thought of as the point at which new manufacturers enter the market, attracted by rising margins. If the value of the aircraft falls, this lost profitability is also shared between the airline and manufacturer. The lower bound to price is the manufacture's variable cost. A scaling constant can be used to determine the extent to which the above sharing in profits occurs. The constant can be set to zero in which there is no price movement at all. When we do this, we are modelling the case where the holder of the natural option to wait can always demand the same pricing as that previously negotiated by the delivery option holder. This is useful as it can be used to determine the proportion of the option value that is attributed to both queue length uncertainty and price uncertainty.

Because aircraft price (X) rises more slowly than aircraft value (PV) during an economic upturn in the airline industry, the natural option to wait becomes valuable, but is still less valuable than the delivery option in which price has been fixed during a lower level of industry profitability. This is different from a call option on a traded security, where the non-option holder forgoes any upside by waiting.

Figure 20 shows option values from the model, for an A320 aircraft with a four-year expiration date (T) and an 18-month manufacturing lead time (L_d). An annual volatility

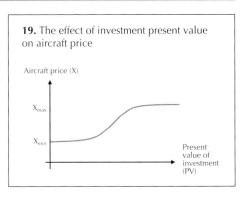

19. The effect of investment present value on aircraft price

Aircraft price (X)

X_{max}

X_{min}

Present value of investment (PV)

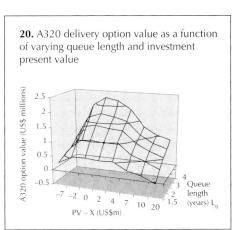

20. A320 delivery option value as a function of varying queue length and investment present value

A320 option value (US\$ millions)

PV – X (US\$m)

Queue length (years) L_q

(σ) in aircraft PV of 20% and a mean reversion time of three years have been used. For a constant queue length, the value of the option has a maximum around PV = X. This is because the delivery option, compared to the natural option to wait, is most valuable when the investment is marginal, ie, when the option is "at the money". If the NPV (PV – X) is strongly negative, no amount of delivery flexibility will help, and if the NPV is strongly positive, the investment will go ahead regardless of the value of the flexibility. In contrast, options on securities increase in value, as the option becomes more and more "in the money". Options that are "at the money" are still valuable, as the stock price can rise up to the point where the option must be exercised (the expiration date). As would be expected, the value of the delivery option, relative to the natural option, increases with increasing queue length (L_q). An up-cycle in the industry would be represented by a diagonal path (bottom left to top right) across the surface of the graph (increasing queue length and PV).

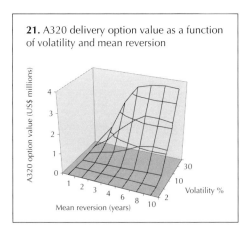

21. A320 delivery option value as a function of volatility and mean reversion

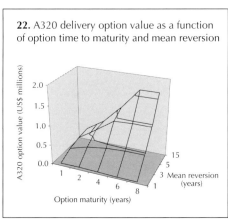

22. A320 delivery option value as a function of option time to maturity and mean reversion

Figure 21 shows the effect of volatility (σ) and mean reversion on the value of the same A320 delivery option. As would be expected, the value of the option increases with increasing volatility and decreasing mean reversion. Mean reversion has the effect of reducing the amount the PV can wander from its base value. Figure 22 shows the effect of option maturity time (T) and mean reversion on the value of the option. With stock options, the value increases dramatically with time to exercise. However, in the case of the aircraft delivery option, mean reversion – as expected – has a significant impact on this. With very strong reversion, the option does not significantly increase in value with time to exercise. With realistic levels of mean reversion (eg, three years), the option value does increase with increasing time to exercise, but not to the same extent as a stock call option.

Finally, how much value have manufacturers created for airlines by reducing manufacturing lead times from, for instance, an average of two and a half years to 18 months? Figure 23 shows the value of an A320 delivery option as a function of lead-time (L_d). The volatility has been fixed at 20%, the mean reversion at three years, the time to exercise (T) at three years, and the queue length today (Q_t) also at three years. The option value decreases with increasing lead time, and, as expected, the option value becomes zero as the lead time approaches the current queue length. By reducing purchasing lead times from, for instance, three years to 15 months, a value of approximately US$0.9 million per aircraft has been created. A further reduction in purchasing lead time to one year would create another US$0.2 million in value for airlines. Lead times of less than one year have little – if any – value, because, as discussed, lead times on other items become the constraining factor.

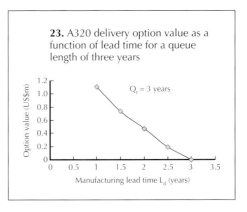

23. A320 delivery option value as a function of lead time for a queue length of three years

PRODUCT COMMONALITY AND DELIVERY FLEXIBILITY

Until now, the uncertainty an airline faces has been characterised somewhat simplistically in terms of its overall fleet size requirement, ie, the number of aircraft needed.

Uncertainty can be considered to be driven by both the overall supply-demand equilibrium in the industry as a whole, and the competitive moves airlines make at the hub and market level. At this level, airlines see a positive relationship between market share (frequency) and yield. This creates a tendency to add capacity. However, the sum total of these endogenously created shocks to the supply–demand balance is additive to the exogenous shocks created by overall consumer spending changes created by macro-economic trends, and historically, this has reinforced the volatile nature of the industry.

To demonstrate this volatility, Figure 24 shows the historical trend in total passengers flown on a typical domestic US transcontinental mission over the last 20 years. The volatility around the mean (σ) is approximately 21% annually. However, the variation in passengers flown by the three major players over the same period are as follows:

Airline X:	43%
Airline Y:	36%
Airline Z:	23%
Overall market:	**21%**

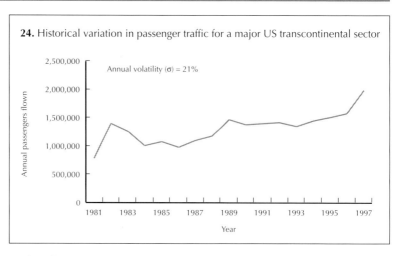

24. Historical variation in passenger traffic for a major US transcontinental sector

Therefore, one can postulate that contested markets are more volatile than monopoly markets, and that this is specifically due to competitive moves at the market level, and that specific market volatility is greater than overall demand volatility that the airline faces.

Because airlines compete predominantly on the basis of frequency, the clear preference for managing market-level volatility is through aircraft size and not number of flights flown. In other words, in a contested market, if the players are faced with an overall market decline, they would prefer to manage this through a reduction in average aircraft size rather than frequency. Consequently, an airline needs flexibility not only in terms of its overall fleet size, but also in terms of the size of aircraft in its fleet.

The ability to choose between a family of different sized aircraft, manufactured on the same production line, at option exercise, can be termed a *switching option*. Options are not additive. For example, the option to choose between an A320 and an A319 for a particular option delivery position cannot be characterised as the sum of an A319 and A320 option with the same characteristics. Additionally, it cannot be characterised as a straight delivery option (call option) on the A320, plus an A320 put option and an A319 call option. The A319/A320 switching option is an option on the maximum of the two aircraft PVs (see Stulz, 1982 or Johnson, 1987). Therefore, we need to develop a separate model for the switching option.

For the sake of the more academic readership, the straight delivery option can be characterised as a binomial risk-adjusted option-pricing model incorporating mean reversion and one degree of uncertainty: aircraft PV (queue length and aircraft price are deterministic). The two aircraft switching option model can be characterised as a three-dimensional binomial model (two degrees of uncertainty, plus time) with similar characteristics. This model may be unique in that it has been successfully implemented on a spreadsheet. A three aircraft switching option, such as that offered by

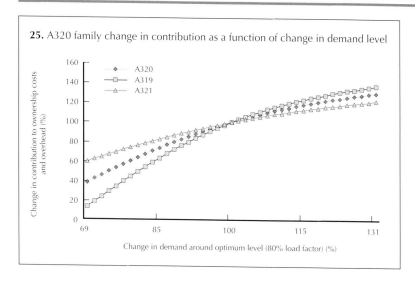

25. A320 family change in contribution as a function of change in demand level

Airbus with the A319, A320 and A321 family of aircraft, is a four-dimensional tree, which poses some not insignificant problems if it is to be modelled as a decision tree on conventional spread-sheet type PC software.

In order to calculate the value of a switching option, we need to determine the volatility and PV specifically associated with each aircraft type. Both aircraft manufacturers and airlines use what is known as profit profiles to describe the fact that for each aircraft size, there is an optimum range of demand for which contribution is maximised. In this case, we have used a two-class spill model and standardised the operating cost and revenue ground rules used to compare different aircraft. Figure 25 shows profit profiles for the A320 family. The profiles are shown in terms of the variation in contribution compared to each aircraft's optimum contribution defined as a load factor of 80%. For each aircraft, there is an optimum range of demand which will maximise profit compared to operating another member of the family. The profit can then be discounted over the predicted economic life of the aircraft to give an aircraft present value (PV) as a function of average demand. It can be seen that the smaller the aircraft, the larger the variation in contribution for a given change in demand. This is because for a given change in passenger demand, the effect on profit is larger. The larger the aircraft the wider the range of passenger demand that can be operated profitably.

Passenger demand is, of course, uncertain, and is affected both by overall market demand and competitive factors at the market level such as frequency, price and branding. As discussed earlier, we now assume that frequencies are predominately driven by market competitive factors, rather than being set so as to operate an aircraft within its optimum range of demand. For example, if demand falls in a contested market with five daily

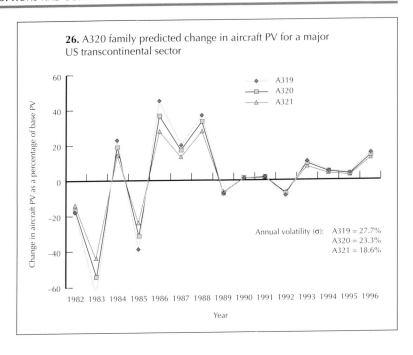

26. A320 family predicted change in aircraft PV for a major US transcontinental sector

Annual volatility (σ): A319 = 27.7%
A320 = 23.3%
A321 = 18.6%

A320 frequencies, an airline would prefer to downscale to the A319 rather than reduce frequency. In order to determine the variation in aircraft PV with time and not demand, we need to determine a market demand volatility. This can be determined from US DOT reports, (eg, that shown in Figure 24). Once an estimate of the demand volatility with time is made for a specific market type, the volatility in aircraft PV with time for each aircraft can be determined through Monte-Carlo simulation techniques.

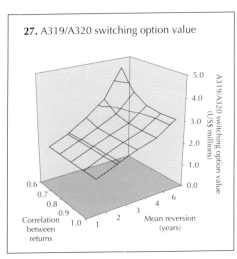

27. A319/A320 switching option value

Figure 26 shows the predicted variation in PV for the A320 family of aircraft on this specific US transcontinental sector. As expected, the smaller the aircraft, the higher the volatility of earnings and therefore PV. These aircraft specific volatilities, along with prices (X) and base PV's values, can then be input into the model.

Figure 27 shows the value of an A319/A320 switching option, as a function of mean reversion and the covariance of the aircrafts' returns. The lead-time (L_d) is 18 months and the current queue length (Q_t) is three years. The value of the option increases with increasing mean reversion time in a similar way to the straight delivery option. In fact, the switching option has many of the same characteristics as the straight delivery option.

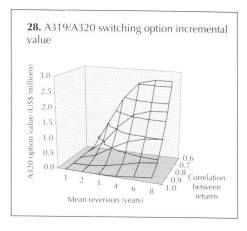

28. A319/A320 switching option incremental value

Figure 28 show the incremental value of the same switching option over and above the straight delivery option, ie, solely the switching value. The value can be seen to be dependent upon the correlation between the two aircraft's returns. The coefficient of correlation can vary from plus one (+1) to minus one (–1). Plus one can be interpreted as 100% of the variation in one aircraft's PV, can be explained by the variation in the other aircraft's PV, and is a measure of how the two returns move together with changes in demand level over time. Minus one would be a completely inverse correlation, and zero no correlation. If the two aircraft are to be used on an identical route, then the correlation will be relatively high, as the variation between returns is only driven by the variations in contribution as a function of passenger demand level as shown by Figure 25. However, if the aircraft are to be used on routes with different demand characteristics over time, the correlation will be much less, and the value of the switching option consequently much greater. For example, the A330 and A340 aircraft are manufactured on the same production line, allowing Airbus to offer A330/A340 delivery flexibility. Some versions of the A330 can be used in a domestic or transcontinental mission, while the A340 is a long-range intercontinental aircraft. It is likely that the demand profile with time would be significantly different for both types of routing. For example, a domestic recession or competitive moves by other domestic airlines which would effect future demand could be un-correlated to changes in the international environment. This type of delivery flexibility could be worth several million US dollars per aircraft. Even in the domestic environment, there can be a significant lack of correlation between long and short haul routes.

Another way of looking at the value of aircraft delivery switching options is as follows. An airline today may have a network requirement for 50 120-seat aircraft (A319s) and the same number of 150-seat aircraft (A320s). Let's assume that aircraft are on average retired at 22 years of age, and that the predicted industry growth is 3%. Therefore, the airline needs to negotiate a delivery stream of five aircraft a year for retirement and three aircraft a year for growth, or a total of eight aircraft (8% of the fleet) annually. As we have stated, time resolves uncertainty and the airline may actually find that it needs somewhat fewer 150-seat aircraft and somewhat more 120-seat aircraft than it had originally predicted when making the order. As it is turning over approximately 8% of its fleet every year, the ability to swap A320 delivery positions for A319s allows the airline to significantly change the character of its domestic fleet over time. The value of the switching option can then be considered the NPV of the avoided cost of operating a 150-seat aircraft in a 120-seat market. However, returning to the option-pricing framework, it should be noted that one of the compelling attributes of this theory is that we do not need to predict the actual outcome in order to value the option (however, we do need some idea of the *expected* outcome). We only need to estimate the volatility of the underlying asset; the stochastic process models all possible outcomes and their respective probabilities. The logic of only exercising outcomes that are profitable in the model then gives us the value of the option, and thus its PV.

EMPIRICAL EVIDENCE

Since aircraft delivery positions are not openly traded, there is little, if any, empirical evidence to confirm the valuations of aircraft delivery options derived from the above models. However, there is supporting evidence. For example, the US Government pays airlines a significant fee for the right but not the obligation to use their fleets in times of war, when aircraft are wet-leased from the airline to transport troops and provisions around the world. The airlines receive an annual fee for this right, which allows the US government to avoid maintaining a large fleet of transport aircraft that would only be used in times of war. In other words, the airline has sold a non-expiring call option on part of its fleet in return for the annual fee. If the option is exercised, it will have to adsorb the cost of the disruptions to its network until the aircraft are returned.

The most compelling evidence supporting the value of delivery flexibility is that airlines do indeed use the flexibility given to them. Airlines that have committed themselves to a family of aircraft have in fact subsequently taken delivery of a significantly different portfolio of aircraft to that which they originally anticipated. This clearly demonstrates both the dynamic nature of the airline competitive environment and the value of delivery flexibility in this uncertain environment.

SUMMARY

The airline industry has historically been highly volatile. In response to this, airlines intuitively build in margins, and this can be seen in the required spread between an airline's cost of capital and its hurdle rate. Hurdle rates of return for new investments are often significantly higher that the cost of capital. A study by Summers (1987), looking at a variety of industries, showed that hurdle rates were often two to three times a company's cost of capital allowing for the deductibility of interest expense.

Traditional economic theory would say that in doing this, airlines are passing up investments that would provide an adequate return to shareholders. However, airlines realise that capital investments are often not fully reversible, and what looks like a good investment today, as shown by the now-or-never choice given by conventional NPV analysis, may turn sour tomorrow.

The static NPV analysis fails to capture the true dynamics of the investment decision. Academics have for some time now been critical of classical Capital Budgeting (NPV) techniques that do not address flexibility in response to the resolution of uncertainty over time. In fact, this spread between an airline's cost of capital and its hurdle rate is simply the value of flexibility not accounted for in their classical Capital Budgeting analysis. The flexibility is created by the project's embedded options, including those provided by asset flexibility, and management's heuristic learning.

Recently, manufacturers have provided increased asset flexibility through both reduced lead times and product commonality. This flexibility can be seen in the value of aircraft purchase and switching options. The above analysis has demonstrated the very significant value of this to the airlines, which should now benefit from being better able to manage the economic cycle. This should result in more stable returns, and reduce their required hurdle rates to invest in new equipment.

BIBLIOGRAPHY

Benninga, S., 1994, *Numerical Techniques in Finance*, MIT Press, Cambridge, Massachusetts.

Black, F. and M. Scholes, 1973, "The Pricing of Options and Corporate Liabilities", *Journal of Political Economy*, 81, May–June, pp. 637–54.

Brearly, R.A. and S.C. Myers, 1996, *The Principals of Corporate Finance*, 5th edition, McGraw-Hill Companies Inc., New York.

Chriss, N.A., 1997, *Black Scholes and Beyond – Option Pricing Models*, Irwin, Chicago.

Copeland, T.E. and P.T. Keenan, 1998, "How Much is Flexibility Worth", *The McKinsey Quarterly*, 2, pp.38–49.

Cox, J., S. Ross and M. Rubinstein, 1979, "Option Pricing: A Simplified Approach", *Journal of Financial Economics*, 7, September, pp. 229–63.

Dixit, A.K. and R.S. Pindyck, 1994, *Investment under Uncertainty*, 1st edition, Princeton University Press.

Hallerstrom, N. and J. Melgaard, 1998, "Going Round in Cycles", *Airfinance Journal*, March, pp. 49–52.

Hull J. and A. White, 1990, "Pricing Interest Rate Derivative Securities", *Review of Financial Studies*, 3(4), pp. 573–92.

Hull, J.C., 1997, *Options, Futures and Other Derivatives*, 3rd edition, Upper Saddle River, NJ: Prentice Hall.

Johnson H., 1987, "Options on the Maximum or the Minimum of Several Assets", *Journal of Financial and Quantitative Analysis*, 18, March, pp. 277–84.

Jordan, W.S., 1992, "New Aircraft Orders: Still a Leading Indicator of Airline Profits", *Airfinance Journal*, 139, June, pp. 42–7.

Merton, R., 1973, "Theory of Rational Option Pricing", *Bell Journal of Economics and Management Science*, 4, Spring, pp. 141–83.

Stulz R., 1982, "Options on the Minimum or the Maximum of Two Risky Assets: Analysis and Applications", *Journal of Financial Economics*, 10, July, pp. 161–85.

Summers L.H., 1987, "Investment Incentives and the Discounting of Depreciation Allowances", in *The Effects of Taxation on Capital Accumulation*, ed. Feldstein, M., Chicago University Press, Chicago, Illinois.

Trigeoris, L., 1995, *Real Options in Capital Investments*, Praeger, Westport, Connecticut.

8

Real Option Valuation for E-Business: A Case Study

Richard Chatwin, Yann Bonduelle, Anne Goodchild, Franchee Harmon and João Mazzuco

PricewaterhouseCoopers

Real Option Valuation (ROV) can help determine the value of start-ups in the light of the uncertainties they face and the options they can exercise in the future. In this chapter, we present a case study of the valuation of an e-business start-up, which is planning to provide a transactional, Internet-based business-to-business service.

We describe how the key decisions, real options and uncertainties faced by the company are identified through a structured discussion process with the company's management. We then discuss the development and implementation of a *learning model* that captures changes in the level of uncertainty about the adoption of the new service over time, as information about early adoption rates is obtained. This model drives the valuation of the capacity expansion investment options available to the company's management.

In the case illustrated, an important component of the ROV process is the development of a consumers' choice model that uses a conjoint analysis to forecast sales of the proposed new service under various pricing schemes and adoption rates. We describe the process by which the choice model is assembled and its interaction with the company decision model. Finally, we describe the key information that results when the decision tree output is used in a financial model in order to value the company under various scenarios.

INTRODUCTION

One of the key challenges facing young companies and their investors is the evaluation of the potential market for their products and services; the composition, potential evolution and rate of adoption of their customer base; and the ways in which these factors will affect their strategic options and decision-making processes. Nowhere is this truer than in e-commerce and e-business today.[1]

The strategic decision-making process is critical for both the company and its investors. In the early stages of development, a company's management and investors have many real options to consider. For example, a start-up company must decide on which market it should focus, how to modify its concept to meet the demands of the marketplace, and what resources it should buy or build in order to win potential customers over. Potential investors, for their part, must decide if, when and how much to invest.

However, deciding which of these real options should be exercised, and when to do so, is no easy task. The future is highly uncertain, especially for start-up high-tech companies. How effective will the technology be? Will the market adopt the new solution? How will the competition respond? The company and its investors need to have confidence that their answers to these questions are well informed, realistic and up-to-date; they also need to have confidence that they understand what these answers imply in terms of decision making. This will only be the case if the answers are grounded in a solid understanding of the market, and if the decisions are made in the context of a clearly defined, strategic plan that can be adapted dynamically as the environment changes.

Start-up businesses typically have more insight into some of these areas than others. High-tech companies typically understand the technological situation and options very well, but may have less idea about the market and business environment. This lack is exacerbated by the inadequacy of conventional analytical tools to address these areas.

Because e-commerce and e-business are relatively new, fast-evolving areas, there is often little historical information of particular relevance to a specific company available. For example, two factors of critical importance to a business's development are the size of the potential market for its products or services, and the share of that market it can expect to win. It may be difficult to find relevant historical data on either or both of these two factors. Without it, the business might still be able to control for differences, but this assumes a degree of market efficiency that is frequently considered unrealistic where early-stage companies are concerned. This means that comparative, or peer, analysis is usually difficult and once completed is often severely lacking in credibility.

It may sometimes be possible to apply other traditional analytical techniques, such as market research and discounted cashflow modelling, to operations that simply offer an e-commerce version of an existing bricks-and-mortar business. However, e-businesses that represent a genuine evolutionary advance – ie, those which could not exist without the new technology – cannot be addressed in these ways. For these businesses, there are typically few reliable indicators as to the potential value of the business or the potential adoption pattern of the product or service, and sometimes there are none at all.

At PricewaterhouseCoopers, we have been valuing early-stage technology businesses since January 1996. The expertise we have gathered in the process has resulted in the development of a "high-tech toolkit" that employs a number of non-traditional techniques to perform market, financial and strategic analysis for early-stage businesses.

Among the most important of the toolkit instruments is Real Option Valuation (ROV). Unlike conventional valuation approaches, ROV recognises that there is more than one route that a company can take in order to achieve and provide value, and that the alternative routes each need to be assessed in order to plan effectively for an uncertain future. The key is to avoid trying to predict what the future will be, and instead to understand the range of outcomes that might be experienced. ROV recognises that potential investment comes with embedded options that allow alternative responses in different future circumstances (see Dixit and Pindyck, 1995, and Luerhman, 1998, for interesting discussions of the real options framework to value investment decisions). Because ROV identifies and values these options explicitly, it taps into a more complete and realistic view of the business environment than traditional investment analysis tools do. Under ROV, the investment decision is not binary, but is drawn from a dynamic "roadmap" that shows its users how to navigate over time for greatest value. For an example of ROV application in the oil and gas sector, see Walkup and Chatwin, 1999.

The principle for understanding the value of a real option is analogous to methods of valuing financial options. For example, a financial call option gives its owner the right, but not the obligation, to purchase the underlying asset (eg, a share of stock) at a specific price, either before (if it is an American option) or upon (if it is European) a specific date. However, real options generally do not possess some of the key characteristics of financial assets that underlie the financial options pricing models. For example, the price of real assets does not follow a random walk model, nor can real assets be openly traded in a similar fashion to financial assets.

Decision trees are an alternative to financial option pricing for modelling the flexibility of strategic decisions (see Gertner and Rosenfield, 1999). A decision tree is the tool used in decision analysis for the explicit modelling of decisions and uncertainties. Smith and Nau, 1995, contrast the application of decision analysis and option pricing methods to value risky projects. Decision trees can be attached to discounted cashflow models to value different real assets' investment scenarios. When we have future decisions – which we call "downstream decisions" – modelled in a decision tree, such that the downstream decision depends on the resolution of uncertainty, we have in effect an investment option in a real asset. Panel 1 contrasts the use of financial option pricing tools and decision trees for valuing real options.

FINANCIAL OPTION PRICING MODELS
VS. DECISION TREES

Real Option Valuation (ROV) is concerned with valuing management's flexibility to take different courses of action in response to different future scenarios. This flexibility comes in the form of real options, that management may or may not exercise depending on the way relevant uncertainties are resolved. The existence of real options gives management the potential to maximise upside gains and minimise downside losses.

To be able to exercise real options, it is necessary to learn over time about some of the key aspects that underlie the option value. Take the case discussed in the main text: an option to wait a few years to launch the new product would have no value if over those few years nothing could be learnt about the market for the product, the competition movements, technology development, costs of launching the product, etc. It follows then that, to properly value an option it is essential to capture the dynamics of uncertainty evolution over time, meaning not only the distribution of values for relevant uncertainties, but also how those distributions change over time.

Financial option pricing methods are based on modelling the dynamics of uncertainty. For example, the value of a call option on a stock given by the Black–Scholes model is derived from the random walk model of the stock price. This model is parameterised by the current stock price, the volatility of the stock price, and the risk-free rate of return. Together with the option characteristics (its exercise price and its time to expiration), these parameters determine the value of the option.

One of the problems of using financial option pricing models to value real options is that the basic assumptions of the models may not hold for real assets: real assets cannot be continuously traded in the market, real asset prices do not change continuously, and the return on real assets does not generally follow a lognormal distribution. Furthermore, standard financial options have a specified maturity, whereas the best time to exercise a real option is typically unclear.

Where appropriate one can track the value of a real option to a traded asset that has the same risks as the investment in question. It can then be argued that the resultant real option value reflects the market value of the investment opportunity. However, most real asset investments have some unique aspect, so that a perfect correlation with a market security can never be established, which is also to say that real options have "private" risks that are not priced in any comparable traded security.

Decision trees offer an alternative to financial option pricing models for valuing real options. Decision trees model the uncertainties and decisions associated with an investment, including downstream decisions. Downstream decisions are conditioned by the preceding uncertainties, so that some learning about the uncertainties occurs before the decision is made. Downstream decisions are nothing more than investment options. At the end of each path in a decision tree is a value associated to that path, normally calculated by a cashflow model that is linked to the tree. It makes an almost perfect fit to use decision trees to structure and value real options. The value of the option will fall out from the paths in the decision tree in which the option is exercised.

One of the criticisms of decision trees is that the assessment of uncertainties in a decision tree normally relies on a subjective rather than on a market interpretation of the world, in which case the calculated option value may differ from the value that would pertain in the marketplace. That is not to say, however, that decision trees cannot capture the value of market risks. When carrying out a Real Option Valuation we categorise risks into market and private risks. Market risks are the risks that have already been priced by the market, such that this risked valuation can be incorporated in the cashflow. A typical example is the use of oil futures and options market prices to model the oil price risks inherent in an upstream oil investment. On the other hand, risks that are not correlated with the market are assessed by experts, and these values are also included in the cashflow calculation.

Both decision trees and financial option based methods have their advantages. When an existing traded asset portfolio can be correlated well to the real option in question, the method may be reduced to determining the parameters that go into the option price equation, thus avoiding the lengthy exercise of estimating cashflows and probabilities of associated future scenarios.

Decision tree analysis is particularly suitable to investments where market data cannot be identified, such as R&D investments where similar products are not valued in the market. One of the main advantages of decision trees over financial option pricing models is in their transparency. The almost intuitive language of decision trees contrasts sharply with the "black-box" approach of the complex differential equations used in financial options analysis. Decision makers are much more likely to rely on a method that they understand to inform their decision making process.

In the case of high-tech companies, the development of the market is one of the major sources of uncertainty. Therefore, the ROV process is often informed by another tool from the high-tech toolkit, namely Market Strategy Analysis (MSA), which helps to more closely define what the future may look like in this respect.

In this chapter, we will outline the steps taken in carrying out a project using both ROV and MSA on behalf of a client intending to provide a transactional, Internet-based business-to-business service.

BEGINNING THE PROJECT: OPENFRAMING

The client[2] was a start-up e-business founded by the ex-employees of a major commercial organisation (not an investment vehicle) with a natural inclination towards this kind of service. That major organisation was one of two founding investors in the business, having provided the seed funding that had allowed the product to be developed to the point of commercialisation. The same two investors also stood ready to provide launch funding and were likely to become involved in future rounds of investment if the product won a market.

Through their knowledge of the industry, the client and its investors had a good idea of their product's potential market. However, as with many start-up e-businesses with an evolutionary technology product, it had little idea of how its market share might evolve – ie, just how likely the product was to win customer favour and how its chances of success might be optimised.

In our experience, many proprietors and investors of early-stage technology businesses have little feel for the true value of the business and where this may be created in the future. Most entrepreneurs know a great deal about their technology and the associated issues, and some also have a good understanding of how the target market should be defined. However, they may not fully appreciate the business environment and can find it difficult to keep up to date. Furthermore, they may be wedded to a particular view of the world, or find it difficult to think much beyond a particular chain of events that maximises their chances of success.

We have developed a structured discussion process called OpenFraming that seeks to free the principals from this kind of thinking. In some cases, it may be used even earlier in the process to assist the start-up with the development of its business proposition, but typically, as in this case, it is brought into play in order to assess the value proposition once potential business models are in place. Details of the OpenFraming process are given in Panel 2.

The end result of OpenFraming should be a precise description of the problem – or problems – that need to be addressed in the next stage, the modelling process.

DEFINING THE PROBLEM

At the conclusion of the OpenFraming session in our case study, we had obtained the information required to outline the key decisions, real options and risk variables. Three parties were relevant to the problem at hand: the

PANEL 2

OPENFRAMING

OpenFraming is a structured discussion process that aims to define the Real Option Valuation (ROV) problem for a company by identifying the business risks as well as the options available for converting those threats into opportunities, and then establishing a framework for analysing the risks and options. ROV involves an ongoing dialogue between decision makers and the valuation team: OpenFraming provides the foundation for this dialogue (Figure A).

A. The OpenFraming workshop is the start of the organisational process required by Real Option Valuation (ROV)

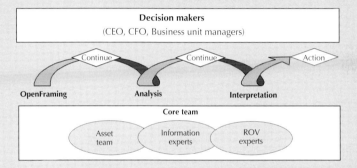

The "open" part of OpenFraming refers to the effort to shed preconceptions and received wisdom in favour of an exploration of all possibilities. As such, we seek to ensure that no single person or perspective dominates the discussion, and that different opinions and perspectives are given as much of an airing as possible – in essence, allowing those involved to argue the issues without any prejudice as to the "correct" conclusions. The "framing" part refers to the structuring of the problem, with the goals being to identify the right problem; focus on the most important aspects; agree on the level and scope of the analysis; clarify the objectives; and identify the alternatives and uncertainties. This is achieved through the gradual evolution of a more structured discussion over the course of the OpenFraming session.

Typically, the OpenFraming session is a two-day workshop, ideally attended by all those who will eventually be involved in the project. The project and its background will be outlined, and a "team charter" defined for what the valuation team is trying to accomplish. The team charter, a kind of mission statement, determines the rules of engagement, what the project needs to be successful, and what the failure modes could be, together with corresponding contingency factors.

The next stage is to encourage the team to discuss the issues and challenges facing the business as well as potential solutions and alternative approaches. This is superficially similar to the exercises commonly practised by companies preparing to enter a new line of business, but OpenFraming differs from simple brainstorming in the degree of structure brought to the discussion. OpenFraming has a very specific goal: it is to identify the key uncertainties, real options and decision points associated with the development of the business, so that these may subsequently be used as the foundations for model-building. The techniques used in fostering the discussion reflect this goal.

For a detailed description of the OpenFraming process, see the paper by Claeys and Walkup Jr. (1999).[1] The major steps and tools employed can be summarised as follows. After focusing the team by defining a team charter, the process of discovering options is facilitated by the utilisation of various brainstorming tools, including SWOT analysis, headlining and back-casting. SWOT analysis is used to identify the key factors affecting the business's value, both positively and negatively. Headlining and back-casting help to expose the assumptions made in an individual's or the team's view of the world, and thus to identify key areas of uncertainty and devise alternative scenarios. In headlining, people are asked to imagine a headline from the future that encapsulates what the relevant part of the world looks like at that time. In back-casting, they are then asked to explain what chain of events had to happen and what decisions had to be made for that world situation to be reached.

Once the risks and options inherent in the business have been uncovered, the structuring process begins, with the goal being to formulate the valuation as a management strategy problem. Various tools are used in this process, and outputs may include a Policy Wheel, a DreamTree, and an Influence Diagram.

The final step in the OpenFraming process is to communicate the conclusions and insights to the decision makers. Two useful communication devices are the Waterfall Chart and the Valuation Hierarchy. The Waterfall Chart expresses the real option concept in a simple manner by breaking down the total value of the business into its "standard" value – the value of the business including risks and uncertainty, but ignoring the flexibility to respond to changing conditions – plus the value provided by each option. A Valuation Hierarchy is used to display the options and key assumptions that will be included in the analysis phase, identifying decisions that are outside the scope of the analysis, those that are the focus of the analysis, and those that can be considered implementation issues as they are too detailed to be major value drivers.

1   Clayes, J. and G.W. Walkup Jr., 1999, "Discovering Real Options in Oilfield Exploration and Development", paper SPE 52956 presented at the 1999 Society of Petroleum Engineers Hydrocarbon Economics and Evaluation Symposium, March.

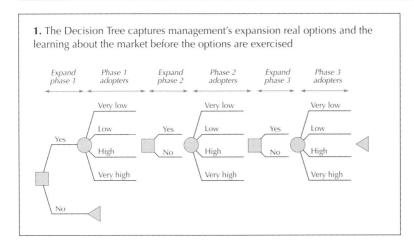

1. The Decision Tree captures management's expansion real options and the learning about the market before the options are exercised

company itself, its investors and its potential customer base. Given the company's sizeable lead in developing the technology and its industry expertise, it was determined that a fourth party – potential competitors – need not be included in the analysis.

OpenFraming revealed that the key decision for the company was to be the exercise of its real options to expand operational capacity at the end of each of the three phases of the business plan. Such expansion would require fresh investment, but would allow the customer base to expand, and this would then have a direct bearing on both the costs and the revenues (and thus the value) of the company thereafter. There were three distinct stages of capacity expansion that the company might progress through in sequential order.

We modelled these decisions with a fairly simple decision tree, comprising a decision point fixed in time at the end of each of the three phases of the company's development, as illustrated in Figure 1. At each decision point, the company would have to consider the level of adoption at that point and decide whether to step up capacity or not; uncertainty would arise from the adoption rate by customers. (From a theoretical point of view, we could equally well have framed the question the other way, by defining the decision points as the points at which a particular level of adoption had been achieved and extra capacity was needed. In that case, the key uncertainty would have been the time at which this occurred).

We chose not to directly model the investors' decision to invest at these key decision points, taking the stance that the investors would be interested in investing further if the expected value of the company was positive each time, as it subsequently proved to be. This stance was informed by the OpenFraming exercise, which also determined that other scenarios and factors that might have been relevant to the investors' decisions – return on investment targets, willingness to tolerate negative value over the short term, etc – were not germane to the analysis in this case and so did not need to be modelled.

In the absence of competition, each customer's key decision was simple: whether to adopt the product or not. Assessing the likelihood of such adoption using traditional techniques such as market research would not be easy or accurate: there was great uncertainty about how likely potential customers were to buy into the product, when they might do so, and how many users there might eventually be.

However, such information would be very valuable to the company, whose initial business model called for revenues to be generated as an annual fee paid by users, with the possibility of transaction fees being introduced sooner or later, depending on adoption patterns. Clearly, the company would want to tailor the price (and possibly other features) of its product in order to optimise the customer adoption rate. The adoption rate was also the key factor in the company's choice to exercise its capacity options.

We concluded, therefore, that a second model would be necessary, this one to assess the likelihood of the product actually being adopted by its potential users. We therefore devised a plan in which the potential market would be mapped and potential customers surveyed to build up probabilistic information about their preferences and decisions to adopt or otherwise.

THE MODELLING PROCESS

To summarise, the key problem had been identified during OpenFraming as the evaluation of the company's options to expand capacity, based on the adoption pattern that might be expected from its potential customers in the absence of third-party competition. In order to analyse these options, it would clearly be necessary to model the customer adoption pattern, so the first step would be the development of a market model that would produce probabilistic information about potential customers' attitudes to the product.

This information could then be converted into adoption rates and fed into the company's decision model, which would estimate the size of the customer base under various scenarios and thus indicate whether the company should expand its operational capacity at various times or not. The outcomes of those decisions could then be fed into a financial model of fairly standard (spreadsheet-based) construction, in order to provide sample financial information for each of the various scenarios. The cost structure for this e-business, like many others, was relatively simple. The resulting information would offer some guidance and perspective to the company and its investors.[3]

THE MARKET MODEL

The first task in developing the market model was to build up an idea of the total population of potential users of the product – ie, the size and make-up of the potential market. Given the industry background of this company, we began with a reasonable idea of the population; more generally, the potential market can often be sized and identified by referring to external sources of information, such as published records and secondary research providers, consulting firms, think-tanks and industry organisations. We used some of these tools to bolster our understanding in this case.

We began our primary research by identifying and interviewing some of the company's industry contacts and potential users who had already been exposed to the product. This provided us with an understanding of the proposition, in principle, and supplied qualitative information about the issues likely to be important to potential customers.

There were two key pieces of information obtained from this qualitative discussion. The first was that not all users were equally significant in terms of adoption or product revenues. Rather, there were a number of "driver companies" with the muscle-power to make their smaller trading partners adopt the product. After conducting the interviews we felt it reasonable – and this was confirmed by our later research – to assume that if a driver company adopted the product, so would its "satellites". Under the proposed pricing structures for the product, the driver companies would pay a large fee, while its satellites would each pay a smaller fee. We therefore assumed in our subsequent analysis that the adoption of a single driver company would bring in not only its own (large) fee, but also the sum of the smaller fees paid by the average number of satellites per driver. The second piece of information that we obtained from the qualitative interviews was that the potential users would be interested in the product's existing market share, as well as in its pricing. Being network-based, the product's value would grow rapidly if and when more companies used it. There would be some innovators who would buy in quickly, believing in the eventual value of the product; some pragmatists, who would not adopt until it had achieved what they saw as "critical mass"; and some laggards who would not adopt until they could no longer ignore it. This helped us to identify the five key attributes of the product that we needed to ask other potential users about – four of these related to pricing features and one to the existing market share.

We had thus identified the companies whose preferences we needed to evaluate in the next stage of the market analysis, and the issues we needed to ask them about. We carried out the evaluation by asking key decision makers at these companies to complete a standardised, structured questionnaire designed to explore their reactions in a fair and objective way. A number of potential users who had not been exposed to the product completed this questionnaire, which asked them repeatedly to choose between two alternatives that differed in two of the five key attributes. We also conducted focus groups with these respondents. More details of this process are given in Panel 3.

The interview responses were subsequently analysed and utilities derived for each of the five attributes for all respondents. Having calculated the utility values for each attribute, it was then possible to define any

MARKET STRATEGY ANALYSIS

One of the major problems facing a company looking to launch a new product or service is the likely composition and evolution of the potential market. The newer or more revolutionary the product or service, the more difficult the market assessment. Part of the high-tech toolkit developed by PricewaterhouseCoopers comprises a process known as Market Strategy Analysis (MSA), which uses Individual Choice Modelling (ICM) to produce accurate and flexible forecasts of revenues and market share.

The first step in developing an MSA model involves the collection of primary market research data from those individuals who would ultimately decide whether to buy into the product or service. Consequently, the formulation stage of an MSA project includes the development of a detailed sampling plan. The aim is to collect sufficient data from each decision-maker to simulate their purchase decisions. The next step is to model each customer's purchase decision, resulting in extremely accurate predictions of revenues and market share by capturing the full diversity of customer preferences. These predictions can also be broken down by market segment.

The data gathered to support the market model are collected through computer-administered interviews, using our proprietary measurement system, which employs highly adaptive conjoint analysis to extract the necessary information. Computer-administered interviewing allows for a personalised, interactive interview, and results in higher quality data. In conducting a project of this type, it is very important – and very difficult – to walk the line between introducing potential users to the product in order to gain their unbiased feedback, and "selling" them on the product and thus prejudicing their reaction. A carefully designed computer interview can minimise the possibility of bias.

The interview comprises a number of questions intended to collect quantitative information about attitudes to the product and the conditions under which potential users would adopt the product. To achieve this, a number of key "attributes" are defined for the product – those features on offer that may impact on the likelihood of a customer taking up the product offered. The interview measures values for these characteristics by asking purchase decision-makers to choose between, or "trade-off", product offerings that differ in respect of one or more attributes.

For example, the potential customer might be asked to decide between two different pricing schemes, or between circumstances they would require before adopting the product. In this case, our preliminary qualitative discussions with knowledgeable contacts indicated that potential users would probably recognise that the product represented the shape of

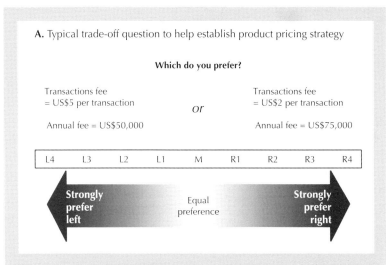

A. Typical trade-off question to help establish product pricing strategy

Which do you prefer?

Transactions fee = US$5 per transaction	*or*	Transactions fee = US$2 per transaction
Annual fee = US$50,000		Annual fee = US$75,000

| L4 | L3 | L2 | L1 | M | R1 | R2 | R3 | R4 |

Strongly prefer left — Equal preference — **Strongly prefer right**

things to come, but the industry context made existing market share more important than stand-alone value. Therefore, some of the questions that were asked used market share as one of the conditions of the trade-off. Examples of these two types of question are shown in the Figures A and B.

Some of this process might seem superficially similar to traditional market research, but it is distinct in several important ways. The structure of the interview questionnaire differs from conventional market research in that it is not intended to establish a consensus or quorum of opinion on particular static questions. Rather, it is intended to extract probabilistic information about individual respondents' preferences and potential adoption behaviour with respect to specific product attributes.

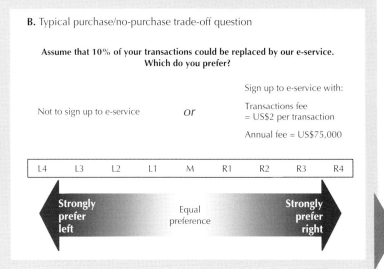

B. Typical purchase/no-purchase trade-off question

Assume that 10% of your transactions could be replaced by our e-service. Which do you prefer?

Sign up to e-service with:

Not to sign up to e-service	*or*	Transactions fee = US$2 per transaction
		Annual fee = US$75,000

| L4 | L3 | L2 | L1 | M | R1 | R2 | R3 | R4 |

Strongly prefer left — Equal preference — **Strongly prefer right**

Consequently, the information gleaned is more accurate and can be used more flexibly than conventional market research data. It is more accurate because it infers customer preferences from choices made in realistic purchase decisions, rather than by asking direct questions about importance or value. It is more flexible because product attributes are considered rather than complete offerings. This means that any offering that can be described as a combination of the attributes can be evaluated – including competing products or services, where necessary. In conventional market research, by contrast, a question cannot be answered unless it has been asked in the initial round of interviews.

In this case, the value of the market model came from its ability to address growth in total market size – ie, the adoption rate of the new technology – and the extent to which the adoption of the new technology would depend on the chosen pricing scheme and the pricing level. Being able to accurately gauge the relationship between the adoption rate, pricing structure and market penetration was crucial in making the right decisions about the introduction and pricing of the new technology.

The flexibility of the model and the typical longevity of the data's relevance allows it to be used to help not only with the initial "go–no go" decision, but also to make downstream decisions as the product nears or even proceeds past launch. It can be used to identify product enhancements that are likely to increase adoption by customers; to make pricing decisions; to identify target markets of high potential; or, in the case of the e-service described here, to plan for capacity expansion.

variation on the product and "add up" the value of that variation to a given respondent on the basis of his or her reported utilities. (This is unlike conventional market research, which produces static information: a question can only be addressed if it was part of the original questionnaire).

FROM UTILITIES TO ADOPTION RATES

Although we could now evaluate the value of any variation on the product to the customer, it did not automatically follow that a respondent would choose a given variation just because it had a higher utility than another. Given superficially similar circumstances, human beings do not always make the same decision, and nor is the decision always determined by a simple value judgement.

A Logit choice model is a standard model used to predict how a particular individual will choose between a number of alternatives, given the utilities of these alternatives. By comparing the actual responses with predicted ones, it is possible, using our proprietary methodology, to parameterise the "noise" in each respondent's set of answers, and thus garner probabilistic information about the decision making process. The probability of choosing or not choosing the product then feeds into a distribution of

2. The Market Model combines product descriptions in terms of attributes with respondents' values to produce the respondents' choice probabilities

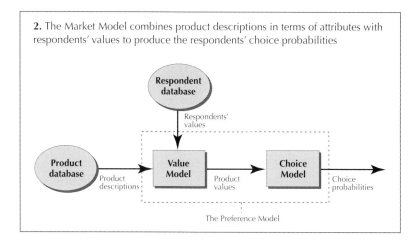

The Preference Model

adoption probabilities for the respondent population, given that particular scenario (Figure 2).

In this case, the result was that there was a group of early adopters who would adopt quickly because they believed it to be a good product, as predicted by the qualitative interviews. There was then additional information about the levels of market penetration that would attract pragmatic and laggard users, and about the effects that altering the pricing scheme would have.

However, there was little solid information about exactly when potential users would adopt the service, only about how likely they were to do so. The output of the market model had, therefore, to be combined with an estimated curve for the uptake over time, which was done on the basis of technology diffusion rates for similar products drawn from one of the major investors. This yielded the target variable: adoption rates and revenue as a function of time, product pricing and existing market share.

THE DECISION MODEL

We were now in a position to run the company decision model. Because the model only took in one piece of information – the adoption rate and its bearing on the company's options to expand operational capacity – it was a fairly simple problem. We began by making the reasonable assumption that the market was fairly homogeneous: if 70% of the market had already adopted, 70% of each respondent's trading partners would already have adopted. We also assumed that each respondent represented a sector of the entire population and that their responses could be scaled up accordingly.

Given these assumptions and the information derived from the market model, we could then construct a "learning model" of the evolution of the market, and hence of the need for extra capacity at each of the three decision points (the concept of learning models is presented in more detail in Gallant et al, 1999). We considered the first phase to begin "today", with no users of the product. Because the adoption rate of the product was uncertain, we could not be sure how many users of the product there would be at the end of the first phase. However, we could describe the number of users at the end of the first period in probabilistic terms. Using information from the market model, we derived the distribution for the number of adopters at the end of the first period.

It was then necessary to assess the number of people who might adopt in the second period. This number would depend in turn on the number who adopted in the first period. The next step, therefore, was to examine each respondent and assess the probability that they had already adopted in the first period, and, if they had not, the probability that they would do so in the second period.

This process was important because we knew that those who adopted in the first period would mostly come from the group of aggressive "early adopters" already noted. Hence, by the second period, most of the people most likely to adopt the product would already have done so, while the remaining potential users' adoption would be extremely sensitive to the market share that the product had already won. These remaining users would now be somewhat more likely to buy into the product.

To put it slightly more technically, each respondent could be thought of as tossing a biased coin in each period to determine whether or not they would adopt the product, or not. The bias of the coin would reflect the respondent's probability of adoption. The result of that coin-flipping process would be a Bernoulli distribution. Each respondent is considered to represent a segment of the potential customer base, and so each of the potential customers identified by that segment will in turn be flipping a coin with the same bias. The sum of all of the associated Bernoulli distributions will be a binomial distribution. Consequently, at the end of the first period, the distribution of the number of adopters would be the sum of binomial distributions with parameters set by the adoption probabilities obtained for each respondent from the market model.

In the second period, the distribution for the number of adopters must reflect the adoption that is already known to have occurred, and so it is a conditional distribution. The adoption probability associated with each segment of the potential user base will have to be adjusted to account for the probability that they have already adopted – the early adopters will have to be adjusted downwards quite substantially, while those waiting for market share to increase will be adjusted upwards slightly. Hence the weights of these segments will alter and the distribution for the number of adopters will change accordingly. Mathematical details are given in Panel 4.

The result is a probabilistic estimate of the adopted base at each of the decision points, which will give the company an insight into what extra capacity might be needed and whether it should exercise its real option at

PANEL 4

THE COMPANY DECISION MODEL

The company decision model considers three different adoption periods which correspond to the different phases of the business plan. The decision to expand capacity at the end of each phase will depend on the number of companies that have already adopted the product at this time. The main uncertainty in our decision-modelling problem is therefore the number of companies that will adopt the product in each phase.

This uncertainty was addressed by the market analysis, in which probabilities were calculated that each of the R respondents would adopt the product (under a given pricing scheme), given that 10%, 30% or 70% of the total population had already adopted. We define $P_i(z)$ to be the probability that a respondent adopts the product in the next phase, given that $z\%$ of all potential users of the product have already adopted (under the particular pricing scheme). From the market analysis, we have values for $P_i(10)$, $P_i(30)$, and $P_i(70)$ for each respondent i. We compute the other values as shown below. Specifically, when between 10% and 70% of the potential user base have adopted, we use linear interpolation for proportions, and we map to 10 or 70 outside this range as appropriate.

$$P_i(z) = \begin{array}{ll} P_i(10) & \text{if } z \leq 10 \\ (30-z)/20 * P_i(10) + (z-10)/20 * P_i(30) & \text{if } 10 \leq z \leq 30 \\ (70-z)/40 * P_i(30) + (z-30)/40 * P_i(70) & \text{if } 30 \leq z \leq 70 \\ P_i(70) & \text{if } z \geq 70. \end{array}$$

We need to generate the distributions of the number of adopters in each of the three phases. From these distributions we can derive the data for each of the three uncertainties in the decision tree of Figure 1. Note that the distribution of the number of Phase 1 adopters is unconditional as no one has adopted as yet. However, the distribution of the number of adopters in Phase 2 is conditional on the number of adopters in Phase 1. Likewise, the distribution of the number of adopters in Phase 3 is conditional on the number of adopters in Phase 1 and in Phase 2. We determine these distributions through simulation.

CONDUCTING THE SIMULATION

Let M represent the total population of potential users. No one can have adopted the product at the beginning of the first phase (the product launch date), so at this time $z = 0$. Let X_{pj} be a random variable that takes on value 1 if the jth potential adopter adopts during the first phase p (p = 1, 2, 3), and value 0 otherwise. Now define $X_p = X_{p1} + X_{p2} + \ldots + X_{pM}$ to be the total number of adopters in phase p.

177

Let $N = M/R$. We assume that the first N potential adopters are represented by the first respondent, the next N potential adopters are represented by the second respondent and so forth. When potential adopter j is represented by respondent i, we assume that the probability of potential adopter j adopting the product during a phase when z% of the population has adopted the product is given by $P_i(z)$. Thus, for the first phase we have:

$$X_{ij} \sim \text{Bernoulli } (P_i(0))$$

We now define the following:

$$Y_{pi} = \sum_{j=1+(i-1)N}^{i(N)} X_{pj}$$

so that Y_{pi} represents the total number of actual adopters in the first phase p from the market segment represented by respondent i. We assume the potential adopters adopt the product independently, so in the first phase Y_{1i} is the collective outcome of a number of independent Bernoulli trials with the same parameter. It can therefore be described by a binomial distribution:

$$Y_{1i} \sim \text{Binomial } (N, P_i(0))$$

For each market segment i we can then simulate a random drawing (call it y_{1i}) from the appropriate binomial distribution to determine the number of adopters during the first phase from that segment, and hence the total number of adopters $(x_1 = y_{11} + y_{12} + ... + y_{1R})$ during the first phase. Define $z_1 = 100 * x_1/M$ to be the percentage of the population that adopted during the first phase.

Now in market segment i there are $N - y_{1i}$ potential adopters who have yet to do so, and each will adopt during the second phase with probability $P_i(z_1)$. Then:

$$Y_{2i} \sim \text{Binomial } (N - y_{1i}, P_i(z_1))$$

Once again, for each market segment i we simulate a random drawing (y_{2i}) from the appropriate binomial distribution to determine the number of adopters during the second phase from that segment, and hence the total number of adopters $(x_2 = y_{21} + y_{22} + ... + y_{2R})$ during the second phase. Define $z_2 = 100 * (x_1 + x_2)/M$ to be the percentage of the population that adopted during by the end of the second phase.

Finally, for the third phase we have

$$Y_{3i} \sim \text{Binomial } (N - y_{1i} - y_{2i}, P_i(z_2))$$

And through simulation we obtain y_{3i}, the number of adopters during the third phase from segment i, and hence the total number of adopters $(x_3 = y_{31} + y_{32} + ... + y_{3R})$ during the third phase.

OBTAINING THE PARAMETERS FOR THE DECISION TREE UNCERTAINTIES

Suppose that we perform 10,000 simulation runs. Each simulation can be characterised by the triple (x_1, x_2, x_3) representing the number of adopters in each of the three phases. These runs give us an approximation of the distributions for the number of adopters in each phase. We want to further approximate these distributions to fit the uncertainties of our decision tree, ie, a four-branch distribution with appropriate probabilities and values on each branch.

We begin by looking at the distribution for the number of adopters in the first phase. We compute the first three moments (equivalently, the mean, variance, and skew) of this distribution from the simulation runs. Then we use the Miller-Rice algorithm (see Miller and Rice, 1981) for moment matching to fit a four-branch approximating distribution. This tells us the probabilities and values associated with each of the four branches of the uncertainty Phase 1 adopters.

Now we look at the distribution for the number of adopters in the second phase. This is conditional on the number of companies who adopted in the first phase. We divide the simulation runs into four groups, corresponding to the four branches of the Phase 1 adopters' uncertainty. Suppose that the probabilities associated with the four branches are: Very low 20%, Low 40%, High 30%, and Very high 10%. Then we divide the simulation runs according to the number of adopters in the first phase, with the 20% of runs with the smallest number of Phase 1 adopters in the Very low group, etc. Within each group of runs we compute the first three moments of the distribution for the number of adopters in the second phase. As before, the Miller-Rice algorithm tells us the probabilities and values associated with each of the four branches of the uncertainty Phase 2 adopters, conditional on the outcome of the uncertainty Phase 1 adopters. We can similarly obtain the probabilities and values associated with each of the four branches of the uncertainty Phase 3 adopters, conditional on the outcome of both of the uncertainties Phase 1 adopters and Phase 2 adopters.

RUNNING THE DECISION MODEL

With all elements of the decision tree now defined, the decision model can be linked to the financial model to determine the capacity expansion strategy that management should follow, as a function of the proportion of the market that has adopted the product. This requires that the financial model has the flexibility to consider the multiple different capacity expansion and product adoption scenarios that the decision tree can prescribe. The cost implications of installing additional capacity at different times must be captured, as well as the revenue impact of different adoption scenarios in the context of the capacity expansion strategy which determines the company's ability to handle increased demand for its services.

that point. In the first period – the early adoption phase – the initial position was that the company's probability of success (in terms of market share) had a very large variance around it. Yet as the company moved from phase to phase, more and more was learnt about its probability of success, effectively reducing the variance around the company's performance in this and subsequent periods.

The consequences of those decisions could then be fed into the financial model. As it turned out, the eventual implication was that the company would probably want to expand at each of the three decision points.

THE FINANCIAL MODEL

The financial model used in this project was not too different from a standard spreadsheet model presenting information on the balance sheet, profit and loss statements, free cashflows, etc. The difference really came down to the flexibility it offered for considering different scenarios. By taking the adoption rate and the capacity expansion decision information, accompanied by the relevant pricing information and the estimated technology diffusion curve, we could assess the actual revenues and costs across the period under each scenario.

This then led to an expected value of the business, the variance (or standard deviation) of the range of potential business values and the risk profile of the company, given the model's parameters and scope. We found that there was only a small probability that the company would make a great deal of money; however, there was also only a small probability that it would lose money. The value range therefore proved to be quite tight, which was intuitively consistent with the adoption probabilities derived from the market analysis. There were small groups of early adopters and laggards, but a significant percentage of pragmatists who were likely to adopt within a reasonable timeframe.

In this particular situation, we modelled just one of the risk variables associated with the product – the probability of adoption. In general, however, there would actually be a number of inhibitors for the adoption of a product – competition, length of track record and proof of reliability, regulatory environment, etc – which might also be modelled, making the analysis somewhat richer. These would probably also have the effect of adding some more depth and dispersion around the risk profile.

Nonetheless, the exercise proved valuable for the client, because even this relatively streamlined analysis provided the following three sets of key information.

Customer preferences

The first set of information was the output from the market analysis and the dynamic market model. Customer preferences are obviously of key importance in the case of a new product launch.

Capacity expansion strategy

The second set of information pertained to the advisability of preparing to expand capacity in all three phases of business development, as predicted by the company decision model. Had the modelling indicated that it might in some circumstances be inadvisable to expand at one of the three decision points, we would have been able to construct a "roadmap" to guide the company through alternative decision-making scenarios.

Likelihood of success

The third set of information was the relatively narrow range of the value of the business as predicted by the financial model. This indicated that the business was likely to succeed – at least in respect of market share and associated revenue. It also indicated that the company and its investors were not extensively exposed to risk – either in terms of the opportunity costs associated with unanticipated enormous growth, or with the losses associated with failure to win market share.

CONCLUSION

In this chapter we have presented some of the latest thinking behind the valuation of start-up e-businesses. Even relatively well-established e-businesses are notoriously hard to value – when the company is still at a nascent stage, the task is that much harder. However, it is a critical task because important decisions rest on the valuation, for the company itself and its investors.

In this case study, we have focused on two of the areas that make e-business valuation so hard: namely the lack of understanding of the market, and the fact that much of the value of an e-business is embedded in real options. We have described how we use Market Strategy Analysis to develop a model of the marketplace that determines the range of possible future outcomes, and how the output of the market model informs a Real Option Valuation process. In turn, this ROV model identifies the business's real options, places a value on those options, and creates a dynamic roadmap that shows how to adapt the business strategy over time to achieve that value.

The description of this case study was deliberately kept relatively simple so that we could most effectively illustrate the concepts behind our approach. Of course, both the market model and the ROV model can be (and most often are) considerably more complex. In our experience, there are three important points to bear in mind when designing the analytical models.

1. The analysis is predicated on an integrated suite of models, so it is important that the level of complexity is commensurate across the models, and that the models are designed in an integrated manner.
2. The real purpose of the analytical models is to inform decision-makers, and as such it is critical that the conclusions and their justifications can

be clearly communicated to the decision-makers. Therefore, it is important that the analytical process supports this communication, rather than this being subsumed at the expense of analytical complexity.

3. Last, but by no means least, we have found that the most important part of the process is usually the OpenFraming session, because this sets the stage for the entire analysis. OpenFraming provides a common, comprehensive understanding of the potential value of the business. This provides the structure for the analysis by identifying the risks and opportunities that affect value and facilitates the ongoing communication that will result in confidence in the conclusions, and hence confidence in the decisions being taken.

The very nature of the e-business environment suggests that a real options approach would be more appropriate than traditional valuation approaches. We have found that an integrated approach combining market, options and financial models provides our clients with the clarity and insight to make business decisions, confident in the knowledge that they understand the value of their business. While this chapter describes a simple model, we have developed more complex models where appropriate, and recognise the need for further research to expand the robustness and applicability of our valuation models.

1 The work described in this paper was carried out in mid-1999; the paper was prepared in October 1999.

2 We have made our description of the client and the analysis anonymous – and, in some places, generic – in order to protect client confidentiality. Specific details about this client or about PricewaterhouseCoopers services should not be inferred from this information, which is provided as an illustration only.

3 This analysis is conceptually simple, although complex to put into practice. We have chosen a simple case because it allows the processes involved in the analysis to be described more transparently. Considerably more complex analyses are possible and have been carried out by PricewaterhouseCoopers.

BIBLIOGRAPHY

Clayes, J. and G.W. Walkup Jr., 1999, "Discovering Real Options in Oilfield Exploration and Development", paper SPE 52956 presented at the 1999 Society of Petroleum Engineers Hydrocarbon Economics and Evaluation Symposium, March.

Dixit, A.K. and R.S. Pindyck, 1995, "The Options Approach to Capital Investment", *Harvard Business Review*, May–June.

Gallant, L., H. Kieffel and R. Chatwin, 1999, "Using Learning Models to Capture Dynamic Complexity in Petroleum Exploration", paper SPE 52954 presented at the 1999 Society of Petroleum Engineers Hydrocarbon Economics and Evaluation Symposium, March.

Gertner, R. and A. Rosenfield, 1999, "How Real Options Lead To Better Decisions", *Financial Times*, Mastering Strategy supplement, March 25.

Luehrman, T.A., 1998, "Strategy as a Portfolio of Real Options", *Harvard Business Review*, September–October.

Miller, A.C. and T.R. Rice, 1983, "Discrete Approximations of Probability Distributions", *Management Science*, 29(3).

Smith, J.E. and R.F. Nau, 1995, "Valuing Risky Projects: Option Pricing Theory and Decision Analysis", *Management Science*, 41(5), May.

Walkup Jr., G.W. and R.E. Chatwin, 1999, "Case Studies of a Real Option Approach to Asset Valuation in the Petroleum Industry", paper SPE 52952 presented at the 1999 Society of Petroleum Engineers Hydrocarbon Economics and Evaluation Symposium, March.

9

Using Real Options to Frame the IT Investment Problem*

Nalin Kulatilaka, P. Balasubramanian and John Storck

Boston University

Investment in IT has become a dominant part of the capital expenditure budget of many organisations in both the service and manufacturing sectors. As a result decision-makers are faced with difficult questions: How should IT investments be designed and managed to ensure alignment with corporate strategy? How should such investments be justified prospectively, and how can success be measured retrospectively? What more (than technology) is needed to realise the full potential of IT? What are the risk implications of these investments? How can the value of IT investments be managed over time? These questions are not new, but they have not been answered satisfactorily. In this chapter we develop a formal and practical methodology to evaluate investments in information technology infrastructure.

Determining the value of IT investments is inherently difficult. Although the costs seem readily identifiable, many of the benefits are elusive. For example, consider the investment in an electronic mail system within a geographically dispersed workgroup. As with many other infrastructure investments, attempting to justify e-mail on the basis of efficiency alone is likely to fail. E-mail may be a substitute for other forms of communication, but its real value comes as its use expands throughout the organisation and as other, more sophisticated applications are added to the basic e-mail platform. Specifically, e-mail *within* a workgroup may develop into a workflow management system *across* workgroups, which in turn can evolve into

*An earlier version of this chapter appeared as Boston University Working paper 96-35, "Managing Information Technology Investments: A Capability-based Real Options Approach". This research was sponsored by the Internal Revenue Service and the Systems Research Center (SRC) at Boston University. We would like to thank John Henderson, N. Venkatraman, Martha Amram and conference participants at the SRC Spring 1996 meeting for helpful comments and insights. We would also like to thank Robert Materna and Janet Wilson for their help with the case study. Finally, we would like to thank George Wang for his excellent research assistance on this project.

a knowledge-sharing Lotus Notes database for the *entire organisation.* Typically, the diffusion of e-mail across the organisation and the evolution of e-mail to higher forms of knowledge sharing takes substantial time. Thus there is a significant time gap between the point of initial investment and the day when value is derived. As the example suggests, the investment may be staged so that its ultimate scope becomes organisation-wide although the initial investment point may have been a single department. The complexity of valuing IT investments arises not only because it is difficult to quantify the value but also because it is difficult to predict the trajectory and pace of the technology investment across the organisation.

In this chapter we propose a novel way of thinking about these elusive benefits, which leads to a new way of managing IT investments. Our proposal draws on two strands of thought about such investments: considering them as a way of bridging the gap in business capabilities and considering capabilities as providing options to cope better with uncertainty. By characterising business capabilities as arising from a set of operating drivers, we offer a way to improve the alignment between the project manager's technology view and the general manager's business view. We also view the initial investment in terms of the options it creates for the firm. Exercising these options, which usually requires further investments, then allows the firm to capture a greater set of benefits.

Both business and project managers must recognise that value is derived from business capabilities, not merely from specific investments in technology. Continuing with the e-mail example, when viewed simply as a technology, e-mail provides the ability to speed up asynchronous communication, replacing or supplementing memos, phone calls and face-to-face meetings. However, to derive higher value from the e-mail investment, work must be reorganised around this technology. There may be opportunities to improve document handling and coordination of tasks. Frequently, there is greater participation in decision-making. Additionally, higher-order benefits may result when the simpler, less formal mode of communication engendered by e-mail leads organisations to form new alliances with their customers and suppliers. This can create new opportunities for mass customisation and reduction in new product development times, both of which are examples of new *business capabilities* that may arise as a result of considering e-mail as more than just an investment in technology.

We summarise the first part of our proposal by arguing that the design and justification of an investment in technology must begin with the desired set of business capabilities that unfold from the overall business goals of the firm. The investment problem can then be interpreted as the transformation of today's business capabilities into those desired for the future. By focusing on capabilities, we broaden the scope of investment to include not only physical investment (eg, technology), but also changes to human capital (eg, training) and organisational form (eg, partnerships).

The second conceptual underpinning of our methodology recognises the real options created by the staging of investments.[1] These options create value by enabling management to react to changing conditions by altering the timing, scale and configuration of follow-on investments, thereby modifying the risk–return pattern of the investment outcomes. Using real options, decision-makers are able to evaluate not only the value of an investment but also its risk profile.

In the e-mail example, for instance, if after the first stage (implementation of within-group e-mail) business conditions turn out to be ideal, the project roll-out to other groups in the organisation can be accelerated. If conditions are good but not ideal, then a more conservative expansion plan may be pursued. If there are adverse conditions the project may need to be postponed, reconfigured or even abandoned. The procurement of the final business capability is often structured as a multistage process so that management can retain the ability to react to changing conditions on an ongoing basis. In fact, it is the very uncertainty about future business conditions that makes the option valuable. Recent developments in the theory of real option pricing can, with suitable modifications, be adopted to evaluate the flexibility that is inherent in such staged investment programmes.

We link the concepts of business capability and real options using the neoclassical economist's notion of a production possibility frontier. Business capabilities allow a firm to transform its input factors into a set of products and services. Although products and services – the outputs – can be valued, any valuation is contingent on market conditions and the degree of success in attaining the capability. The capability-based real options approach provides the basis for making an investment decision that incorporates the effect of contingencies on the transformation of the input factors into the desired outputs.

We formalise our approach in a four-step process of investment design and analysis (Figure 1) that improves the alignment of the goals of information technology projects with a firm's overall business vision: (1) identify current and desired business capabilities; (2) design an investment programme to achieve the desired capabilities; (3) estimate costs and benefits (in terms of cashflows) resulting from realised capabilities; and (4) fold-back of the cashflows to obtain the market value of the investment.

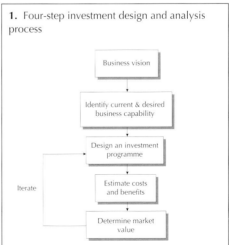

1. Four-step investment design and analysis process

Implementing the real options approach requires periodic monitoring, re-evaluation and redesign of the investment programme. Investment decisions are not simply made once and handed over to project managers for execution but, rather, investments are managed over time. This is in sharp contrast to some current practice where, first, investment decisions are made and, then, projects are managed with a focus on implementation of the technology without adequate consideration of the appropriateness of the project in light of changing business conditions. This shift from a *project management* to an *investment management* view requires that firms put in place a capability to enact an investment management process with the requisite measurement metrics, monitoring schemes and decision-making authority.

The rest of the chapter is organised as follows: in the first section, we elucidate the concept of a business capability and describe it in terms of the constituent *operating drivers* of technology, organisation and process. The second section develops the four-step methodology and presents the rudiments of the real options valuation technique. In the third section, we illustrate the proposed investment management process by analysing how a Canadian mortgage banking firm leveraged imaging technology to build several important business capabilities. Finally, the fourth section concludes with the lessons learned and future research plans.

CHARACTERISTICS OF IT INVESTMENTS

IT infrastructure investments are highly risky to make but can offer huge rewards to a firm. Current practice in evaluating such investments falls into two traps: the trap of negative net present value (NPV) or the trap of vanishing *status quo* (Clemons, 1991). The first trap arises from the difficulty of identifying future benefits and of estimating them accurately in terms of cashflows. This results in conservative estimates of the benefit stream, which, coupled with large investment costs, results in negative NPVs. The second mistake that firms make is in assuming a static market and rejecting valuable opportunities. This could result in loss of market share and other bad outcomes due to actions by competitors.

In this chapter we introduce a methodology that explicitly takes into consideration market uncertainties and determines the value of investments on the basis of their impact firm-wide and over time. Further, we deal with IT investments at an organisational level and argue that IT, along with other operating drivers whose effects are influenced by uncertainties, enables the organisation to achieve a set of capabilities. These capabilities in turn have an effect on the value that a firm derives from its products and services. This link between the operating drivers and value is explained using the capability-based real options approach, which can also be used to manage the investment process.

Capabilities

A business capability is a distinctive attribute of a business unit that creates value for its customers. Capabilities are measured by the value generated for the organisation through a series of identifiable cashflows. Thus, business capabilities distinguish an organisation from others and directly affect its performance.

For example, Boeing's new concurrent design and manufacturing approach gives it the ability to deliver the 777 jetliner much more rapidly than under the conventional "design-then-build" paradigm (Norris, 1995). Engineers, marketing personnel and financial analysts from Boeing's airline customers actively participated in the design of this aircraft almost from the beginning of the project. Concurrent design and manufacturing has become a business capability for Boeing.

In the consumer product sector, micro-marketing at Frito-Lay has been widely publicised (Applegate, 1993). The initiative was designed as a response both to local competition and to the increased information that supermarket scanners had made available to large chains. This had a direct impact on Frito-Lay's revenue stream. Over seven or eight years its micro-marketing skills developed to the point where a major competitor – Annheuser Busch – withdrew from the market. Thus, micro-marketing evolved into a major business capability.

We suggest that a business capability such as concurrent engineering or micro-marketing is built by investment in "operating drivers". It is important to note that investment decisions take place at the level of these drivers. Two firms may obtain the same business capability through investing in different kinds of operating drivers, which include not only tangible infrastructure but also process and organisational components.

The effectiveness of a technology investment depends to a great extent on how work is organised around that technology (Kogut and Kulatilaka, 1994; National Academy Press, 1994). Furthermore, the structure of the organisation, including outsourcing relationships and alliances, must be aligned with the technology and the work processes that are in place (Henderson and Venkatraman, 1993). Thus, the operating drivers are the set of technologies, processes and organisational elements that are necessary for a firm to achieve a business capability. For the purpose of this discussion, we assume that the technology component of a business capability is information technology; by the process component we mean procedures, workflows, management controls and human resources practices; and the organisational component includes relationships with other firms as well as the internal management structure. Figure 2 shows the relationship between business capabilities and operating drivers. It is the interaction of these business capabilities with market forces that creates value.

2. Business capability components

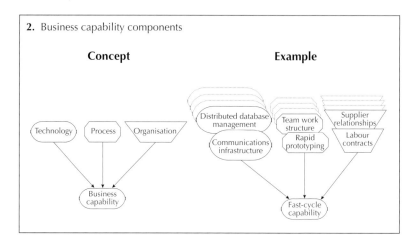

Dealing with uncertainty

In order to move from their current business capabilities to their desired capabilities, firms have to invest resources to make technology, process and organisational changes. The benefits from investments depend on the capabilities that are actually achieved and also on prevailing economic conditions. Thus, firms are faced with two types of investment uncertainties: project-related and market-related. Project-related risk is determined by how the firm chooses to design, implement and manage the operating drivers. For example, the investment may not pan out as expected because the technology may not deliver on all its promises, or integrating the technology into the organisation may be more difficult than foreseen, or there may be cost overruns and time delays. The second type of risk, market-related, is based on customer acceptance, competitor actions and other factors that affect market demand for the firm's products and services. In this case, even if the project unfolds as expected, the resulting business capabilities may not be appropriate for the realised market conditions. For example, a system that is successfully built to handle one million inquiries per month will be inappropriate if demand halves (or doubles). Hence, to achieve the desired capabilities, firms must periodically identify, analyse and manage both sources of risk and manage them over time.

From capabilities to future cashflows

Capabilities alone do not generate cashflows. External market conditions and the firm's operating policies are also determinants of cashflows. Capabilities, however, determine management's ability to react to evolving market conditions.

More specifically, investing in operating drivers and acquiring a set of capabilities influence the firm's cost structure (eg, by increasing fixed costs and reducing variable costs) and its revenue sensitivity (eg, market share).

The capability analysis forms the foundation for building the cashflow models that are essential to any pro-forma cost–benefit analysis. Typical practice, however, entwines the cashflow effects of investments with a particular market scenario. For example, the cost reduction derived from an imaging project is closely tied to the volume of documents processed. Volume is projected by assuming a particular demand for the firm's products or services. In contrast, our approach makes explicit a cashflow model which includes the exogenous market conditions as variables. For instance, if uncertainty stems from the total size of the market for the product, a new capability may affect the firm's fixed cost, the variable (per-unit) cost and the market share. As a result, we can create a map of the incremental cashflows that are generated under all potential future capabilities, investments and market contingencies.

Valuation of contingent cashflows

If a conventional discounted cashflow (DCF) valuation analysis were followed, we would first forecast the future cashflows, compute the expected cashflows, and then discount at the risk-adjusted opportunity cost of capital to obtain the present value. With a model that links capabilities to cashflow in hand, the valuation model requires only the growth rate (to forecast expected future cashflows) and the "beta" of the cashflows (to capture the systematic risk for the opportunity cost of capital). When an equilibrium market model (eg, a capital asset pricing model – CAPM) is used to derive the discount rate, the resulting net present value gives the *market* value of the project.

The contingent nature of the future decisions, however, renders this approach inappropriate for two reasons. First, since the subsequent investment decisions are contingent on the realised business conditions, it is not sufficient to focus on the expected growth rate of the uncertain variable. The future cashflows depend on the management's reactions to the particular realisation of uncertainty. Hence, we must open up the uncertainty to consider all possible future business conditions and assess the optimal investment decisions. This is messy but feasible and can be handled with an event decision tree or a Monte Carlo-type simulation model.

Once the contingent cashflows are mapped out, the valuation and the optimal investment decisions can be obtained simultaneously by solving the event decision cashflow tree as a stochastic dynamic program. The information needed to create the tree includes not only the growth rate of the exogenous variable but also other properties of its stochastic process (eg, volatility) that determine the probability structure of the future cashflow outcomes.

However, a further complication arises in the determination of the opportunity cost used in discounting the expected future cashflows. The risk characteristics of the investment project change every time the business conditions change. Since future business conditions evolve stochastically, deriving the opportunity cost of capital becomes impossible.

The critical insight of financial option pricing gets around this problem by relying on the existence of a traded securities market that spans all exogenous uncertainty.[2] The intuition behind this result is straightforward. Since all risk arising from movements in the underlying asset price contained in the contingent claim can be eliminated by taking appropriate positions in the underlying marketable asset, we can create a portfolio that is riskless relative to the underlying asset. When the contingent payoffs to this portfolio are known, it can be valued using riskless discounting. The presence of the traded asset eliminates the need for risk adjustment and valuation does not rely on a risk pricing model such as the CAPM. This insight forms the foundation of the Black and Scholes (1973) and binomial (Cox, Ross and Rubinstein 1976) option pricing models.

Hence, *with the existence of a traded market for the underlying source of uncertainty*, the information needs are reduced to the volatility of the exogenously uncertain variable and other observable variables, the current price of the asset and the risk-free rate of interest. Any option can be valued by replacing the actual growth rate of the underlying asset with the risk-free rate of interest in laying out the potential future payoffs (the event decision tree) and solving the dynamic program by discounting at the risk-free rate. It is important to note that, although this approach is operationally equivalent to a more traditional decision-tree method, the information needs are different. We rely on market information to adjust for risk by using the volatility, rather than subjective probabilities or CAPM-based risk adjustments, to capture the effects of uncertainty.

In some special cases the investment valuation can use Black–Scholes or other financial option pricing models. We must first draw a correspondence between the option embedded in the investment problem and a known financial option. For instance, the option to wait-to-invest is analogous to an American call option and the option to abandon to an American put. If the underlying source of uncertainty comes from the price of a traded security, the investment project can be evaluated using the appropriate call or put valuation model.

The insight in option pricing can be extended to devise a more general contingent claims valuation model even when the uncertainty arises from sources other than traded security prices (Hull, 1999). In such cases the replication argument must be modified to overcome the risk-adjustment problem. Note that when there are traded securities that can capture this demand uncertainty, we do not need to estimate the mean of the distribution. That is, we do not need to forecast the trend of the demand but only its volatility.[3]

In summary, the real options approach deals with a complete spectrum of risks ranging from, at one extreme, the prices of traded securities and, at the other, unique events. Wherever possible, market information is used.

Table 1. Summary of risk evaluation techniques

Source of risk	Information required to value contingent claims	Analytic method
Prices of market-traded securities	Current prices, volatility	Black–Scholes and other financial option pricing models
Product/service or input market-related risk (eg, prices of goods and services, market size)	Traded prices as proxies, volatility of proxy variable OR Actual growth rate, measure of systematic risk (β), volatility and convenience yield of the risky variable	Risk-neutral "decision trees" (eg, binomial models)
Unique events affecting the firm (project-related risk)	History-based or subjective probability estimates of events	Risk-neutral decision trees

The information requirements, as well as how the information is processed, are markedly different from the more traditional DCF, decision-tree or simulation models. Table 1 summarises the spectrum of risks and the valuation methods.

A METHODOLOGY FOR IT INVESTMENT MANAGEMENT
Our methodology consists of four steps: identification of current and desired business capabilities; design of a contingent investment programme to achieve the desired capabilities; estimation of the costs and benefits of realised capabilities in terms of cashflows; and evaluation of cashflows to obtain a value for the investment.

Identification of current and desired capabilities
The planning effort involves translating the vision into a set of specific desired business capabilities. In addition, the firm must decide what operating drivers are needed to support each of the business capabilities. This involves taking stock of the firm's current operating drivers and determining how to enhance, substitute and build on these drivers to enable the firm to deliver the desired business capabilities. For each business capability there is an associated value and, similarly, for each of the operating drivers there is usually an associated investment.

The business capability analysis has several important implications for the valuation of IT projects. End business capabilities are secured by making a series of investments, where the go/no-go decision at each stage is contingent on the *success of the preceding stages* and the *business conditions*. The investment manager reacts to changing conditions by changing the scope, timing and scale of the investment stages to mitigate downside losses and capture (or even enhance) the upside benefits.

3. First stage of e-mail project

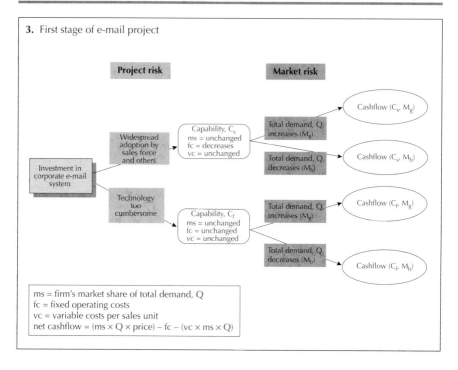

ms = firm's market share of total demand, Q
fc = fixed operating costs
vc = variable costs per sales unit
net cashflow = (ms × Q × price) – fc – (vc × ms × Q)

Design of an investment programme

So far, the capability definition step may appear to be quite traditional. However, when considering that events in the future are inherently uncertain, the firm needs techniques to characterise the uncertainty associated with capability deployment and associated values. As noted earlier, we identify two sources of uncertainty – market-related (price and demand) and project-related uncertainty – which may cause the firm to achieve different capabilities than those envisioned.

Let us revisit the e-mail project considered at the beginning of the chapter, where the investment is made in two stages. In stage 1, workgroup e-mail is installed in a single-product high-tech company. The objective is to improve communication and reduce costs. In stage 2, the company intends to leverage its e-mail investment by implementing knowledge-sharing practices. This will allow the company to respond more effectively to customer needs.

Using our analytical framework, decision-makers build a decision tree (Figures 3 and 4) by determining the menu of choices at each decision point based on the outcomes of prior states and identifying the internal and external sources of uncertainty. Assuming binary outcomes and binary decisions, this process results in 24 potential cashflow outcomes at the end of stage 2, which the decision-maker should evaluate. This valuation technique is described in the next section.

4. Second stage of e-mail project

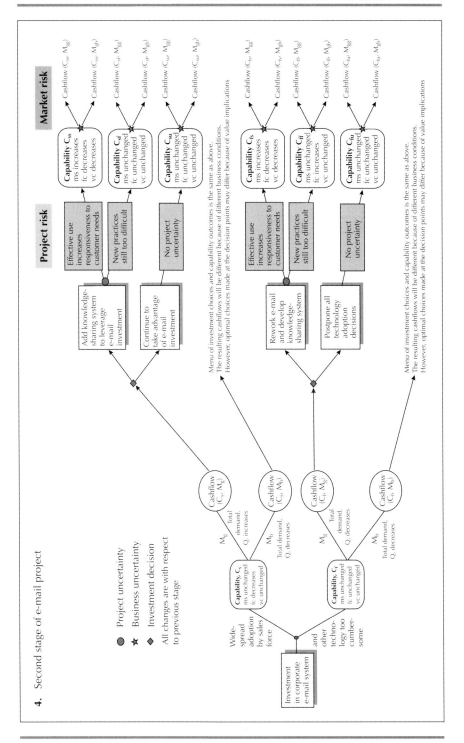

Estimation of cashflows

The third step in the investment management process involves determining the value associated with each business capability. We analyse the value impact at the overall firm level. Although more sophisticated cost–benefit models can be developed, for pedagogic clarity we use a simple cashflow model at each time period. Suppose that the firm faces an industry demand D. The firm's share of the market is ms. The firm's revenues are therefore the fraction, ms, of the total industry demand, D (ie, Revenues = ms × D).[4]

Fixed costs, fc, are the total annual fixed costs of the firm. Since investment costs, I, are explicitly accounted as a cash outflow, neither investment costs nor depreciation allowances are included in fc. Rather, fc represents the portion of operating costs that is unaffected by the firm's output volume. Typical items included in fc are overhead costs that are usually allocated in accounting cost calculations.

Variable costs depend on the firm's output volume. For instance, investing in a more efficient process will reduce the amount of energy and input material consumed, thus lowering variable costs.[5] We capture this effect through the per-unit variable cost parameter, vc. Hence, the total variable cost is vc × ms × D, and the resulting net cashflow, π, is given by (ms × D) − fc − (vc × ms × D).

The parameters ms, fc and vc are influenced by making investments in operating drivers. Since making an investment does not guarantee its success, the realised partakers depend on the success or failure of the investment stage and on the context of the investment.[6] Although the investments position the firm in the market, the realised cashflow depends crucially on the realisation of the exogenous uncertain demand, D.

Evaluation of the cashflows

Finally, using a dynamic programming algorithm, the decision tree can be collapsed to determine an optimal value at each stage. We define value to be the current worth of expected future cashflows computed from the cashflows associated with each terminal node belonging to a stage within the decision tree. The dynamic programming evaluation continues until the initial decision point is reached.

We illustrate the valuation technique using the two-stage investment in e-mail, again with binary sources of uncertainty and binary decision choices (see Figure 4).[7] For instance, suppose that both investment stages are committed as planned and implemented successfully, and that the external business conditions turn out to be advantageous to the firm in both periods.[8] Then the firm will receive net incremental cashflow $\pi_s(M_g)$ in year 1 and $\pi_{ss}(M_{gg})$ in year 2, where the subscripts on π, the cashflow function, denote project success (s) or failure (f), and the subscripts on M denote market outcomes good (g) or bad (b). Figure 4 shows the year-2 cashflows for each of the potential contingencies. Since the benefits of the

5. Value derived at time 1

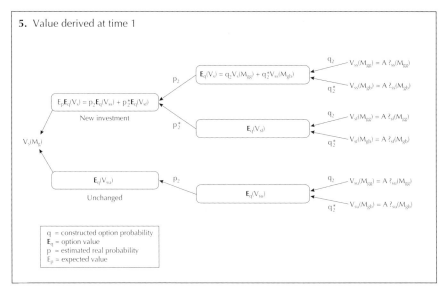

6. Net value at time 0

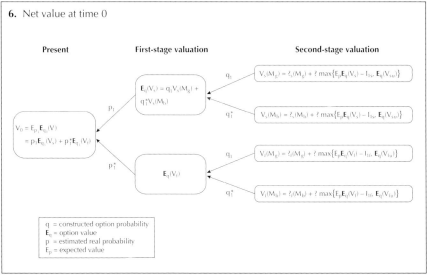

project are likely to accrue for a period of time after the second year, the value, V, of the project at year 2 will be the year-2 cashflow multiplied by the present value annuity factor, A. For example, the year-2 value under the most optimistic scenario discussed above is $V_{ss}(M_{gg}) = A\pi_{ss}(M_{gg})$.

Once the contingent value at the terminal date (planning horizon) is known, we can solve the dynamic programme to fold back the value of the project by taking expectations over each of the sources of uncertainty and building in the decision criteria at each stage (Figures 5 and 6). Consider the year-1 value if the first stage is successful and the market turns out favourably, $V_s(M_g)$. This value would be the incremental cashflow received at year 1 plus the present value of the expected cashflows from following an optimal investment decision thereafter. The menu of decisions at this node is to continue with the proposed expansion at a cost of I_{1s} or abandon the expansion plan. The expected values under the cashflows from the two decisions are as follows.

If expansion is undertaken:

$$V_s(M_g) = \pi_s(M_g) - I_{1s} + \rho\, p_{2s} E_{q_2}\{V_{ss}(M_g)\} + (1 - p_{2s})\, E_{q_2}\{V_{sf}(M_g)\}$$

$$= \pi_s(M_g) - I_{1s} + \rho\, E_{p_1}\left[E_{q_2}\{V_s(M_g)\}\right]$$

and if expansion is rejected:

$$V_s(M_g) = \pi_s(M_g) + \rho\, E_{q_2}\{V_{su}(M_g)\}$$

where $E_p(\cdot)$ is the expectations operator, $E_q(\cdot)$ is the "option value" operator,[9] ρ is the risk-free discount factor, p_{2s} is the probability of successfully implementing the investment I_{1s}, and subscripts s, f and u on V denote values under success, failure and unchanged capability sets, respectively. Management will choose the decision to maximise value. Hence,

$$V_s(M_g) = \max\left[\pi_s(M_g) - I_{1s} + \rho\, E_{p_2} E_{q_2}\{V_s(M_g)\},\ \pi_s(M_g) + \rho\, E_{q_2}\{V_{su}(M_g)\}\right]$$

Similarly, we can obtain the year-1 values under all possible contingencies:

$$V_s(M_b) = \max\left[\pi_s(M_b) - I_{1s} + \rho\, E_{p_2} E_{q_2}\{V_s(M_b)\},\ \pi_s(M_b) + \rho\, E_{q_2}\{V_{su}(M_b)\}\right]$$
$$V_f(M_g) = \max\left[\pi_f(M_g) - I_{1f} + \rho\, E_{p_2} E_{q_2}\{V_f(M_g)\},\ \pi_f(M_g) + \rho\, E_{q_2}\{V_{fu}(M_g)\}\right]$$
$$V_f(M_b) = \max\left[\pi_f(M_b) - I_{1f} + \rho\, E_{p_2} E_{q_2}\{V_f(M_b)\},\ \pi_f(M_b) + \rho\, E_{q_2}\{V_{fu}(M_b)\}\right]$$

By building in the decision criterion (in this case, choosing the maximum of two alternatives), these contingent values incorporate the flexibility to manage the investment programme in the future. Hence, the valuation includes not only direct effects but also the option-like platform value of the investment.

Continuing with the dynamic programme using a similar notation, we can obtain the net present value of the investment I_0 (ensuring that all future decisions are made optimally), the valve function can then be written as

$$V(M_0) = -I_0 + \rho\, E_{p_1} E_{q_1}\{V(M)\}$$

Clearly, we can generalise this approach along several dimensions: a larger menu of alternative decisions; more possible outcomes for the project's successful completion; and more general distributions for the exogenous uncertainty, M. Although the computational complexity will grow rapidly, the methodology remains conceptually similar.

Thus far we have considered one possible investment configuration (ie, design). Typically, we would like to compare several mutually exclusive alternative investment designs.[10] For each such design an analysis similar to the above needs to carried out to arrive at the respective net present value.

While the current value, V_0, appropriately includes the risks of the staged investment programme, this approach provides a much richer picture of the risk characteristics faced by the firm. Since we make uncertainty explicit and consider the firm's possible reactions to future contingencies, the risk profile facing the firm is likely to be significantly modified when compared to a naïve take-it-all-or-leave-it investment design.

For instance, consider the top branch in Figure 4. For the investment stream of I_0 and I_1, to yield $\pi_s(M_g)$ in year 1 and $\pi_{ss}(M_{gg})$ in year 2 (and some residual based on π_{ss} thereafter), stage 1 investment must succeed, the year-1 market must be good, stage 2 investment must be made and be successful, and the stage 2 market must also be good. This has a probability of $p_1 q_1 p_2 q_2$. But the very decision to go ahead with I_1 is determined endogenously within the valuation model. Hence, if the parameter values are such that abandoning the project is preferred at the node {s, g}, this branch may be "trimmed" from the tree of possible values. In effect, the construction of the decision tree and the real options approach for evaluating cashflows provides the organisation with a process for managing risk.

THE METHOD IN ACTION: THE CASE OF NMT

As a testbed for the methodology we use a mortgage bank that was involved in making a large IT investment. In early 1994, National Mortgage Trust[11] (NMT) was a relatively small but aggressive financial institution that specialised in mortgage-backed lending in Canada. Its head office was in Montreal, with branches in Halifax, Toronto and Ottawa. Over the previous seven years NMT's assets had grown from zero to about C$6 billion, and many would say that it was a good example of a successful organisation in the 1990s – flat, fast, customer-orientated, and dedicated to a process of continuous learning and improvement. Within its industry NMT was viewed as a leader in the use of information technology, innovative work processes and management systems. It was also considered to be aggressive in the pursuit of innovative ways of gaining market share and packaging mortgages in ways that are attractive to the funding sources.

NMT's business consisted of three major activities: originating residential mortgages, funding its mortgage commitments and servicing these mortgages. Customers were reached directly through the branch offices, via realtors (estate agents) and with the aid of mortgage brokers. Like other firms in the industry, NMT offered customers relatively few mortgage financing choices. Current offerings were limited to two or three fixed-rate plans and about the same number of variable-rate plans. The following paragraphs summarise the three basic business processes of mortgage origination, funding and servicing.

Mortgage origination begins with the customer reaching agreement on a price with the seller of a property. If the customer has decided to finance the purchase through NMT rather than another financial institution (eg, a commercial bank), an application is submitted. NMT now has to obtain a range of information in order to approve or deny the application. Using the telephone, fax and mail, NMT verifies employment, marital status, credit history and bank balances. Property inspections, surveys, appraisals and title searches are also necessary. If there are no major problems, this process takes two to four weeks. On approval of the loan, a closing date is set. At that time a settlement statement is used as the basis for the exchange of documentation and funds.

The funding process consolidates the potential requirements of the many mortgage applications that are being processed simultaneously. NMT tracks the funding requirements on a daily basis so that a market assessment of funding availability can be continuously made. As deals reach the closing date, mortgages are packaged together for resale to the funding sources. These, of course, require evidence of a careful credit review process and supporting documentation to minimise the risk of non-payment and title defects.

The mortgage servicing process includes dealing with customers both before and after the mortgage is approved. Before they receive approval, customers frequently call NMT with questions relating to status and file completion. These questions are handled by people within NMT who are responsible for each of the major activities in the approval process. Following closing, customers may also call for various kinds of service. In this case, questions are predominantly related to monthly payments (or non-payment!). However, issues relating to refinancing, home improvements and insurance may also arise. Again, answers to these mortgage servicing questions are provided by specialists within the NMT organisation, who often have to call the customer back after retrieving the required documentation.

NMT's capability gap

At the time we began studying NMT, the top management summarised NMT's current state and desired business capabilities as follows (Table 2).

By identifying mass customisation as a desired capability, NMT recognised that with diverse end-user need profiles, there was an opportunity to gain market share by delivering mortgages that were customised in terms of rate, structure and duration. With direct delivery, NMT wanted to

Table 2. Transformation of capabilities

Current state	Desired business capabilities
Small menu of mortgage options	Mass customisation
Branches/brokers/realtors as channels	Direct delivery
Standardised, simple mortgages for resale	MBS placement, including CMOs
Fragmented, activity-orientated servicing	One-stop case servicing

expand the scope of the existing delivery channels to sell mortgages directly to home-owners rather than marketing via mortgage brokers and other intermediaries. The need to build MBS (mortgage-backed security) placement capability was an outcome of mass customisation. Because the make-up of the package of mortgages being sold to funding sources would have changed from mortgages with homogeneous terms to mortgages with varied terms, NMT needed the ability to collateralise these varied term mortgages to secure attractive funding. Further, the dynamic nature of financial market conditions had to be accounted for in determining the rates. Finally, management decided that they wanted NMT to establish long-term relationships with their customers by providing a high level of service before and after a mortgage was approved. The one-stop case servicing approach, with the ability to access customer records while a phone call was in progress, was designed to support this goal.

Business decisions and opportunities

Having agreed on the desired business capabilities, the top management team identified imaging systems as the key technology driver. Imaging systems convert documents and images into digital form so that they can be stored and accessed by the computer. To confirm the view of top management of NMT, we took the facts of NMT's business and presented them to a group of CIOs attending a meeting of the Systems Research Center (SRC) at Boston University. We first asked them to identify the operating drivers for each of the business capabilities identified by the top management. The outcome of this exercise is shown in Table 3.

As indicated in the table, one technology driver that featured in most of the business capabilities was an advanced imaging system, confirming the intuition of top management of NMT.

Proceeding to the next step in the proposed investment methodology, we discussed with the CIOs and the CIO of NMT the staging of the imaging investment and the sources of risk. As a result, we identified two investment stages:

1. Implement the document imaging processing technology in a limited number of offices using off-the-shelf software, but implement it only for new mortgages.

Table 3. Operating drivers

Desired business capabilities	Technology	Organisation structure	Process
Mass customisation	WANs PSNs DBMS Imaging Workflow management software	Alliances with funding sources	Rapid application development Advanced training Market survey/ scanning Performance metrics
Direct delivery	WANs PSNs Imaging	Multiple input sources Alliances with credit reporting agencies	Maintenance/support Performance metrics
MBS placement, including CMOs	Financial model management	Alliances with funding sources	Financial modelling
One-stop case servicing	Imaging Integrated data access	Case-based approach Team-based problem solving	Advanced training Conversion of existing data

2. Expand the data-capture capability to all offices and scan in all pre-existing mortgages. Also, design and implement new workflows throughout the mortgage servicing division.

We then asked both the management and the CIOs to consider the risks that NMT was exposed to. The market risks were clear and identical for all stages. The primary drivers of the overall demand for new mortgages are interest rates and Canadian business cycles. In addition, NMT's "spreads" (between the cost of funds and mortgage interest rates) and market share were affected by regulations concerning the entry of US mortgage banks and the large Canadian commercial banks into the Canadian mortgage market.

The project risks, however, were harder to identify as they were dependent on the technology used. At stage 1, the project risks with the technology were essentially systems integration risks – whether NMT had the expertise to make the technology components work together. NMT also risked not having the expertise necessary to institute process changes that were necessary to keep the imaging system operational. During stage 2 the project risks were somewhat more varied, now including software/hardware performance and scaling issues. Since the data-capture capability was being extended to all offices, NMT could now be faced with a broader range of integration issues. It would also encounter control issues in converting the old documentation – ie, making sure that all documents were accurately indexed and captured by the imaging system. Moreover, since NMT was planning to make changes to the workflows, support requirements would be more complex in stage 2.

We could now define decision points and decision menus for the imaging project. These are summarised in Figure 7. Note that the two alternatives facing the decision-makers were to invest in an imaging system and not to invest in one. The figure describes the potential impact of the internal and external uncertainties on capabilities and cashflows. The combination of internal and external uncertainties implies that there are six possible outcomes at the end of stage 1 and 28 at the end of stage 2 (Figure 8). The probability estimates for each branch in Figures 7 and 8 and the expected cashflows are discussed in the next section. These estimates were obtained in part from the case study at NMT and in part by our analysis of the results of the CIO meeting.

From capabilities to value

The above capability analysis provided the necessary inputs to developing contingent cashflow. Following the simple cashflow-modelling structure presented in the third section, the aggregate (firm-wide) cashflow effects of an investment on the resulting business capability were captured via the three parameters fixed costs, fc, variable costs, vc, and market share, ms. As the exogenous demand for mortgages, D, fluctuated, the net cashflows to the firm were affected according to the capability that was in place.

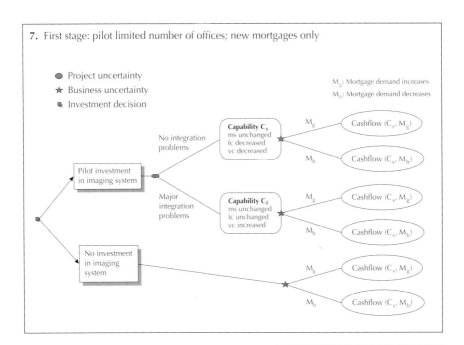

7. First stage: pilot limited number of offices; new mortgages only

8. Second stage: expand to all offices

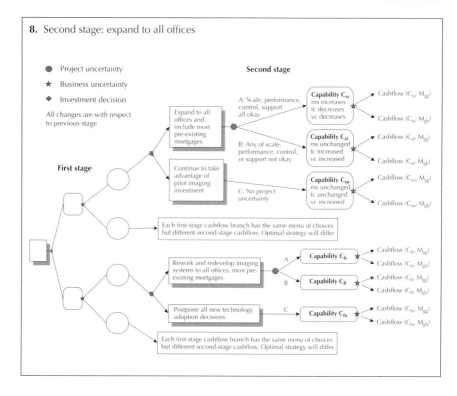

At the time of the case study, NMT generated annual revenues of C$200 million. Its fixed costs were 20% of revenue and the total variable costs were 70% of revenue.

From the capability analysis, NMT estimated that if the first stage were successfully implemented, the fixed costs would increase by 2% because of new support and maintenance processes associated with the introduction of imaging technology. Because the efficiency effects of the investment would be felt only for new mortgages in a limited number of offices, NMT estimated that variable costs firm-wide would be reduced only by 2%. Management did not expect any change in market share, again because improvement in mortgage servicing would occur only for new mortgages in a few geographical markets. If stage 1 failed, the increased overhead of the imaging systems would be carried without any productivity improvements; hence, the fixed costs would increase by 2%, but the variable cost reductions would not materialise.

Estimates for the second stage of investment were developed as follows. If success in stage 1 were followed by success in stage 2, new firm-wide support and maintenance requirements would double fixed costs. Variable costs, however, were conservatively estimated to decrease by 10%. This relatively small change was attributed to the fact that paper processing comprises a small part of the variable cost (review and analysis of the credit application are the major components of variable cost). Finally, with success in stages one and two, management estimated there would be a 50% increase in market share as a result of NMT being viewed as a service leader in the industry.

If success in stage 1 were followed by failure in stage 2, fixed costs were projected to increase by 80%. Management believed that variable costs would fall by 5% in the case of a stage 2 failure, compared to a 10% decrease if stage 2 was successful. Market share was projected to decrease by 5%, principally because staff would be preoccupied with making the new systems work and because of negative customer perceptions about NMT's ability to service their accounts.

NMT also made estimates of impacts on cashflow in the situation where stage 1 failed and stage 2 was successful. In this case, as with success in both stages, the new firm-wide support and maintenance requirements would double fixed costs. Variable costs were conservatively estimated to fall by 5%. This reduction is less than that achieved with success in both stages because of lower levels of efficiency gains. Finally, management estimated there would be a 50% increase in market share.

If failure in stage 1 were followed by failure in stage 2, fixed costs were, again, projected to increase by 80%. Also, variable costs were projected to remain the same because of the continued use of the old systems. Market share was projected to decrease by 5%, again mainly because staff would be preoccupied with making the new systems work and because of negative customer perceptions.

The impact of procuring capabilities is modelled via changes in the cost structure and the ability to generate revenues ("market share"). These assumptions are summarised in Table 4.

As described in the second section, in addition to modelling cashflows we also modelled sources of uncertainty, as follows. Total market demand for mortgages was assumed to follow a lognormal distribution with an annual standard deviation of 35% – ie, if the current demand for mortgages is D_0 and the time-t demand is D_t, then $\ln(D_t/D_0)$ is normal distributed with standard deviation of 0.35. Our estimate of volatility, σ, was based on the volatility of Canadian interest rates. If instead we had used GNP as a proxy for the mortgage demand, the volatility around the mean growth rate would have yielded similar volatility estimates.

For purposes of our discrete-time model we developed a risk-neutral binomial approximation of the lognormal distribution. Specifically, over a time interval τ

$$D_\tau = u D_0 \qquad \text{with probability } q$$
$$= d D_0 \qquad \text{with probability } 1 - q$$

Table 4. Summary of cashflow impacts

	Time–cashflow impact				Time–cashflow impact		
Stage 1	*ms*	*fc*	*Vc*	**Stage 2**	*ms*	*fc*	*vc*
				Success p = 0.8	50%	100%	−10%
Success p = 0.8	0%	2%	−2%	Failure p = 0.2	−5%	80%	−5%
				Not invest	−5%	0%	0%
				Success p = 0.7	50%	100%	−5%
Failure p = 0.2	0%	2%	0%	Failure p = 0.3	−5%	80%	0%
				Not invest	−5%	0%	0%
Not invest	0%	0%	0%	Not invest	−5%	0%	0%

Notes: All cashflow effects are incremental over prior-period cashflows.

Stage 2 cannot be done without having done stage 1.

If stage 1 fails, stage 2 investment cost increases by 25% (to account for redoing parts of stage 1).

If stage 1 is not undertaken, it can be accelerated and implemented together with stage 2 at 50% higher cost and a lower probability of success (70%).

where u and d are the coefficients, chosen such that, for time interval τ, the expected return from the investment in time τ is $u\tau$ and the variance of the return is $\sigma^2\tau$. Also, $u = 1/d = e^{\sigma\sqrt{\tau}}$ and $q = (e^{r\tau} - d)/(u - d)$, where r is the risk-free rate of interest. Under this structural assumption the only two pieces of market information that we require are the volatility of demand (35%) and the riskless rate of interest (5%).

Project uncertainty was estimated using subjective measures. Utilising the real options methodology, we assumed that stage 1 would fail with probability 10% and stage 2 with probability 20%. For the analysis reported here, we assumed that success of the second stage is independent of the outcome of the first stage. This assumption can easily be relaxed. The cost of the stage 1 investment was estimated to be C$500,000; stage 2 was projected at C$5 million.

Using the real options approach and the data discussed above, we modelled the investment programme using a spreadsheet and estimated the value of the imaging project to be C$2.1 million. This result is quite different from that given by the most simplistic traditional NPV technique, which yields a *negative* project value (C$380,000). The real options valuation includes not only the NPV obtained by following the optimistic path of assumed success, but it also adds the contingent value of the project at each decision point on all possible paths.

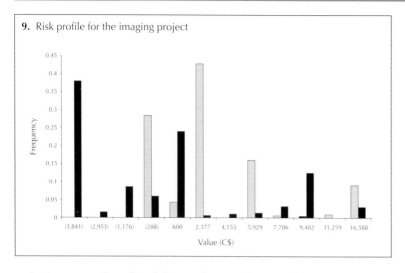

9. Risk profile for the imaging project

An important benefit of this analysis is that in addition to a value, decision-makers are provided with a risk profile. We used the spreadsheet model to produce a histogram which conceptually compares the probability of obtaining a range of values through the NPV technique and the real options approach (Figure 9). By staging the investment and making the follow-on decisions contingent on the realisation of the external (market demand) and internal (project) uncertainty, the firm is able to protect itself against some of the most undesirable outcomes. At the same time, if the future market conditions turn out to be good, the firm can use its investment flexibility to capture the upside benefits. Nevertheless, the project may still end up making a loss. Tracking through the decision tree, managers can identify the scenarios that bring about these losses and may be in a position to redesign the project to minimise such losses.

The project value is most sensitive to the assumption of market share enhancement as a result of acquiring the business drivers. Figure 10 shows the sensitivity of value to this assumption. In fact, this was one of the most contentious assumptions within the firm's top management. Even when a project is deemed successful (the technology works, the processes run smoothly and organisational changes are enacted without a hitch), competitive conditions may prevent the firm from realising the planned gain in market share. If a conventional DCF analysis had been used, the project would have had to generate nearly a 75% increase in market share to be viable. A business case built around such an assumption is likely to be looked at with suspicion by senior management, who would be concerned about possible reactions by competitors. In the case of NMT, the initial C$500,000 outlay for the first stage was tantamount to purchasing an option to undertake the second stage.

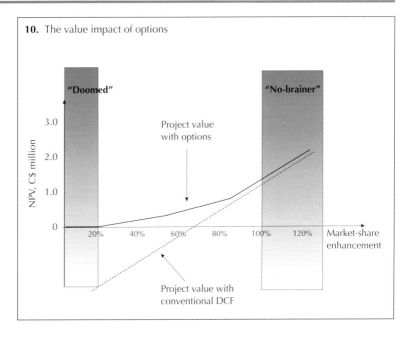

10. The value impact of options

"Doomed"

"No-brainer"

Project value
with options

NPV, C$ million

3.0

2.0

1.0

0

20%   40%   60%   80%   100%   120%   Market-share
enhancement

Project value with
conventional DCF

We note that in fact a third stage of investment was identified by NMT management. They considered using optical character recognition (OCR) technology to automate the conversion of the information in the images into digital form for their transaction processing systems. The OCR investment would have built on the process and organisational drivers that were needed for the first two stages of the imaging project. However, using the real options approach, the nature of the project risks in this case revealed that investment in OCR was not justifiable.

LESSONS LEARNED

As it turned out, NMT reached the decision point for the stage 2 investment when economic conditions in Canada were not conducive to further development of its mortgage business. However, by staging the imaging investment, NMT had explicitly hedged this risk. The structure of the project enhanced the value of upside gains that would have been achieved if the economy had been stronger and it protected NMT against downside losses. It may be argued that this is the advantage of any pilot or prototyping approach, where management may decide to abort a project due to cost. However, we suggest that the real options methodology allowed NMT management to quantify both its initial and periodic assessments of project value, taking into account internal risks and market risks. The four-step cycle of identifying desired business capabilities, designing the investment programme, valuing realised capabilities in terms of cashflow and solving the decision tree provided a basis for decision-making. If it had not used the four-step methodology, NMT might have made a different decision at stage 1 (eg, given the strong economy prior to stage 1, they might have elected to deploy the imaging technology for all mortgages rather than new mortgages only). The real options method helped NMT to design an investment programme that was consistent with the vision of the organisation and took into account the unpredictability of future business conditions. Moreover, the methodology motivated the definition of the business capabilities and associated operating drivers. It was necessary to identify the operating drivers in order to develop estimates of the impact on future cashflows.

In the NMT case, the classic IT investment questions seem to have been answered. To apply the methodology, the infrastructure investment question was recast in terms of the capabilities that could be achieved. As a result of this, decision-makers could perform "what-if" types of analysis, keeping in mind alternative design configurations, investment timing decisions, etc. This helps decision-makers to evaluate different ways of achieving a particular capability, thereby providing them with different perspectives on the investment in infrastructure. Furthermore, the methodology highlighted the need for policy planners, project managers and financial analysts to work together to manage the investment process.

Prospectively, investments were justified by a combination of "think wide" and "think long" behaviour. Management focus on investment in operating drivers (the technology, process and organisational components of the investment) accomplished two objectives. First, cost estimates across the entire organisation were fully specified. Second, by thinking broadly about operating drivers, not only did the impact on business capabilities become more clearly defined but new and broader capabilities were also identified. For example, relationships with funding sources (an organisational driver) might support a new, critical business capability such as home equity lending, which is not in the current list of desired capabilities. As indicated in Table 2, some drivers support the development of more than one capability. Hence, interdependencies are vital.

"Think long" behaviour also helps to prospectively justify IT investment. The NMT case shows clearly how the staging of investments helped this organisation to cope better with uncertainty. Stakeholders were able to capture the option value of managerial flexibility, which, as it turned out, increased with increasing uncertainty. This more explicitly quantified long-term view provides a stronger basis for strategic planning.

The fourth classic IT investment question – What more is needed to realise the investment's full potential? – is in part answered by the identification of the technological, process and organisational operating drivers necessary to create the business capability. In addition, the real options methodology allows management to understand the dynamic impact of internal and external risks in the project design as well as the contingent nature of follow-on investment decisions.

The investment management process itself provides an answer to the second question: how do we design and manage investments to ensure alignment with corporate strategy? Obviously, the concept of periodic reassessment of *investment* decisions, and not just operating decisions, is not new. However, we also suggest that the real options methodology motivates consideration of alignment as a bidirectional process. The traditional direction is to go from investment decisions to business capabilities to operating drivers. Using the real options approach, operating drivers are considered on a broad scale in the organisation, so their potential for enhancing business capabilities is clearly identified. As a result, investment decisions may be modified on the basis of either view of alignment.

Finally, the real options methodology provides a means of measuring success retrospectively. In particular, the methodology considers external business risk and internal project risk separately. The separation of risk provides organisations with an opportunity to assign management accountability. Project managers cannot control external conditions but they do have responsibility for identifying internal risks and possible outcomes of implementation. Further, by asking business managers to specify market scenarios and other changes in competitive dynamics, they take responsibility for monitoring external factors. By partitioning the retrospective analysis of outcomes into internal and external factors, planning and decision-making should improve.

The capability-based real options approach described in this chapter suggests two important questions for further research: will decisions change if real options thinking replaces the traditional discounted cashflow-based approach for evaluating investment in IT infrastructure? And, can we apply the real options approach to other contexts – eg, across divisions in a multidivisional firm, or to capabilities that are delivered by an alliance of firms?

In particular, the first question becomes increasingly relevant in a environment where the evolution of capabilities is discontinuous. For example, almost any organisation has multiple options to change the way it delivers value to its customers. Such changes can be radical. There can be new technologies, operating units can be outsourced and processes can be totally re-engineered. Technology drivers of particular interest include those built around intranet technology, videoconferencing or data warehousing technology. Intranet technology represents both a major infrastructure investment for many firms and a potential solution to information access and intra-firm communication issues. We believe that intranet technology is especially interesting for real options thinking because substantial uncertainty is still associated with the technology with respect to standards and potential applications (Gartner Group, 1996). Moreover, the market has assigned substantial value to this technology. Videoconferencing is rapidly emerging as a medium for connecting dispersed workgroups at all organisational levels. Again, the investment required to make video broadly available on the desktop is substantial, primarily because of support (ie, process) costs. The major uncertainty with respect to video is that people do not yet have sufficient experience to understand applications issues. Data warehousing is a technology with similar characteristics (Inmon, 1996). Effective deployment is dependent on understanding these uncertainties, and a systematic study will therefore help organisations to develop and manage investment programmes. In these situations we need to evaluate whether the DCF approach, with its focus on investments and specific paybacks rather than timing, will identify outcomes similar to those obtained with the real options approach.

In considering the real options approach in other contexts, we believe that it might have particular value in interdivisional settings and interorganisational relationships. In particular, the approach will be useful for evaluating investments when capabilities are transferred from one division to another or when capabilities are developed jointly by two or more divisions. Evaluating the potential for capability transfer is interesting because one would have the experience and data from the first implementation to apply to the second. The second situation raises issues that are similar to those faced in an inter-organisational relationship.

Organisations are increasingly using alliances and partnerships to develop business capabilities. Although on the surface the methodology may appear to be directly applicable, there may also be a third category of risk – namely, interaction risk. This is the risk that participating firms cannot or will not meet their obligations to their partners. In addition to technological incompatibilities, the firms share a second-level of market risk in that they share each other's exposure to market uncertainties.

In this chapter, we have presented a framework for dealing with the complexities of large information technology projects. By providing a means of capturing and analysing the many internal and external uncertainties that are inherent in such projects, we are offering organisations the opportunity to derive greater value from these investments.

---

1 The term "real options" is used to stress the analogy with options on financial assets and to highlight the fact that they provide opportunities to acquire real assets. See Amram and Kulatilaka (1999).
2 Note that it is the existence of the market and the possibility of replication, rather than actually carrying out the replication, that allow options to be priced in an arbitrage-free fashion.
3 For additional information see Amram and Kulatilaka (1999).
4 Where the output price is normalised to 1, without loss of generality.
5 These do not include an allocated portion of fixed cost.
6 More generally, there is a continuum of degrees of project success/failure. For now we will treat this as a binary outcome.

7 If we need a richer set of outcomes, we can take smaller time steps between stages. As a result, the event tree unfolds with thicker foliage. Investment decisions, however, are made only at periodic (annual) intervals.

8 Although this outcome is contingent on a particular sequence of events occurring, many business plans are based on equally specific scenarios. Even in this highly simplified example, this is only one of 24 potential outcomes that are explicitly considered in the valuation.

9 This is operationally equivalent to taking risk-neutral expectations over the possible market outcomes and discounting at the risk-free rate of interest. When the uncertain market variable, M, is a traded security price, the Black–Scholes options price can be used to value the option-like project. When M is a non-traded asset, a similar computational technique can be adopted by first transforming the probabilities into their risk-neutral equivalents using an equilibrium asset pricing model. See Hull (1999) or Dixit and Pindyck (1995). A tutorial on the risk-adjustment techniques is presented in Kulatilaka and Marcus (1992).

10 One such choice is to recognise the ability to postpone the project.

11 National Mortgage Trust is a pseudonym for a real organisation. The events described here are based on a case study conducted by one of the authors together with John Henderson, Robert Materna and Janet Wilson. Also, we note that some of the data for stages 2 and 3 came out of the CIO meeting and some are derived from the case study performed at NMT in 1995.

BIBLIOGRAPHY

Amram, M. and N. Kulatilaka, 1999, *Real Options: Managing Strategic Investment in an Uncertain World*, Boston, MA: Harvard Business School Press.

Applegate, L.M, 1993, "Frito-Lay, Inc.: A Strategic Transition (A)", HBS, 9-193-129.

Black, F. and M. Scholes, 1973, "The Pricing of Options and Corporate Liabilities", *Journal of Political Economy*, 81(3), pp. 637–54.

Clemons, E.K., 1991, "Investments in Information Technology", *Communications of the ACM*, 34(1), pp. 22–36.

Clemons, E.K. and B.W. Weber, 1990, "Strategic Information Technology Investments: Guidelines for Decision-making", *Journal of Management Information Systems*, Fall, pp. 9–28.

Cox, J.C., S.A. Ross and M. Rubinstein, 1979, "Option Pricing: A Simplified Approach", *Journal of Financial Economics*, 17(2), pp. 145–60.

Davenport, T., 1993, *Process Innovation: Reengineering Work Through Information Technology*, Boston, MA: Harvard Business School Press.

Dixit, R.S. and R.S. Pindyck, 1994, *Investment Under Uncertainty*, Princeton, NJ: Princeton University Press.

Gartner Group, 1996, *Mining the Internet*, Proceedings.

Hammer, M. and J. Champy, 1993, *Reengineering the Corporation: A Manifesto for Business Revolution*, Harper Business.

Henderson, J. and N. Venkatraman, 1993, "Strategic Alignment: Leveraging Information Technology for Transforming Organizations", *IBM Systems Journal*, 32(1), pp. 4–16.

Hull, J.C., 1999, *Options, Futures, and Other Derivative Securities*, Fourth edition, Englewood Cliffs, NJ: Prentice Hall.

Inmon, W.H., 1996, *Building the Data Warehouse*, John Wiley and Sons.

Kambil, A., J.C. Henderson and H. Mohsenzadeh, 1993, "Strategic Management of Information Technology Investments: An Options Perspective", Chapter 9 in R. D. Banker, R. J. Kauffman and M. A. Mahmood, eds, *Strategic Information Technology Management: Perspectives on Organizational Growth and Competitive Advantage*, Idea Group Publishing, pp. 161–78.

Kogut, B. and N. Kulatilaka, 1994, "Options Thinking and Platform Investments: Investing in Opportunity", *California Management Review,* 36(4), pp. 52–71.

Kulatilaka, N. and A. Marcus, 1992, "Project Valuation Under Uncertainty: When Does DCF Fail?" *Journal of Applied Corporate Finance*, 5, pp. 92–100.

Markus, L. and D. Robey, 1988, "Information Technology and Organizational Change: Causal Structure in Theory and Research", *Management Science*, 34(5), pp. 583–98.

National Academy Press, 1994, *Information Technology in the Service Society: A Twenty-First Century Lever*, Washington, DC.

Norris, G., 1995, "Boeing's Seventh Wonder", *IEEE Spectrum*, October, pp. 20–30.

Quinn, J.B. and M.N. Baily, 1994, "Information Technology: Increasing Productivity in Services", *Academy of Management Executive*, 8(3), pp. 28–51.

Quinn, J.B., 1992, *Intelligent Enterprise*, The Free Press.

10

Software Design as an Investment Activity: A Real Options Perspective*

Kevin Sullivan, Prasad Chalasani, Somesh Jha and Vibha Sazawal

University of Virginia; HBK Investments
Carnegie Mellon University; University of Washington

Many important software design guidelines remain without adequate theoretical or conceptual foundations. Important but inadequately formulated concepts include information hiding (Parnas, 1972 and 1985) and its modern version in software architecture (Shaw and Garlan, 1996); risk-reducing spiral processes models and other phased project structures (Boehm, 1988); and guidelines on the timing of commitments to product and process design decisions (Habermann, Flon and Cooprider, 1976). These ideas, which are so central to software design and engineering, remain in their current formulations more akin to folk wisdom than science.

In practice, the lack of scientific or mathematical foundations for software product and process design significantly impedes software development. First, it is hard to teach and understand software design. The body of knowledge of the field appears as informal, unrelated rules of thumb, rather than as principles based on an underlying theory. What is the connection between information hiding and spiral development models, for example? Second, it is hard to justify trade-offs and other key decisions in design. Debates about economically important design issues end up as arguments about whose heuristics are better, with little or no theory to help resolve such debates. Third, the lack of an adequate conceptual model makes it hard to recognise flaws in or boundaries of applicability of informal heuristics, and thus to correct or extend them.

In this chapter, we outline an integrated view of software design as being largely a process of decision-making under uncertainty and incomplete knowledge, including threats of competitive entry. We then appeal to

*This work was supported by the National Science Foundation (USA) under grants to Kevin Sullivan numbered CCR-9502029, CCR-9506779 and CCR-9804078

decision theory and finance for mathematical foundations for key design guidelines. We take utility maximisation, generally, and wealth creation, in particular, as the basic objective of the software design decision-making process in a business context, and we try to explain how we might develop an account of the value-enhancing aspects of a number of software design guidelines in terms of mathematical utility and finance theories.

In particular, we outline a theory of software design based on the idea that part of the value of a typical software product, process or project is in the form of embedded options. These real options provide design decision-makers with valuable flexibility to change products and plans as uncertainties are resolved over time. We apply some basic ideas emerging from the study of real options to try to establish the plausibility of using such concepts to develop a better account of important software design ideas in three areas:

❏ timing of important design decisions;
❏ designing the modular structure of a system (information hiding); and
❏ the use of phased or iterative project structures (the spiral software development model).

We are less concerned here with the use of arbitrage techniques to develop market-based valuations for real options than in developing a case for an options-based rethinking of key ideas in software design and engineering. In some cases, arbitrage pricing is possible, but it depends on knowledge of current asset values and complete markets: that there are traded assets whose risks are closely related to those in the given options. The first step for software engineering is to understand the nature, role and value of options. The second is to develop pricing tools. Here we take the first step.

ECONOMICS-DRIVEN SOFTWARE DESIGN AND ENGINEERING

Before plunging into our discussion of the creation and management of options in software design, we take a step back to address the notion of software design and engineering as a value-driven activity. We put this view in context with traditional software engineering thought, which focuses more on structure and technical perfection than value added. Then we give a brief overview of current software engineering economics.

We take the view that the software design and engineering activity is one of investing valuable resources under uncertainty with the goal of maximising value added (Sullivan, 1996). It is possible to adopt a complex view of value. One could characterise software design as a multi-objective optimisation activity in which one trades safety for performance, or in which one satisfies multiple stakeholders (Boehm, 1989) for example. In this chapter we take a narrow view: that value is measured in terms of market value added to the design firm.

Although this view might have shortcomings, it is a plausible basis for developing a theory of software design for modern business environments.

The view approximates to much industrial practice, embodying the core axiom of corporate finance theory: the objective of the management of a publicly held firm is to make decisions that maximise owners' wealth (Brealey and Myers, 1996). Second, seeing engineering design as a value-seeking activity is not new. Baldwin and Clark state that: "Designers see and seek value in new designs" (Baldwin and Clark, 1999). Third, some of the most successful software companies make wealth the explicit goal. "Everybody in a business unit has exactly the same ... job description, and that is to ship products. Your job is not to write code, your job is not to test, your job is not to write specs. Your job is to ship products ... You're trying not to write code. If we could make all this money by not writing code, we'd do it" (Cusumano and Selby, 1995, p. 45). Fourth, some prominent managers, such as Strassmann, now bemoan software design that fails to focus on value added:

> The proper measurement of the success of software investments requires more than compliance with models of technical perfection. Technical excellence of programming code is highly desirable, but clearly insufficient. Nowadays, the most profitable and popular software in the world is notorious for its bugs and glitches. Economic utility and independent measures of customer satisfaction must be the ultimate arbiters of all judgement about the utility of software (Strassmann, 1997, p. 147).

From structure to value added as desideratum

Our critique of current software design thinking is that no strong links are made from the use of technical design concepts to the goal of economic value added. The design concepts that we discuss are formulated, not in terms of value added, but in purely structural terms. How should a designer go about structuring a product, project or development process?

Consider information hiding. The guideline promotes designs in which aspects of a system that are likely to vary over time or across a product line are "hidden" within modules that can be accessed only through stable interfaces (Parnas, 1972, 1976 and 1985). The concern with software architecture largely addresses the same issue, with a clear emphasis on structure. The important book of Shaw and Garlan on software architecture begins, "As the size and complexity of software systems increase, the design and specification of overall system structure become more significant issues than the choice of algorithms and data structures ..." (Shaw and Garlan, 1996, p. 1). This statement is true, without a doubt. The problem in the field is that no serious attempt is made to characterise the link between structural design decisions and value added.

Process criteria tend to be formulated in structural terms, as well. They define stages of design, their ordering and transition criteria (Boehm, 1988). The waterfall model, in which design begins with requirements analysis and then proceeds mechanically through specification, modular decomposition, module implementation, module integration, system testing and deployment, pays little regard to value added. The spiral model is at least implicitly value-based in that a project "get[s] started by a hypothesis that a particular operational mission (or set of missions) could be improved by a software effort" (Boehm, 1988). We see this as a hypothesis that such an effort is expected to add value. Nevertheless, value remains implicit. No clear link is made in the formulation of the spiral model to a clear notion of value maximisation.

In timing of design investments, we also rely on informal rules of thumb. One such rule says that a designer should delay decisions for as long as possible to maximise the information available when the decision is made. Later in this chapter we show that this heuristic is not correct, in general. We need a principled basis for reasoning about the timing of design investment decisions in order to have a better founded approach to managing complex software projects. More generally, we need a sound basis for reasoning about the conditions under which important heuristics are valid.

Structure and flexibility in software design

The structure of a software product, process or project influences its economic value in critical and often decisive ways. The reason is that structure largely determines the flexibility that the designer has to make changes in a product or development process over time; and in the face of changing and uncertain future conditions, flexibility can have great value. It can provide both protection against downside risk and exposure to upside opportunity. The ability to cancel a project early in the face of unfavourable new information provides downside protection. The ability to make such decisions more effectively promises substantial economic payoffs (Boehm and Sullivan, 1999). The flexibility to adapt a product to a new market or to select the best of a set of compatible components for use in a given design, by contrast, provides upside potential.

By contrast, the "year 2000 problem" illustrates the enormous cost incurred when the flexibility to make needed changes is missing due to an inadequate design structure. The problem is not a result of designers using only two digits to represent dates, as commonly believed. Rather, it is that, in each case, designers failed to *hide* this design decision within a module that is accessed using a single date manipulation interface. If that had been done, the two-digit representation used privately within the module could be changed at low cost, without impact on the remainder of the system. Unfortunately, the lack of modularity in date management code in many programs led to a situation in which many parts of a system came to depend on the decision to use a two-digit representation. When that representation had to change, entire systems had to be scrubbed by hand to find far-flung dependencies on the assumption of two-digit dates.

Uncertainties in software design

Our goal, then, is to develop a better economic account of the value of structure and its exploitation in software products and process. We seek to provide software designers with intellectual tools, and ultimately prescriptive guidance, for understanding when to invest in flexibility and how to exploit it effectively.

Good software designers and software design concepts recognise that uncertainty and incomplete knowledge are critical issues. Uncertainties that have been addressed by researchers and that are reflected in well-known decision-making guidelines include the cost and schedule required to develop a product; aspects of a system that are likely to change in the future or across a product line; the presence of faults in a product and thus the risk of operational failures, and technical risks in building complex software systems. Other uncertainties have been addressed less well, including those about future technology and standards developments; user needs and the value that users are likely to ascribe to products and features; the impact of process changes on cost and scheduling estimates, and others.

A good designer sizes up relevant uncertainties; designs products and projects to provide flexibility to handle them, to the extent that such investments are expected to maximise the value of the project; and continually evaluates the flow of information into the project and takes decisions, within the bounds of flexibility afforded by the product or project, to track the value maximisation goal. Exogenous uncertainties, such as the risk that a standard on which a project is betting will not be accepted by the market, are resolved only by waiting for external processes to reveal themselves. Endogenous uncertainties, such as the feasibility of building a solution on a given platform, are resolved through active inquiry, eg, experimental prototypes.

A key phrase is *within the bounds of flexibility afforded by the project or product*. Here is the link back to structure. The freedom to take actions at a reasonable cost is often missing unless a product or process was designed for it from the outset. It is thus not surprising that much of software design thinking today is about how to design for flexibility. Information hiding design criteria and software architecture to a considerable extent focus on the use of modularity to provide flexibility in design. Similarly, the spiral software development process model provides flexibility in at least two important dimensions. First, it imposes a phased structure on a project, where the goal of each phase is to reduce a key uncertainty facing the project, with decisions about whether or how to invest in subsequent phases based on information from earlier phases. Second, within each phase it stresses the development of alternatives, creating an option to pick the most promising one.

Having designed for flexibility, the designer is in the position of having to manage it. A key issue is knowing when to take an action that is available, but not mandatory, as a result of the project structure. Under threat of competitive entry, for example, when should a designer decide to take a product to market even though it still has bugs due to incomplete testing?

In the face of increasing upgrade costs because of a decaying modular structure, when should a designer invest in restructuring the system to reduce costs? Does it make sense always to wait until forced? When a designer has flexibility to invest or wait, the question is how to time the decision to maximise the project value.

Traditional software engineering economics

The software designer clearly faces two difficult questions concerning the economics of flexibility. First, when should the designer invest to create flexibility that can be exploited later by means of a follow-on investment, if necessary (eg, by designing a module interface to hide a data representation)? Second, given a degree of flexibility to make such a follow-on investment, what strategy should the designer use to decide whether – and if so when – to make it (eg, in changing the data representation hidden within a module).

In deciding whether or not to invest in flexibility, the designer has to weigh its cost against its value to make the value-maximising decision. The problem that the designer faces is that the cost is usually tangible, but the value hard to grasp. For example, hiding a data format in a module incurs an up-front design cost; but, on the other hand, the *present* value of the flexibility so obtained is elusive. The value is in the ability to respond to uncertain future conditions, if necessary. The payoff occurs in the future, contingent on uncertain future conditions. For example, the flexibility obtained by hiding two-digit date codes pays off only if the system is used after 2000.

How can the designer make the intangible present value of flexibility tangible so that the real value can be compared with the real, tangible cost? Software designers generally lack the means to do this. It is thus perhaps not surprising that designers tend to overlook the value of flexibility. Without a sound basis for reasoning about its value, tangible cost often trumps a hard to quantify but real economic benefit.

Before turning to the options approach for making the value of flexibility tangible, we discuss current work in software engineering economics and the difficulties that it would have with this issue. Can we use existing work to get a handle on the value of flexibility? We believe that the basic answer is *no*.

Boehm (1981) pioneered the use of economics to reason about software. The most influential work was on cost and schedule estimation. Boehm also developed the idea of using finance concepts to reason about software design decisions. He developed the idea of using statistical decision theory, in particular, to reason about the value of investments in risk-reducing software prototypes. However, in most early work and the best work since, economic approaches to software design appeal to the concept of *static* net present value (NPV) as a mechanism for estimating value (Boehm, 1981 and Favaro, 1996). A fundamental problem is that static NPV does not capture the value of flexibility under uncertainty.

The static NPV of an investment opportunity is computed by discounting a projected cashflow stream for time and risk. Uncertainty can be factored in by taking a probability-weighted average over a set of projections for a range of scenarios. The static NPV of a possible project is taken to be the amount by which the value of the firm would be changed if the investment were make. The associated investment decision rule is that the investment should be made if the NPV is positive, otherwise not, since making such an investment increases the expected value of the firm by the NPV amount (Brealey & Myers, 1996).

It is now widely accepted in the finance community that static NPV does not capture the value of managerial or design flexibility and that it thus tends to underestimate the value of flexible assets when flexibility is important because of prevailing uncertainty. The problem is that the NPV technique values assets as if they were passively held, having terms that cannot be changed by the owner no matter how well or poorly the future turns out. Real assets are not as passively held. To the extent that an asset is flexible, its owner can intervene actively to optimise value as the uncertain future is revealed. Averaging cashflow streams over all possible futures ignores the value of the flexibility to avoid negative outcomes and to leverage positive ones, eg, by abandoning a project if markets dwindle (Brealey and Myers, 1996; Dixit and Pindyck, 1994; Kester, 1984; Trigeorgis, 1995; Trigeorgis, 1996). The bottom line is that static NPV is generally not a good measure for valuing software because it tends to overlook one of the key sources of value in software assets: the flexibility to adapt to newly revealed and changing information, markets and circumstances.

DYNAMIC APPROACHES TO ACCOUNTING FOR THE VALUE OF FLEXIBILITY

A number of alternative valuation techniques are now available that can help to make the value of flexibility tangible. Teisberg surveys the conditions for applicability and relative merits and difficulties involved in three approaches: dynamic discounted cashflow analysis, decision analysis (utility theory) and real options (Teisberg, 1995). Each technique is appropriate in some conditions and not others; and each has its strengths and weaknesses.

In this chapter, we focus primarily on the concept of real options. The basic idea is to treat flexibility in capital investment decision-making as an option and to value it as such. An option is an asset that provides its owner the right without a symmetric obligation to make an investment decision under given terms for a period of time into the future ending with an *expiration* date. If conditions favourable to investing arise, the owner can *exercise* the option by investing the *strike price* defined by the option. A *call* option gives the right to acquire an asset of uncertain future value for the strike price. A *put* option provides the right to sell an asset at that price. An American option provides the right to exercise at any time up to expiration.

A European option provides the right to make a decision only on the expiration date. A *financial* option is an option on a financial asset, such as a share of stock. A *real* option is an option on a non-financial (real) asset, such as a parcel of land or a new product design.

The notion that options value must be considered in capital investment is now widely accepted. Speaking on the value of flexibility to defer making investment decisions until more information is available, for example, Ross concludes that,

> ... when evaluating investments, optionality is ubiquitous and unavoidable. If modern finance is to have a practical and salutary impact on investment decision-making, it is now obliged to treat all major investment decisions as option pricing problems ("Uses, Abuses and Alternatives to the Net-Present-Value Rule," 1995, p. 101, quoted by Flatto, 1996).

The contribution of this chapter is to view a software product, process or project as a portfolio of assets, some part of the value of which is in the form of real options, and to interpret some critical software design concepts as having implicit options-based rationales. Real options in software provide the designer with flexibility to respond dynamically to information as it emerges over time by making an ongoing sequence of investment decisions. Investing in flexibility is seen as buying options, and exploiting flexibility as exercising them. This view is not new in the real options literature, but it is quite unusual in software design and engineering.

Deciding when to invest in creating flexibility and then exploiting it are transformed into decisions about both when to buy options and how to exercise them to maximise the expected present value of a project or product. This view helps because it reduces the problem of reasoning about the value of flexibility to one of reasoning about the value of options; and much work has been done over several decades to develop techniques for computing options values, including the groundbreaking work of Black, Merton and Scholes, for which a recent Nobel Prize was awarded.

Our primary concern is with understanding options in software design, and only secondarily with the techniques by which values can be computed. Some work in real options assumes that options are valued using arbitrage-based techniques related to those of Black, Scholes and Merton. Arbitrage techniques can only be used when strong assumptions hold. They will not hold for some, perhaps many, software design decisions. We take a somewhat broader view of option pricing based on event trees and dynamic programming. In practice, a range of techniques will be useful in valuing options embedded in software projects, products and processes.

The rest of this chapter elaborates the idea that it is revealing to think about software design and design guidelines in options terms. Panel 1 introduces financial options concepts. In the next section we move from these concepts to those of real options. Next, we discuss one approach to valuing options in a simple but general setting based on event trees. The five sections thereafter then sketch links between options concepts and software design. In the first, we address the timing of design decisions. In the second, we derive qualitative design guidelines from a sensitivity analysis of option values to changes in key parameters. Third, we discuss an options interpretation of information hiding in modular software architectures. Fourth, we outline an options-based interpretation of the spiral model. Finally, we return briefly to the issue of timing, where we discuss the role of options in decisions about time to market under threat of competitive entry, and the engineering tradeoffs that are appropriate in such circumstances. We touch on related work, discuss practical and theoretical difficulties using an options framework to reason about software design, and finally summarise, outline future work and conclude.

BASIC REAL OPTIONS CONCEPTS

Real options theory addresses the problem that investment valuation based on static discounted cashflow tends to overlook the value of decision flexibility. The person who lacks an understanding of the role, value and characteristics of options is not only unable to justify investments in assets that would add value but where a significant part of the value is in the form of decision flexibility. Perhaps more importantly, that person lacks a critical set of intellectual tools for reasoning about strategy and value creation in an uncertain world.

The real options field opened in 1977 when the economist Myers noted that, "part of the value of a firm is accounted for by the present value of options to make further investments on possibly favourable terms" ("Determinants of Corporate Borrowing", 1977, p. 148). Myers saw that, all else equal, a firm that is in a position to exploit potentially lucrative opportunities, eg, by dint of early strategic investments, is worth more than the firm that is not. He also saw that that such assets took the form of *options*, and that options pricing techniques might be used to measure their value, thereby making them tangible.

Today the options Myers saw are called growth options (Kester, 1984, and Myers, 1977). Many other real options are now recognised. Types of real options that have been analysed include the following, Dixit and Pindyck (1994) and Trigeorgis (1996):

❏ Option to defer decisions to invest until optimal to do so; Dixit and Pindyck (1994), Madj and Pindyck (1987) and Myers (1977).
❏ Option to default early on a project that is structured in phases or abandon a project for its salvage value; Geske (1979), McDonald and Siegel (1986) and Myers and Madj (1990).
❏ Option to expand or contract production if favourable or unfavourable conditions emerge; Pindyck (1988).

BASIC FINANCIAL OPTIONS CONCEPTS

The first advantage of formulating uncertainty-related software design concepts in terms of options is that the theory provides a framework for reasoning about the value of decision flexibility under uncertainty. Understanding even the basic behaviours of options under varying conditions provides intellectual tools that we believe can help designers to reason about the value of flexibility in their products and processes. In this panel, we provide very basic background to financial options.

Underlying random process: The potential payoff of an option is largely determined at each point in time by the value, at that time, of an underlying random process. For example, the payoff of a call option on a stock is largely determined by the price of the stock, which can be modelled as a random process. If the stock price is higher than the strike price, the payoff is the price of the stock minus the strike price paid to buy it. When the underlying value is greater than the strike price, we say that the option is *in the money*. When the value is less than the strike price, the option is *out of the money*.

Non-linear payoff: A fundamental characteristic of an option is that its potential payoff is non-linear in the value of the underlying random process. Consider a stock option. As the stock price rises above the option strike price, the option payoff rises with the stock price. However, no rational investor would ever choose to exercise an out-of-the-money option, since doing so would require paying more for the stock than it sold for in the market. Thus, the potential payoff for all values of the underlying process less than the strike price is zero. The graph of the function is flat up to the strike price and then it rises directly with the asset value thereafter.

Options have value: An option has value because it gives its owner the flexibility to decide in the future whether or not to pay the strike price for an asset whose future value is not known today. An option provides a right to decide *after* finding out how things turn out. Such a right has value because owning the option not only has no downside risk (because its minimum payoff is zero), but it also provides exposure to any upside potential. Thus, for example, even an out-of-the-money option has value if it is possible that the asset value will exceed the strike price before the expiration. Thus, for example, the right to buy a stock for US$100 any time in the next three months has value, even if the current stock price is US$70, provided that there is enough variance in the stock price over time and enough time left before expiration to create the possibility that the stock price will surpass US$100 before the option expires.

Factors influencing value: The precise value of an option depends on a number of factors. First, it depends on the current value of the underlying asset, since a payoff is that value minus the strike price. Second, for the same reason it depends on the strike price. Any drop in the value of the asset would be reflected in the value of the option on that asset. That point is important for understanding the impact of dividend-like phenomena, in which the asset value drops in a sharp step. Third, the option value depends on the underlying uncertainty, with the value increasing with the variance or risk in the underlying random process. Greater variance exposes the option owner to a greater upside but leaves the payoff in the unfavourable case unchanged, making the option more valuable. Fourth, the value of an option depends on the time left to expiration. The value decreases as the time dwindles, because the option provides less flexibility. Another way to view it is that less time to go means less likelihood of a significant upside move in the asset value. Option values also depend to a degree on macro-economic factors, such as the interest rate at which money can be borrowed.

Optimal exercise policy: Although an option being out of the money means that it should not be exercised at the moment, being in the money does not necessarily mean that it should. The reason is that in addition to requiring payment of the strike price, exercising kills the option, which, in general, has additional value. Exercising is an irreversible decision that incurs as a cost the strike plus the additional opportunity cost of not being able to wait any longer to decide whether to invest. It is worthwhile to exercise an option only if the asset obtained is worth at least the strike price plus the option value (Dixit and Pindyck, 1994). It can be optimal to hold rather than exercise an option, even one that's in the money.

The role of dividends: The best time to exercise an option is not always obvious. Options theory addresses optimal policies for timing these investment decisions. A complicating factor is that of dividend payments. A dividend payment on a stock is a cash distribution of part of the asset value represented by the stock. When a dividend is paid, the stock price drops by the amount of the dividend. For a call option on an asset that is not subject to dividend payments, it is known that it is best to wait as long as possible – until just before expiration – to decide whether or not to invest (Dixit and Pindyck, 1994; Hull, 1993). Nothing is lost by waiting, and valuable information might be gained. However, if the asset is subject to dividends, then early exercise is sometimes justified. The reason is that dividends go to the asset owner; holding an option alone forgoes the benefits of owing the asset. For such assets, there is an opportunity cost not only to investing early, but also to waiting. With real options, any discrete drop in the asset value can be thought of as a dividend. A competitor's entry into a market, grabbing a part of it, is an example. Options thinking provides a way to reason about timing in the face of countervailing incentives to hurry or delay investment decisions (Dixit and Pindyck, 1994).

❑ Option to switch materials used in a product, or switch to producing another product as supply and demand conditions change; Kulatilaka, 1993.

❑ Compound options, or options on options, which can be used to model phased investments, in which investing in one phase buys an option to invest in the next; Triantis and Hodder, 1990.

❑ Option to pick one of several risky assets; Stulz, 1982.

❑ Interactions among real options have also been explored; Brennan and Schwartz, 1985; Trigeorgis, 1993.

To help make the real option idea more concrete, we consider a simplified version of an example from the literature involving the flexibility to switch the materials used in an electricity generating plant. Suppose a manager has to decide between investing in a less expensive but inflexible power plant that burns only oil, or a more expensive one that has the flexibility to switch between oil and coal (Kulatilaka, 1993). The price of coal is stable, but the future price of oil is uncertain. Is it worthwhile to pay more for flexibility?

Clearly there is a price at which the flexible plant is too costly, despite the risk of a price rise in oil. The value-maximising decision is to invest in the inflexible plant. On the other hand, flexibility has value today because it confers the ability to save future expenses contingent on a more or less probable price rise. So the manager should be willing to pay somewhat more for the flexible plant. How much more? What are the relevant factors that must be considered in making the decision? And on what data can the decision be based?

The manager should assess the expected NPV of each of the two choices and select the better one, factoring in the cost and value of the option created by the flexibility to change fuels for a defined switching cost. The expected value V_I of the inflexible plant is its expected benefits B_I minus its expected costs C_I adjusted for time and risk: $V_I = B_I - C_I$. For the flexible plant the value is its benefits B_F plus the value of the option O_F to switch to coal should future oil prices be unfavourable, minus its costs: $V_F = B_F + O_F - C_F$. The best choice is the flexible plant if $V_F > V_I$. Assuming that the benefits are the same when the two plants burn oil, ie, $B_F = B_I$, then we find that the flexible plant is best when the value option exceeds its cost, $O_F > C_F - C_I$. The flexible plant is best when the option is worth more than its cost.

That is pretty simple. The difficulty is in evaluating O_F. What is flexibility worth? What factors influence its value and how are they related? How do you reason properly quantitatively, or even just in a rigorous qualitative way, about the value of flexibility?

One must clearly give up static NPV as a valuation measure and use a dynamic technique, such as decision analysis, dynamic NPV, or options pricing. The first insight behind real options theory is that flexibility in real assets is analogous to a financial option, such as a call option on a stock, in that it gives the decision-maker the right, without a corresponding obligation, to make an investment decision in the future. The second insight was that techniques related to those for pricing financial options might be used to estimate real options values quantitatively.

In the preceding example, the owner of the flexible plant has an option to pay a certain amount (a strike price) to reconfigure the plant from oil to coal. In return, the manager acquires the cashflow stream comprising the cost savings accrued by the decision to switch. When the price of oil is high, that asset is valuable. Even if the price of oil is low today, there is a risk that it will go higher, so the right to claim the cost savings in that case has value. The flexible plant thus comprises a portfolio of valuable assets including an embedded option. If the price of oil goes high enough, then it will be worthwhile to exercise the option. The dynamic nature of decision-making becomes clear. At first the decision-maker has an option to buy an option, then, having bought it, to exercise it.

Having formulated the flexibility as an options problem, a major challenge is to find an appropriate technique for pricing the option, so that the first decision (whether to buy it or not at a given price) can be made rationally. One starting point is the Black–Scholes equations (Black and Scholes, 1973), the seminal result in the field. The approach is based on the concept of arbitrage. Arbitrage-based techniques require knowledge of the current value of the asset in question, and on the option on that asset being *in the span of the market*. This phrase means that market-traded, and thus also market-priced assets, are available that could, in principle, be assembled into a portfolio that tracks the option payoff closely as the underlying random process evolves. Because the portfolio payoff tracks that of the option, the market should value both assets equally. The market has already priced the portfolio; so a market-calibrated option price is obtained. The key benefit of such techniques is that market-based valuations of real options are derived without the subjective probability estimates required in decision analysis (Amram and Kulatilaka, 1999).

The likelihood that oil prices will rise, for example, has already been "calculated" by the information-integrating operations of the market, and is reflected in the prices of oil futures for some period into the future. Moreover, there is a considerable body of historical data for calibrating models of the random process of oil prices. The availability of such data provides an empirical basis for estimating the parameters of options pricing formulas.

If the conditions for using arbitrage-based techniques (in particular, spanning) do not hold, then other methods for estimating values must be used: dynamic programming, for example (Dixit and Pindyck, 1994). Although there are considerable data on movements in the price of oil over time, there might be few or no market data on which to base estimates of the likelihood that a particular well will turn out dry. So, if one has an option on that risky asset, how should it be valued?

Some real options researchers define the real options approach as requiring arbitrage-based pricing, and would assert that an approach that uses anything other than market data is essentially decision analysis or some other technique. Others see that option-pricing techniques can be used even if spanning conditions do not hold, albeit with the need to use subjective estimates of certain parameters. This approach loses the benefit of objective, market-based valuations, but many of the benefits of "options thinking" (to use Amram's phrase) nevertheless are preserved.

In our view, the critical step is to begin to think in terms of options: to view projects and products as portfolios of assets that can be designed to include valuable options, and then to manage such portfolios dynamically as uncertainties are resolved and new information is acquired over time. The next step is to decide how to model different kinds of options for valuation, and to understand how much confidence can be placed in the reliability of valuations, based on the valuation approach used and the adequacy of any empirical data used for setting the model parameters.

Implicit in our view is the idea that even qualitative reasoning with options thinking is important. The intellectual framework is most critical, because it provides a designer with a sound structure for reasoning about decisions that have to be made anyway. Moreover, back-of-the-envelope calculations based on a powerful model can have real value. For example, a quantitative model permits a systematic analysis of the sensitivity of computed value to variations in subjective assumptions or parameter values estimated from empirical data.

FORMALISING UNCERTAINTY, OPTIONS AND VALUATION

In this section we discuss one approach to reasoning about option values. Although some important options in software design will satisfy the required conditions for the use of arbitrage-based pricing techniques, others will not. There will be options on risky assets for which the risks have not been priced directly or indirectly by the market. In other cases, market assessments of the risks will be aggregated in the market prices of assets exposed to several risks, sometimes making it impossible to separate out the data on the specific risk at issue. Such options are essentially not in the span of the market and so cannot be priced using arbitrage-based techniques. Therefore, we present an account of option pricing that does not depend on spanning conditions or arbitrage, but which can be adapted to exploit market data if they are available.

In particular, in this section, we describe basic concepts in options theory, with a focus on the interplay between the value of an option and the optimal exercise strategy. First we define the mathematical notions and notation that we use. Then we show formally how option pricing is related to optimal stopping times. For more basic information on options the reader is referred to any of several excellent texts, including Hull (1993) or Luenberger (1998). Merton (1990) provides an advanced treatment.

Modelling uncertainty with event trees

Uncertainty and the value of flexibility in the face of uncertainty are at the heart of both software design and finance. Options pricing and related techniques are financial applications of general mathematical techniques used to support optimal decision-making under uncertainty. There are both discrete- and continuous-time formulations of the key issues. In this chapter, we employ a very simple, discrete-time formulation. Our goal is to get at the key concepts, not to present a complete mathematical theory.

We model uncertainty about the future value of a single parameter (random variable) with a discrete event tree of finite depth N, with N the maximum number of future time steps that we wish to model (eg, months, years, etc). The root node, at depth 0, represents the present time. The set of nodes at depth k represent possible states of the world at time k. Given a depth k node v, the children of v are the possible next states at time k + 1, given that the state at time k is v. If a node w is a descendant of v, we write $v \rightarrow w$.

For k = 0, 1, ..., N, a random variable X is a mapping (or function) that associates with each node v, a real number X(v). A random process is a sequence of random variables $\{X_k\}_{k=0}^{N}$, (often referred to briefly as the "process X_k") where for each k, $X_k(v)$ has non-zero values only for nodes at depth k. When we want to refer to the value of a random process X_k at a specific node v, we will often drop the subscript and just write X(v). We define the special random variable $\delta(v)$ to be the depth of v.

As an example, consider tossing a fair coin N times. For each toss there are two outcomes, each equally likely. We represent the uncertainty in outcomes by a simple event tree, called the binomial tree. Each non-leaf node has two children. Each of the 2^N paths represents a sequence of coin-toss outcomes. On any path, for k = 1, ..., N, the kth branch is an up-branch if the kth coin-toss lands heads (H), and it is a down-branch if it lands tails (T).

To each branch in an event tree, we associate a probability. The sum of the probabilities of the branches emanating from a node is 1. In the example above, the probability of each branch is 0.5. For any node v, the probability that state v occurs, denoted $\mathbf{P}(v)$, is the product of the probabilities of the branches from the root node to v. If a node v has a branch to node w, we denote its probability by $\mathbf{P}(w \mid v)$. Clearly,

$$\mathbf{P}(w|v) = \mathbf{P}(w)/\mathbf{P}(v)$$

The expectation of a random variable X is the probability-weighted sum of possible outcomes, denoted by $\mathbf{E}(X)$, and defined precisely as

$$E(X) = \sum_v X(v)\mathbf{P}(v) \tag{1}$$

The concept of conditional expectation is important. Imagine we are in some state at time k, eg, at depth k node v. Then the conditional expectation of a random variable X, given that we are at v, is denoted by $E(X \mid v)$, and is defined as

$$E(X|v) = \sum_{w:v \to w} X(w) \frac{P(w)}{P(v)} = \sum_{w:v \to w} X(w)P(w|v) \tag{2}$$

This is just a form of the familiar Baye's rule. Clearly this conditional expectation will in general be different from EX, and will depend on the given depth k node v. For instance in the coin-toss tree above, suppose the random variable H_k is the number of heads up to time k, on the path to a specific node in the tree. Then if v is at depth k and $m \geq k$, the conditional expectation $E(H_m \mid v)$ will be higher if the path to v consists of more heads.

Decision rules

We will use decision rules in this chapter to model the timing of various investment decisions. For instance we might want to decide *when* (ie, at which nodes in the tree) and *how much* to invest in building a software prototype. In general let us assume that at any node we are allowed c possible levels of investment, numbered 1, 2, ..., c. We consider level 0 to represent no investment. A decision rule τ with respect to an event tree T is a mapping from the set of nodes of T to the set $\{0, 1, ..., c\}$, with the restriction that on any path of the tree, there is at most one node v with a non-zero value of $\tau(v)$. In other words, a decision rule specifies a rule that we can follow as the state of the world changes along the tree. Whenever we are in a state v for which $\tau(v) \neq 0$, we invest at level $\tau(v)$. In the coin-toss binomial tree, an example of a decision-rule would be: "invest at level 1 when the coin has landed heads three times", or more formally: $\tau(v) = 1$ if $H(v) = 3$, and $\tau(v) = 0$ otherwise. Those familiar with stochastic processes will recognise that decision rules are closely related to *stopping times*.

American call options

One of the simplest kinds of option is an American call option. As we discussed earlier, an American call option on an asset, say a share of stock, is a contract that gives the holder of the contract the right, but not the obligation, to buy a share of the stock at a predetermined price called the strike price, which we will call L, on or before a certain expiration date, T time units in the future. In other words, the option gives its holder the flexibility to decide whether or not to exercise the contract, ie, buy a share of stock for L after uncertainty about its future value has been resolved. Such flexibility has value. When the option is exercised or if it expires without being exercised, it ceases to exist. Exercising an option is thus an irreversible decision. Conversely, we can think about discretionary but irreversible investments as options.

We model opportunities to make discretionary but irreversible investments in real assets as call options. There are other dimensions of flexibility that are modelled by other kinds of options. Although our approach includes the range of options, we will focus primarily on call options in this chapter.

Uncertainty and payoff

To describe an American call option formally, we need a model of the underlying uncertainty. It is typical to model the price of a stock as a depth-N event tree, with N being the time to expiration, and $\{S_k\}$ a random process modelling the uncertain stock price.

Given such a model, we can reason about when, if ever, to exercise an option. It makes no sense to exercise at any node v where the value of the asset is no more than the strike price $S(v) \leq L$. However, if $S(v) > L$, the option holder can but is not obliged to exercise by investing L to obtain the asset. In the case of a share of stock, the holder could then immediately sell the asset in the market for $S(v)$ making a profit of $S(v) - L$. The profit that can be realised by exercising the American call option at time k is thus $\max(S(v) - L, 0)$, which we refer to as the payoff $G(v)$. It is standard to denote $\max\{x, 0\}$ by x^+, so we can write the payoff as the random variable

$$G_k = (S_k - L)^+ \tag{3}$$

In other words, for any node v, the payoff $G(v) = S(v) - L^+$.

Optimal exercise strategy

What is the best strategy for deciding whether to exercise an American call option held at time k? An exercise strategy can be described by a decision rule τ that maps each node to the set $\{0, 1\}$. If we are in state v, we exercise if and only if $\tau(v) = 1$. An example of an exercise strategy is "exercise when the stock price reaches a threshold λ or when the expiration date is reached", which is formalised by the decision rule τ, where $\tau(v) = 1$ if $S(v) \geq \lambda$ or the depth $\delta(v)$ of the node v is N, and $\tau(v) = 0$ otherwise.

In reasoning about payoffs, it is necessary to account for the time value of money: a dollar tomorrow is worth less than one today. To discount future cashflows to the present time, we have to assume that money can be borrowed or lent at a risk-free interest rate of r. Thus a dollar lent or borrowed at time k is worth $R = 1 + r$ dollars at time $k + 1$. It is common to refer to R as a discount factor since a dollar at time k, discounted to the present time (ie, time 0) is worth $1/R^k$.

The optimal exercise strategy is the strategy with the highest expected payoff. At a depth k node v the expected value of a strategy τ discounted to time k is denoted V_k^τ. It is computed as follows. At any node w, a descendant of v, if the option is exercised (ie, $\tau(w) = 1$), the payoff is $G(w) = (S(w) - L)^+$, and if it is not exercised the payoff is 0. Thus in general at any node w we can write the payoff as $G(w)\tau(w)$, which is worth $G(w)\tau(w)R^{k-\delta(w)}$ at time k. Therefore the expected value of the strategy τ, discounted to time k, given that we are at a node v, is

$$V_k^\tau(v) = E(G\tau R^{k-\delta}|v) \tag{4}$$

The rational option holder wants to use the strategy τ that maximises this expectation. We denote this maximum by the random variable V_k:

$$V_k(v) = \max_\tau V_k^\tau(v) \tag{5}$$

V_k is the greatest expected present value at time k realisable over all possible exercise strategies. We take the option value at time k to be precisely V_k. The reasons for this definition will become clear shortly. The point is that we now have a technique for valuing options provided that assets are modelled in this event tree framework.

Since immediate exercise is a valid strategy at any time, the option value $V(v)$ must be at least as large as $(S(v) - L)^+$. A situation in which immediate exercise is not optimal is one in which $(S(v) - L)^+ < V(v)$. In this case, some other strategy will yield a strictly greater expected present value of payoff, under our assumed asset model, so it is beneficial not to exercise but to wait. On the other hand, if the payoff now is equal to the best expected payoff, $(S(v) - L)^+ = V(v)$, nothing is gained by waiting, and it is optimal to exercise immediately. Indeed it can be shown rigorously that the decision rule τ that achieves the maximum in equation (5) above is given by

$$\tau(v) = \begin{cases} 1 & \text{if } (S(v) - L)^+ = V(v) \text{ or } \delta(v) = N \\ 0 & \text{otherwise} \end{cases} \tag{6}$$

We can think of the strike price L as the cost of an asset obtained by exercising the option, since this is the price one must pay to obtain the asset. Similarly, S_k is the benefit from exercising at time k, since this is the price one could obtain by selling the asset, if obtained. It is useful to view the option value V_k as representing the value of the right to choose whether or not to invest. It is often the case that this right is worth more than the payoff that could be obtained by exercising immediately. That is obviously true if the option with time remaining to expiration is out-of-the-money. One would decline to exercise immediately, for a payoff of zero; yet the option would still have value, because it would provide the potential for a future positive payoff contingent on a rise in value of the asset. The statement also can be true if the payoff that one can obtain by exercising immediately is small in relation to the value of the option to wait for a bigger payoff.

When an option is exercised, the option is killed and the flexibility created by the right to decide is lost. An opportunity cost is incurred in addition to the strike price. V_k, the option value, is that opportunity cost. From the discussion above, the optimal strategy is to exercise when $(S_k - L)^+ = V_k$: *Exercise only when the benefit* S_k *equals the direct cost* L *plus the opportunity cost* V_k. This is the viewpoint most useful in this chapter.

In terms of real options and software design, this analysis suggests that if there is some uncertainty about the future, is might not be optimal to invest in an opportunity (eg, to port a computer program to a new platform or to restructure a legacy system) even if doing so would yield a small expected payoff. Delaying preserves a valuable option to make the decision in the future when the expected payoff might be greater.

Dynamic programming algorithm for valuing options

In our formulation, with its finite time horizon, we can compute V_k for all k by a *dynamic programming* procedure (Corman, Leiserson and Rivest, 1990). First observe that $V_N = (S_N - L)^+$. This is clear both from equation (5) and from observing that, since the option expires at time N, there can be no advantage in waiting to decide whether or not to invest. Stepping backward in time in the decision tree, we compute $V_k(v)$ at any depth k node v by

$$V_k(v) = \max\{(S_k(v) - L)^+, \mathbf{E}(V_{k+1}|v)/R\} \qquad (7)$$

In other words, the option value $V_k(v)$ at a depth k node v is the maximum of the immediate payoff $(S_k(v) - L)^+$ and the expected present value of the option value one time step ahead given that we are at v. It can be shown that this backward-recursive formula for V_k and equation (5) are equivalent, regardless of the specific process that the stock price S_k follows.

OPTIONS IN TIMING SOFTWARE DESIGN INVESTMENTS

We have introduced the idea of applying options-based thinking to software design decision-making, and have presented a simple framework for modelling uncertainty and valuing options. The rest of this chapter is concerned with making concrete, through several examples, the link from real options concepts to some key issues in software design. The examples are highly idealised, so that we can focus on the essential concepts. Options models of actual software design decisions are likely to be much more complicated.

The decision to restructure a legacy system

We first present an example that illustrates how real options concepts might be used to reason about when to reorganise a software system to reduce the costs of enhancing and maintaining it. A central objective of the software designer is to select a modular structure for the system that makes it easy to understand and to change over time as corrections are needed and requirements evolve. The choice of modular structure, or architecture, is the key mechanism for achieving ease of understanding and evolution. The designer will try to modularise a system to separate conceptually independent parts so that they can be understood independently, and to ensure that potential changes will have a module-local (and thus inexpensive) impact on the system, rather than a system-wide (and thus costly) impact.

A major problem in software design is that designers cannot always anticipate how a system will have to change. Thus a modular structure that makes one set of potential changes easy by localising their impact might not localise the impacts of changes that turn out to be needed in practice. Such a change incurs a larger up-front cost relative to the functional increment achieved than a change that is facilitated by the existing design structure.

The additional up-front cost of such a change is, however, just the beginning of a long-term cost stream. Making a change that does not fit well into the existing design structure often ends up compromising that structure to some extent. Two modules that previously could be understood independently might end up more tightly coupled, for example, as a result of the need to incorporate into both, different but interconnected aspects of an unexpected enhancement. Over time, the accumulation of such changes lead to ever-increasing disorder in the structure of the system, and thus ever-increasing costs to achieve given increments in function. At some point, a restructuring of the system to "clean up" its degraded modular structure might be the economical choice (Belady & Lehman, 1976).

The decision about when to restructure a system is one that many designers face. It is often a very costly prospect. Much of the many tens of billions of dollars being spent on software in the telecommunications sector each year, for example, is spent on restructuring legacy systems for a new deregulated, network-centric environment.

Not only are such investments costly. They are often also risky in the sense that the payoffs are uncertain, most likely in multiple dimensions. The ability to enter a new market successfully with a restructured system is not necessarily given. Similarly, if the payoff is simply in the form of a reduced cost to make future changes, the stream of changes that will be needed might not be certain. To illustrate options reasoning about these kinds of issues, we take uncertainty over future changes as an example.

Suppose that restructuring will cost US$1,600.[1] The benefit, if any, will come in the form of reduced future costs. If the benefits were certain, the decision would be easy: the designer would compare the present value of the future benefits, represented as a cashflow stream, against the present value of the cost of US$1,600.

The issue is more complex when the payoff depends on uncertain future conditions. Suppose that the demand for future changes is uncertain. For one reason or another, the system will have to be changed either often or hardly at all. Perhaps the uncertain success of a partial replacement system in development would reduce the need to change the existing system.

As a simplification, let us assume that there are two possible futures: one in which many changes are needed, which is thus favourable to an investment in restructuring; and an unfavourable future, in which so few changes are required that it would have been better not to pay to restructure. We represent the possible payoffs as cashflows. Suppose that the payoff in the favourable scenario is 3,300, and just 1,100 otherwise.

The nature of the uncertainty

We model the uncertainty with a one-level event tree, rooted at the present, with the payoff of 1,100 at one leaf and 3,300 at the other. Next, we assign probabilities to each branch. Suppose that at present it is our expert judgement that each outcome has a probability of occurring of 0.5. Finally, we account for the depreciation in the value of money over time by assuming a discount factor of 1.1 per time period – a 10% discount rate. Thus, for example, a cashflow of US$1,100 one period from now is worth US$1,000 today.

In this example we are using subjective estimates rather than market data based on an arbitrage construction to set the probability parameters of the event tree. Some real options theorists would state that we have moved from a real-options-based approach to one more resembling decision analysis. Our concern is first to recognise the options in any given situation and thus the need to use techniques other than static NPV to reason about value. Our second concern is to select the best valuation technique for the given situation. Satisfaction of spanning conditions that permit the use of market-based data in a no-arbitrage construction rather than subjective probability estimates is an enormous advantage, but, as we have noted, in some cases it won't be possible.

In this chapter, we present the concepts in a setting that does not assume that spanning conditions hold. The same kinds of event trees and dynamic programming algorithms can be used for both arbitrage and non-arbitrage approaches. The interpretations of the probabilities and discount rates of the formulations are vastly different in the two cases, with synthetic *probability-like* numbers derived from market data and the risk-free discount rate being used for the arbitrage approach. Amram (1999) provides an excellent introduction. In this work, we must be satisfied to present the outline of a method in a setting based on subjective estimates. A comprehensive approach to software design investment decision-making under uncertainty would have to incorporate multiple valuation techniques, some requiring subjective data, with others based on market data, when available.

Static net present value

The central point is that the traditional static NPV decision strategy does not produce an investment that is optimal for expected value added. Recall that the traditional rule states that the investment should be made if the static NPV is positive. The decision under this rule is to restructure immediately, because the static NPV of the investment is 400 – for a present value added of 400 – as shown in the following computation.

$$NPV = 0.5(-1,600 + 1,100/1.1) + 0.5(-1,600 + 3,300/1.1) = 400$$

Suppose, however, that the designer can wait to invest until more is known about how much the requirements will have to change (eg, whether the related project succeeds). The flexibility to wait is tangibly valuable. The reason is that investing now risks a loss of $-1,600 + 1,100/1.1 = -600$ should the unfavourable scenario emerge (the related project succeeds and fewer changes are needed). Waiting allows the designer to invest only in the favourable scenario for a profit of $-1,600/1.1 + 3,300/1.1 = 1546$. Given that the likelihood of a favourable outcome is estimated at 0.5, the expected value of the dynamic strategy $(0.5)(3,300/1.1 - 1,600/1.1) = 773$, is significantly greater than that of investing today. It's clearly better to wait.

Making the option explicit

Real options thinking suggests that the software designer should view products and projects as portfolios of assets that include valuable options, that options can have significant value, and that their value should be factored into decision-making. To make the analogy between the restructuring decision and options clear, we recast our analysis into an options formalism.

We formulate the cost to restructure as the strike price $L = 1,600$ of an American call option on the expected benefits. This asset is worth S_t, the expected value of the profit stream from restructuring at time t. S_t is a random variable. Letting subscripts denote time and discounting to the present, S_1 is either $3,300/1.1 = 3,000$ or $1,100/1.1 = 1,000$, each with probability $p = 0.5$, and so $S_0 = 0.5 * (1,100/1.1) + 0.5 * (3,300/1.1) = 2,000$.

Net of cost, the payoff of exercising now is $S_0 - L = 400$. A month from now it is $\max(S_1 - L, 0)$, since the option is not exercised in the unfavourable future. With even odds this is either $3,300/1.1 - 1,600/1.1 = 1,546$, or 0, for an expectation of 773. Recall that the value V_t of an option at any time t is the expected present value of future payoffs under the optimal exercise strategy. In our example, all uncertainty is resolved in the first period, so there are only two strategies: exercise now or in the next period. The value V_0 of our option is thus 773, since this is the expected payoff from the best exercise strategy of the two available at time $t = 0$.

The software designer is in the position of holding an option to invest, and of having to manage that option carefully. A design decision to commit to restructuring must be viewed as a decision to exercise that option. Restructuring today kills the option, which is worth 773, for an expected value added of only 400. Despite the apparent profitability of investing today, it is clearly suboptimal for expected value added to the firm.

Incorporating cashflow streams

In practice, restructuring a system might yield a benefit (savings) each time a change is made. The benefit is thus a cashflow *stream*. Extending the model and analysis to include cashflow streams in multiple time periods is straightforward. The traditional static NPV is computed as the expected present value S_0 discounted to time 0 of the stream of profits B_n, $n \geq 0$ from the investment, with the cashflow in each period discounted in the standard fashion at a rate compounded by the number of periods:

$$S_0 = \sum_{n=0}^{\infty} EB_n / R^n \qquad (8)$$

As we noted above, even if the NPV is positive, it might be better to wait to find how the underlying uncertainty is resolved. The optimal approach is to decide at any time k whether the value of expected profits discounted to time k (ie, S_k) is sufficiently above the direct cost L to offset the additional cost of losing the option. Thus a designer must compare the value of investing now against that of investing at *all* future times. The question is not just whether to invest, but when, if ever.

At any time k, the designer has the right but not the obligation to invest L (the strike price) to receive a stream of profits (the savings) with an expected present value S_k (the asset price). The random variable S_k is the expected benefit of restructuring at time k, ie, the value of the future profit stream resulting from investing at time k discounted to time k.

We computed S_0 above. The payoff from exercising at time 0 is $G_0 = (S_0 - L)^+$, since one would not invest if $S_0 < L$. This is the same equation (3) for the payoff from an American call option on a stock at time 0. S_0 is analogous to the stock price at time 0, hence our choice of notation.

How do we generalise the equation (8) for S_0 to an arbitrary node v in the tree? To compute the benefit $S(v)$ at node v, we proceed as in equation (8), except that we discount the profits to time corresponding to the depth of node v rather than time 0, and we replace the expectation by the conditional expectation. Finally, we only perform the summation from $\delta(v)$ to ∞. Recall that $\delta(v)$ denotes the depth of node v which also corresponds to the time associated with node v. So $S(v)$ is given by the following expression:

$$S(v) = \sum_{w:v \to w} E[B(w)R^{\delta(v) - \delta(w)}|v] \qquad (9)$$

The expected benefit of restructuring at node v is then

$$G(v) = (S(v) - L)^+ \qquad (10)$$

which is the same as equation (3) for the payoff from a call option. The value V_k of this option represents the value of the investment opportunity, which would be lost if we were to exercise at time k. As described above, V_k can be computed for any k using dynamic programming. Also, as mentioned, it is optimal to exercise when the value V_k equals or exceeds the payoff G_k. Thus it is optimal to restructure when $S_k - L \geq V_k$, or $S_k \geq L + V_k$.

Informally, we should exercise our option to restructure when the benefit S_k is at least as much as the sum of the direct cost L and the opportunity cost V_k. What we end up with is an option-based rule for committing to design decisions under uncertainty:

If at any time k, S_k, *the expected value of future profits discounted to time* k *is at least* V_k *more than the direct costs,* L, *then commit to the design decision, otherwise do not.*

Trading evolvability for market share and an option to restructure

We consider another simplified example involving the design of internet agents (Maes, 1994; Mitchell, Caruana, Freitag and McDermott, 1994; Sycara, Decker, Pannu and Williamson, 1996). Agents are specialised autonomous software entities that provide services to people, such as finding inexpensive airline tickets or filtering news. It often makes sense for one agent to use another to accomplish its task. Indeed, the dynamic composition of such service-providing agents executing in the internet is an emerging model for future software systems. We imagine a system of agents in which each agent has a capability, and in which the capabilities of available agents are stored in some kind of capability directory. For the sake of being concrete, consider a financial portfolio management agent that might want to find another agent to get company reports. The agent-based system is expected to evolve primarily by the addition of new agents over time. The designer is considering two designs:

Distributed directory (D). A copy of the directory is wired into the code of each agent. An agent that wants to find another agent consults its local directory at essentially zero cost. This approach does not follow the information hiding design criterion in that a likely kind of change (adding an agent) will have a costly system-wide impact. Whenever an agent is added to the system, the directory code in each agent has to be changed. We denote the total cost of the changes required when an agent is added at time n by the random variable D_n.

Centralised directory (C). There is a *yellow pages* agent that implements the capability directory. All other agents access directory information through an interface with this agent. We let C denote the total cost of initially hard-coding the centralised directory and its associated interfaces. When a new agent is created, only the yellow-page agent needs to be changed. Also, an agent requiring a capability needs to query the yellow-page agent. We let the random variable C_n denote the total query and update costs at time n.

Which approach should the software engineer choose? If starting from scratch, as in a start-up company, there is no flexibility to delay a decision. The decision must be made now. The trade-off might be increased design and runtime costs for a centralised design that reduces future maintenance costs.

Because there is no flexibility to wait, a static NPV valuation approach might be appropriate. We assume that the costs common to both approaches are 0. Thus, the only relevant costs are C and C_n for choice C, and D_n for choice D. We view the problem as one of deciding whether or not to use choice C, and express the costs and benefits relative to choice D. There are two quantities of interest when choice C is compared with D: the direct cost of choice C, ie, the immediate cost of implementing it, which is L = C; and the monthly profit of choice C relative to D in month n for $n \geq 0$: $B_n = D_n - C_n$.

We view the design problem as an investment decision problem: Should L dollars be invested in choice C? Let us assume a discount factor R. Consider the traditional NPV approach. We first compute the expected present value S_0 (discounted to time 0) of the stream of profits B_n, $n \geq 0$ from the investment:

$$S_0 = \sum_{n=0}^{\infty} EB_n / R^n \tag{11}$$

which we refer to as the expected benefit of choice C relative to D at time 0. The NPV of the investment at time 0 is

$$NPV = S_0 - L = S_0 - C$$

The traditional NPV rule states that if the NPV is positive, then the investment should be made, otherwise not. When there is no flexibility, the NPV rule is correct. Thus a decision rule that might be used when there is no design to start with is the following:

If the expected present value of the future profits S_0 that would flow from choice C exceeds the direct cost C of implementing it, then go ahead and implement choice C, otherwise implement choice D.

However, the analysis might not be that easy. If there is competition, the optimal strategy might be to invest in a capability that can be brought to market as quickly as possible. This would mitigate the threat that the market share meant to be acquired by the investment will disappear as the result of entry by a competitor. The best strategy might be to get to market quickly, and, if successful, to make a follow-on investment in restructuring to keep long-term costs manageable and to create additional value through greater design flexibility.

If for certain technical reasons the centralised design is harder and will take longer to get running initially, the value-maximising choice might be to sacrifice a design with long-term maintenance benefits for a shot at market share, augmented with a plan for a possible second phase beginning with a restructuring for long-term success. This is an example of a situation in which a heuristic, such as *always use information hiding design techniques*, might conceivably not be valid. Thus it is an example of where options thinking can inform design strategy.

In practice, we suspect that some start-ups pursue such a strategy initially, but either lack a plan for a follow-on phase for restructuring, or fail to execute such a phase. In these cases, initial successes can run into difficulties in the longer term because their software designs cannot sustain long-term correction and enhancement effectively.

Of course, the decision to invest in that second phase is one that can be delayed. So when, if ever, should it be made? Suppose the existing system has the distributed structure (D), and the designer is deciding whether or not to invest in restructuring to switch to choice C. In addition to the cost C of creating the yellow-pages agent, there might be a cost C^s to scrap the distributed design. Each agent must be changed so that it queries the yellow pages instead of its own local directory. Thus the direct cost of choice C is $L = C + C^s$. It is tempting to propose the following strategy (compare it with the previous decision rule):

If the expected present value of future profits S_0 that would flow from restructuring exceeds the direct cost of restructuring, L, then go ahead and restructure, otherwise do not.

By now we recognise the flaw in this analysis: the designer has the option to wait in hopes of making a better decision in the future. In addition to the direct cost L, there is an opportunity cost that represents the loss of the value of flexibility. At any time k, the value of the expected profit discounted to time k (ie, S_k) must be sufficiently more than the direct cost L to justify switching. The designer should compare the value of investing now (at time 0) versus investing at *all* possible future times.

Numerical calculations

We make the analysis of this decision concrete with a numerical example. Suppose the cost C to restructure is 9,000, and the cost C^s of scrapping the distributed directory structure is 1,000. Thus the total direct cost L of restructuring is $C + C^s = 10,000$.

For simplicity, we assume that building the yellow-page agent and scrapping the distributed directories takes 0 time. Each time step in our model represents 1 month. Time n represents the beginning of the nth month, for n = 0, 1, 2, ... We imagine that during the current month, or month 0, several new agents will be created, and that the associated updating cost under the distributed approach is $D_0 = 2{,}000$. We assume that the total query/update cost under the centralised approach is $C_n = 500$ at all time n. Thus if we move to a centralised directory at the beginning of month 0, the monthly profit for month 0 would be

$$B_0 = D_0 - C_0 = 2000 - 500 = 1500$$

Suppose that if our designer's system beats the competition (probability $p = 0.5$) then several new agents will be added each month, starting in month 1. This outcome is favourable for approach C and we will therefore superscript variables under this scenario with the letter f. Suppose that if this event occurs the total maintenance cost under approach D, is $D_n^f = 3{,}000$ for all $n \geq 1$. On the other hand, if the technology does not achieve dominance in the marketplace, few agents will be created, a situation unfavourable for approach C: the cost to switch to a centralised directory will not be paid back by the cost-savings of the information hiding restructuring. Thus, we superscript variables in this scenario by the letter u, for *unfavourable*. We suppose that the corresponding update cost under choice D in this case is much lower, at $D_n^u = 400$ for all $n \geq 1$.

Thus from month 1 onward, the monthly profit from restructuring for information hiding would be

$$B_n^f = D_n^f - C_n = 3000 - 500 = 2500, \quad n \geq 1$$

in the favourable scenario, and

$$B_n^u = D_n^u - C_n = 400 - 500 = -100, \quad n \geq 1$$

in the unfavourable scenario, each case occurring with probability 0.5. Therefore, for $n \geq 1$,

$$EB_n = EB_1 = pB_1^f + (1-p)B_1^u$$
$$= 0.5(2500 - 100) = 1200$$

Our model is represented by the event tree in Figure 1. There are just two possible paths in this event tree, which we denote by ω_f (favourable) and ω_u (unfavourable). Note that for $k \geq 1$ and $n \geq k$, on the favourable path,

$$E(B_n | \omega_f) = B_n^f = B_1^f = 2500$$

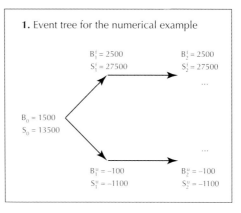

1. Event tree for the numerical example

$B_1^f = 2500$
$S_1^f = 27500$

$B_2^f = 2500$
$S_2^f = 27500$

$B_0 = 1500$
$S_0 = 13500$

$B_1^u = -100$
$S_1^u = -1100$

$B_2^u = -100$
$S_2^u = -1100$

and on the unfavourable path,

$$E(B_n | \omega_u) = B_n^u = B_1^u = -100$$

Assuming a monthly discount factor of $R = 1.1$, we calculate the benefit of switching at time k. For $k = 0$, we use equation (8) to compute

$$
\begin{aligned}
S_0 &= \sum_{n=0}^{\infty} E(B_n)/R^n \\
&= B_0 + \sum_{n=1}^{\infty} E(B_1)/R^n \\
&= B_0 + E(B_1)/(R - 1) \\
&= 1500 + 1200/0.1 \\
&= 1500 + 12000 = 13500
\end{aligned}
\tag{12}
$$

For $k = 1$, from equation (9), the benefit from switching at time k in the favourable scenario (or on the favourable path) is

$$
\begin{aligned}
S_k^f &= \sum_{n=k}^{\infty} E(B_n | \omega_f) R^{k-n} \\
&= \sum_{n=k}^{\infty} B_1^f R^{k-n} \tag{13} \\
&= R \sum_{n=0}^{\infty} B_1^f / R^n \tag{14} \\
&= B_1^f \frac{R}{R-1} \tag{15} \\
&= 2500(1.1)/0.1 = 27500
\end{aligned}
$$

which is bigger than the direct cost $L = 10{,}000$. Thus in the favourable scenario the expected benefit of switching is always greater than the cost. Similarly,

$$S_k^u = B_1^u \frac{R}{R-1} = -100(1.1)/0.1 = -1100, \quad k \geq 1 \tag{16}$$

which is smaller than the direct cost $L = 10{,}000$, so in the unfavourable scenario the expected benefit of switching is smaller than the cost. Note that from the definitions of S_0, S_1^f and S_1^u it follows that

$$S_0 = B_0 + (p/R)(S_1^f + S_1^u) \tag{17}$$

Should the designer invest $L = 10{,}000$ and restructure to switch to design C now, or would it be better to wait for a month and invest only if the situation favours a switch? There is no uncertainty after the first month, so these are the only strategies to consider.

We first approach this question by computing the net present value of these two strategies. The NPV of strategy 1 is

$$NPV(1) = S_0 - L = B_0 + E(B_1)/(R - 1) - L = 13500 - 10000 = 3500 \tag{18}$$

Since the NPV is positive, the NPV rules indicates that the designer should invest. However, let us calculate the NPV of investing under strategy 2: Wait one month, and invest in switching to the yellow-page agent only if the technology succeeds. Since the technology succeeds with probability $p = 0.5$, the net present value of strategy 2 is

$$NPV(2) = (p/R)(S_1^f - L)$$

$$= (p/R)\left(B_1^f \frac{R}{R - 1} - L\right) = (0.5/1.1)(27500 - 10000) = 7954 \tag{19}$$

which is significantly greater than the NPV of investing immediately. This shows that it is better to wait.

We now approach the question by computing the value V_k of the investment opportunity at times $k = 0$ and $k = 1$. The payoff if we exercise our option to invest at time k is given by $G_k = (S_k - L)^+$ which is identical to the expression for the payoff from an American call option. Since there is no uncertainty after time 1, it is easy to see that $V_k = G_k = (S_k - L)^+$ for all $k \geq 1$. In particular, if our designer's system succeeds, the option value at time 1 is

$$V_1^f = (S_1^f - L)^+ = (27500 - 10000)^+ = 17500 \tag{20}$$

and if it fails,

$$V_1^u = (S_1^u - L)^+ = (-1100 - 10000)^+ = 0 \tag{21}$$

From the backward recursion in equation (7) we conclude that

$$
\begin{aligned}
V_0 &= \max\{G_0, (1/R)E(V_1)\} \\
&= \max\{G_0, (1/R)(pV_1^f + (1 - p)V_1^u)\} \\
&= \max\{(S_0 - L)^+, (p/R)(S_1^f - L)^+\} \tag{22} \\
&= \max\{(B_0 + E(B_1)/(R - 1) - L)^+, (p/R)(B_1^f R/(R - 1) - L)^+\} \tag{23} \\
&= \max\{3500, (1/1.1) \times 0.5 \times (17500 + 0)\} \\
&= \max\{3500, 7954\} \\
&= 7954 \tag{24}
\end{aligned}
$$

The values 3,500 and 7,954 in the max above are exactly the NPVs of strategy 1 and strategy 2, respectively. Also, $V_0 > G_0 = 3,500$, so it is not optimal to invest right away. However, after 1 month, if the technology succeeds, $V_1 = G_1 = 17,500$, so it is then optimal to invest at that time. Thus we have shown in two different ways that strategy 2 is optimal. In general when the uncertainty lasts several periods, computing NPVs for the exponentially many strategies is impractical. The dynamic programming approach from option pricing theory would be a method of choice.

QUALITATIVE DESIGN PRINCIPLES

Software design strategy is based today almost entirely on experience and heuristics. The information hiding principle exhorts the designer to *hide within stable modules design decisions that are likely to change*. The spiral development approach urges the designer to *identify and rank risks and take a phased, iterative approach in which the greatest risks are mitigated first and plans reconsidered after each phase*. One heuristic on timing suggests that all decisions should be delayed for as long as possible.

To the first order, none of these heuristics is based on documented scientific or mathematical models or theories. We see in options theory the potential to begin to understand better why these principle seem to work, to explore conditions under which they are and are not valid, and to develop normative models for software design decision-making based on solid foundations.

The insight is that real options thinking makes key variables explicit in relation to the value of decision flexibility under uncertainty. It thus enables reasoning about the sensitivity of value to the relevant parameters. A designer who understands the mathematical relationships in the theory is better equipped to reason about the critical issues of decision flexibility, uncertainty and value in software design.

In this section we explore this view, using the example from the previous section to keep the discussion concrete. In particular, we investigate the sensitivity of options values to variations in the cost to invest, uncertainty over benefits, likelihood of a favourable outcome, and uncertainty over cost. As we vary parameters, we continue to assume that the two scenarios retain their favourable/unfavourable status:

$$S_1^f > L > S_1^u$$

Effect of direct cost

From equation (22), we notice that the value V_0 of the option is the maximum of two quantities: the NPV of strategy 1, namely $(S_0 - L)^+$, and the NPV of strategy 2, $(p/R)(S_1^f - L)^+$. Note that since $p/R < 1$, as L decreases, the former NPV increases faster than the latter. Thus, if all other parameters remain the same, there is a critical value for the direct cost L below which it is optimal to restructure immediately, ie, at time 0. Consider the quantity EP = NPV(2) − NPV(1). EP represents the benefit achieved by waiting, or in other words the difference between the value of strategy 2 (where one waits until the next period) versus strategy 1 (where one makes the decision at the initial node). Larger values of EP mean higher benefits of waiting. The graph of EP with respect to the direct cost L is shown in Figure 2.

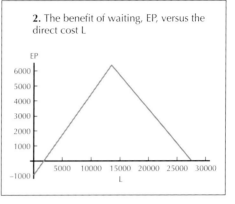

2. The benefit of waiting, EP, versus the direct cost L

Another way to state this principle is that if the direct cost L is sufficiently low, the cost of waiting (the profit S_0 − L one would forgo) outweighs the value of waiting (the value V_0 of the flexibility to reverse the decision not to invest). Since there is nothing special about time 0, this statement applies at any time. Thus we have an options-based justification for what would otherwise remain an informal software design guideline:

If the cost to effect a software decision is sufficiently low, then the benefit of investing to effect it immediately outweighs the benefit of waiting, so the decision should be made immediately.

Although this design decision-making rule of thumb seems obvious, it contradicts the heuristic, always delay design decisions as long as possible. The plausible reasoning behind that rule is that you should wait until all information is in before investing. The options approach shows that that is wrong in general. This conclusion makes the point that by reducing costs, new technologies, such as restructuring tools (Griswold and Notkin, 1993), can change a situation from one in which it is best to delay to one in which it is optimal to invest.

Effect of uncertainty over benefits B_n

In the numerical example of the previous section, the two possible values of B_n for $n \geq 1$ were $B_n^f = 2,500$ in the favourable case and $B_n^u = -100$ in the unfavourable case. Now suppose we keep all parameters the same, except that we change B_n^f to 3,000 and change B_n^u to −600. Notice in particular that the expectation of B_n,

$$E(B_n) = 0.5 \times (3000 - 600) = 1200, \quad n \geq 1$$

is the same as before, but that the variance of B_n is larger. This new parameterisation models greater uncertainty about the range of future benefits without any change in the net expected benefit, ie, a "higher risk, higher return" project.

Since the expectation remains the same, the NPV of strategy 1, ("restructure at time 0"), given by equation (18), is the same as before, because (see equation (12)) the expected benefit S_0 of switching at time 0 depends only on the expectation of each B_n. On the other hand, if the designer waits for 1 month and switches only if the situation is favourable (strategy 2), the net benefit S_k^f (see equation (15)) is

$$S_k^f = B_1^f R/(R - 1) = 3000 \times 1.1/0.1 = 33000, \quad k \geq 1$$

which is bigger than the previous S_k^f value of 27,500. Thus the NPV of strategy 2 (see equation (19)) is bigger than before.

This shows that the incentive to delay the decision to invest in restructuring increases with project risk, manifested as uncertainty over future benefits B_n, as long as all else, including the *expected* benefit, stays the same. Conversely, as uncertainty about future value diminishes, it becomes clearer whether it would pay to invest. The option value preserved by delaying diminishes. In the limiting case, you can decide immediately based on the static NPV.

Consider again the quantity EP = NPV(2) – NPV(1). The graph of EP against B_n^f (such that $E(B_n) = 1,200$ or $B_n^u = 2400 - B_n^f$) is shown in Figure 3. The options formulation makes the issue clear. The expected payoff of restructuring immediately is the same as before, since the values $E(B_n)$ are the same. However, if restructuring is delayed, then one of two outcomes occurs. In the unfavourable case (see equation (21)) the payoff V_1^u is still zero, because the design option will not be exercised. However, in the favourable case, the payoff V_1^f (see equation (20)) is greater than before. Thus the option value V_0 given by equation (22) increases.

These conclusions make sense intuitively. Uncertainty over the value of investing in a users' manual, for example creates an incentive to wait for information. If a manual is very likely to be profitable, there is less benefit to waiting. Similarly, if its value is clearly minimal or negative, a decision not to invest can be made immediately. Thus we can conclude with the following qualitative design guideline.

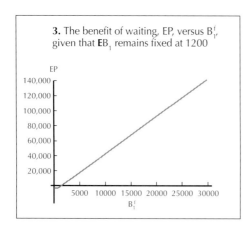

3. The benefit of waiting, EP, versus B_1^f, given that EB_1 remains fixed at 1200

With other factors, including the static NPV, remaining the same, the incentive to wait for better information before effecting a design decision increases with risk – ie, with the variance, or spread, in possible benefits.

Effect of the probability of a favourable outcome

In the example of the previous section, we assumed that at time 0 the likelihood of favourable and unfavourable outcomes was equal, with $p = 0.5$. This probability distribution represents the risk that the favourable outcome will not be actualised. We now examine how the value V_0 of the real option depends on the probability p of a favourable outcome.

Consider the payoff $G_0 = (S_0 - L)$ from immediate exercise, ie, the NPV of strategy 1 (see equation (17)):

$$G_0 = B_0 + (pS_1^f + (1 - p)S_1^u)/R - L = (p/R)(S_1^f - S_1^u) + B_0 - S_1^u/R - L$$

If we plot G_0 against p the slope would be $(S_1^f - S_1^u)/R$. The discounted expected value of the option V_1 is thus (equation (22))

$$EV_1/R = (p/R)(S_1^f - L)$$

This is the NPV of strategy 2. If we plot this value against p, we find the slope to be $(S_1^f - L)/R$. Since we have assumed $S_1^u < L$, we see that as we increase p, the NPV of strategy 1 grows faster than that of strategy 2. Thus as the probability p of a favourable outcome increases, at some point the strategy of investing right away becomes optimal. To put it differently, as the risk of an unfavourable future decreases, so does the incentive to wait. The graph of $EP = NPV(2) - NPV(1)$ versus p is shown in Figure 4. We have thus given a rigorous basis for the following design decision-making heuristic:

The incentive to wait before investing increases with the likelihood of unfavourable future events occurring.

Notice that this decision-making heuristic addresses uncertainty and risk in a different way from the previous rule. The previous rule addresses the variance in the payoffs under different outcomes. This rule addresses variation in the uncertainty about the likelihood of future events that influence outcomes. These are two important but distinct dimensions of risk.

Effect of uncertainty over direct cost

We now examine the possibility of the cost L being uncertain. This aspect of uncertainty is critical in software engineering, especially if delaying design decisions is an

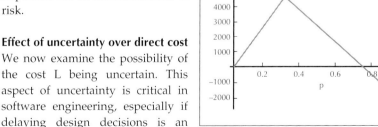

4. The benefit of waiting, EP, versus the probability p of a favourable outcome p

accepted strategy: It goes to the question of estimating project costs, which is widely known to be subject to significant uncertainties. Uncertainty about costs might reflect uncertainty about availability of skilled labour in the future, or about changes in technology, such as the development of automated tools or new methods that could reduce costs.

To simplify matters, let us assume that the monthly profit B_n from restructuring is 1,500 at all times $n \geq 0$ (there is no uncertainty in this regard). Thus the expected benefit of switching at time k, for any $k \geq 0$, is given by an expression analogous to equation (15) (in either scenario):

$$S_k = B_k \frac{R}{R-1} = 1500(1.1)/(0.1) = 16500, \quad k \geq 0$$

However, now assume that the direct cost L_0 at time 0 is known to be 10,000, but that it is uncertain at time 1. Let us assume that L_1 is either $L_1^f = 5,000$ (a favourable situation) or $L_1^u = 20,000$ (an unfavourable situation). The NPV of strategy 1, investing now, is

$$NPV(1) = S_0 - L_0 = 16500 - 10000 = 6500$$

which is positive. The traditional NPV rule suggests switching right away. Again, this rule is faulty because it ignores the contingent, option strategy: wait a month, and switch only if the direct cost is $L_1^f = 5,000$. The NPV of this strategy is

$$NPV(2) = (p/R)(S_1 - L_1^f) = (0.5/1.1)(16500 - 5000) = 11500$$

which is considerably greater than the NPV of the first strategy. Thus it is optimal to wait a month in this case before deciding whether to invest.

Now let us go a step further, and see what happens if we keep L_0 the same and increase the uncertainty (in particular, the variance) of L_1, while keeping its expectation EL_1 the same. This would mean L_1^f is smaller, and NPV(2) larger. In this case, the value of waiting is even greater. This situation is analogous to the one in the section headed "The effect on uncertainty over benefits". When the uncertainty over direct costs is larger, and the expectation remains the same, the potential profit in the favourable scenario increases, while in the unfavourable scenario it remains the same at 0. Thus we have provided a justification for another heuristic:

All else being equal, the value of the option to delay increases with variance in future costs.

AN OPTIONS INTERPRETATION OF INFORMATION HIDING

Having discussed the application of real options to reasoning about the value of being able to decide when to invest in software design decisions, we now turn to the value of modularity. Although real options have had little impact on software engineering to date, it is fascinating that concepts from software engineering have made their way into serious work in the real options literature. Here, we discuss the work of Baldwin and Clark. Based on Parnas's seminal concept of information hiding modules, which hide internal design details that are likely to change (Parnas, 1972 and 1985), Baldwin and Clark interpret modular designs (for computer hardware) as creating real options (Baldwin and Clark, 1999).

They aim to develop a theory of the evolution of the computer industry. Before 1960 or so it was highly centralised. Now it is very decentralised. They see firms as being driven by the options value of modularity to modularise designs, but that published modular architecture enables competitors to compete for slots in the design (eg, disk drives). Thus, modularity in design drives decentralisation of the industry structure.

In more detail, modules create options to select the best implementation from a set of implementations for a given slot in a modular design. Variants are produced by experimentation, whether internal to a firm or in the marketplace. Modules thus create real options for designers to change hidden module details without impacting the rest of a system. The investment in the design of the module thus has a benefit that can be expressed as the value of such an option. (Modularity does have other benefits, as well, which are not necessarily captured in an options formulation, eg, supporting large-scale development through the concurrent efforts of designers working on separate modules.)

More generally, modularising a system involves the selection of a portfolio of options. The choice of modular architecture for a system should be based on the goal of maximising its value, which includes options values. Information hiding concepts having informed real options thinking, it now appears that real options thinking can inform software design theory. Taking the options perspective suggests ways to broaden the traditional view of information hiding.

Recall that the idea of information hiding is to hide within stable module boundaries aspects of a system that are *likely* to change (likelihood is rarely quantified). As a bet on future conditions, it might make sense to hide design aspects that are *unlikely* to change, but where the risk is high. An option created by a module will have some value even if the likelihood of payoff is small, provided that the payoff in the unlikely event is sufficiently high and the cost of the option small. We are thus driven at least to consider using information hiding to speculate on *unlikely* changes. More broadly, the options perspective allows us to integrate the information hiding concept into a more comprehensive understanding of software design as a strategic activity.

Baldwin and Clark model the value of a system as a sum of the values of the modules in the system. They take value maximisation as the goal of design and derive design investment policies under which such maximisation is achieved. They assume that a given system has already selected a module implementation for each slot and that the other implementations (produced by investments in experimentation) have values that are normally distributed around that of a currently selected implementation, with a variance determined by the number of design parameters that are bound within the module. Among other aims, they seek to gain a better understanding of optimal levels of investment in experimentation and testing to produce and evaluate variant module implementations. They conclude that firms generally under-invest in experimentation.

This work is encouraging for software design and engineering. It substantiates our insight that options thinking can help to model, analyse and explain basic issues in software design, including information hiding. Their work leaves many questions unanswered (as does ours). First, although they draw heavily from software design, appealing to information hiding and structured design, they do not try to develop an investment or options-based view of software design principles themselves. Second, their additive model of the value of a system is simple. It might be a reasonable model of systems that are essentially collections of largely independent features. Some shrink-wrapped software packages have roughly this structure (Cusumano and Selby, 1995). However, the model does not capture other systems well, in which the value of the system is not a simple sum of module values. Nor are software module implementations necessarily created by a random walk around the current module, as Baldwin and Clark assume. In future work, we plan to investigate the ways in which real options in real software systems interact, more convincing models of module-based options in *software*, and the extent to which such options might be valued in an arbitrage style using market data.

AN OPTIONS INTERPRETATION OF THE SPIRAL MODEL

The spiral model (Boehm, 1988), is generally regarded as a risk-based process model. We sketch an account of the spiral model as a value-maximising rather than just a risk-minimising model, based on real options concepts.

Risks in the spiral model are addressed by a phased project structure in which, in each phase, important risks are mitigated, often by investing in prototypes, user surveys or other such experimental efforts. In addition, investments are made at the beginning of each phase to develop and evaluate a range of solution approaches for meeting the objective of the phase. At the end of each phase, the project is re-evaluated, and plans are developed for the next phase.

The spiral model is often held up against the waterfall model, historically the most important software development project model and one that is still widely used; and the relative benefits of the spiral model are stressed. The waterfall model begins with a feasibility study, after which there is decision to proceed or not. Once there is a decision to proceed, the project goes forward mechanically through elaboration of requirements and specifications, design of a modular system architecture, parallel implementation and testing of the individual modules, system integration, system testing, release and maintenance. Investments of tens or hundreds of millions of dollars are often handled using this process model.

Today, researchers and many practitioners acknowledge the chief deficit of the waterfall model: it does not recognise risk or uncertainty as critical issues in the development of complex software-intensive products. It includes no serious strategy to address uncertainty. It is thus not surprising that beyond the initial feasibility study, the model does not promote investment in options; it is not designed to have embedded options for the designer to change course; nor does it suggest a dynamic approach to managing projects in uncertain conditions as new information continually arrives.

By contrast, the central elements of the spiral model have clear interpretations in real options terms. Analysing the model in this way provides a valuable way of seeing this process model as one concerned with value maximisation under uncertainty.

First, the *implicit* message in the model is that decisions should be made that create the most value. Boehm states that the designer begins with a hypothesis that a project will "*improve the operational mission*" of an enterprise. Recasting this point in economic terms leads to the position that the designer begins with a hypothesis that investing will *maximise value added*. This formulation is consistent with Boehm's description and makes the model consistent with standard corporate finance theory. Similarly, Boehm states that the designer should terminate the spiral (cancel a project) when the mission improvement hypothesis is rejected. Our interpretation is that one should decline to invest in the next phase when doing so is not optimal for maximising added value.

Second, the model exploits options extensively. Developing and evaluating variant approaches in each phase creates option to pick the best of n approaches identified. Perhaps most important, the phased project structure creates value in the form of compound options: the investment in each phase creates an option to invest (or not) in the next phase.

What we have done is to interpret software development process models as implicit investment strategies, and we sketched an explanation in options terms for why one model (spiral) is so much more effective than another (waterfall). We elaborate this idea after introducing a concept important for understanding the treatment of uncertainty by the spiral model, but one not based mainly on options concepts. The issue is the value of information that can be obtained by investing.

Value of flexibility versus value of information

One of the most important tactics that Boehm emphasises for mitigating risk is use of prototyping to gain information. In software design it sometimes pays to invest a little in design and implementation early to resolve uncertainties that might affect future outcomes, (Boehm, 1981). There is a significant difference between prototyping and options that needs to be understood. Although prototyping seeks value maximisation under uncertainty, it does not do so by waiting for the resolution of exogenous uncertainty, but rather by investing now in a controlled way. For example, when a designer invests in a prototype to resolve a risk, it is investing itself that resolves the uncertainty. By contrast, you cannot learn how much a stock is going to be worth tomorrow by investing a little today.

The essence of prototyping is thus not in the value of flexibility (VOF) to respond to uncertain exogeneous conditions, but in the value of information (VOI) obtained by investing. The idea is that an investment in a prototype is justified when the information revealed is worth more than it costs – eg, when it helps to avert a costly commitment to an unworkable design. Hillier and Leibermann (1995) provide an introduction and references to the mathematical formulation in terms of statistical decision theory.

The distinction is important. For example, while VOF considerations can drive one to delay investing early, VOI is just the opposite. Because important information won't be obtained until it is "purchased," it can make sense to buy it early. The fact that the two situations are so different suggests that a comprehensive approach to managing uncertainty in software design will require an integrated set of tools, including tools for modelling and analysing both options (using arbitrage and non-arbitrage methods) and the value of information. Ultimately, we need process models that go beyond the spiral in taking a comprehensive approach to the modelling of, analysis of, and decision-making under uncertainty in software design.

Real options in projects based on the spiral development model

A key element of the spiral model is the generation of alternative solution approaches at the beginning of each phase. Generating alternatives is related to the generation of alternative module implementations in Bladwin and Clark's real options analysis of the value of information hiding. Generating a set of n solutions provides the designer with the option to select the best. The options view suggests qualitative guidelines for deciding how much to invest in the exploration that leads to new alternatives: when the risk is high, options are worth more, so spend more on options.

Phased projects as compound options

Phased project structures are an essential part of the spiral model. The goal is to keep investments small until risks are resolved. Such a structure provides an ability to manage risk by embedding options in a project to change course or even to abandon it as uncertainties are resolved over time. One way to think about phased projects is that they contain embedded options to scale back or to abandon the project if conditions turn out to be unfavourable (Trigeorgis, 1996). Such options are *put* as opposed to *call* options, giving holders the right to sell assets at a specified price (eg, to abandon a project in return for the market value of its assets or avoidance of future costs). Embedding such options in the project increases its value relative to one without options.

A second interpretation is that investing in one phase of a project buys the designer an option to make a follow-on investment should the situation be favourable at that time. A designer considering such initial investment thus has an option on an option, called a compound option. Similarly, a second phase can yield an option on the third, and so on. Real options theory has been applied to value such phased projects as compound options (Geske, 1979).

A striking insight emerges from the options view: it can be optimal to invest in the first phase of a project even though the overall project has a negative *static* NPV (Brealey and Myers, 1996). The key idea is that spending a little on one phase can yield an option to invest in the next if conditions turn out to be favourable. If the upside potential of the second phase is high, the option value today can outweigh its cost, even if the entire project currently has a negative NPV. Although this concept is familiar to those who have studied modern corporate finance, including options concepts, it is not the way that software designers are taught to think.

Extending this insight to the spiral model we infer that it can be optimal to begin a spiral not on the hypothesis that the project *will* improve the operational mission of the firm, but that it *might*. In other words, we infer that it can pay to begin a spiral process as a *strategic bet* on favourable future conditions. It might be worthwhile to invest in learning a standard even before it is widely adopted, if doing so makes it possible for the designer to respond quickly if the standard does become widely adopted, for example.

A concrete example

We make the preceding point concrete with a simple example. Suppose that the designer can restructure in two phases. The first phase costs 1,000. With probability 0.5, that is the total cost incurred; but with probability 0.5 serious difficulties will be encountered, and 3,000 more dollars will have to be invested to produce a satisfactory design. Perhaps the selected restructuring tool has unforeseen shortcomings that require some manual restructuring. More generally, a project might contain risks that are resolved by investing in the first place.

Suppose that the profit from restructuring, at each step t, is 200. Summing up the sequence, the present value of this stream, at any time, with the discount rate at 10%, turns out to be $200R/(R - 1) = 2,200$. NPV analysis compares the expected cost, $1,000 + (0.5)(3,000) = 2,500$, with the present value of profits, 2,200. Owing to the risk, the static NPV is –300. Not investing appears to be advised: the project does not improve the mission of the firm.

However, this analysis ignores the value of the option to cancel the project after the first phase if a second phase costing 3,000 turns out to be necessary. The traditional NPV analysis ignores the contingent strategy enabled by the embedded option to cancel the project. The dynamic NPV is $(0.5(2,200) - 1,000 = 100$. In other words, for 1,000 the designer can buy an asset – an option on the second phase – that with even odds will be worth either 2,200 or 0. It's a good bet, with an expected value of 100.

Traditional software engineering economics using static NPV overlooks the value of the options – ie, flexibility – embedded in development projects and products. The options approach is superior to static NPV analysis for quantitative reasoning about projects and assets with embedded options. More importantly for our purposes in this chapter, it provides a framework for understanding strategic design, by which value is created with intelligent bets on uncertain future outcomes.

REAL OPTIONS IN TRADE-OFFS RELATING TO TIME TO MARKET

Finally, we discuss an options-oriented approach to reasoning about an issue that troubles many software engineering researchers: the rush to market with software products that are not engineered to the highest standards. In the internet economy, in which technology is evolving at a tremendous pace and lock-in is a serious issue, opportunities to exploit new markets are fleeting, and the threat is always looming that a competitor will take that market away by getting there first. There is thus a powerful heuristic commonly employed by software designers: "be first". The designer often sacrifices some quality to be the first with a new product.

The threat can be understood in options terms. The entry of a competitor can reduce the share of a market that would otherwise be available for a designer to exploit, and thus the value of the cashflow stream from sales that the designer gets by shipping a product. Such a discrete drop in asset value can be seen as a dividend – similar to the dividend that a stock pays, with an immediate, corresponding drop in share value.

It is known in options theory that it is optimal to delay exercising an American call option on a stock that does *not* pay dividends until expiration. In other words, there is no opportunity cost to delaying, and you know most about the value of the stock just before your right to buy it expires. In this case, waiting as long as possible is the right strategy. However, when a stock pays a dividend the share value drops and the option owner is not entitled to the dividend. The payoff from exercising after a dividend is reduced. That is, there is an opportunity cost to waiting. In these cases, it can be optimal to exercise early to capture value that would be lost otherwise.

Consider a software designer developing a product under threat of competitive entry. The designer has an option to ship the product, ie, to exercise an option to capture a share of the market, even if the product is not yet perfect. The entry of a competitor, reducing that share, is a dividend (Trigeorgis, 1996). To capture that benefit the designer might ship early. More generally, dividends create a countervailing incentive: not to delay, but to exercise early to capture benefits that flow from actually owning an asset. We do not advocate designers shipping shoddy products. That is not likely to maximise value over time. However, we can see why in some cases trading some quality for time could be the right *engineering* choice. The purpose of design is value, not perfection.

RELATED WORK

To begin our summation, we address related work in several areas: flexibility in software; options; software engineering economics; software reuse investment analysis; and real options in the analysis of information technology projects. In the following section, we discuss theoretical difficulties in taking an options approach to computer related issues.

Flexibility in software product and process design

We are obviously not the first to notice that flexibility is critical in software design and that it has both costs and benefits that have to be weighed against each other. Information hiding (Parnas, 1972), extension and contraction (Parnas, 1978), and program family concepts (Parnas, 1976), were seminal. More recently, Fayad and Cline (1996), emphasise that flexibility has costs, that it should be designed in where it is economically the most effective. They see *design patterns* (Gamma, Helm and Vlissides, 1995), as providing "hinges" needed for flexibility in particular dimensions. They even state that such hinges provide "opportunities" to make changes that might be necessary – reflecting an implicit options mode of thinking. However, to the best of our knowledge there have been few attempts to connect such concepts explicitly to precise notions of the value added by flexibility.

Financial options theory

Real options theory is based on financial options theory. The options literature is immense. It is not feasible to cite all relevant work. Financial options have been studied since 1900; however the seminal modern results, which provided long-sought closed-form mathematical formulations for valuing financial options, are due to Scholes, Merton and Black, Black and Scholes (1973) and Merton (1973). Scholes and Merton received the 1997 Nobel Prize in economics for their work on this topic. Many other results, which are now elements of basic finance, have been produced since (Brealey and Myers, 1996; Cox and Rubinstein, 1984 and 1979; and McDonald and Siegel, 1986). For the past 20 years, researchers have been building the theory of real options (Brealey and Myers, 1996; Dixit and Pindyck, 1994; Trigeorgis, 1995).

Software engineering economics

The idea of finance-based decision criteria for software design is not new. Boehm wrote on it in his *Software Engineering Economics* (1981). In general, he emphasised static net present value as the basic concept of value and how it might be taken as the objective of software design. He appealed to statistical decision theory as well to reason about the value of investments in information under uncertainty.

Boehm's emphasis on static NPV is understandable. Static NPV was the standard measure of value added taught in business schools. Moreover, real options were hardly known when Boehm's book was published. Boehm mentions options in the colloquial, but it does not analyse software design concepts in terms of real options.

The software reuse literature reports applications of finance theories to software reuse investment analysis (Lim, 1996). Favaro has argued that much work in this area uses techniques known to have technical problems. He has argued that NPV is the proper basis for such analysis (1996). That view is consistent with the traditional academic view, but it does not consider the value of flexibility.

Withey (1996 – and more recently Favaro *et al*, 1998) considers flexibility in options terms in work on investment analysis of product line architectures. He shows how economies of scope achieved through investments in product-line design can be interpreted as options on uncertain markets. Withey did not invoke real options because of questions about its broader validity for analysing software design decisions (personal communication). We agree with Withey that it is critical not to take real options or other such investment concepts as silver bullets for software design decision-making. It is especially important to understand the conditions under which arbitrage pricing techniques can legitimately be used.

It bears mentioning that Boehm (1981) warns of the pitfalls of adopting financial criteria for software design. Focusing exclusively on *quantifiable* economics can compromise attention to human economic issues that in the long run are critical to success. Our work is meant to provide intellectual tools to help designers think more effectively about important issues in design decision making, and to provide a basis for the eventual development of modelling and analysis tools. But models are prone to incompleteness and inaccuracy. They can improve but not replace human judgement.

Information technology project valuation

Henderson and Kulatilaka are developing an approach to investment analysis of information technology (IT) projects based on real options (Kulatilaka, 1996). The proposed approach appears to be a standard use of real options for investment analysis at the project level. The work does not address software design. Flatto (1996) reports on a survey of whether managers use real option concepts in IT investment analysis, which showed that options concepts are not used.

PRACTICAL AND THEORETICAL DIFFICULTIES

The quantitative use of real options theory to support software design decision-making is an attractive possibility, but one that will clearly require the careful treatment of practical and theoretical problems. In this section, we enumerate some of these problems and discuss possible solution strategies.

Arbitrage-based valuation techniques require knowledge of the current asset values and of the risks of assets determined by appeal to market data. They do not require subjective estimates of cashflows. When arbitrage-based techniques cannot be applied, estimates of cashflow streams and discount rates are needed. Estimating software costs remains a highly imprecise exercise, and little work has been done on benefit estimation. We provide a framework within which to explore the implications of various estimates. Having such a framework in addition to sheer intuition is likely to be better than not. However, the problem of estimating parameters will remain a serious impediment to accurate valuation of some software options.

Second, formulating design issues in options-oriented terms can be hard because each possible product or process design is likely to contain a set of embedded options, each of which should be valued to value the design. Building options-based models is a challenge. Tool support would help. The feasibility of building real options-based models of industrial-scale software projects has yet to be determined, and is the subject of a case study that we are pursuing.

Another challenging problem is to identify and model quantitatively the underlying uncertainties that determine future costs and benefits. When the uncertainties have been priced by the market in cases where traded stocks reflect the market judgement of the uncertainty, then market data can be used as a basis for estimates. In cases where the uncertainty is private to a given project, expert subjective estimates will be needed, and it will be hard to provide reliable and justified estimates.

The distinction between options that are in and not in the "span of the market" might help explain Strassmann's reservations about Henderson's use of options in valuing IT investments (Strassmann, 1997). Strassman objects that in richly traded markets there is information on values and uncertainty. However, he notes that computer projects occur in low volumes, and he argues that therefore getting valid data, treating them consistently, and dealing with non-quantifiable effects makes IT project valuation different. Strassmann then concludes that "... there is no true resemblance between trading in financial options and planning computer projects", (Strassmann, p. 159).

Strassmann is correct that arbitrage-based techniques (which many people define as options pricing techniques) cannot be used for options not in the span of the market. He is also clearly correct that estimating valid inputs for options that are not in the span is difficult. Lack of spanning can be a problem, but options are present whether they can be priced by arbitrage or not. As Dixit and Pindyck state that "whether or not spanning holds, we can obtain a solution to the investment problem, but without spanning, the solution will be subject to an assumed discount rate" (1994, p. 152). Furthermore, the assumed discount rate is not itself subject to theoretical justification. In essence, when markets are incomplete (spanning does not hold), the data required for pricing using dynamic programming will be subjective estimates. Strassmann's valid objection is that getting valid estimates will be hard.

The pessimist will claim that we are back to where we started, with design reasoning being based on no more than expert opinion. In cases where arbitrage-based pricing is possible, market-based valuations of real options are possible without the need for subjective projections and estimates. Even in cases where market-based data are not available, the options perspective appears to be useful, because it highlights the role of flexibility in software design and gives the designer a way to think about that value as being tangible. Software designers have to estimate such quantities as "likelihood of change" today, in any case, in order to apply existing concepts such as information hiding. However, these estimates are treated without the benefit of any kind of well-grounded mathematical model. Options concepts identify the parameters in the underlying investment decisions and tells us how they relate to optimal strategy for value added. At a minimum, it provides a framework for back-of-the-envelope models, with support for sensitivity analysis. We expect real gains as researchers and designers explore the implications of the options view for *strategic software design*.

Software strategy is the term that we use to refer to software design techniques in which uncertainty, incomplete knowledge, competition, and related issues are treated systematically and consciously in a sound manner designed to maximise the expected value of a given product or project. A designer will use techniques such as modularity and phased project structures with a conscious understanding of how they provide hedges, bets, and the flexibility to respond to new information. Ideally, designers will be able to engineer projects for selected levels of exposure to risk and reward. The options framework provides a powerful language in which to develop this idea. We are exploring the idea of managing software projects as portfolios of assets whose value includes the values of embedded real options. A card game might be a good metaphor. As uncertainty is resolved over time, investment decisions are made on the basis of the options held at the time: cards are bought, assessed, played, and discarded in a dynamic and strategic game against both nature and adversaries.

CONCLUSION

Existing software design principles, such as information hiding and spiral processes, can be quite effective. To a considerable degree they operate by serving as (imperfect) proxies for value-maximising decision criteria for investing under uncertainty. We have tried to make this insight precise by relating a range of important software design heuristics to options theory. This approach has enabled us to present a somewhat unifying analysis of a set of previously disconnected design principles. In addition to merely analysing such concepts, we have provided some support for the claim that a value-based perspective that accounts for the value of flexibility in terms of real options can lead to a better understanding of, and new insights into software design. For example, we see the spiral model not merely as a risk-reducing model, but as a value-maximising model, with equal emphasis on profitable reduction of downside risk and upside opportunities.

We are taking several additional steps to develop this work. First, a comprehensive approach to scientific uncertainty management for strategic software design requires an integrated set of modelling and analysis methods appropriate for valuing different kinds of decision flexibility under different conditions: arbitrage or not; value of information or flexibility; etc. We are working to elaborate the models.

Second, we are investigating whether real designers change how they make design decisions as they learn about the nature, role, and value of decision flexibility and its options interpretation.

Third, we are developing new, normative development models based on the idea of scientific uncertainty management and strategic design. The idea is that software development should be driven not by risk reduction, *per se*, but value-maximisation. We see an *active investment management* approach, in which software systems and projects are treated as portfolios of assets with embedded options, as a promising start on such models.

Fourth, we are designing software tools for use in such processes. Among other functions, these tools have to support mathematical modelling and analysis of real options in software and continuous monitoring of technical, market and other issues for new information that might change asset valuations in ways that require dynamic decision-making.

We are also working to identify options in software design for which arbitrage-based valuation techniques can be used. The availability of market-calibrated valuations of decision flexibility structures would be enormously useful. The value of portability to new computing platforms, for example, seems amenable to such an approach. Market data are often available on prospects for platforms, for example Apple Corporation's iMac.

1 Our numbers are fictional, and largely from Dixit and Pindyck, 1994, "Investment Under Uncertainty", Princeton University Press.

BIBLIOGRAPHY

Amram, M. and N. Kulatilaka, 1999, *Real Options: Managing Strategic Investment in an Uncertain World*, Cambridge, Massachusetts: Harvard Business School Press.

Baldwin, C.Y. and K.B. Clark, 1999, *Design Rules: The Power of Modularity*, Cambridge, Massachusetts: MIT Press.

Belady, L.A. and M.M. Lehman, 1976, "A Model of Large Program Development", *IBM Systems Journal*, 15(3), reprinted in Lehman, M.M. and L.A. Belady, 1985, *Program Evolution*, London: Academic Press, pp. 165–200.

Black, F. and M. Scholes, 1973, "The Pricing of Options and Corporate Liabilities", *Journal of Political Economy*, 81(3), pp. 637–55.

Boehm, B.W., 1981, *Software Engineering Economics. Advances in Computing Science and Technology*, Prentice Hall.

Boehm, B.W., 1988, "A Spiral Model of Software Development and Enhancement", *IEEE Computer*, 21(5), pp. 61–73.

Boehm, B.W. and R. Ross, 1989, "Theory-W Software Project Management: Principles and Examples", *IEEE Transactions on Software Engineering*, 15(7).

Boehm, B.W. and K.J. Sullivan, "Software Economics: Status and Prospects", invited paper, *Information and Software Technology*, special millennium issue, forthcoming.

Brealey, R. and S. Myers, 1996, *Principles of Corporate Finance*, New York: McGraw-Hill, fifth edition.

Brennan, M. and E. Schwartz, 1985, "Evaluating Natural Resource Investments", *Journal of Business*, 58(2), pp. 135–57.

Corman, T.H., C.E. Leiserson and R.L. Rivest, 1990, *The Design and Analysis of Computer Algorithms*, Cambridge, Mass.: MIT Press.

Cox, J. and M. Rubinstein, 1984, *Options Markets*, Englewood Cliffs, NJ: Prentice-Hall.

Cox, J.C., S.A. Ross and M. Rubinstein, 1979, "Option Pricing: A Simplified Approach", *Journal of Financial Economics*, 7, pp. 229–63.

Cusumano, M. and R. Selby, 1995, *Microsoft Secrets*, New York: Free Press.

Dixit, A. and R. Pindyck, 1994, *Investment under Uncertainty*, Princeton Univesity Press.

Gamma, R.J.E., R. Helm and J. Vlissides, 1995, *Design Patterns*, Reading, Massachusetts: Addison-Wesley.

Favaro, J., 1996, "A Comparison of Approaches to Reuse Investment Analysis", *Proceedings of the Fourth International Conference on Software Reuse*, 4.

Favaro, J., K.R. Favaro and P.F. Favaro, 1998, "Value based software reuse investment", *Annals of Software Engineering*, 5, pp. 5–52.

Fayad, M. and M. Cline, 1996, "Aspects of Software Adaptability", *Communications of the ACM*, 39(10), October, pp. 58–9.

Flatto, J., 1996, "The Application of Real Options to the Information Technology Valuation Process: A Benchmark Study", PhD thesis, University of New Haven.

Geske, R., 1979, "The Valuation of Compound Options", *Journal of Financial Economics*, 7, pp. 63–81.

Griswold, W. and D. Notkin, 1993, "Automated Assistance for Program Restructuring", *Transactions on Software Engineering and Methodology*, 2(3), July.

Habermann, A., L. Flon and L. Cooprider, 1976, "Modularization and Hierarchy in a Family of Operating Systems", *Communications. of the ACM*, 19(5), May, pp. 266–72.

Hillier, F. and G. Liebermann, 1995, *Introduction to Operations Research*, McGraw-Hill, sixth edition.

Hull, F., 1993, *Options, Futures, and Other Derivative Securities*, Prentice Hall, second edition.

Kester, C., 1984, "Today's Options for Tomorrow's Growth", *Harvard Business Review*, March/April, pp. 153–60.

Kulatilaka, N., 1993, "The Value of Flexibility: The Case of a Dual-Fuel Industrial Steam Boiler", *Financial Management*, 22(3), Autumn, p. 271.

Kulatilaka, N., P. Balasubramanian and J. Storck, 1996, "Managing Information Technology Investments: A Capability-based Real Options Approach", Boston University School of Management Working Paper No. 96-35, June.

Lim, W., 1996, "Reuse Economics: A Comparison of Seventeen Models and Directions for Future Research", *Fourth International Conference on Software Reuse*.

Luenberger, D., 1998, *Investment Science*, New York: Oxford University Press.

Madj, S. and R. Pindyck, 1987, "Time to Build, Option Value, and Investment Decisions", *Journal of Financial Economics*, 18(1), pp. 7–27.

Maes, P., 1994, "Agents that Reduce Work and Information Overload", *Communications. of the ACM*, 37(7), July, pp. 31–40.

McDonald, R. and D. Siegel, 1986, "The Value of Waiting to Invest", *Quarterly Journal of Economics*, 101(4), pp. 707–27.

Merton, R., 1973, "Theory of Rational Option Pricing", *Bell Journal of Economics and Management Science*, pp. 141–83.

Merton, R.C., 1990, *Continuous-Time Finance*, Cambridge, Mass.: Blackwell.

Mitchell, T., R. Curuana, D. Freitag and J. McDermott, July 1994, "Experience With a Learning Personal Assistant", *Communications of the ACM*, 37(7), pp. 81–91.

Myers, S., 1977, "Determinants of Corporate Borrowing", *Journal of Financial Economics*, 5, pp. 147–75.

Myers, S. and S. Majd, 1990, "Abandonment Value and Project Life", *Advances in Futures and Options Research*, 4, pp. 1–21.

Parnas, D., 1976, "Program Families", *IEEE Transactions on Software Engineering*, SE-2(1), March, pp. 1–9.

Parnas, D., 1985, "The Modular Structure of Complex Systems", *Transactions on Software Engineering*, SE-11, March, pp. 259–66.

Parnas, D.L., 1972, "On the Criteria to be Used in Decomposing Systems into Modules", *Communications of the Association of Computing Machinery*, 15(12), December, pp. 1053–8.

Parnas, D.L., 1978, "Designing Software for Ease of Extension and Contraction", *Proceedings of the Third International Conference on Software Engineering*, pp. 264–77, IEEE.

Pindyck, R., 1988, "Irreversible Investment, Capacity Choice, and the Value of the Firm", *American Economic Review*, 78(5), pp. 969–85.

Ross, S., 1995, "Uses, Abuses, and Alternatives to the Net-Present-Value Rule", *Financial Management*, 24(3), Autumn, pp. 96–102.

Shaw, M. and D. Garlan, 1996, Software Architecture: Perspectives on an Emerging Discipline, Upper Saddle River, NJ: Prentice-Hall.

Strassmann, P., 1997, *The Squandered Computer: Evaluating the Business Alignment of Information Technologies*, New Canaan, Connecticut: The Information Economics Press.

Stultz, R., 1982, "Options on the Minimum or the Maximum of Two Risky Assets: Analysis and Applications", *Journal of Financial Economics*, 10, pp. 161–85.

Sullivan, K.J., 1996, "Software Design: the Options Approach", Second International Software Architecture Workshop (ISAW-2), in *Joint Proceedings of the SIGSOFT'96 Workshops*, L. Vidal *et al*, ed., New York, NY: Association for Computing Machinery.

Sycara, K., K. Decker, A. Pannu and M. Williamson, 1996, "Distributed Intelligent Agents", technical report, Carnegie Mellon University.

Teisberg, E., 1995, "Methods for Evaluating Capital Investment Decisions under Uncertainty", in *Real Options in Capital Investment: Models, Strategies, and Applications*, L. Trigeorgis, ed., Westport, Connecticut: Praeger.

Triantis, A. and J. Hodder, 1990, "Valuing Flexibility as a Complex Option", *The Journal of Finance*, XLV(2), June, pp. 549–65.

Trigeorgis, L., 1993, "The Nature of Option Interactions and the Valuation of Investments with Multiple Real Options", *Journal of Financial and Quantitative Analysis*, 28(1), pp. 1–20.

Trigeorgis, L., editor, 1995, *Real Options in Capital Investments: Models, Strategies and Applications*, Westport, Connecticut: Praeger.

Trigeorgis, L., 1996, *Real Options: Managerial Flexibility and Strategy in Resource Allocation*, Cambridge, Massachusetts: MIT Press.

Withey, J., November 1996, "Investment Analysis of Software Assets for Product Lines", Technical Report CMU/SEI-96-TR-010, Carnegie Mellon University – Software Engineering Institute.

11

The Valuation of Natural Resources

Gonzalo Cortazar*

Pontificia Universidad Católica de Chile

Natural resources can be seen as *the* natural candidates for real options valuation methodology. Their investments and their contingent claim markets have all the correct characteristics to fully take advantage of this new approach. Promising as it is, however, its use by the practitioner community has been rather slow.

This chapter's aim is to show why the real options approach is a much better valuation method for natural resource investments than the traditional net present value (NPV) technique, and to illustrate some of the recent modelling advances that enhance its value for practitioners.

NATURAL RESOURCE INVESTMENTS AND THE USE OF THE NET PRESENT VALUE

The importance of choosing the right valuation tool is highly dependent on the characteristics of the problem. Good decision makers handle a portfolio of alternative techniques and assign the most appropriate one to each problem. Variations of the net present value (or discounted cashflow) methods are among the most popular for very good reasons, including sound theoretical justification and user friendliness. This simplicity can become dangerous because it may not be justified by the structure of the problem being addressed. In what follows we illustrate this point by highlighting common pitfalls that arise when using the net present value method for investment valuation. We then discuss why many natural resource investments justify the use of more sophisticated valuation tools like option theory.

Some pitfalls of NPV

The NPV method for capital budgeting has strong theoretical backing and, if properly used, maximises wealth. However, we show three common

*The author thanks Eduardo S. Schwartz for introducing him into the real option approach and for almost a decade of joint work applying it to valuing natural resources. The financial support of FONDECYT-1990109 is acknowledged.

types of misuse of NPV for capital budgeting. Panel 1 presents examples of these problems.

Pitfall 1: incorrect computation of cashflows

Discounted cashflow methods determine the present value of risky cashflows by computing their expected values and discounting them at an appropriate rate. One common mistake when implementing this approach is to compute cashflows using the expected value of all risky variables, instead of computing the expected value of the cashflows under the distribution of all risky state variables. From Jensen's inequality it is well known that the expected value of any non-linear function of random variables is not equal to the function valued at the expected value of each of the random variables.

Non-linear cashflows arise in many natural resource investments. For example, if commodity prices decrease enough to make it optimal to stop the production, cashflows must be modelled as a convex function of price. Similarly, increases in prices may induce an optimal production expansion that again leads to convexity in the cashflow function. The same effect can arise with uncertainty in factors such as costs, ore grades, or reserves. Whenever expected cashflows are computed using expected prices, costs, ore grades and reserves, a bias is introduced into the present value calculation. Managerial flexibility, which allows managers to react optimally to varying market and project conditions, may be worth a considerable proportion of total project value and is neglected if the impact of uncertainty on cashflows is not adequately modelled (see Panel 1).

Pitfall 2: incorrect decision to invest

A blind application of the decision rule "positive NPV projects should be undertaken" is a very common mistake of decision makers. Many times it is forgotten that the rule applies only to independent investments – those that do not interact with other investment projects. Whenever these interactions (or externalities to the project) do exist it does not suffice to have a positive NPV: it must be the maximum among all available alternatives. One way of understanding this is by noting that if developing project A prevents project B from being undertaken, the NPV of B is actually an opportunity cost for A.

Many natural resource investments have mutually exclusive projects that should be considered in the capital budgeting process. One of the most common is the same project but developed later in time. The option to postpone a project must be carefully considered when valuing an investment project and is the reason why many positive-NPV projects are delayed, especially in times of high uncertainty.

THREE EXAMPLES OF MISUSE OF
THE NET PRESENT VALUE DECISION RULE

The net present value (NPV) approach to capital budgeting has a well-deserved reputation of being a simple optimising decision rule. However, the robustness of the procedure to changes in its underlying assumptions is somewhat exaggerated, as shown in the following three examples.

EXAMPLE OF INCORRECT COMPUTATION OF CASHFLOWS

A manager is considering an investment project to expand production of a mine lease that expires next year. An investment of US$80 million would allow production of 1 million additional units next year. Next year's expected commodity unit price is US$400, with an annual return volatility of 25%. Marginal unit cost of production is US$320 and the appropriate project discount rate is 10%. Should the project be undertaken?

A common, but incorrect, application of the NPV rule computes expected cashflows by using expected commodity prices. Thus:

$$NPV = -80 + 1(400 - 320)/(1.10) = -7.27 \text{ million}$$

which would seem to imply that this is an unprofitable project and should not be undertaken.

The simplicity of the above calculation sometimes obscures the underlying assumption of total lack of managerial flexibility to cut losses in the event of low commodity prices. If we recognise that 25% commodity return volatility implies that half of the time the price could be US$500 and the other half US$300 (keeping the mean of US$400), *and* if we allow the project to be flexible enough to stop production when prices are low, then the present value for each scenario becomes:

	500	$NPV = -80 + 1(500 - 320)/(1.10)$	= 83.64 million
400			
	300	$NPV = -80 + 0$	= -80 million

Thus, project NPV, computed as the expected value for each scenario, is:

$$NPV = 0.5 \times 83.64 + 0.50 \times (-80) = 1.82 \text{ million}$$

and the project *should* be undertaken.

EXAMPLE OF INCORRECT DECISION TO INVEST

A manager is considering an investment project to develop and extract all resources in a natural resource lease that expires next year. If the manager invests US$80 million, then 1 million units of commodity could be produced and sold immediately. Next year's expected commodity unit price is US$400, with annual return volatility of 25%. Today's unit commodity price is also US$400. Marginal unit cost of production is US$300 and the appropriate project discount rate is 10%. Should the project be undertaken today?

The application of the discounted cashflow approach concludes that to invest today is a positive NPV decision:

$$NPV = -80 + 1(400 - 300) = 20 \text{ million}$$

This calculation may induce suboptimal decision making by neglecting the possibility of postponing the same project so that it may be undertaken under more favourable market conditions. We should always compare the value of investing now with the value of the same project undertaken later in time if commodity prices rise.

	500	$NPV = (-80 + 1(500 - 300))/(1.10)$	$= 109.09 \text{ million}$
400			
	300	$NPV = 0$	$= 0 \text{ million}$

$$NPV = 0.5 \times 109.09 + 0.50 \times (0) = 54.54 \text{ million}$$

which is greater than the value of undertaking the investment project now, so the project should not be undertaken today but management should wait to see whether next year's price rises or not.

EXAMPLE OF INCORRECT DISCOUNT RATE

A manager is considering an exploration investment project that requires

Pitfall 3: incorrect discount rate

Compounding an interest rate is simple to do, but is based on a strong assumption: that uncertainty is resolved over time at a constant rate. In other words, to discount a year one cashflow using a 10% discount rate and a year two cashflow using a 21% discount rate assumes that first and second year risk are the same (per year). This may or may not be the case, but for most natural resource investments it will not.

Appropriate discount rates may be obtained by adding to the risk-free interest rate a risk premium that depends on the volatility and the correlation of cashflows with some priced risky factor in the economy. The capital asset pricing model (CAPM) considers that the only priced risk is market an upfront investment of US$1 million. The project is risky and half of the time will be abandoned after one year of exploration with no residual value; the other half of the time a profitable ore will be found, which will require an additional US$5 million investment, but will provide a perpetuity of US$1 million.

Many times, in cases like this, decision makers look for some kind of "average" annual risk that may grossly bias the calculation. For our example, the volatility of outcomes may induce us to use high discount rates, like 20%. In this case:

	Find ore	−5	1	1	1	1	...
−1							
	Abandon	0					

$$NPV = -1 + 0.5\,(-5 + 1/0.20)/1.2 = -1 \text{ million}$$

and the exploration project looks like a bad project.

The fact that uncertainty evolves over time at a non-constant rate has profound implications for the value of many projects. For example, this exploration project resolves all its uncertainty at the end of the first year. Thus, conditional on finding ore, risk is very low and from year one on should be discounted at a low rate (ie, 10%). Our valuation could then be

	Find ore	−5 + 1/0.1 = 5 million
−1		
	Abandon	0

and the exploration project is very valuable because with a US$1 million investment the project has an expected cashflow of US$2.5 million one year later.

uncertainty. Other models like the arbitrage pricing model decompose risky cashflows by correlating them to several risky factors (like unexpected inflation or unexpected changes in productivity) and determining a unit risk premium for each of them.

Whichever pricing model is used, most investment projects will find that their risk structure changes over time. In the same way as financial leverage changes equity riskiness, operational leverage, by changing cost structure, modifies cashflow volatility. Moreover, whenever cashflow is a non-linear function of uncertainty, cashflow volatility will not be constant, making the computation of risk premiums an extremely difficult task (see Panel 2). This cashflow non-linearity may arise from the optimal exercise of options available to the project manager as well as from the possible occurrence of discrete technical or economic events, like the discovery of a rich ore in an exploration project, or the marketing success of a new product.

REAL OPTION VALUATION OF NATURAL RESOURCE INVESTMENTS

The similarity in the cashflow functions between financial options and many investment projects has been recognised since the early 1980s. Financial options are defined by their non-linear cashflow function induced by the holder's right to choose the most favourable among several alternatives. For example, a call option that gives its holder the right but not the obligation to obtain a given asset at a fixed cost (strike price) exhibits convex cashflows by taking advantage of scenarios of high asset prices while limiting downside risk. Similarly a put option also has convex cashflows providing the right to sell the asset at a fixed price, being valuable for low asset prices but being worthless for high prices.

Many natural resource investments exhibit cashflows with functional forms similar to those of financial options. For example, a mine-extraction project with costless opening/closing may be seen as a call option written on the output commodity price with marginal cost of extraction as its strike price. Another example is a development project, which can be viewed as a call option written on the value of the developed project with the development investment as the strike price.

Once the analogy between financial options and real investments is settled, it becomes clear that what has been learned about how to value the former can be successfully applied to the latter. The valuation of natural resource investments as real options is based on the use of:

❑ arbitrage valuation; and
❑ futures prices.

This new valuation approach takes care of the major pitfalls in NPV valuation by adequately computing relevant cashflows, providing optimal operational decisions during the life of the project and correctly discounting cashflows.

Arbitrage valuation

Financial theory privileges relative over absolute pricing. Market efficiency implies that market prices provide a reliable benchmark that can be used for pricing other assets. This idea prevails in most financial reasoning including bond pricing, NPV valuation, risk premium determination, and option pricing. Computing the term structure of interest rates, for example, is an exercise in relative pricing by assuming that all bonds that pay a given cashflow at a given date must provide the same return. Moreover, when applying this idea to bonds, and even to real investments in a NPV calculation, the assumption is that every dollar received at any given date has a current price equal to a bullet bond with maturity on that date. Even the CAPM, which computes risk premiums for financial assets, prices assets relative to benchmarks by determining total return in relation to those of a risk free asset and a market portfolio.

Arbitrage valuation follows the same idea by also valuing an asset in relation to a benchmark. In this case each asset has its own benchmark: a perfectly correlated asset. The CAPM has a similar reasoning. If we decompose total asset risk into its diversifiable and non-diversifiable components, CAPM states that only the latter matters for pricing, and this component is also perfectly correlated to its benchmark asset: the market portfolio.

Arbitrage valuation is a very robust approach, provided a perfectly correlated is found. The reasoning is simple but powerful: whenever it is possible to construct a risk-free portfolio by combining perfectly correlated assets with adequate weights, this portfolio should earn the risk-free return. Otherwise any investor, without regard to his or her preferences, would benefit by trading this portfolio against a risk free bond, and continue doing so until prices adjust.

Unfortunately most assets do not have an adequate perfectly correlated benchmark to price them by arbitrage. Some do, however, like financial options, with returns perfectly correlated to those of their underlying assets. Natural resource investments also have these perfectly correlated benchmark portfolios, because most non-diversifiable risk is perfectly correlated to commodity prices. Thus it should be straightforward to apply this arbitrage principle to valuing natural resource investments. Panel 2 explains why it is so much easier to value option-like cashflows by arbitrage instead of by the discounted cashflow methods.

Futures prices

Discounted cashflow methods aim to determine a present value equivalent to a stream of future cashflows. Even if these cashflows are deterministic (with no risk), time preference makes them less valuable further into the future. When uncertainty is introduced, risk aversion induces a further devaluation of expected cashflows. The most common approach to computing current value of risky flows is to increase the discount rate to include an adequate risk premium.

There is, however, an alternative approach to obtaining the present value of future cashflows that consists of penalising risky cashflows in order to obtain their *certainty equivalents*. This certainty equivalent is a fixed cashflow that is as valuable for asset holders as the original risky flows. With this approach, the present value of the original cashflows can be obtained by discounting their certainty equivalent at the risk-free interest rate. Thus we have transformed the problem from computing return risk premiums into obtaining certainty-equivalent cashflows.

ARBITRAGE VERSUS DISCOUNTED CASHFLOW VALUATION: COMPUTING RISK PREMIUMS FOR FLEXIBLE INVESTMENTS

WHY IT IS BETTER TO USE ARBITRAGE VALUATION INSTEAD OF NPV

In this panel we illustrate how to value by arbitrage a contingent claim and the difficulty of correctly determining risk premiums whenever cashflows are a non-linear function of uncertainty. We start with a very simple case in which the underlying asset has no risk premium, and we value a derivative asset by both procedures. Then we show how difficult it is to correctly implement the NPV approach whenever the underlying asset has a risk premium.

A manager needs to bid for a lease to exploit a developed natural resource. The lease gives the right to produce 1 million units of a commodity next year at a marginal cost of US$150 each. After the first year the lease expires independently of the amount produced. The current commodity price is US$150, but next year's price is uncertain and has 33% return volatility. The risk-free interest rate is set, for simplicity, to zero.

The manager recognises that if commodity price is less than US$150, the natural resource should be closed and cashflows will be zero, making this project look like a one-year-maturity call option written on production revenues with a US$150 million strike price. Given this financial option analogy, the project may be valued using both NPV and arbitrage valuation techniques. We analyse two cases for commodity price uncertainty: with and without commodity risk premium.

CASE 1: COMMODITY PRICE HAS NO RISK PREMIUM

If we assume no risk premium, zero risk-free interest and 33% commodity return volatility, next year's commodity price should have an expected price equal to this year's price, and the lease could be modelled as follows:

Commodity price uncertainty	Net value of production
S_1 = US$200	US$50 million
S_0 = US$150	
S_1 = US$100	0 (Abandon)

with a 50% probability for each price scenario.

$$NPV = \frac{0.5(0) + 0.5(200 - 150)}{1} = 25$$

Thus, using the net present value approach, the value of the lease is US$25 million.

Arbitrage valuation is based on the ability to hedge commodity price risk by forming a portfolio including the lease and a position in the commodity market (spot or futures).

Let n be the short position on the commodity that hedges project risk. We determine n by equating the value of holding one unit of the lease and shorting n units of the commodity:

S_1	100	200
Lease	0	50
Portfolio	$0 - n\,100$	$= \quad 50 - n\,200$

Thus, $n = \frac{1}{2}$.

Given that the portfolio has no risk, arbitrage valuation requires that portfolio return should be the risk-free interest rate. So

$$\frac{\left(0 - \frac{1}{2}100\right)}{\left(\text{Lease} - \frac{1}{2}150\right)} = 1$$

from which the value of the lease becomes US$25 million.

This example shows that when commodity price does not have any risk premium, and expected cashflows are computed correctly, arbitrage and NPV valuation procedures provide the same value estimate.

CASE 2: COMMODITY PRICE HAS A NON-ZERO RISK PREMIUM

In this case we maintain all assumptions, but introduce an annual risk premium for commodity prices of 10%. Thus next year's expected commodity price should be 10% higher than this year's price, and the lease could be modelled as follows:

Commodity price uncertainty	Net value of production
$S_1 = \text{US\$200}$	50 million
$S_0 = \text{US\$150}$	
$S_1 = \text{US\$100}$	0 (Abandon)

To achieve an expected price rise of 10% we have to assume prices will rise with a 65% probability and decrease with a 35% probability.

If we now want to use arbitrage valuation for this case we can easily replicate the procedure used for Case 1 and again will obtain a value of US$25 million for the lease. The only difference between both cases is the probability vector on each price scenario, and, given the hedging arguments used, this information is not relevant for determining lease value.

On the other hand, one of the difficulties of computing project value using discounting cashflows is that expected project cashflows obviously change when scenario probabilities change, increasing now to US$32.5 from US$25 million of Case 1. This could induce us to think that now the lease is more valuable, which is not the case. The fact that expected cashflows are higher is perfectly offset by the increased riskiness of the project. This can be confirmed by computing return volatility of investing in the commodity and in the lease:

	Return		Return
S_1 = US$200 33%		50 million	100%
S_0 = US$150	25		
S_1 = US$100 −33%		0 (Abandon)	−100%

Given that lease volatility is three times higher than commodity volatility, and that commodity and lease returns are perfectly correlated, it is easy to show that lease risk premiums should be three times higher, which means that the correct lease risk premium should be 30%. Now we can compute the net present value of the project:

$$NPV = \frac{0.35 \times 0 + 0.65 \times (200 - 150)}{1.30} = 25 \text{ million}$$

We have shown that if we correctly compute expected cashflows and risk premiums for option-like projects it is possible to use discounted cashflow methods for valuation. However, it is evident that as long as project cashflows are not a linear function of commodity risk, computing risk premiums is a very difficult task and arbitrage valuation is a much more robust approach.

Most of the theory for dealing with risk has been developed to determine return risk premiums (CAPM and APT models) instead of certainty equivalent cashflows. However, recent developments in the financial markets and increased trading of futures contracts on many commodities are now providing market data for these certainty equivalents. The futures contracts price represents what we agree today to exchange for a given commodity at a future date and is, by definition, the certainty equivalent of the underlying asset price at delivery.

The use of futures prices, whenever available, is a very robust way of valuing risky cashflows. It makes it unnecessary to estimate expected commodity prices by providing a direct market price. Moreover, by using only riskless discount rates it does not rely on any risk premium calculation (which is very noisy). This approach is consistent with traditional sound financial advice, which recommends the use of direct market data over estimations, which are always the subject of bias and noise. Natural resource investments have a natural advantage in using real options because of the existence of these active futures markets.

Natural resource investments as options

Real option methodology is not an important tool for *all types* of investments. It is certainly more sophisticated than naïve applications of discounted cashflow, and as such requires, in many cases, a more detailed modelling of the available uncertainties and flexibilities, which makes it undesirable for some kinds of investments.

There are several ways to classify investments. One classification is related to their strategic nature. We consider an investment project to be strategic if it is large enough to be relevant and irreversible enough to induce significant switching-back costs. Investment size is obviously a strong determinant of how much effort (and decision-making cost) an organisation is willing to commit to make a good decision. Managers often consider it unprofitable to spend significant resources on small projects. On the other hand, irreversibility of resource deployment is a main determinant of the optimal amount of valuation effort. If decisions are reversible then the optimal decision rule is essentially myopic and consists of comparing marginal costs and benefits over the next unit of time. Given the higher valuation effort of using the real option approach, strategic investments are much more prone to be valued using this new methodology.

Natural resource projects frequently have a strategic component. For example, the development of a mine involves huge resources, a large proportion of which are tied up to the project and cannot be recouped if the project fails. Many projects of this type can greatly benefit from refining the valuation process.

A second way of classifying investment projects is by their behaviour under uncertainty. Some projects behave in essentially the same way under all states of nature, for example, projects that reduce fixed costs (administrative overhead that is independent of production level). This type of project typically does not benefit from a very detailed valuation process because the optimal decision making becomes somewhat trivial. A second type of project is one which is exposed to uncertainty in a linear fashion. This means that there is essentially the same probability of increasing their value by a fixed percentage as there is of decreasing it by the same amount.

Some natural resource investments with no operational flexibility because of contractual, technological or economic ties may not require the use of a fully fledged real-option methodology, but only the use of futures prices for valuing the present value of cashflows. For example, if we are committed (for whatever reason) on producing a barrel of oil twelve months from now we should value that commitment using the risk-free discounted value of the current futures price for delivery in twelve months. There is no benefit from going through the cumbersome (and error-prone) process of estimating the spot oil price in a year and then discounting it using a risky return rate, but neither does this project have any flexibility that should be valued as a financial option.

Most natural resource investments belong to a third type of project – those that are very risky but also have embedded operational flexibilities that make them behave very well in good scenarios while limiting their downside risk by allowing their managers to take appropriate remedial actions. Typically a natural resource investment project may expand production when commodity prices increase, but is able to limit or shut down production when prices are low. Development investments are also sometimes postponed or accelerated, and even extraction sequencing may depend on market or project conditions. These are the projects that have been, and will continue to be, those that benefit the most by using real-option methodology.

Natural resource investments also possess the very important feature of having a market for their major source of non-diversifiable risk. The fact that futures maturity is shorter than the production horizon may be dealt with by assuming an adequate futures-pricing model. The increasingly developed commodity futures market makes implementation of this real option procedure for investments in this sector a much easier task than for others.

RECENT ADVANCES IN NATURAL RESOURCE VALUATION USING REAL OPTIONS

There are now hundreds of academic papers on using real option methodology for valuing natural resources. Probably one of the seminal works is Brennan and Schwartz (1985) in which an investment project to extract copper is valued using arbitrage arguments. The source of uncertainty is output price and firms can respond by delaying production temporarily or permanently depending on price levels and volatility. Given that futures prices are used, the project value is determined without requiring predictions of spot prices, one of the main sources of error in natural resource investment valuations. The optimal response by the firm (the decision when to delay or resume production) is obtained jointly with firm value. In this setting the value of the firm is a function of the available resources to be extracted (output to be produced in the future) and the commodity spot price. In order to maximise its value, the firm manager can respond by modifying the production level. Many academic works have discussed the application of this approach to topics including the valuation of oil reserves (Ekern, 1985; Paddock, Siegel and Smith, 1988), copper contingent investments (Cortazar, Schwartz and Salinas, 1998) and gold mines (Moel and Tufano, 1998).

Despite the wide consensus on the benefits of using the real option approach to valuing commodity contingent claims, its adoption by practitioners has been rather slow. Many firms that use this new approach limit themselves to restricted formulas developed for financial claims, like Black and Scholes (1973), without taking full advantage of its potentialities. In our opinion, more work has to be done if we want to increase its use in real-world applications.

Recently there have been modelling advances that may enhance real option applicability. The first issue that has benefited from recent research is the modelling of commodity-price uncertainty. Commodity prices are very volatile, with typical annual variations of 20% to 40%. This price uncertainty has a major effect on asset valuation and should be modelled accordingly. Futures contract markets provide risk-free estimates of commodity prices and are critical in any real option implementation.

Initial applications of the real option methodology modelled the dynamics of commodity prices using one-factor random walk specifications. This means that uncertainty can fully be described by one state variable and that any two perturbations of this variable are independent of each other. This type of model has three major drawbacks:

❑ it does not take into account mean reversion in commodity prices, which is a standard assumption in the natural resource industry;

❑ it is not consistent with empirical evidence on term structure volatility of futures contracts that has declining return volatility with contract maturity; and

❑ it induces a perfect correlation among all derivatives of a commodity and all contract maturities.

Increasingly, in the 1990s, better commodity price models have been proposed. One-, two- and three-factor mean reverting models have been developed and estimated for major commodities like oil, copper and gold (Gibson and Schwartz, 1990; Ross, 1995; Bessembinder, Coughenour, Seguin, and Monroe Smoller, 1995). Recent papers improve model specifications, propose alternative parameter estimation procedures, and actualise parameter values. Typically these models consider two or three correlated risk factors like spot prices, convenience yields, interest rates and deviations from long-term drifts. They find significant mean reversion and decreasing volatility with maturity and a much better fit with existing futures market prices, making real option models of natural resource investments more credible for industry use (Schwartz and Smith, 1997; Schwartz, 1997; Cortazar, Schwartz and Riera, 1999). The use of these models is critical for estimating:

❑ long-maturity futures prices for which there are no markets;
❑ price volatility that is relevant to value managerial flexibility; and
❑ hedging ratios required to implement risk management strategies.

The development of richer stochastic process specifications for uncertainty, like the two- and three-factor models just described, poses an additional challenge to derivative valuation techniques because of added complexity. It must be noted that most natural resource investments can be seen as American-type options because investment and operational flexibility can be exercised at any moment within a given time frame. If so, cashflows on a given date depend not only on past information but also on expectations of future events. It has long been known that whenever a markovian process (one where all past information may be embedded in current state variable values) can describe uncertainty, the value of a security must be obtained by some kind of backward induction. This procedure works its way into the present starting from some known value, typically at option expiration.

A number of backward induction procedures have been proposed for valuing assets, from dynamic programming, to binomial and multinomial trees, to finite-difference procedures for solving partial differential equations. These procedures start from boundary conditions and solve simultaneously for asset value and for the optimal exercise policy, determining the shape of the cashflow function in such a way as to maximise asset value. One problem is that it is increasingly difficult to implement them when uncertainty is modelled as multifactor processes, because complexity grows exponentially. This can be a major deterrence to using sophisticated uncertainty modelling.

One way of handling uncertainty in a much simpler way is to use Monte Carlo simulation methods. Recent advances in this area have allowed its use to be extended to value not only traditional European-type options, but also American-type ones, which is very relevant for natural resource real-option models. Examples of simulation techniques for valuing American options include Barraquand and Martineau (1995), Broadie and Glasserman (1997a and 1997b), Broadie, Glasserman and Jain (1997), Raymar and Zwecher (1997), Longstaff and Schwartz (1998), and others. These methods try to combine the simplicity of forward induction typical of simulation with the ability to determine the optimal option exercise of backward induction. An example of the application of Monte Carlo simulation procedures to the valuation of the decision regarding when optimally to develop an oilfield can be found in Cortazar and Schwartz (1998).

Finally, there are some encouraging signs that the real option approach to valuation is making inroads into the mainstream. Real-world applications are being published much more frequently (Tufano and Moel, 1997; Cortazar and Casassus, 1998), academic and practitioner-oriented conferences are being regularly organised (such as the Real Options Conferences, 1997–9), and more companies are increasingly making use of this new approach. Natural resource companies are leading the way to what will probably become the central paradigm for corporate valuation in the near future.

BIBLIOGRAPHY

Barraquand, J. and D. Martineau, 1995, "Numerical Valuation of High Dimensional Multivariate American Securities", *Journal of Financial and Quantitative Analysis*, 30(3), pp. 383–405.

Bessembinder, H., J. Coughenour, P. Seguin and M. Monroe Smoller, 1995, "Mean Reversion in Equilibrium Asset Prices: Evidence from Futures Term Structure", *Journal of Finance*, 50(1), pp. 361–75.

Black, F. and M. Scholes, 1973, "The Pricing of Options and Corporate Liabilities", *Journal of Political Economy*, 81, pp. 637–54.

Brennan, M. and E. Schwartz, 1985, "Evaluating Natural Resource Investments", *Journal of Business*, 58(2), pp. 135–57.

Broadie, M. and P. Glasserman, 1997a, "Pricing American-Style Securities Using Simulation", *Journal of Economics Dynamics and Control*, 21, pp. 1323–52.

Broadie, M. and P. Glasserman, 1997b, "Monte Carlo Methods for Pricing High-Dimensional American Options: An Overview", Working Paper, Columbia University.

Broadie, M., P. Glasserman and G. Jain, 1997, "Enhanced Monte Carlo Estimates for American Option Prices", *Journal of Derivatives*, 5(1), pp. 25–44.

Cortazar, G. and J. Casassus, 1998, "Optimal Timing of a Mine Expansion: Implementing a Real Options Model", *The Quarterly Review of Economics and Finance*, 38, pp. 755–69.

Cortazar, G., E. Schwartz and F. Riera, 1999, "Market-based Forecasts of Commodity Prices using Futures", *1999 FMA European Conference*, Barcelona, (June).

Cortazar, G. and E. Schwartz, 1998, "Monte Carlo Evaluation Model of an Undeveloped Oil Field", *Journal of Energy Finance and Development*, 3(1), pp. 73–84.

Cortazar, G., E. Schwartz and M. Salinas, 1998, "Evaluating Environmental Investments: A Real Options Approach", *Management Science*, 44(8), 1059–70.

Ekern, S., 1985, "An Option Pricing Approach to Evaluating Petroleum Projects", *Energy Economics*, 10, pp. 91–9.

Gibson, R. and E. Schwartz, 1990, "Stochastic Convenience Yield and the Pricing of Oil Contingent Claims", *Journal of Finance*, 45(3), pp. 959–76.

Longstaff, F. and E. Schwartz, 1998, "Valuing American Options By Simulation: A Simple Least-Squares Approach", The John E. Anderson Graduate School of Management at UCLA, Finance Working Paper No. 25–98.

Moel, A. and P. Tufano, 1998, "When are Real Options Exercised? An Empirical Study of Mine Closings", 2nd Annual Conference on Real Options, Chicago, (June).

Paddock, J.L., D.W. Siegel and J.L. Smith, 1988, "Option Valuation of Claims on Real Assets: The Case of Offshore Petroleum Leases", *Quarterly Journal of Economics*, 103(3), pp. 479–508.

Raymar, S. and M. Zwecher, 1997, "A Monte Carlo Valuation of American Call Options on the Maximum of Several Stocks", *Journal of Derivatives*, 5(1), pp. 7–23.

Real Options Conference: Theory Meets Practice, Annual Conferences Organised by L. Trigeorgis, New York (1997), Chicago, (1998), Wassenaar/Leiden (1999).

Ross, S.A., 1995, "Hedging Long Run Commitments: Exercises in Incomplete Market Pricing", Working Paper.

Schwartz, E., 1997, "The Stochastic Behaviour of Commodity Prices: Implications for Valuation and Hedging" *The Journal of Finance*, LII(3), (July).

Schwartz, E. and J. Smith, 1997, "Short-Term Variations and Long-Term Dynamics in Commodity Prices", The John E. Anderson Graduate School of Management at UCLA, Finance Working Paper No. 14-97.

Tufano, P. and A. Moel, 1997, "Bidding for Antamina", Harvard Business School, Case N9-297-054.

12

Learning and Exercising Options to Reduce Capital Project Risk

Larry Chorn and Peter Carr

American Graduate School of International Management;
Banc of America Securities LLC

Successful investment management of capital-intensive, long-term energy projects requires an understanding of the associated economic uncertainties, or risks, as well as the mechanisms to resolve them. Industry traditionally manages these risks by purchasing information (such as seismic studies, well testing, appraisal drilling, reservoir simulation, market capacity and price studies) about the project and making incremental investments as new information reduces the uncertainties to acceptable levels.

Traditional discounted cashflow analyses cannot readily value information. We suggest that the purchase of information about a project has considerable value and can be treated as purchasing an option on the project. As with options on equities, if the information leads to the expectation of a positive investment outcome, the project should be funded. Similarly, options on capital investment projects also have a time factor dictating value and the proper time to undertake the investment.

This chapter discusses the application of real options techniques to value information. We show how real options are used to value the information surrounding a production capacity decision for an offshore gas field development. In this example, we value the field development alternatives and the acquisition of incremental information for the alternative selection process. As a further extension of real options to capital investment projects, we create a dynamic model to identify investment alternatives to capture additional value over the project's lifetime. The dynamic model uses information acquired in development drilling and field operations to maximise the investment outcome.

In the 1990s the energy industry added value creation to its traditional set of performance metrics, which consisted of reserve replacement and production volume. Within the same period, the industry's universe of investment opportunities grew rapidly. However, increasingly, many attractive opportunities consist of complex field and infrastructure developments requiring the expenditure of billions of capital dollars over the project's life. These frequently contain extensive uncertainties regarding timing, technical and financial dimensions, depend on synergies between upstream and downstream activities, and resulting in large positive cashflows distributed over 20 or more years. These uncertainties and complexities make the financial analysis of a project much more demanding. In particular, the financial analysis must properly reflect the opportunity to create value in a project by resolving the uncertainties and by defining an investment approach to maximise the project value.

Traditional financial tools, such as discounted cashflow (DCF) may undervalue the upside associated with these long-term and uncertain projects relative to management's intuitive sense of their value (Kulatilaka and Marcus, 1992). Discounted cashflow is unable to value management's insight regarding changing technologies, market conditions and the impact of leveraging. These projects are then often defined as "strategic" and accepted for inclusion into the company portfolio despite an unfavourable valuation.

Why does DCF fail to consider upside value? We believe that traditional approaches do not adequately value the flexibility in investment behaviour created by management's use and acquisition of new information. New information about a project allows management to adjust, for example, project scope, investment rate and production rates, to accommodate uncertainties related to price, market, cost, and reserve size (Nichols, 1994).

MIMICKING INVESTMENT BEHAVIOUR

Flexibility in investment behaviour means that options exist to adjust the timing and size of the investment profile as new information becomes available. Economists agree that flexibility has value, but it is difficult to quantify flexibility in a manner that can guide management action. A remedy is to identify and value the outcome of an intelligent decision pathway for the project. An intelligent decision pathway maps an optimal sequence of choices through multiple decision points. The choices maximise the return on the investment and are based on the values of key variables at each decision point. So, maximising the return from an uncertain investment requires building and retaining flexibility - or options - in the investment programme. The value of those project options is the difference between the maximised return from a flexible investment programme, net of incremental expenditures for reducing uncertainty in key variables, and the return from an inflexible programme constructed using only the information available at the project's initiation.

From an applications perspective, economic theories for optimising investment behaviour are problematic if they involve estimating unknown parameters with little or no guidance. However, real options techniques are a branch of finance theory that has made the most progress towards describing optimal behaviour in investments incorporating uncertainty (Dixit and Pindyck, 1994). Financial instruments, shares and options, are claims on uncertain future cashflows as are investments in real assets like gas plants, pipelines, or offshore platforms (Paddock, Siegel and Smith, 1988). The critical questions for buyers and sellers of such claims are: "what are their values?" and, for options, "when should they be exercised?" The value and optimal exercise of a real option can be modelled in the same way as a financial option. Solutions to these problems depend on the rate at which key variables' uncertainties are resolved, the discount rate, and the time remaining in the option's life. Real options analysis improves the upside valuation for a long-term, uncertain project.

REAL OPTIONS PRINCIPLES

The distinction between the real options approach and traditional DCF analysis often boils down to the difference between the expectation of a maximum and the maximum of expectations. For example, a real options valuation of the option to purchase a stock is valued as the expectation of the maximum:

$$C_0 = E_0 \max\left[0, (S_T - K)e^{-rT}\right] \tag{1}$$

where E_0 is the time 0 expectation, S_T is the terminal stock value, K is the strike price, r is the discount rate and T is the time to maturity. The expectation is calculated using the risk-adjusted (also called risk-neutral) probability measure. In the now standard analogy with capital-budgeting decisions, is treated as the value of the project's cashflows at T and K as the investment required to undertake the project. The maximum is taken over the two possible operating modes: the project is taken if $S_T > K$ (net present value (NPV) at T_1 is positive), and not taken at T_1 if $S_T \leq K$ (NPV at T_1 is 0 or negative). In this standard analogy, it is assumed that if the project is not taken at T_1, then there is no ability to exercise (invest in the project) later. Thus the decision to not take the project at T_1 is tantamount to abandonment.

The traditional DCF approach not only ignores the ability to maximise outcomes during a project's life but also ignores the option to wait and undertake the project later. The flaw is that DCF assumes the decision to be made at the current time, rather than at the last time the decision can be made. As a result, the value under the traditional approach is a maximum over expectations E_0 using information at time equals T_0:

$$\text{Value} = \max\left[0, (E_0 S_T - K)e^{-rT}\right] \tag{2}$$

In words, the traditional DCF approach compares the NPV of the expected project outcome, $(E_0 S_T - K)e^{-rT}$, with 0. If NPV is positive, the project is taken; if NPV is negative, it is abandoned.

In the terminology of real options, the difference in value between the call option analogy (1) and the NPV analysis (2) is the time value. Time value reflects the incremental value due to the ability to condition decisions on future acquisition of information about the project's outcome. Time value is never negative. Thus, in the real options analogy, the project is taken if $S_T > K$, whereas in the NPV analysis, the project is taken if $E_0 S_T > K$. If uncertainty is 0, then $S_T = E_0 S_T$ and the two approaches are equivalent – the time value is 0 and incremental information has no value.

Even when the current project NPV is positive, the real options analogy suggests that it may still be better to defer the investment decision and acquire information that reduces uncertainty in the cashflow projections, rather than going ahead with the project and extinguishing flexibility. The value of the additional information can be described as:

$$\text{Value} = E_0 \max\left[0, (S_T - K)e^{-rT}\right] - (E_0 S_T - K)e^{-rT} \tag{3}$$

As long as there is time remaining before investment is required and significant uncertainties can be resolved, it may be better to defer the investment than to accept the positive NPV project immediately. This is only valid if management can actively acquire uncertainty-resolving information. Passive information acquisition, such as waiting for higher certainty in product sales price, will only result in continuous deferrals and project value destruction.

Strictly speaking, the previous discussion applies only to European-style options – options that can be exercised only at the end of their contract period. In reality, most firms have many highly complex American-style options, which can be exercised at any time during their contract period. When exercising now confers some benefit that exercising later will lose, it makes financial sense to invest in the project immediately. Examples of such benefits include a technological advantage by being first to market in a highly competitive environment, capturing, for example, low front-end investment costs. These effects can be valued by

$$\text{Value} = \max\left[C_0(K_T), (S_0 e^{-(r-\delta)T} - K_0)e^{-rT}\right] \tag{4}$$

where δ may be interpreted as a downward force on value due to competitive pressures and K_0 and K_T are the magnitude of investments required now and at T respectively.

Similarly, immediate investment is also justified if additional information will not change the investment decision or uncertainty-reducing information will not be available before the investment must be taken or abandoned. As information is acquired in a discontinuous fashion, management should be prepared to regularly revisit the valuation analysis to determine if the uncertainty threshold has been achieved and, if so, the investment should be undertaken (or abandoned) without further delay – an American-style option.

It is apparent then that real options analysis is not a substitute for traditional DCF analysis but an enhancement of DCF principles that allows the analyst to properly value managerial flexibility. Real options analysis also provides insight into the existence of project upsides. If a project has limited flexibility, real options will, as a consequence, reveal limited option value. Further, a real options model provides guidance in executing the investment programme whereas a traditional DCF analysis cannot. It assumes that there are no decisions remaining once the project begins. The dynamic nature of real options encourages management to return to the model during the project's life to post-audit prior decisions and prepare for future decisions by valuing the acquisition of new information.

APPLICATION TO ASSET DEVELOPMENT

We now demonstrate the merit of a real options analysis to identify the highest valued development scenario for an offshore gas field. Production capacity, or facility-sizing, applications have been identified by a number of organisations as their principal use of real options in capital budgeting. We illustrate this application in some detail. However, both gas price and recoverable volumes are uncertainties in this analysis. To our knowledge this is the first demonstration of a real options model using more than one variable. Further, the focus on using real options to value incremental information appears to be a new concept.

The preliminary development programme encompassed several distinct fields, zones within fields and numerous nearby exploration opportunities. The project was envisioned as incrementally developing reserves adequate to sustain a base production level, q, of 400 million cubic feet per day of sales gas over a 20-year contract. As the initial development begins to decline in production rate, subsequent volumes will be developed from the remaining proved, undeveloped assets to maintain contract production levels.

The investment, K, required to undertake the project, includes:

❏ drilling and well costs;
❏ unmanned platforms for most production facilities;
❏ one large processing platform with limited separation capability and compression;
❏ platform-to-shore multiphase pipeline; and
❏ slug catcher, separation, and liquid storage facilities on shore.

There are many investment decisions to be made through the life of the project associated with these facilities. This real options analysis is only concerned with sizing of production capacity. The analysis evaluates the economic merits of q = (400, 600) million cubic feet per day (MMCFD) and a subsequent increase in production capacity of Δq = (0, 200, 400) MMCFD.

The issue of timing is important in every economic analysis. It is very important in a real options problem because time can be a variable. This

1. Intelligent decision pathway for gas field development

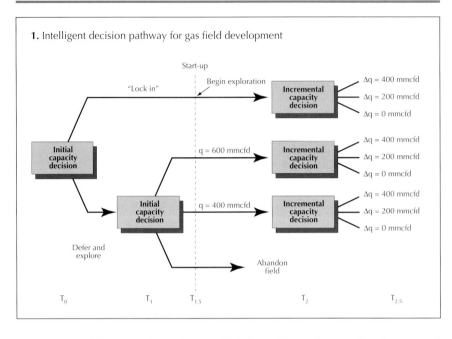

project has two fixed dates with information gathering timeframes and decision points preceding them. The project is assumed to begin production at $T_{1.5}$. Construction lead times require a decision point at T_1, at least three years prior to $T_{1.5}$, to fabricate and install facilities and wells. The second fixed date, $T_{2.5}$, occurs five years after $T_{1.5}$, at which additional production capacity may be added, or not, depending on gas price and remaining reserves. Again a decision point, T_2, at least three years prior to $T_{2.5}$, is required to accommodate construction constraints.

The intelligent decision pathway for the project is shown in Figure 1 for clarity. Decisions can be taken or deferred as indicated. Only $T_{1.5}$ is fixed. The branches on the pathway indicate the possible cases that management can select for the development programme. Each branch is evaluated independently using real options modelling principles. The highest NPV branch reflects the optimum approach to develop the gas fields. A base case analysis using traditional DCF analysis techniques is performed to value the preliminary project development programme without option considerations – using only the knowledge of price and recoverable volumes that exists at T_0.

GAS PRICE AS A VARIABLE

Annual gross revenue, $S_t q_i$, from the project depends upon spot gas prices over the 20-year life of the known fields and exploration opportunities. As with reserves, gas prices are highly uncertain. However, there is extensive market information available on gas price trends and volatility, from which a

Table 1. Inputs to the real options model for a gas field development

Deterministic input variables

- ❑ Risk-free rate (% per year)
- ❑ Convenience yield (% per year)
- ❑ Condensate price (US$/bbl)
- ❑ Condensate ratio (bbl/mmcf)
- ❑ Time interval (years) between
  - Today and initial capacity decision deadline
  - Deadline for initial and incremental capacity decisions
  - Initial capacity decision and start of production
  - Deadline for incremental capacity decision and start-up of that capacity
- ❑ Set of initial production capacities allowed (mmcfd)
- ❑ Set of incremental production capacities allowed (mmcfd)
- ❑ Investment required for each initial capacity (US$)
- ❑ Investment required for each incremental capacity (US$)
- ❑ Unit production costs (% of spot price)
- ❑ Exploration costs estimates (US$)
  - if exploring at T_0
  - if exploring at $T_{1.5}$

Probabilistic input variables

- ❑ Price of natural gas
  - current spot price (US$/mcf)
  - price volatility (% per year)
- ❑ Reserves volume in known fields
  - expected recoverable volumes
  - variance around expected volumes
  - variance after 5 years of production
- ❑ Speculative potential volume
  - expected recoverable volumes
  - variance around expected volumes, pre-exploration
  - variance around expected volumes, post-exploration
  - variance after 5 years of production

distribution of future expectations can be constructed. Previous real options analyses (Paddock, Siegel and Smith, 1988; Lohrenz and Dickens, 1993) have focused exclusively on price, so this paper will only briefly review the standard stochastic process recognised as governing spot prices of natural gas and use that approach to build a future expectation distribution for reserves.

At time T_0, the current spot price of natural gas is known with certainty to be S_0. Given all of the available information at T_0, the spot price at any future date T_1 is unknown. The standard model quantifies the uncertainty surrounding the time T_1 spot price by assuming that the natural logarithm of the price is normally distributed with mean $\ln S_0 + \mu T_1$ and variance $\sigma^2 T_1$. Here, μ is the assumed constant drift rate of the diffusion process for price and σ^2 is the assumed constant variance rate of the process. Table 1 presents the model parameters for spot price. Figure 2 illustrates a discretised gas price distribution as a function of S_0 and time.

As time increases, the variance of $\ln S_T$ increases. The current spot price must reflect expectations of future spot prices. If near-term future prices

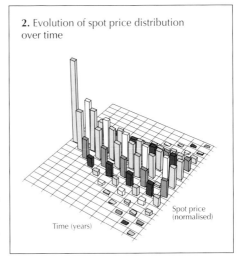

2. Evolution of spot price distribution over time

Spot price (normalised)

Time (years)

are expected to be significantly higher than current prices, rational buyers would increase their present purchases and decrease expected future spot purchases using gas storage. The resulting surge in demand for immediate delivery would push up current spot prices until equilibrium was reached. These economic forces are always present, so it is true that spot prices at T_1 also reflect the expectations at T_1 for spot prices at T_2.

RESERVE VOLUME AS A VARIABLE
The known fields have a limited production history and therefore retain a residual uncertainty surrounding the recoverable volumes. This uncertainty is represented with a composite probability distribution. Similarly, a probability distribution exists for the composite of the exploration opportunities' speculative potential volumes that may contribute to the sales gas volumes at some time in the life of the project. This probability distribution is shown in Figure 3.

From a modelling perspective, the essential differences between the known fields and the exploration opportunities are:

❑ there is a 100% certainty that there is a positive minimum economic reserve volume in the known fields, whereas there is a significant probability that there are no reserves in the exploration opportunities;

❑ by expending capital on exploration, the uncertainty surrounding the speculative potential volumes in the exploration opportunities can be reduced, whereas uncertainty regarding the reserves in the known fields can only be further reduced by developing the fields.

Complexity and accuracy may be added to the model by allowing individual state variables to represent the reserves in individual fields and exploration opportunities. This additional complexity does not significantly alter the valuation of the overall project but does complicate the investment profile and the timing of commitment to capacity by adding several more decision points to the intelligent decision pathway.

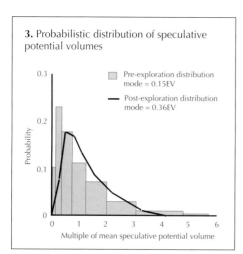

3. Probabilistic distribution of speculative potential volumes

Pre-exploration distribution mode = 0.15EV

Post-exploration distribution mode = 0.36EV

Probability

Multiple of mean speculative potential volume

RESOLVING RESERVES UNCERTAINTY
Just as the known current spot price is a standard input for real option models, we assume by analogy that the known current expectation of remaining reserves is an input for the valuation model. Formally, the input is $Q_0 \equiv E_0\widetilde{Q}$, where the

subscript 0 on the expectation operator E indicates that expectations are as of T_0 and the tilde over Q recognises that the reserve volumes and speculative potential volumes are uncertain. For simplicity, further use of the term "reserves" will imply discovered reserves and speculative potential volumes. This expectation for Q also follows a process over time. Letting $\overline{Q}_t \equiv E_t\tilde{Q}$, we define $\tilde{Q}$ as the remaining reserves at time t. For $t > T_0$, the mean reserves at t, $\overline{Q}_t$, is itself a random variable based on the information that we have at T_0. As a result we can describe the evolution of $\overline{Q}_t$ as a stochastic process.

The parameters of the $\overline{Q}_t$ stochastic process depend upon the project's operational status:

$$d\overline{Q}_t = \mu(q_t)dt + v(q_t, l_e)dW_t \qquad (5)$$

where
$d\overline{Q}_t$ is the change in the mean reserves over a short time interval;
$q_t \geq 0$ is the production rate at time t;
$\mu(q_t) \equiv -q_t$ is the drift rate of the mean reserves;
ll_e is an indicator variable, equal to 1 when exploring and to zero otherwise;
$v(q_t,l_e) \equiv \sqrt{v_q^2 q_t + v_{e,t}^2 l_e}$ is the volatility rate of the mean reserves;
$v_q^2 > 0$ is the variance rate per unit of production (assumed constant);
$v_{e,t}^2 > 0$ is the variance rate due to exploration at time t; and
dW_t is the increment of a standard Brownian motion.

As a consequence, we have $E_t d\overline{Q}_t = \mu(q_t)dt$, or equivalently $\mu(q_t) = E_t d\overline{Q}_t / dt$, so that the drift rate μ is the expected change at t in the mean reserves per year. We also have $Var_t d\overline{Q}_t = v^2(q_t,l_e)dt$, or rearranging, $v^2(q_t,l_e) = Var_t d\overline{Q}_t / dt$, where the variance rate v^2 is the variance at t of changes in the mean reserves per year. In the absence of absorption, the Brownian shock implies that, based on the information at any time, the mean reserves at any later time are normally distributed. An absorbing barrier is imposed on the evolution of $\overline{Q}_t$ at the origin to avoid the possibility of creating a probability of negative mean reserves. That is, once the mean reserves fall to 0, they can no longer rise or fall stochastically because the fields have been fully depleted. The resulting distribution for future mean reserves is no longer normally distributed. There is a strictly positive probability for a realisation of 0 with the remaining probability smoothly distributed over all positive reserve volumes.

Reducing the uncertainty surrounding the reserves is accomplished through two actions that acquire information: exploration and production. Each action impresses a different variance rate on a different volume, either in exploration opportunities through the conversion from speculative potential volumes to reserves or in known fields through confirmation of a recovery factor through production history. Modelling the uncertainty reduction requires defining the operator's activities relative to their effect on speculative potential or reserves. For this analysis, there are four operational phases that may occur in any of five time periods $\{T_1 - T_0, T_{1.5} - T_1, T_2 - T_{2.5}, T_{2.5} - T_2, > T_{2.5}\}$. Table 1 also presents the model parameters for mean reserves.

PHASE I

The project's operational state is at phase I when the operator is neither exploring nor producing. At T_0, the operator can decide to lock in the initial capacity now at T_0 or defer the decision until T_1. If the capacity decision is made at T_0, there is no rationale for exploring so the project is in a phase I state between T_0 and $T_{1.5}$. If the initial capacity decision is postponed until exploration results are available, the project moves into phase I between T_1 and $T_{1.5}$. Similarly, the project will be in phase I once all the reserves have been extracted. For phase I, the parameters in equation (5) become:

$$q_t = 0, l_e = 0, \mu = 0, \text{ and } \nu = 0$$

As a result, the mean reserves do not change with time. If the reserves have been extracted, Q_t equals 0. If the project is between T_0 and $T_{1.5}$ and there is no exploration under way, Q_t equals Q_0. Note that spot prices continue to evolve in phase I. Consequently it may be reasonable to defer capacity until T_1, rather than locking in at T_0, but deferral beyond T_1 cannot be justified by claims of improving price knowledge.

PHASE II

The project is in phase II when the operator is exploring but not producing. If the capacity decision is deferred to T_1 so that the operator can explore and optimise the production capacity, the project is in a phase II state between T_0 and T_1. The parameters for this phase are:

$$q_t = 0, l_e = 1, \mu = 0, \text{ and } \nu = v_{e,1}^2$$

This formulation assumes 0 mean reserve drift because exploring does not affect mean reserves, except after the fact. This *ex post* movement is captured by the positive variance rate, $v_{e,1}^2$. This rate is fixed by prompting for the reduction in variance of the total reserves due to exploring continuously over the time frame for the exploration programme. Estimates of variance reduction magnitudes must be obtained from experienced exploration staff familiar with probabilistic reserve assessments and in resolving uncertainty through the purchase of information – for example, seismic data acquisition and exploratory drilling. The variance rate $v_{e,1}^2$ is computed by dividing this reduction in variance by the timespan. If the operator does choose to defer the capacity decision to T_1 and explore over the $T_1 - T_0$ time frame, the project moves into a phase I state post-T_1, because exploration is concluded and production has not commenced.

PHASE III

As the operator begins production, the project progresses into phase III. This stage of uncertainty reduction in reserves begins at $T_{1.5}$ and continues until the fields are depleted. The parameters of the $\bar{Q}_t$ stochastic process in phase III are:

$$q_t > 0, l_e = 0, \mu = -q_t, \text{ and } \nu = \sqrt{\nu_q^2 \, q_t}$$

The variance rate per unit of production must be obtained from experienced reservoir engineering staff familiar with probabilistic reserve assessments and resolving recovery factors from reserve estimates and production history. Initially, the reduction in total variance due to production at the base rate of 400 MMCFD over a base case time interval $(T_2 - T_{1.5})$ is determined. This reduction must be annualised and further transformed to the variance rate per unit of production using the annualised production rate. The model assumes that the resulting variance rate per unit of production is a constant. Total variance is reduced in proportion to production capacity, assuming that available production capacity is fully exploited and is equal to the fields' production rate.

PHASE IV

A fourth phase is possible if the operator chooses to defer exploration until after a production capacity is fixed, facilities and wells are in place and the known fields are producing. Reserve uncertainties in known fields and exploration opportunities are simultaneously addressed. Phase IV can occur between $T_{1.5}$ and T_2 with these parameters for the stochastic process:

$$q_t > 0, l_e = 1, \mu = -q_t, \text{ and } \nu = \sqrt{\nu_q^2 \, q_t + \nu_{e,2}^2}$$

The variance rate $\nu_{e,2}^2$ is calculated assuming the same decrease in reserve variance due to exploration as that used for phase II, but the rate in phase IV is computed based on the time interval $(T_2 - T_{1.5})$, rather than $(T_1 - T_0)$ that is used for phase II. The variance rate, ν_q^2, associated with production activities, is the same in phase IV as in phase III.

OPTIMISING THE PROJECT VALUE

Management's principal impact on the value of this offshore gas field is limited to timing the investment and selecting a production capacity to maximise the present value of cashflows. The production capacity level is selected from a set of several discrete choices, which maximises project value at the decision times T_0, T_1, and T_2. At decision time T_0, if the operator decides to lock in the initial production capacity, the allowable choices are $q_l = 400$ MMCFD and $q_h = 600$ MMCFD. Within the lock in now alternative, capacity is built at the level chosen at T_0 even if conditions change at T_1 or if the resulting NPV is negative at T_1. Therefore, T_1 is a decision date only if the decision is deferred at T_0. If the decision deferral occurs, the allowable choices at T_1 are 0, $q_l = 400$ MMCFD and $q_h = 600$ MMCFD. A choice of 0 production capacity implies project abandonment. At both T_0 and T_1, the initial capacity level chosen is conditional on the information available then, which includes spot price and mean reserves as well as the optimal decision to be made at T_2. At T_2, two incremental capacity levels of $\Delta q_l = 200$ MMCFD and $\Delta q_h = 400$ MMCFD are available, as well as maintaining current capacity or abandoning the project. Thus the decision at T_2 chooses from seven discrete production capacity levels available from $T_{2.5}$ until the gas reserves are depleted, namely $\{0, q_l, q_l + \Delta q_l, q_l + \Delta q_h, q_h, q_h + \Delta q_l, q_h + \Delta q_h\}$. For each potential outcome – spot price and mean reserves – an optimum choice from this set is taken at T_2, after accounting for any incremental investment. An analytic formula is used to compute the project value for $t \geq T_2$, conditional on the time T_2 spot price, mean reserves, initial capacity, and incremental capacity.

Computational approach

The simplest method to evolve the mean reserves and spot price into the future and to discount the maximised project value from T_2 back to T_0 is to employ a bivariate binomial lattice. Details regarding binomial lattices for real options can be found in other articles (Chorn, 1996; Cox and Rubinstein, 1985). It is also necessary to value the cashflows associated with the production and sale of reserves between $T_{1.5}$ and T_2. This requires a second analytic formula that utilises the current spot price, the current mean reserves, and the initial production capacity. "Current" refers to time T_0 if the initial capacity decision is locked in then, or T_1 if the decision is deferred. The formulas are predicated on the assumption that production at full capacity continues until the reserves are depleted, even if spot prices fall below extraction costs during this time. Extraction costs are low relative to current spot prices, so the option to shut in gas production is not modelled. Extraction costs are assumed to be a constant percentage of spot price over the project's life.

The binomial lattice is used to discount the cashflows back to prior decision points, retaining evolution of the gas spot price and reserve volumes over time. The maximised project value at T_2 is discounted back from T_2 to T_1 and summed with the analytic value of the cashflows between $T_{1.5}$ and T_2. The present value of the investment is also subtracted from that sum to form the NPV for each of the two initial capacities. If the initial capacity decision is deferred to T_1, the larger of the two project NPVs is also compared with 0, the abandonment option. The optimum decision at T_1 is chosen and its associated value is discounted back to T_0 again using the binomial lattice. For the lock in now scenario with the capacity decision made at T_0, the larger of the two project NPVs at T_0 is reported.

The output of the model is the project NPV at T_0 based on the optimal development pathway, the expectation of a maximum. This value is, in essence, the expected value of the discounted cashflows, after adjusting for the market price of gas price risk (implicitly embedded in the gas spot price), and the risk associated with the recoverable reserves and speculative potential volume estimates. By comparing the real options' NPV values for several pathways with the traditional discounted cashflow analysis for the project, the values of spot price information, information from exploration, and information from production can be computed.

RESULTS

The model was used to investigate two issues and the timing associated with them:

❑ How should the offshore gathering facilities be sized?
   • initial size
   • incremental capacity additions
❑ When should the sizing decision be made?
❑ How much is the exploration information worth?
❑ When should more exploration be undertaken?

The results reflect the full project size, not partners' share, sizes and are computed before taxes, but after royalties.

Table 2 shows the model results for the evaluation of two development pathways compared with the "no-options" base scenario computed using a traditional discounted cashflow analysis. The base scenario assumes no decision deferral and no additional exploration or capacity additions.

Real options case 1 evaluates a pathway with no initial capacity decision deferral but with exploration and additional capacity options retained for future exercise. This case 1 pathway reflects a management decision to design the facilities with the option to deliver additional gas, if and only if the information acquired from exploration and production activities is favourable. Exploration results will not be available, in this case, to influence the initial capacity decision. By following the case 1 pathway, management can potentially add 6% to the project NPV as compared to the base case pathway.

Real options case 2 evaluates a pathway with an initial capacity decision deferral, while exploration is underway, and an additional capacity option. This pathway reflects a management decision to retain two options. The first option is to design the initial production facilities to deliver additional gas above the anticipated capacity, if and only if the information acquired from

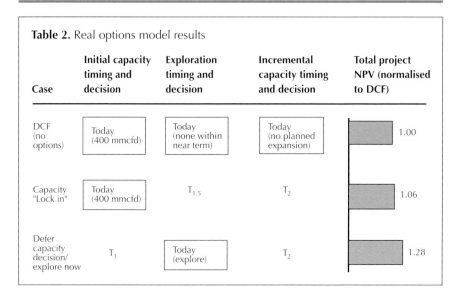

Table 2. Real options model results

Case	Initial capacity timing and decision	Exploration timing and decision	Incremental capacity timing and decision	Total project NPV (normalised to DCF)
DCF (no options)	Today (400 mmcfd)	Today (none within near term)	Today (no planned expansion)	1.00
Capacity "Lock in"	Today (400 mmcfd)	$T_{1.5}$	T_2	1.06
Defer capacity decision/ explore now	T_1	Today (explore)	T_2	1.28

exploration is favourable. The second option is to purchase additional gas production capacity if information from production activities indicate that this decision adds value. By following the case 2 pathway, management can potentially add 28% to the project NPV as compared with the base case pathway.

A sensitivity study was performed to measure the impact of variables whose values are not directly measurable, such as regional gas price volatility, reserve size and speculative potential uncertainty, and gas price at initial production. The results of the sensitivity study are presented in Figures 4 to 7. The real options results suggest where management should focus attention, as well as how to proceed in the field development process. Of particular interest are:

❏ Near a break-even gas price the options' values are at their peak, and at high gas prices, options' values decrease to 0.
❏ The degree of uncertainty in reserves and speculative potential has greatest impact on the value of initial capacity deferral option.
❏ High spot price volatility encourages initial capacity deferral and accelerated exploration.
❏ Incremental capacity option value is a weak function of both price and volume uncertainty.

A particularly interesting result is shown in Figure 7. This illustrates the sensitivity of the analysis to resolution of the uncertainty surrounding the speculative potential in the exploration opportunities. The independent variable is a measure of uncertainty reduction between pre-exploration expectations and post-exploration expectations. The variable is plotted as a percentage change in the standard deviation of the speculative potential

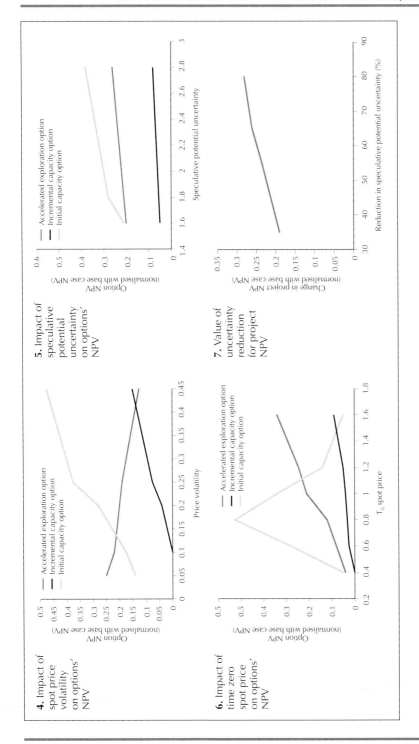

4. Impact of spot price volatility on options' NPV

5. Impact of speculative potential uncertainty on options' NPV

6. Impact of time zero spot price on options' NPV

7. Value of uncertainty reduction for project NPV

volume. The dependent variable is the fractional change in the project NPV relative to a base case analysis in which there was no reduction in the uncertainty. The sensitivity is relatively high at low reductions in the uncertainty but quickly becomes insensitive above about 50%. One interpretation of the curve, if the dependent variable is converted to exploration expenditures in dollars, is that it is the upper limit for the present value of the exploration budget. Spending more than the upper limit will gain information that does not improve the project value. In fact, it will probably decrease the NPV.

CONCLUSION

Real options analysis techniques are evolving from their equity origins to become powerful tools in evaluating and managing capital investments. This chapter illustrated a step in that evolution. Despite the intuitive nature of a real options analysis, the complexity of the mathematics and the need for new perspectives on existing economic and technical data have slowed its adoption in most industries.

The value of real options analysis is most commonly recognised during the project justification stage, but with a dynamic model, as described here, management can guide the investment project through its early stages where all the major capital expenditure and information gathering activities occur.

This chapter introduced the use of real options to price the purchase of information that could improve a project's value. The effect is twofold. First, managers can purchase information that will affect the upcoming decisions, if the value increase justifies the cost of the information. Second, managers should invest now or abandon the project if there is there is no information to be gained (or if its expense is too great) that will significantly change the project's outcome or affect the investment decision process.

BIBLIOGRAPHY

Chorn, L.G., 1996, "Managing Investments in the Energy Industry, Valuing the Options", paper IPA96-3.0-204 presented at the Indonesian Petroleum Association Meeting, Jakarta, October 2–4.

Cox, J.C. and M. Rubinstein, 1985, *Options Markets*, Englewood Cliffs, NJ: Prentice-Hall.

Dixit, A.K. and R.S. Pindyck, 1994, *Investment Under Uncertainty*, Princeton, NJ: Princeton University Press.

Kulatilaka, N. and A.J. Marcus, 1992, "Project Valuation Under Uncertainty: When Does DCF Fail?" *The Continental Bank Journal of Applied Corporate Finance*, 5(3).

Lohrenz, J. and R.N. Dickens, 1993, "Options Theory for Evaluation of Oil and Gas Assets: The Upsides and Downsides", SPE 25837, SPE Hydrocarbon Economics and Evaluation Symposium.

Nichols, N.A., 1994, "Scientific Management at Merck", *Harvard Business Review*, 72(1).

Paddock, J.L., D.R. Siegel and J.L. Smith, 1988, "Options Valuation Claims on Real Assets: The Case of Offshore Petroleum Leases", *The Quarterly Journal of Economics*, 103.

13

The Value of Market Research When a Firm is Learning: Real Option Pricing and Optimal Filtering

David Epstein*, Nick Mayor, Philipp Schönbucher, Elizabeth Whalley and Paul Wilmott*

*Mathematical Institute, Oxford; Hoare Govett; University of Bonn; Warwick Business School; Wilmott Associates

This chapter is motivated by the well-established use of option pricing methods in evaluating firms' market opportunities. The key reference in this area is Dixit and Pindyck (1994). Amongst a firm's other valuation and control problems, they model the value of the option to invest in a product at a later date, given that the intrinsic value of the project is uncertain. Other authors have evaluated research and development projects and investment opportunities under conditions of uncertainty. Grossman and Shapiro (1986) derive the optimal time path of R&D outlays when the difficulty of a project is unknown and its benefits will only accrue upon completion. Brennan and Schwartz (1985) use option pricing to value a copper mine as a derivative claim on future revenues. In more general models, McDonald and Siegel (1986) value a "perpetual option" offered to a firm by the right to launch a product at some later date, and Newton and Pearson (1994) discuss the general application of option pricing theory to R&D valuation.

Such real option pricing models are shown by Quigg (1993) to have strong empirical support. She shows that a model of land values which includes the option value of waiting to develop a site has significant predictive power for transactions and prices over and above simple intrinsic value. Empirical work by Pakes (1986) has also looked at the option value of the right to a later investment offered by a patent, and demonstrated evidence for a large amount of inherent option value.

The crucial factor in the specification of a model of the value of any derivative claim is the specification of the process followed by the underlying variable on which the derivative claim rests. In exact analogy to financial option models, the underlying value of the investment opportunity in all the real option models is assumed to follow a constant variance process; either a geometric random walk or a simple mean-reverting process.

In many of these models, the firm can only decide to invest at one later date; this feature is also common to European options. Yet while these models capture the value of the increase in information until the exercise date, they are unrealistic in assuming that there is only one possible and fixed time to invest which cannot be chosen by the management.

The endogenous time to invest was developed within later models, allowing a firm to observe how a project's potential value evolves before locking into an especially favourable value; this development is also present in the early exercise of American options. In these models, the firm's management is always perfectly informed about the current value of the state variable. The option to wait derives its value from the firm's ability to wait for an even more favourable value, rather than from information acquisition by the management.

This is undesirable for many projects, as it implies that the firm does not learn about the actual level or process for intrinsic value with any greater certainty. Admittedly, in some cases the firm can actually observe the underlying variable on which the value of its project rests. However, in many real world situations this is not true: a product may have a certain but unobservable value, or its prospects may depend on a variable whose process is not observable. Throughout the period during which a product is being investigated, it seems reasonable that the investigating firm would be learning about the processes involved, meaning that the uncertainty inherent in its environment is not constant, and the choice of time to invest is endogenous.

Models of firms' activities in which the stochastic environment, although not given, can be influenced, have been developed before. Cukierman (1980) demonstrates a model in which a firm decides which of a range of investment projects to undertake and "buys" information by waiting, thus reducing the probability of losses from launching an unsuccessful product. Demers (1991) has a model of a firm which is uncertain about the demand in a particular market, and updates its beliefs according to a Bayesian rule after receiving informational signals. In both cases, the firm learns about its environment with greater accuracy as time goes by.

It would seem worthwhile to combine these two aspects - learning about the true state of the economy and endogenous timing of the investment - in a single approach. This was first undertaken by Roberts and Weitzman (1981): they model the value of an R&D project and entry/exit boundaries as information develops. Our approach is more general than that taken by Roberts and Weitzman. The learning and its intensity are endogenised, and we do not assume a finite time horizon for the R&D project.

Here, we aim to introduce information acquisition in a real option framework. In the model we present, it is assumed that the firm does not know the payoff of the project under investigation (which may even be negative). However, it can observe a costly, noisy signal of this payoff. Given this signal, the firm has three choices: it can start the project, continue collecting signals, or abandon the project altogether and stop collecting signals. The second option, to investigate the project, is valuable because it allows the firm to reduce the risk of undertaking a project with negative payoff.

Drawing on the theory of optimal filtering of noisy signals, we derive the process to achieve the firm's best estimate of a project's value. This is then regarded as the underlying variable for a model of the value of market research along option pricing lines. The general result, apparent from considering the more general real option pricing literature - and indeed suggested in a different context by Bernanke (1983) - is that the presence of a learning effect decreases option values over and above net present value (NPV).

In this modelling framework, we also consider the situation in which the firm has some control over the intensity of its signals: it can control the amount of information it buys over time. The firm's problem now begins to look like the two-armed bandit problem studied by Rothschild (1974) and Bellman (1956). The firm must decide whether to continue its project (and if so, at what pace), or enter the market, or drop out completely. It must therefore decide which of three "slot-machines" offer the most favourable outcome, given that obtaining more information is expensive. However, this analogy is not exploited here. Our intention is not to build a complete theory of optimal research behaviour, but rather to model this control problem specifically within the real option pricing framework.

The structure of the chapter is as follows. First, we discuss the general framework of optimal filtering. We then apply this to the valuation of market research projects. Finally, a situation in which the firm can control the "intensity" of its market research is considered, and the optimality condition is derived.

OPTIMAL FILTERING

In physics and engineering, a great deal of consideration has been given to the processing of noisy signals, ie, to situations in which we are concerned with the value of a process which we cannot directly observe. An analogy would be the act of tuning in a radio, when we cannot observe the various factors which distort the signal.

One approach taken to such a problem is the theory of optimal filtering, in which the optimal contemporaneous estimate in a continuous time framework is derived. The optimality criterion used in this case is to formulate the best estimate (ie, the minimum variance) of the unobserved system. The ideas in this section are clearly not new; the treatment is based on

Arnold (1974) and Oksendal (1992). The basic model and some results are discussed heuristically in one dimension, using stochastic differential equations. An interpretation is also given in discrete time. Finally, it is worth mentioning that it is assumed that all key model parameters are known. The situation in which they are not is that of "adaptive filtering" (Goodwin and Sin, 1984, and others); such a situation adds little to the analysis described here.

The optimal filtering model

In the general model, there is some magnitude V which is of interest to us, but which we cannot observe directly. We can only observe a noisy signal of V. Our problem is to estimate the current state of the "system" V on the basis of the observations we have.

At the highest level of generality, we can model our observations H(t) as a disturbed functional of V. There are then two components to this model. The first is a systematic function of V. The second is pure noise. This is assumed for simplicity to be white noise; extensions to coloured noise have been made (Brown and Hwang ,1992). Thus we can write the model as

$$H(t) = \mu(V, t) + \sigma(t)\varepsilon \tag{1}$$

where μ represents the mapping from (V, t) to the real line, $\sigma(t)$ is a variance parameter, and ε is assumed to be white noise. With no loss of information, we can define the "signal representation" $Z(t)$ as the cumulative past history of our observations:

$$Z_t = \int_0^t H_s ds \tag{2}$$

This then allows us to specify the stochastic differential equation which this signal must satisfy:

$$dZ = \mu(V, t)dt + \sigma(t)dW \tag{3}$$

where dW is a Wiener process, $Z(0) = Z_0$ given and $t \geq 0$. To enable results to be couched in terms of stochastic differential equations, the signal process is used from now on.

We now have a model for the signal we observe; to allow for cases in which the system variable also changes over time, we need a general model for the evolution of V. The model suggested is the generalised Itô process

$$dV = \alpha(V, t)dt + \xi(V, t)dX \tag{4}$$

where dX is a simple Wiener process, $V(0) = V_0$ and we assume that dX, dW, V_0 and Z_0 are all independent.

A special case

The most famous special case of the filtering problem is the Kalman-Bucy theorem for linear systems (Bucy and Joseph, 1968, and Kalman, 1963). Linearity in this application is defined as being "in the narrow sense", which boils down to the variance of the processes involved being free of V and Z. This will be important in the next section.

In this special case, we model the system with the equation:

$$dV = \alpha V dt + \xi dX \tag{5}$$

and the signal process by the equation

$$dZ = \mu V dt + \sigma dW \tag{6}$$

Given the white noise assumption, it can be shown (Oksendal, 1992) that our optimal estimate of V is the mean of the conditional distribution of V, conditional on the set of observations $Z[t_0, t]$, ie,

$$\hat{V}(t) = E[V(t)|Z[t_0, t]] \tag{7}$$

Furthermore, if V(0) and Z(0) are normally distributed or constant, it can be shown that V and therefore Z are Gaussian processes. Therefore all conditional distributions are normal.

It therefore follows that the conditional density $f_v(Z[t_0, t])$ of V on the basis of our observations is a normal distribution with mean $\hat{V}$ and conditional variance:

$$S_t = E[(V_t - \hat{V}_t)^2 | Z[t_0, t]] \tag{8}$$

The Kalman-Bucy theorem states that the dynamic equations for the updating of these parameters as new information arrives are

$$d\hat{V} = \alpha \hat{V} dt + S\frac{\mu}{\sigma^2}(dZ - \mu V dt) \tag{9}$$

and

$$\frac{dS}{dt} = 2\alpha S + \xi^2 - S^2 \frac{\mu^2}{\sigma^2} \tag{10}$$

The second equation is a deterministic Riccati equation. S is independent of the observations $Z[t_0, t]$, and, for a non-negative initial value, it can be shown that there exists a unique global solution for S (Bucy and Joseph, 1968). This equation for S clearly shows the emergence of a "learning effect": the precision of the optimal estimate increases over time.

The Kalman-Bucy filter as the limit of a discrete time problem

To illustrate the workings of the model, consider a discrete time example. Given an initial guess $\hat{V} = E[V]$ with variance σ_V^2, and a signal $H = V + e$, where e is the noise term (assumed to be white noise). Define the "precisions" $\pi_V = \sigma_V^{-2}$ and $\pi_e = \sigma_e^{-2}$. We are looking for the best linear approximation of V given our current information $\hat{V}$ and H. In other words, we are looking for the minimising arguments a, b such that

$$E[(a\hat{V} + bH - V)^2]$$

is minimised. Expanding, we get

$$E[(a\hat{V} + bH - V)^2 = E[(a\hat{V} + be - (1 - b)V)^2]$$

$$= E[(a\hat{V} + be)^2] - 2E[a\hat{V} + be)(1 - b)V] + (1 - b)^2 E[V^2]$$

$$= a^2\hat{V}^2 + b^2\sigma_e^2 - 2a(1 - b)\hat{V}^2 + (1 - b)^2\sigma_V^2 + (1 - b)^2\hat{V}^2$$

$$= (a - (1 - b))^2\hat{V}^2 + b^2\sigma_e^2 + (1 - b)^2\sigma_V^2$$

The first order conditions are then

$$0 = a - (1 - b)$$
$$0 = b\sigma_e^2 - (1 - b)\sigma_V^2$$

The first condition means that we will have a weighted average of $\hat{V}$ and H in the new estimate $\hat{V}^1$; substituting into the second condition, the first condition implies that

$$b = \frac{\pi_e}{\pi_V + \pi_e}$$

$$a = \frac{\pi_V}{\pi_V + \pi_e}$$

This gives a new best estimate

$$\hat{V}' = \frac{\pi_V}{\pi_V + \pi_e}\hat{V} + \frac{\pi_e}{\pi_V + \pi_e}H$$

which (by substitution into the original equation) has a precision of

$$\pi' = \pi_V + \pi_e$$

The above analysis is now heuristically extended to continuous time. For simplicity, suppose the system process is given by $dV = 0$. Also, suppose that signals are of the simple form

$$dZ = \mu V dt + \sigma dW \tag{11}$$

with parameters defined as before.

The estimate $\hat{V}$, its variance $S(t)$ and its precision $\pi(t)$ are given, and we want to update them given dZ. Write (heuristically) for the observation H,

$$H \equiv \frac{1}{\mu} \frac{dZ}{dt} = V + \frac{\sigma}{\mu} \frac{dW}{dt} \tag{12}$$

where the error e now has the variance

$$\sigma_e^2 = \frac{\sigma^2}{\mu^2} \frac{1}{dt}$$

and the precision

$$\pi_e = \frac{\mu^2}{\sigma^2} dt$$

The precision is therefore well defined as we move into continuous time, whereas the variance is not. The problem is now identical to the discrete time example, and we can substitute in directly to obtain the weights

$$a = 1 - \frac{S\mu^2}{\sigma^2} dt + O(dt^2) \tag{13}$$

and

$$b = \frac{S\mu^2}{\sigma^2} dt + O(dt^2) \tag{14}$$

Finally, we reach:

$$\hat{V}' - \hat{V} = d\hat{V} = -\frac{S\mu^2}{\sigma^2} \hat{V} dt + \frac{S\mu}{\sigma^2} dZ \tag{15}$$

$$\frac{d\pi}{dt} = \frac{\mu^2}{\sigma^2} \tag{16}$$

and

$$\frac{dS}{dt} = -\frac{\mu^2}{\sigma^2} S^2 \tag{17}$$

These equations are in exact agreement with the Kalman-Bucy filtering formulae (equations (9) and (10)).

Thus, the optimal filtering theorems represented by equations (9) and (10) can be seen to be simply the continuous time analogues of finding the best linear estimator of an unobserved V given a discrete set of observations. As mentioned above, under the Gaussian assumption, it can be shown (see Brown and Hwang, 1992) that the Kalman-Bucy theorem finds the conditional mean of V as well as the best linear estimator; in more general cases, it finds the best estimator, but not necessarily the conditional mean. This fact means that in order to obtain the most robust results from the use of the Kalman-Bucy theorem, we should try to model at the level of a process that satisfies this assumption: a stochastic process which is linear "in the narrow sense", and is subject to a Gaussian noise process. This will become a consideration in the next section, when a normalising transform is used to work with a variable which we would rather not assume to be normally distributed. In this next section, the theory of optimal filtering is used to model the evolution of a firm's best estimate of product value, to represent an underlying state variable for a model of the value of market research.

MODELLING THE VALUE OF MARKET RESEARCH

This section applies the theory of optimal filtering to the valuation of market research. We assume that a firm can enter a market and receive an amount V for a fixed entry cost I. The firm is assumed to be risk neutral. Prior to entering the market, the firm cannot observe V directly, but must estimate it on the basis of a noisy market research signal. The entry cost I is known. The firm must decide whether to continue with the costly market research, enter the market, or drop the project completely. Given that its optimal estimate of V is changing over time, this flexibility offers it a certain real option value.

The optimal estimate of market value

We make four key assumptions made in our model of market research.

1. It is assumed that there is a deterministic component to such a signal which is proportional to the true value of the market opportunity. This corresponds to an average "reply rate" of those surveyed. We might suppose that 50% of people who are sent a market research questionnaire will reply, or that 90% of people who respond to a drug will do so during testing. Therefore, if we send out 100 questionnaires and receive 50 back, of which 30 are favourable, we would use 60% as our estimate of potential market share.
2. In the interest of simplicity, it is also assumed that there is just one true value V; that is, $dV = 0$.
3. The signal process Z observed by a firm undertaking market research is assumed to be noisy. As well as the component correlated with V, there

is a disturbance term. The response rate to the questionnaire will not be exactly 50% – or whatever figure generally prevails – at any given time.
4. Finally, it is assumed that the signal Z is distributed lognormally. This is assumed because Z is a function of V, the actual value of the product. Given that V cannot be less than zero, it seems that responses to questionnaires cannot be below zero, since this implies a respondent assigning a negative willingness to buy to the product. Moreover, the empirical literature on the market research response rates (in terms of product sales) suggests that a lognormal distribution should be appropriate (Garbrowski and Vernon, 1983, Garbrowski and Vernon, 1991, Sanders, Rossman and Harris, 1958). Garbrowski and Vernon (1991) demonstrates the stylised fact that pharmaceutical companies undertaking R&D have tended to rely on the occasional "blockbuster" product to support a mass which performs very poorly, while Scherer (1958) shows that the empirical distribution of the data from Sanders et al implies a strongly skewed and leptokurtic distribution, with a possibly unbounded mean; he suggests a Pareto-Levy distribution.

The Paretian distribution is not hugely useful for modelling purposes, but the assumption that market research results will be lognormally distributed at least reflects the skew and kurtosis implied by the data. It also avoids the situation in which our estimate of V is negative – it never can be, given that the information that $V \geq 0$ is contained within our information set. In reality, if we were actually estimating V on the basis of Z, this nonnegativity constraint on V would not matter, since we would be very unlikely to obtain a negative estimate of V for a given realisation of the signal process. However, given that we want to solve an equation over all possible ranges of variables, from a modelling point of view we want to ensure that the variables are within the correct ranges. The assumption of lognormal signals does just this.

Since the Kalman-Bucy theorems are couched in terms of normally distributed variables, we define our "variables of interest" as $v =: \ln V$ and $z =: \ln Z$. These assumptions then give rise to a model for the modified market research signal of the form

$$dz = \mu v dt + \sigma dW \qquad (18)$$

where μ is the average reply rate, σ is the continuous variance of the noise, and dW is a Wiener process. From standard results in probability theory, it must be recognised that $\hat{V}$ is not simply $\hat{V} = e^{\hat{v}}$, but

$$\hat{V}(t) = \exp(\hat{v}(t) + \tfrac{1}{2}S(t)) \qquad (19)$$

For the moment, we will regard the problem as being framed in terms of $\hat{v}$.

Lastly, it is assumed that when starting a project, a firm knows "almost nothing". This is represented by the assumption that S_0^{-1} can be approximated by 0. This assumption is made in order to remove the influence of initial S on the model; it can easily be modified, and indeed must be for the optimal control model presented later.

The value of market research

In the model presented in this section, it is assumed that the firm must maintain a constant continuous payment flow $m \geq 0$ in order to receive its market research signals, allowing $m = 0$ as a special case. For cases where $m > 0$, we have a problem with the same structure as a perpetual instalment American option. We must pay to keep the option open, but can terminate the option to receive either nothing, or whatever the positive intrinsic value of the market opportunity is. In other cases, we have a simple perpetual American-style option valuation problem. We write the value of the firm's real option F.

Assuming for simplicity that the actual value of the product is fixed, we are working with the system

$$dv = 0, \; v_t = v_0 \tag{20}$$

We have assumed that the firm observes the process

$$dz = \mu v dt + \sigma dW$$

By the Kalman-Bucy theorem of optimal linear filtering, the optimal estimate $\hat{v}$ of v satisfies

$$d\hat{v} = -\frac{\mu^2}{\sigma^2} S \hat{v} \, dt + \frac{\mu}{\sigma^2} \, dz \tag{21}$$

and the instantaneous variance S of $\hat{v}$ satisfies

$$\frac{dS}{dt} = -S^2 \frac{\mu^2}{\sigma^2} \tag{22}$$

This equation for S has a straightforward solution

$$S_t = \frac{\sigma^2 S_0}{\sigma^2 + S_0 \mu^2 t} \tag{23}$$

Divide equation (23) through by S_0 to get

$$S_t = \frac{\sigma^2}{\sigma^2/S_0 + \mu^2 t} \tag{24}$$

Initially, S is assumed to be close to infinity: the firm knows almost nothing. S_0^{-1} is therefore approximated by 0. Under this assumption, the first term in the denominator disappears, so that S is given by

$$S_t = \frac{\sigma^2}{\mu^2 t} \qquad (25)$$

This shows how the variance of the error of the optimal estimate of V increases with time, from an initial state of almost zero knowledge.

Substituting the equation for S back into that for $\hat{v}$, it follows that we can now specify the process for $\hat{v}$ as being

$$d\hat{v} = \left(\frac{v}{t} - \frac{\hat{v}}{t}\right)dt + \frac{\sigma}{\mu t} dW \qquad (26)$$

If we take the expectation of $d\hat{v}$ conditional on our information set (the observations Z[...]), it is clear that $d\hat{v}$ has zero drift with respect to this information set. All updates to our estimate of $\hat{v}$ are unpredictable. This corresponds to the fact that if an estimate of an unmoving magnitude required a predictable update at a later date, we would simply include that update now. This follows as a necessary condition of forming an optimal estimate.

With $\hat{V}$ is defined in equation (19) above in terms of $\hat{v}$, it can be verified directly using Itô's Lemma that $\hat{V}$ satisfies the stochastic differential equation

$$d\hat{V} = \left(\frac{v}{t} - \frac{\hat{v}}{t}\right)\hat{V}dt + \frac{\sigma}{\mu t}\hat{V}dW \qquad (27)$$

and we have a lognormally distributed estimate of V, with an expected drift of zero. The updates to $\hat{V}$ are therefore also an innovation process with respect to our information set. With the model (equation (27)) for the evolution of $\hat{V}$, we can now regard the problem as being in terms of V once more.

Given that we cannot observe the ultimate state variable for the option valuation problem, V, the quantity $\hat{V}$ will have to be regarded as being the state variable on which the value of the market research "option" depends. With this in mind, the value of the project is defined as the expected present discounted value of its final or intrinsic value, discounting at an appropriate discount rate ρ. At the end of the project (assuming an optimal choice of termination date T*), we pay I to receive the expected value of the project, $\hat{V}$. So we define the option value F as

$$F(\hat{V}, t) \equiv E\left[F(\hat{V}, T^*)e^{-\rho(T^* - t)}\right] \qquad (28)$$

where

$$F(\hat{V}, T^*) = \max(\hat{V} - I, 0) \qquad (29)$$

Time must be included in this problem, since the volatility on which option value depends is some function of time. Actual calendar time must be included, not just some relative time variable, as there is a singularity in S at $t = 0$. The condition of equation (29) describes the firm's optimal decision at termination time. It can either enter the market and receive $V - I$, or abandon the project (with expected payoff 0). Notice that as the firm bases its decision on expected V, but on entry receives actual V, it is still possible that the firm could enter a market and make a loss.

We are dealing with an optimal stopping problem: the firm is currently undertaking market research, and must determine when it would be optimal to stop, with the aim of either entering the market or abandoning the project completely. There are three regions for which we must describe the behaviour of F, corresponding to the trade-offs the firm faces.

1. In the "out" stopping region, the firm determines that its estimate of product value is so low that it is not worth continuing to pay to hold open its real option in the hope of favourable later information. The option value from waiting is not sufficient to justify the necessary expenditure.
2. In the "in" stopping region, the firm decides to enter the market, since its estimate of product value is sufficiently high to make waiting for further information undesirable. The option value of waiting is outweighed by the estimated profits foregone by not entering now.
3. In the third region, the firm simply waits for more information about the project, paying a sum (assumed to be the constant flow m) to hold its option open. In this region, the option of investing in the project is estimated as being sufficiently valuable to warrant continuing (costly) investigation, but not so lucrative that entering now would be optimal.

In specifying the valuation problem, it is simply observed that F can never fall to below its intrinsic value $\Lambda = \max(\hat{V} - I, 0)$. If it ever did, by terminating its option through entry or abandonment, the firm could reach a higher payoff, and the optimal stopping decision implied by F would be sub-optimal. Therefore, the free boundaries are included in the problem simply by imposing the conditions $F \geq 0$, and $F \geq \hat{V} - I$ on the equation for F. This equation is similarly specified as a weak inequality, and a complementary slackness condition is invoked.

If these conditions hold with equality, the trade-off between the costs and benefits of waiting swings in favour of stopping, thereby receiving the estimated intrinsic value of the project. The loci where this is the case are the free boundaries which the firm determines as the outcome of its optimal stopping problem.

It follows from the imposition of these conditions that the value of this real option to the firm must satisfy

$$F(\hat{V}, t) = \max(\hat{V} - I, (1 + \rho dt)^{-1}E[F + dF] - mdt, 0) \tag{30}$$

over a time-step dt. We know what F is in the "in" and "out" stopping regions. In the interesting region, the continuation region, the equation satisfied by F can again be found straightforwardly. In this region,

$$(1 + \rho dt)F = E[F(\hat{V} + d\hat{V}, t + dt)] - mdt \tag{31}$$

must hold. This implies via an Itô expansion inside the expectation that

$$(1 + \rho dt)F = E\left[F + \frac{\partial F}{\partial t} dt + \frac{\partial F}{\partial \hat{V}} d\hat{V} + \frac{1}{2} \frac{\partial^2 F}{\partial \hat{V}^2} (d\hat{V})^2\right] - mdt \tag{32}$$

Evaluating the expectation, this implies that

$$\rho F dt = \frac{\partial F}{\partial t} dt + \frac{1}{2} \frac{\sigma^2}{\mu^2 t^2} \hat{V}^2 \frac{\partial^2 F}{\partial \hat{V}^2} dt - mdt \tag{33}$$

Dividing by dt and rearranging, F is found to satisfy

$$\frac{\partial F}{\partial t} + \frac{1}{2} \frac{\sigma^2}{\mu^2 t^2} \hat{V}^2 \frac{\partial^2 F}{\partial \hat{V}^2} - \rho F - m = 0 \tag{34}$$

This equation describes the process followed by any derivative claims on V which are dependent on the expected value of V. Since we cannot observe V itself, such a derivative claim must regard $d\hat{V}$ as the underlying process.

In evaluating market research, equation (34) is therefore to be solved under the condition

$$F \geq \Lambda = \max(\hat{V} - I, 0) \tag{35}$$

When equation (35) holds with equality, equation (34) is only satisfied as an inequality. This can be confirmed simply by observing that the intrinsic value or "payoff" Λ is not a solution to equation (34).

This equation, with time included, cannot be solved analytically under these conditions and must be solved by numerical techniques. However, one initial analytic result is apparent from a simple change of the time variable. If we define τ such that

$$\frac{t^2}{dt} = \frac{1}{d\tau}$$

that is, $\tau = -1/t$, then equation (34) becomes

$$\frac{\partial F}{\partial \tau} + \frac{1}{2} \frac{\sigma^2 \hat{V}^2}{\mu^2} \frac{\partial^2 F}{\partial \hat{V}^2} - \tau^2 \rho F - \tau^2 m = 0 \tag{36}$$

Imposing the condition in equation (35) means that the problem now looks like a perpetual US instalment option, with a time-dependent instalment and discount factor. As $t \to 0$, or $\tau \to -\infty$, the discount and cost terms disappear, and it seems that under these conditions, the option value of the project $F \to V$. However, this is somewhat misleading, as in approaching a truly infinite initial variance, the probability of being at any particular value of V goes to zero. Therefore, it could also be argued that, given an infinite diffusion of information, initial option values are everywhere infinite.

Numerical results

The numerical solution of equation (34) subject to condition of equation (35) is now considered. It is in fact difficult to solve numerically for two reasons.

The first reason is that it is a perpetual option, whereas to solve the backwards equation requires some terminal data. In order to supply this, we impose a terminal condition on the valuation problem. The motivation for this is that we can simply say that once the uncertainty surrounding our option has come down to a certain threshold, we will regard the problem as deterministic. In other words, there is some value of S which means that we are no longer interested in the diffusion term in the equation for F. At this point, we (the firm) will either be in or out of the market for definite. All we do by waiting is incur the time cost of discounting the option value into a subsequent period, and the payment flow m necessary to take it there. This would not be optimal. At some time t*, S is below our threshold level of "caring" S*, and so we define a "final condition" as

$$F(\hat{V}, t^*) = \max(\hat{V} - I, 0) \tag{37}$$

As a matter of mathematical necessity, two side conditions are also imposed which accord with the situation modelled are also imposed, namely

$$F(0, t) = 0 \tag{38}$$

$$\frac{\partial^2 F}{\partial \hat{V}^2} \to 0 \quad \text{as} \quad \hat{V} \to \infty \tag{39}$$

These then allow a solution to the equation to be derived.

The second difficulty with deriving a solution to the equation is somewhat more technical and derives from the finite difference solution method used. This method works by approximating the differential equation for F

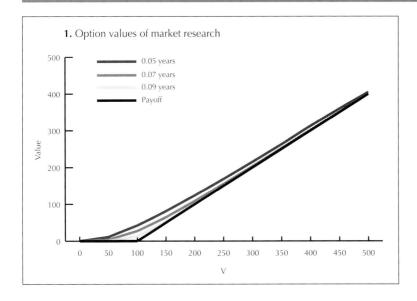

1. Option values of market research

by a difference equation, which is then solved over a "mesh" of points in the t and $\hat{V}$ dimensions.

When t is large and S small, this mesh must be very fine over $\hat{V}$ in order to pick up the small diffusion term. Conversely, as we move back towards the singularity in S, the increments in option value stepping back through time become very large, so that the grid must be very fine over t to avoid instability. A solution was therefore derived by "patching together" grids of different resolution at various points. The solution was not extended completely back to $t = 0$, as at this point S is infinite. The solution begins only after a "tick" of time has taken place.

Option values at various points in time are shown in Figure 1, with parameter values $m = 20$, $\sigma = 0.3$, $\mu = 1$, $\rho = 6\%$ and $I = 100$. Figure 1 clearly shows the "learning effect". Option values diminish over time, moving down towards the intrinsic value (which is also NPV) as time goes on.

The effect of learning on the free boundaries is demonstrated in Figure 2. Early on, there is a great deal of uncertainty and a large amount of value in waiting. For most estimates of $\hat{V}$, the firm should continue to wait for more information before committing itself to a decision. As the uncertainty falls however, projects with very low $\hat{V}$ will be terminated and high $\hat{V}$ entered, as their true intrinsic value becomes increasingly clear and large changes become less and less likely.

The numerical results show clearly that if a firm is learning about the prospects of a particular product, the option value of research into the product declines over time. This is to be contrasted with the standard real option result based on a constant variance model, in which option values are independent of time, and show no tendency to converge to NPV.

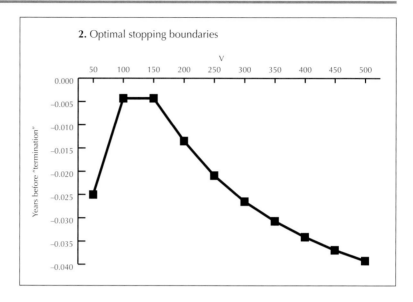

2. Optimal stopping boundaries

The next section extends this model of market research further. The effects of changing m are analysed, and an optimal control problem for situations in which the firm can control the intensity or quality of its information via controlling m is solved.

VARYING THE INTENSITY OF MARKET RESEARCH

An interesting extension of this model is where the amount a firm has to pay for its market research has an influence on the characteristics of the market research itself. For example, suppose that each market researcher out in the street costs one pound. Therefore, by spending m pounds continuously, we are receiving m signals. Each signal is again assumed to be distributed lognormally, and it is assumed that the signal $z = \ln Z$ has a deterministic component, which is a linear function of $v = \ln V$, and a pure Gaussian noise component. So each signal received from each market researcher satisfies

$$dz_i = \mu v dt + \sigma dW_i \tag{40}$$

We assume that $E(dW_i \, dW_j) = 0$ for $i \neq j$. We receive m of these signals, and therefore, assuming all market researchers are identical, the overall observation

$$z = \sum_{i=1}^{'} dz_i$$

which we obtain satisfies

$$dz = \mu m v dt + \sigma \sqrt{m} dW \tag{41}$$

There are m times as many replies on average in the aggregate signal process as there are in each observation itself; and the adding together of m independent normal processes with instantaneous variance σ gives an instantaneous variance for the final constructed process of $\sqrt{m}$ times the original variance.

The value of market research for different intensities

Following the initial method for describing the value of this option to the firm, initially assuming m to be fixed, it follows by the Kalman-Bucy theorem once more that if the outside system is

$$dv = 0 \tag{42}$$

and we observe

$$dz = \mu m v dt + \sigma \sqrt{m} dW \tag{43}$$

then the optimal estimate $\hat{v}$ of v satisfies the stochastic differential equation

$$d\hat{v} = -m \frac{\mu^2}{\sigma^2} S \hat{v} dt + \frac{\mu}{\sigma^2} S dz \tag{44}$$

and S now satisfies

$$\frac{dS}{dt} = -m \frac{\mu^2}{\sigma^2} S^2 \tag{45}$$

Solving for S again and substituting into the equation for $\hat{v}$, it is found that $\hat{v}$ satisfies

$$d\hat{v} = \left(\frac{v}{t} - \frac{\hat{v}}{t} \right) dt + \frac{\sigma}{\mu t \sqrt{m}} dW \tag{46}$$

By equation (19), we can again write the process followed by the optimal estimate of V, $\hat{V}$, as

$$d\hat{V} = \left(\frac{v}{t} - \frac{\hat{v}}{t} \right) \hat{V} dt + \frac{\sigma}{\mu t \sqrt{m}} \hat{V} dW \tag{47}$$

The option value across the three possible regions (in, out, and continue), defined as before, is again

$$F_t = \max(V - I, (1 + \rho dt)^{-1}(E[F + dF] - mdt), 0) \tag{48}$$

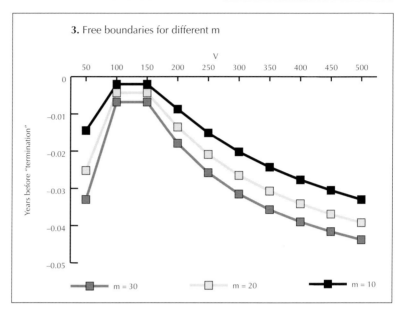

3. Free boundaries for different m

Therefore using the same method as before in the continuation region, it follows that F satisfies

$$\frac{\partial F}{\partial t} + \frac{1}{2}\frac{\sigma^2}{\mu^2 t^2 m}\hat{V}^2\frac{\partial^2 F}{\partial \hat{V}^2} - \rho F - m = 0 \qquad (49)$$

The effect of changing m is clear from this equation. A higher m increases costs, but decreases variance. Two clear results emerge if this equation is solved for different but fixed values of m, subject to the same condition reflecting the structure of the project, and by assertion ensuring optimal imposition of the free boundaries:

$$F \geq \max(V - I, 0) \qquad (50)$$

The first is that a higher m brings forward an earlier optimal entry time for given $\hat{V}$. The results from numerical solutions are shown in Figure 3; parameter values remain as before. Here, the number of time steps before the free boundaries first appear in the numerical solution is plotted for different values of m. The second result is that at any given time, from an initial state of S close to infinity, a higher m gives a lower option value. This is shown in Figure 4. Option values over and above intrinsic value are plotted for the same parameter values after 0.05 years, again for different m. Both these results stem from the same phenomenon: that a higher m means that S decreases more rapidly, giving a lower diffusion term. This explains both the low option value and the early entry, which occurs because of the low option value.

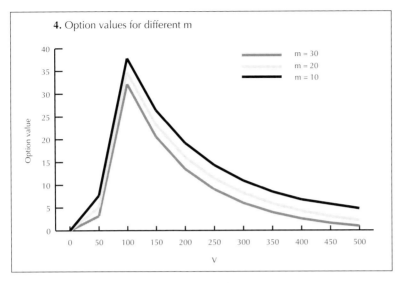

4. Option values for different m

Controlling the intensity of market research

If we now assume that a firm is able to vary its level of market research, there is an interesting optimal control problem. However, in order to consider this problem, we need to alter the set-up of the model. The first change is to remove the assumption of initial variance S being sufficiently close to infinity, so that we can approximate S_0^{-1} by zero. This is in order to remove an apparent paradox. If a firm literally knows nothing about a project, then – with the infinite diffusion of information – the option value of such a project is undefined. As argued above, anything could happen. With fixed m, this is not a problem, since for $m > 0$ we move away from the singularity immediately. However, a firm with a real option and a choice over m could spend nothing on market research, and hold an option with an undefined value; such an option might even be regarded as being infinitely valuable. The infinite option value is in some sense illusory, since with no spending the probability of the firm entering the market is zero.

This paradox is removed if we assume that initial variance is finite. In this case, a firm will spend some money on market research, since with a finite option value (from finite variance), the firm will not be optimising if it has a zero probability of actual entry.

This is an innocuous assumption. For instance, in reality, we know that the value of a project will be at least ten pounds, and less than the GDP of the world. For a finite initial S, the firm will be willing to spend money. Doing so will admittedly have a depressing effect on future option values, but will also bring earlier optimal entry, as discussed above. The key is that the firm cannot change its current S, only future values of S, and so it is not just paradoxically paying to receive a lower option value immediately. It will alter a whole range of future values: expected entry times as well as option values.

The second change to the set-up of the model is to introduce a more general cost function to describe the relationship between the number of researchers and their associated costs. This is done in order to examine what effect different cost structures have on the outcome of the maximisation problem. In particular, it will be seen that the linear case shown above causes some problems, and that in order to obtain a maximum as the outcome to the optimisation problem, marginal costs of information must be increasing in the amount of information. Finally, the problem now requires the inclusion of S as a state variable for the maximisation problem. F will depend on current S, so that in turn the value of S will have an impact on the choice of market research. Since S is a deterministic function of time, and calendar time no longer has any relevance (the optimisation problem is the same for any identical values of S, whatever the date), we remove the time dependence of F.

As before, we assume we have m researchers undertaking our market research; each of their observations is assumed to bear a linear relationship to true market value and contain some noise (assumed to be NIID across researchers). Signals are again assumed to be lognormally distributed, and so again we work from the transformed variables $z = \ln Z$ and $v = \ln V$.

The underlying variables therefore again satisfy

$$d\hat{v} = -m \frac{\mu^2}{\sigma^2} S\hat{v} dt + \frac{\mu}{\sigma^2} S dz \tag{51}$$

and

$$\frac{dS}{dt} = -m \frac{\mu^2}{\sigma^2} S^2 \tag{52}$$

Without solving for S, it can be seen that $\hat{V}$ satisfies

$$d\hat{V} = S\hat{V} \frac{\mu^2}{\sigma^2} m(v - \hat{v})dt + S\hat{V} \frac{\mu}{\sigma} \sqrt{m} dW \tag{53}$$

Costs are represented by the function c(m). Alternatively, we could regard the costs as being a simple linear function of the number of researchers, but with the "quality" or "intensity" of their information as represented by a re-interpretation of m a more general function of these costs. Either interpretation is supported by a one-one mapping from m to c.

We define the value of the option, as a function of m, $\hat{V}$ and S, as the discounted expectation of the payoff on entry:

$$F(\hat{V}, S, m) \equiv E\left[(\hat{V}_{T*} - I)^+ e^{-\rho(T* - t)}\right] \tag{54}$$

and the value of the option to a firm adopting an optimal policy, with respect to the intensity of its market research, as

$$F^* = \sup_m F^m \qquad (55)$$

An optimal policy provides a mapping from $(S, \hat{V})$ to a particular m^*, from which this option value can then be calculated. As noted above, time is not included explicitly as the important aspect of current calendar time is captured by current S, and the optimal entry time will be a function of S and of the optimal policy for m.

The method used to derive the equation satisfied by the value of market research is dynamic programming, deriving the Bellman equation for the problem. We know the value of the project in the two stopping areas. In the continuation region, it must be the case that the value of the real option now is the discounted expected value of the option next under an optimal policy, minus the costs of continuing. Therefore, it must hold that:

$$(1 + \rho dt)F^*(S, \hat{V}) = E\big[F^*(S + dS(m^*), \hat{V} + d\hat{V}(m^*)) - c(m^*)dt\big] \qquad (56)$$

From this, by definition it follows that

$$(1 + \rho dt)F^*(S, \hat{V}) = \max_m \big|E\big[F^*(S + dS(m), \hat{V} + d\hat{V}(m)) - c(m)dt\big]\big| \qquad (57)$$

By Itô's Lemma, this implies that:

$$\rho F^* dt = \max_m E\left[\frac{\partial F}{\partial S} dS + \frac{\partial F}{\partial \hat{V}} d\hat{V} + \frac{1}{2}\frac{\partial^2 F}{\partial \hat{V}^2}(d\hat{V})^2 - c(m)dt\right] \qquad (58)$$

Substituting in for dS and d$\hat{V}$ and evaluating the expectation, we have that

$$\rho F^* dt = \max_m \left(S^2 m \frac{\mu^2}{\sigma^2}\left(\frac{\hat{V}^2}{2}\frac{\partial^2 F^*}{\partial \hat{V}^2} - \frac{\partial F^*}{\partial S}\right)dt - c(m)dt\right) \qquad (59)$$

The first order condition for a maximum is then

$$\frac{\mu^2}{\sigma^2}S^2\frac{\partial F^*}{\partial S} = \frac{1}{2}\frac{\mu^2}{\sigma^2}S^2\frac{\partial^2 F^*}{\partial \hat{V}^2} - \frac{dc}{dm}(m^*) \qquad (60)$$

so that m*(S, $\hat{V}$), the optimal policy rule, solves

$$\frac{dc}{dm}(m^*) = S^2\frac{\mu^2}{\sigma^2}\left(\frac{\hat{V}^2}{2}\frac{\partial^2 F^*}{\partial \hat{V}^2} - \frac{\partial F^*}{\partial S}\right) \qquad (61)$$

The condition for a global maximum is that $c''(m) < 0$. This is satisfied if the marginal cost of extra information is increasing in m. This will be true if we are willing to make some kind of "overkill" assumption: twice as much spending will not result in twice as much information, as the researchers get in one another's way. In the case of linear costs used in the simple model of market research, m is in fact undefined.

For example, take the possibility of quadratic research costs. If $c(m) = 0.5m^2$, then condition of equation (61) becomes

$$m^* = S^2 \frac{\mu^2}{\sigma^2} \left(\frac{1}{2} \frac{\partial^2 F^*}{\partial \hat{v}^2} - \frac{\partial F^*}{\partial S} \right) \tag{62}$$

and m* is now defined. The full Bellman equation for the value of market research is then:

$$\frac{1}{2} \left(S^2 \frac{\mu^2}{\sigma^2} \left(\frac{1}{2} \frac{\partial^2 F^*}{\partial \hat{V}^2} - \frac{\partial F^*}{\partial S} \right) \right)^2 - \rho F^* = 0 \tag{63}$$

which is to be solved again subject to the condition of equation (50):

$$F^* \geq \max(\hat{V} - I, 0)$$

However, this equation is not solved here.

The condition of equation (61) indicates that the optimally researching firm is in effect "reallocating" volatility over time, at a cost. It equates the marginal cost of obtaining another source of information, with the level of current volatility (captured by the second $\hat{V}$ derivative), and the effect of changing m on option value, captured by the S derivative. It "balances" the allocation of volatility over the lifetime of the project.

In a sense, by choosing a higher m, a firm is "squashing" time: S decays more quickly. It was shown above that this effect of a higher m leads to a quicker optimal entry time, and also to a lower option value. Since S is a function of $(1/mt)$, two problems with different levels of m would look the same if viewed over time – if time for the value of the project with higher m is "slowed down" accordingly. A firm following an optimal policy balances the effect of this squashing of time on option value, with its marginal cost and current levels of volatility. It is for this reason that we can drop the time-dependence of F.

However, because of the presence of discounting, this does not mean that time is irrelevant in the sense that we would disregard the difference between spending £40 per day for ten days and £4 per day for 100 days. We still have a well-defined optimal level of current expenditure in terms of a constant flow, given where we want to go in terms of current S.

CONCLUSION

In this chapter, it has been argued that while previous models of the value of research into product opportunities assumed that the underlying state variable on which the value of the project depends follow a constant variance process, this is undesirable. There will be an impact from greater information and learning over time on the variance of estimated product value, and hence on associated option values.

A model has been presented here which includes this learning effect, based on the theory of optimal filtering. The optimal filtering theorem used allows us to specify the stochastic process followed by the optimal estimate of product value, to be used as a state variable for situations in which actual value is unobservable. Optimal filtering is unrealistic because it assumes a continuous observation of the signal process, but it clearly demonstrates how uncertainty, and therefore option value, decreases with time.

The effects of being able to control the intensity of the signal to be filtered have also been demonstrated, and a solution achieved for the optimal policy.

Clearly, this work is by no means comprehensive. Further possibilities would be to alter the assumptions of optimal filtering to allow for lumpier information. Also, different optimisation problems in terms of a firm's preferences over value and uncertainty would be interesting. It is possible that such problems would lead to more intuitively interpretable results. Lastly, it is worth noting that the imposition of different boundary conditions on the partial differential equations used would enable the analysis and evaluation of projects under different decision structures; most notably, a project in which there is a single decision point for the (in/out) decision.

BIBLIOGRAPHY

Abel, A.B., A.K. Dixit, J.C. Eberly and R.S. Pindyck, 1996, "Options, the value of capital, and investment", *Quarterly Journal of Economics*, 3, pp. 753–58.

Arnold, L., 1974, *Stochastic Differential Equations: Theory and Applications*, New York: John Wiley and Sons.

Bellman, R., 1956, "A Problem in the Sequential Design of Experiments", *Sankhya*, 16, pp. 221–9.

Bernanke, B.S., 1983, "Irreversibility, Uncertainty and Cyclical Investment". *Quarterly Journal of Economics*, 98, pp. 85–106.

Brennan, M.J. and E.S. Schwartz, 1985, "Evaluating natural resource investments", *Journal of Business*, 58, pp. 135–57.

Brown, R.G. and P.Y.C. Hwang, 1992, *Introduction to Random Signals*. 2nd ed., Wiley.

Bucy, R.S. and P.D. Joseph, 1968, *Filtering for Stochastic Processes with Applications to Guidance*, New York: Interscience.

Copeland, T.E., T. Koller and J. Murrin, 1994, *Valuation: Measuring and Managing the Value of Companies*, McKinsey & Co.

Cukierman, A., 1980, "The effects of uncertainty on investment under risk-neutrality with endogenous information", *Journal of Political Economy*, 88, pp. 462–75.

Demers, M., 1991, "Investment under uncertainty: irreversibility and the arrival of information over time", *Review of Economic Studies*, 58, pp. 333–50.

Dixit, A.K. and R.S. Pindyck, 1994, *Investment Under Uncertainty*, New Jersey: Princeton University Press.

Fisher, A.C. and W.M. Hanemann, 1987, "Quasi-Option Values: Some Misconceptions Dispelled", *Journal of Environmental Economics and Management*, 14, pp. 183–90.

Garbrowski, H.G. and J.M. Vernon, 1983, "Studies on Drug Substitution, Patent Policy and Innovation in the Pharmaceutical Industry", *Final Report to the NSF*, Duke University.

Garbrowski, H.G. and J.M. Vernon, 1991, "Pharmaceutical research and development: returns and risks", *CMR Annual Lecture*.

Goodwin, G.C and Kwai Sang Sin, 1984, *Adaptive Filtering, Prediction and Control*, Prentice-Hall.

Grossman, G.M. and C. Shapiro, 1986, "Optimal Dynamic R&D Projects", *Rand Journal of Economics*, 17, pp. 581–93.

Kalman, R.E., 1963, "New Methods in Filtering Theory" in *Proceedings of the First Symposium on Engineering Applications on Random Function Theory and Probability*, eds. J.L. Bogdanoff and F. Kozin, New York: John Wiley.

Lund, D., 1991, in *Stochastic Models and Option Values*, eds. Lund, D. and B. Oksendal, New York: North Holland.

McDonald, R.L. and D.R. Siegel, 1985, "Investment and the Valuation of Firms When There is an Option to Shut Down", *International Economic Review*, 26, pp. 331–49.

McDonald, R.L. and D.R. Siegel, 1986, "The Value of Waiting to Invest", *Quarterly Journal of Economics*, 101, pp. 707–28.

Newton, D.P., 1991, "R&D Investment Decisions and Option Pricing Theory", A. M. S. Working Paper, R&D Research Unit, Manchester Business School.

Newton, D.P. and A.W. Pearson, 1994, "Application of Option Pricing Theory to R&D", *R&D Management*, 24, pp. 83–9.

Oksendal, B., 1992, *Stochastic Differential Equations*, Springer.

Pakes, A., 1986, "Patents as Options: Some Estimates of the Value of Holding European Patent Stocks", *Econometrica*, 54, pp. 755–84.

Pindyck, R.S., 1988, "Irreversible Investment, Capital Choice and the Value of the Firm", *American Economic Review*, 78, pp. 969–85.

Quigg, L., 1993, "Empirical Testing of Real Option Pricing Models", *Journal of Finance*, 48, pp. 621–39.

Roberts, K. and M.L. Weitzman, 1981, "Finding Criteria for Research, Development and Exploration Projects", *Econometrica*, 49, pp. 1261–88.

Rothschild, M., 1974, "A Two-Armed Bandit Theory of Market Pricing", *Journal of Economic Theory*, 9, pp. 185–202.

Sanders, J., J. Rossman and L. Harris, 1958, "The Economic Impact of Patents", *Patent, Trademark and Copyright Journal of Resources and Education*, 2, pp. 340–62.

Scherer, F.M., 1958, "Firm Size, Market Structure and the Output of Patented Innovations", *American Economic Review*, 55, pp. 1097–125.

14

Valuing the Operational Flexibility of a Multinational Enterprise (with Implications for Investment Location and Capacity Choice Decisions)

Arun S. Muralidhar[1]

JP Morgan

As the global economic environment undergoes a rapid transition, firms are presented with a situation where doing business, whether in a national or international context, is fraught with uncertainty. Previously centrally planned economies are gravitating towards a free-market system and traditionally less-developed economies are undergoing a metamorphosis towards fiscal prudence and an emphasis on growth. This chapter will attempt to illuminate business risks that arise from volatility in specific markets and show how these may affect strategic decisions that firms must make once they choose to be multinational in this dynamic business environment.

Multinational enterprises (MNEs) that can respond rapidly to changing business conditions will gain a competitive advantage in the global market. As competition between MNEs takes place along a number of dimensions, the competitive position of the organisation will be affected by:

❑ uncertain demand for products;[2]
❑ changes in the cost of mobile and immobile inputs in different countries;
❑ volatile exchange rates;
❑ revisions in government policy agendas; and
❑ innovations in process and product technology.

The strategic management literature has focused its attention on encouraging managers in MNEs to implement strategies that provide operational flexibility.[3] For example, multiple sourcing relationships allow MNEs to mitigate losses that stem from unanticipated changes in input costs in a particular country or from adverse exchange rate movements. Firms have also been encouraged to invest in flexible technologies that allow automated production lines to switch from the production of one product to another with minimal stoppage time.[4] An example of firms adopting flexibility in production techniques to deal with shifts in demand between models comes from the Japanese auto industry. Japanese auto manufacturers have been praised for their investment in flexible technologies, and part of their success was attributed to their ability to exploit this flexibility.

Flexibility is desirable in the face of future uncertainty, but investing in flexibility is a resource-allocation decision. As with all resource-allocation decisions, the crucial question is whether committing scarce resources to acquire certain types of flexibility will result in substantial increases in expected value of the organisation. This chapter fills a gap in the existing literature on flexibility by showing how static investment valuation techniques may be inadequate for the task of project valuation when costs, including exchange rates, are stochastic and MNEs can manage capacity utilisation, and it offers an adjustment to the traditional "net present value" (NPV) rule. Once the investment rule is modified, it is possible to show how the MNE's strategic decisions regarding the location of economic activity and the maintenance of excess capacity (and possibly even investment timing) are affected.[5]

Pindyck (1991) demonstrates how a firm should value the option to invest when *investment is irreversible*. Pindyck (1988) and Pindyck and He (1990) present a methodology for valuing incremental capacity. The critical idea is that when demand/costs are stochastic, the firm has the option in every period to decide whether or not to use a unit of capacity. The firm acquires this portfolio of options when it invests in a unit of capacity. However, the key decision for the firm is the investment decision – the decision whether it should pay a sunk cost to acquire a unit of capacity today or else wait until some future period. In the presence of stochastic demand (and/or unit costs or production) firms may postpone investment rather than invest today.

While this view is acceptable for *national* firms, this approach fails to recognise that many firms are multinational. Multinational enterprises locate plants in a host of countries and have the ability to manage capacity utilisation in every plant depending on the variability of local conditions and exchange rates. This chapter concentrates on valuing operational flexibility as it pertains to the MNE's ability to exploit its global spread to produce a substantial share of its output at lowest cost. It shows that the important variable for a MNE is not the variability of domestic environments considered in isolation, but instead the *co-variability*, or lack thereof, of unit costs of production (in the numeraire currency) in the different geographical regions in which the MNE has a factory.

Kogut and Kulatilaka (1991) show how a MNE can produce *all* the output at the lowest cost. This is an overstatement, as MNEs are capacity constrained in the various locations, and hence may be able to only shift capacity utilisation. The current chapter first demonstrates how a MNE should value projects that provide it with the flexibility to shift production. Thereafter, the rigorous model derived in the third section of the chapter is tested with hourly wage data from various countries. The simulations demonstrate that for US-domiciled MNEs, the value of excess capacity as a percentage of the adjusted present value of cashflows in countries like Germany, the UK and Ireland is significant when compared with the fraction of excess capacity to total capacity. For projects in Canada, the value of excess capacity (flexibility) is less significant because cost increases in the US and Canada seem to be strongly correlated. This conclusion will clearly affect the investment location (invest in the US or invest abroad) and capacity-choice (expand capacity in the US or invest in excess capacity abroad) decisions of US-based MNEs.

The first section of this chapter introduces a new approach by arguing that having operational flexibility is tantamount to holding a portfolio of real options. A stylised scenario is presented to demonstrate how options-pricing techniques can be used to value this type of flexibility. The second section provides a review of related literature and shows how this chapter departs from previous work. The third section provides a rigorous method for estimating the value of operational flexibility. In the fourth section simulations are performed based on different parameter values to demonstrate the sensitivity of the value of operational flexibility to various variables, and the significance of the value of real/operational flexibility in different countries. The fifth section suggests extensions to this approach, and the sixth section posits some implications and conclusions.

OPERATIONAL FLEXIBILITY: AN ANALOGY WITH AN OPTIONS PORTFOLIO

The motivations for valuing operational flexibility is best demonstrated by two simple examples. Consider a US-based shoe manufacturer with a global market that has a factory in the US and one in SE Asia. Should the cost of US labour increase substantially because the firm is expected to make mandatory health insurance payments to its workers, management may scale back operations in the US and expand operations abroad.[6]

Alternatively, consider a car manufacturer that has factories around the world that produces its car engines. If exchange rate changes make it more expensive to import these engines from Latin America and less expensive to import them from Europe, there may be a significant benefit to redistributing capacity utilisation in favour of European locations. However, these strategies are feasible only if there is excess capacity in the foreign locations, and if the costs of switching are not excessive. These examples may seem to be very simplistic, but MNEs are aware of the benefits of shifting capacity utilisation when faced with increased costs in a particular

Table 1. Hourly wages in manufacturing (US$)*

Year	Canada	France	Germany	Ireland	Mexico	Spain	UK	US
								10.84
1989	11.69	6.33	11.27	7.91	1.22	7.11	7.88	10.49
1988	10.77	5.76	10.20	7.30	0.98	6.47	8.15	10.19
1987	9.38	6.23	10.97	7.79	0.55	6.23	7.85	9.91
1986	8.66	5.18	8.66	6.30	0.35	4.70	5.85	9.73
1985	8.29	4.17	6.57	5.21	0.85	3.66	5.33	9.54
1984	8.44	2.98	4.89	3.84	1.22	2.94	3.93	9.19
1983	8.49	3.13	5.43	3.92	1.03	2.92	4.54	8.83
1982	8.34	3.60	6.23	4.48	1.06	3.20	4.84	8.49
1981	7.76	3.62	6.15	4.36	2.42	3.55	5.58	7.99
1980	6.95	4.07	6.73	4.40	1.69	3.60	6.36	7.27
1979	6.39	3.99	7.20	4.69	1.40	3.66	5.07	6.70
1978	5.76	3.35	6.34	3.42	1.24	2.81	3.92	6.17
1977	5.84	2.72	5.39	2.90	1.13	1.94	3.33	5.68
1976	5.75	2.25	4.41	2.16	1.11	1.99	2.67	5.22
1975	5.00	2.21	3.73	2.24	1.24	1.76	2.85	4.83
Average wage (US$)	7.83	3.97	6.94	4.73	1.17	3.77	5.21	8.02
Standard deviation (US$)	1.92	1.35	2.33	1.86	0.47	1.66	1.77	1.91

Sources: *Yearbook of Labor Statistics* (various issues) and *World Currency Monitor Annual* (1975–89).

*See Appendix A for the data used to derive Table 1.

location. Management of Black & Decker for example, actively shift capacity utilisation when exchange rates change to prevent an erosion of profit margins[7]. Table 1 and Figure 1 provide indicative hourly wages (in US$) for the US and a few foreign countries.

The two hypothetical examples and Black & Decker's strategic decisions demonstrate that MNEs gain operational flexibility by diversifying their production locations. By virtue of their international spread, they, presumably, are able to access immobile inputs in different markets and produce goods at the lowest possible cost. The existence of these different entities in a host of countries creates a situation where management's evaluation of foreign projects must transcend the static net present value (NPV) rule to incorporate the unique relationship that foreign investments have with existing investments. This chapter first demonstrates how simple NPV rules that discount expected after-tax cashflows may not capture an essential characteristic of multinational projects. Once the valuation technique is corrected, a comparison is performed between investing at home and investing in more than one location.

In order for the MNE to be able to switch production from one country to another, it has to be willing to have idle capacity in the desired location. The problem is structured so that a national firm has experienced an increase in worldwide demand that can only be met by new investment.[8] This new investment can be made either at home or in a foreign country. Assume that

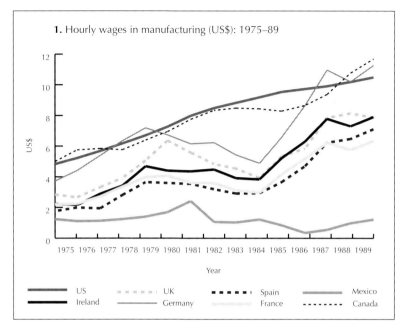

1. Hourly wages in manufacturing (US$): 1975–89

US — UK — Spain — Mexico
Ireland — Germany — France — Canada

capacity expansion is lumpy and hence the firm is forced to invest in excess capacity. However, the key idea is that management may find it preferable to maintain excess capacity abroad, if input prices or exchange rates are volatile.

Management is expected to maximise the expected value of the firm. In evaluating domestic investments, management would have ensured that the present discounted value of all future earnings exceeded the cost of investment. However, if the firm has the opportunity in the future to produce abroad, at lower cost, some output that would have been produced at home, this benefit should be included in the valuation of the foreign project.

Assume that prices are fixed and demand is exogenously determined. Once the foreign investment is made, the increase in demand will be satisfied by production in the foreign location, and one can value the NPV of this aspect of the investment.[9] The excess capacity abroad also allows the firm to consider producing more output abroad if the local currency equivalent of producing abroad[10] is less than the unit cost of production in the home country. The firm *would not* have been afforded this opportunity to lower costs if it had expanded capacity in the original location.

To value this flexibility one must make some assumptions about the volatility and time path of unit costs at home and the local currency equivalent of producing abroad. Figure 2 provides a plot of the difference between hourly wages in the US and Canada, and in the US and Germany (1975–89). Data for this graph are provided in Table 2. The time path of the *difference* between the two costs is modelled as a Brownian motion with no drift, to capture the volatile nature of the costs. In every future period,

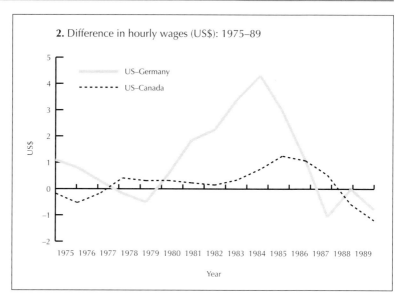

2. Difference in hourly wages (US$): 1975–89

management will observe the unit costs and the exchange rates in the two countries and decide whether or not to exercise the *option* to shift capacity utilisation abroad. The foreign project, in addition to servicing the increase in demand, provides the firm with an option in every period to use excess capacity to increase firm value.

Table 2. Difference between hourly wages in the US and other countries

Year	US–Canada	US–France	US–Germany	US–Ireland	US–Mexico	US–Spain	US–UK
1989	−1.20	4.16	−0.78	2.58	9.27	3.38	2.61
1988	−0.58	4.43	−0.01	2.89	9.21	3.72	2.04
1987	0.53	3.68	−1.06	2.12	9.36	3.68	2.06
1986	1.07	4.55	1.07	3.43	9.38	5.03	3.88
1985	1.25	5.37	2.97	4.33	8.69	5.88	4.21
1984	0.75	6.21	4.30	5.35	7.97	6.25	5.26
1983	0.34	5.70	3.40	4.91	7.80	5.91	4.29
1982	0.15	4.89	2.26	4.01	7.43	5.29	3.65
1981	0.23	4.37	1.84	3.63	5.57	4.44	2.41
1980	0.32	3.20	0.54	2.87	5.58	3.67	0.91
1979	0.31	2.71	−0.50	2.01	5.30	3.04	1.63
1978	0.41	2.82	−0.17	2.75	4.93	3.36	2.25
1977	−0.16	2.96	0.29	2.78	4.55	3.74	2.35
1976	−0.53	2.97	0.81	3.06	4.11	3.23	2.55
1975	−0.17	2.62	1.10	2.59	3.59	3.07	1.98
Average diff. in wages	0.18	4.04	1.07	3.29	6.85	4.25	2.81
Volatility (σ_ω)	0.64	1.16	1.59	0.98	2.12	1.13	1.18

If investments in capacity must exceed existing demand, then we are able to show that there is value to maintaining excess capacity in a foreign location. This value is derived from the fact that the sourcing of inputs has been diversified, and the firm can take advantage of changes in unit costs or exchange rates to lower the total cost of production. Therefore, a national firm that is considering capacity expansion should invest locally only if NPV (invest locally) > adjusted NPV (abroad) where adjusted NPV (abroad) = base NPV (abroad) + portfolio of real options that allow the firm to lower the total cost of production.[11] If we value this portfolio correctly, it should equal the present discounted value of all *expected future cost savings*, given the stochastic process chosen and the exercise rule stated earlier.

Finally, once the investment valuation rule is modified, one can use the new rule to compare competing investment locations. It should be obvious that a correct comparison will involve comparing the adjusted NPVs of these locations to capture the fact that they will contribute some value to the existing organisation by satisfying the increase in demand and, in addition, in the case of a foreign location, through the optimal utilisation of the excess capacity. The next section presents a brief review of related work.

A SYNTHESIS OF PROJECT EVALUATION, FLEXIBILITY AND INVESTMENT

This chapter is an integration of three related strands of analysis; namely, the literature on the correct valuation of foreign projects, the literature on the flexibility of MNEs, and the emerging literature on the option value of investment, when investment is irreversible.

Lessard (1978) has shown that NPV analyses, unless correctly done, may ignore the benefits that a foreign project provides.[12] When foreign projects are undertaken with subsidised financing and under favourable tax treatment, Lessard (1978) recommends that MNEs calculate an adjusted present value (APV) for that foreign project. The APV approach posits that different facets of foreign investments like subsidised financing should be discounted at appropriate risk-adjusted discount rates, and that the present value of these subsidies should be added to the present discounted value of the after-tax cashflows.

In addition, Lessard and Paddock (1980), in a paper on the benefits of valuing international projects by components, argue that there are three distinct components to a foreign project that can be readily identified. Projects produce cashflows that are fixed by contract (*debt equivalents*), respond closely to a set of underlying economic forces (*equity equivalents*), and "respond non-linearly to changes in some underlying cashflows or asset values" (*option equivalents*). Kogut (1985) has emphasised that multinational firms have flexibility that permits them to hedge against the uncertainty over future exchange rates, competitive moves, or government policy. Baldwin (1986) argues that MNEs have location, timing, technology (flexibility) and growth/staging options, and that management should identify, evaluate and exercise these options in an optimal fashion.

These papers capture the importance of flexibility of the multinational enterprise, but they do not provide a methodology to value these options or show the extent to which traditional NPV analyses may fall short of capturing the true value of a foreign investment opportunity.

An emerging literature attempts to value the option equivalents imbedded in certain domestic investments.[13] For example, when future demand is uncertain, shutdown is costless and investment can be postponed, the NPV of investing today should not be taken in isolation, but instead *has* to be compared to the value of postponing the investment to a later date. While the option to shutdown is valuable, having the option to postpone investments may cause a firm to consider investing at a later date when the volatility of either demand or costs does not erode expected future profits.

Trigeorgis and Mason (1987) have used contingent claims pricing methods to value managerial flexibility, and Triantis and Hodder (1990) have used them to value flexible production systems that allow firms to switch their output mix over time.[14] Recent work by Kogut and Kulatilaka (1991) integrates the work on flexibility and the option equivalents in foreign investments. Their paper addresses issues raised in this chapter, but their emphasis is on demonstrating how the sequential process of investment overseas affects the evaluation of all investments that take place after the initial foreign direct investment. They show how the initial investment provides the organisation with growth opportunities and then demonstrate the benefit of maintaining operational flexibility when exchange rates are volatile. This chapter focuses on managing capacity utilisation, but Kogut and Kulitalaka (1991) model the MNE as producing *all* of the output in the lowest cost location, and without any capacity constraints.

Projects in several countries provide MNEs with a productive presence in these countries. When business environments around the world are changing constantly, this diversification of production and/or sourcing of inputs is extremely valuable. The key contribution of this chapter is to focus attention on the *correct* valuation of foreign projects under these circumstances, and to suggest that simple NPV analyses should be complemented with a valuation of the real options that the foreign entity provides. The emphasis is that multinational firms do not close plants and move to another location, but instead are capacity constrained and can only manage capacity utilisation at the margin.

In the next section the analysis is formalised by providing a precise model that is based on the discussion above.

ESTIMATING THE VALUE OF OPERATIONAL FLEXIBILITY

When faced with *input price volatility* (in domestic markets) management must decide whether to

❑ invest domestically today;

❏ wait to invest locally in the future; or
❏ invest abroad.

In this section only, a method to value expanding capacity at home and foreign investments is presented, and the reader is directed to Appendix D for a discussion on the optimal timing of investment.[15]

A simple model is presented below to show how real flexibility can be valued using option pricing theory, and how this should be used in arriving at a correct valuation of a foreign investment opportunity.

Assumptions

A.1   A firm in country A has capacity to produce x units of output per period from a single factory in country A. The factory can produce output for an infinite number of periods.

A.2   Demand has increased to x + d units of output per period and is not expected to increase in the future.[16]

A.3   Capacity expansion is lumpy[17] and the firm can only invest in capacity to produce x more units/period in another factory, either locally, or abroad, say in country B.

A.4   Goal of management is to maximise the value of the firm.

A.5.   Assume that the output is sold on the world market at price p, which is given by the market. (The goal of the firm can now be reduced to cost minimisation instead.)

A.6   Wages in country B are fixed and equal to w^* in every period, where $p \gg w^*$; $p - w^* = b$.[18]

A.7   Wages in country A, w^A, fluctuate randomly and w^A may be greater than or less than w^*, and greater than or less than the price of output p.

A.8   Define $\Delta = w^A(t) - w^*$ and assume that variations in Δ can be captured by the following stochastic process:

$$d\Delta = \sigma_\omega dz \qquad\qquad\qquad (1)$$

where $dz = \varepsilon(t)(dt)^{1/2}$ is the increment on standard Brownian motion. $\varepsilon(t)$ has zero mean and unit standard deviation. $E[dz] = 0$ and $E[(dz)^2] = dt$. σ_ω is the instantaneous standard deviation.[19]

A.9   Assume that the changes in wages have zero beta (uncorrelated with the market portfolio).

A.10   Production technology is such that a single worker produces one unit of output per period – one unit costs w^A if produced in A or w^* if produced in B.

A.11   There is a sunk cost of investment = I, and investment is irreversible.

A.12   Production can be switched from one factory to another costlessly and with no time lag.

A.13   We will ignore transportation costs, and all tax, tariff and foreign exchange issues (refer to A.6 and accompanying note).

A.14   The firm is risk neutral.

A.15   Let r be the real risk-free interest rate and assume that r does not change.[20]

If the firm expands capacity in country A then its costs in every period are $(x + d)w^A$ as long as the unit labour cost is below p. If w^A exceeds p, the firm may want to shut down, unless it is trying to protect its market share. However, if the firm invests in country B to complement its original invest-ment in A, then costs are equal to $\min[xw^A + dw^*, dw^A + xw^*]$. Therefore, a simple NPV analysis to evaluate the investment in B that assumed that the plant in B would produce only one unit of output would underestimate the true value of the foreign investment. A static NPV analysis might assume that the extra unit of capacity will be left unused at all times, given insuffi-cient demand, whereas the approach presented below takes into account the benefit of maintaining that extra unit of capacity when unit costs in one environment are more volatile than they are in another.

If it is assumed that shutdown is costless and that the firm will not pro-duce output in A when the wage rate in A exceeds the price of output, one can find the value of flexibility.

Define

$$b = p - w^* \tag{2}$$

Define

$$w^A = w^* + \Delta \tag{3}$$

This implies that

$$p - w^A = b - \Delta \tag{4}$$

Also, from (1), $d\Delta = \sigma_\omega dz$.

Now the cashflows generated by a national firm

$$= (x + d)(p - w^A)^+ \tag{5}$$

where one can define

$$(p - w^A)^+ = \max[p - w^A, 0] \tag{6}$$

For simplicity assume that $x = 2$ and $d = 1$.[21]

Therefore, if the firm expands capacity at home, the cashflows generated by a national firm in every period (ignoring time subscripts)

$$= 3(p - w^A)^+ = 3(b - \Delta)^+ \qquad (5')$$

because expanding capacity at home will generate additional cashflows

$$= (b - \Delta)^+ \qquad (6')$$

in every period.

Define $N(\Delta)$ = expected present value of a unit of capacity in the home country. From (6') one knows that

$$N(\Delta) = E_t \left[\int_{t=0}^{\infty} e^{-rt} (b - \Delta)^+ \, dt \middle| \Delta_0 = \Delta \right]$$

or

$$N(\Delta) = \max_{j=0/1} E_t \left[\int_{t=0}^{\infty} e^{-rt} (jb - \Delta) \, dt \middle| \Delta_0 = \Delta \right]$$

given that Δ follows the stochastic process specified in (1). In the appendices it is shown that $N(\Delta) = N(b, \Delta)$, and under the appropriate boundary, smoothness and continuity conditions

$$N(\Delta) = \frac{1}{2rg} e^{(-b + \Delta)g} + \frac{b - \Delta}{r} \qquad \text{when } \Delta < b \qquad (7a)$$

$$= \frac{1}{2rg} e^{(b - \Delta)g} \qquad \text{when } \Delta > b \qquad (7b)$$

A brief explanation of (7a) and (7b) is in order. Let us examine (7a) first. When $\Delta < b$, this implies that $p > w^A$ and the firm is producing the additional unit of output at home. If the wage in A were never to change the present value of all future earnings $= b - \Delta/r$. However, should the wage in A rise above p, the firm will shut down and the value of this option $= (1/2rg)e^{(-b + \Delta)g}$.

Equation (7b) states that if the wage in A is higher than p, the firm is not producing output but has the option to produce the additional unit of output when the wage rate in A falls. The value of the option to restart production $= (1/2rg)e^{(b - \Delta)g}$.

On the other hand, determining the cashflows generated by a MNE in every period is an interesting problem. The MNE will produce one unit abroad, produce one in A if the wage in A is below p, and produce the third in the lowest cost location. This approach allows the MNE to minimise the labour costs of producing three units of output. One can express these cashflows, ignoring time subscripts, in equation (8a):

$$\text{Cashflow for the MNE} = (p - w^A)^+ + b + p - \min(w^A, w^*) \tag{8a}$$
$$= (b - \Delta)^+ + b + p - (w^* + \min(\Delta, 0)) \tag{8b}$$
$$= 2b + (b - \Delta)^+ - \min(\Delta, 0) \tag{8c}$$
$$= 2b + (b - \Delta)^+ + \max(-\Delta, 0) \tag{8d}$$
$$= 2b + (b - \Delta)^+ + (-\Delta)^+ \tag{9}$$

Notice, though, that the incremental cashflows of the foreign project = cashflows provided by a MNE less the cashflows that existing investments in the home country will provide. From (5′), (6′) and (9), one finds that the *incremental CFs* from the foreign project

$$= 2b + (b - \Delta)^+ + (-\Delta)^+ - 2(b - \Delta)^+ \tag{10a}$$
$$= 2b - (b - \Delta)^+ + (-\Delta)^+ \tag{10b}$$

Equation (10b) will be crucial for our calculation of operational flexibility.

To value flexibility one must determine the cashflows associated with using the excess capacity in an optimal fashion. One can take the *incremental* cashflow of the foreign project and deduct the cashflows from producing one unit of output abroad. This calculation provides the cashflows that the foreign project will generate (from the unit of excess capacity) *over and above satisfying the increase in demand*. From (10b), the incremental cashflow provided by the foreign project = $2b - (b - \Delta)^+ + (-\Delta)^+$.

Therefore, the cashflows associated with flexibility

$$= 2b - (b - \Delta)^+ + (-\Delta)^+ - b \tag{11a}$$

because b is the guaranteed cashflow produced by the foreign investment from satisfying the unit increase in demand.

Cashflows associated with flexibility

$$= b - (b - \Delta)^+ + (-\Delta)^+ \tag{11b}$$

Define $R(\Delta) = $ value of operational/real flexibility = expected present value of all cashflows that the foreign project generates through the optimal usage of excess capacity. Then from (11b) one knows that

$$R(\Delta) = E_t \left[\int_{t=0}^{\infty} e^{-rt} \left| b - (b - \Delta_t)^+ + (-\Delta_t)^+ \right| dt \middle| \Delta_0 = \Delta \right] \tag{12}$$

A detailed proof is provided in the Appendix, but with appropriate boundary, smoothness and continuity conditions it can be shown that

$$R(\Delta) = \frac{b}{r} - N(b, \Delta) + N(0, \Delta)$$

$$= \frac{b}{r} - \frac{1}{2rg} e^{(-b+\Delta)g} - \frac{b - \Delta}{r} + \frac{1}{2rg} e^{\Delta g} + \frac{-\Delta}{r} \qquad \text{when } \Delta < 0 \qquad \textbf{(13a)}$$

$$= \frac{b}{r} - \frac{1}{2rg} e^{(-b+\Delta)g} - \frac{b - \Delta}{r} + \frac{1}{2rg} e^{-\Delta g} \qquad \text{when } 0 \le \Delta \le b \quad \textbf{(13b)}$$

$$= \frac{b}{r} - \frac{1}{2rg} e^{(b-\Delta)g} + \frac{1}{2rg} e^{-\Delta g} \qquad \text{when } \Delta \ge b \qquad \textbf{(13c)}$$

These equations can be reduced to the following

$$= -\frac{1}{2rg} e^{(-b+\Delta)g} + \frac{1}{2rg} e^{\Delta g} \qquad \text{when } \Delta < 0 \qquad \textbf{(13a)}$$

$$= \frac{\Delta}{r} - \frac{1}{2rg} e^{(-b+\Delta)g} + \frac{1}{2rg} e^{-\Delta g} \qquad \text{when } 0 \le \Delta \le b \quad \textbf{(13b)}$$

$$= \frac{b}{r} - \frac{1}{2rg} e^{(b-\Delta)g} + \frac{1}{2rg} e^{-\Delta g} \qquad \text{when } \Delta \ge b \qquad \textbf{(13c)}$$

Before a detailed interpretation is provided for (13a), (13b) and (13c) one must discuss why there are three regions over which $R(\Delta)$ is defined. The value of flexibility will depend on the value of w^A relative to the foreign wage and the price of output. When $\Delta < 0$, then $w^A < w^* < p$. When $0 \le \Delta \le b$, $w^* \le w^A \le p$, and when $\Delta > b$, then w^A is greater than p.

A brief explanation is now provided for the value of $R(\Delta)$ over the three regions. From (13a) it can be concluded that when $\Delta < 0$, the wage rate at home is less than the wage rate in B, and even though the firm is not using the excess capacity abroad, it has the option to do so in the future. However, if w^A should rise above the price of output, the maximum saving afforded by the foreign investment is = US\$b in every period. When $0 \le \Delta \le b$, then the wage in A is above the foreign wage, but below p. We find from (13b) that if the wage in A were never to change the present value of all cost savings provided by excess capacity abroad $= \Delta/r$. However, if the wage rate in A should fall below the wage rate abroad, the firm will want to switch production back to the home country, and this is a valuable option. In addition, if the wage rate in A rises above p, the maximum cost saving from producing the third unit of output abroad in every period = US\$b. Equation (13c) considers the case where w^A is greater than p and the analysis is similar to that described above for equation (13b); namely, that the firm is presently earning US\$b in every period, and will continue to do so if the wage in A never changes. However, if w^A falls, then the firm would like to change its utilisation of capacity depending on how much w^A falls.[22]

From the discussion above, the value of the foreign investment is more complex than a simple NPV calculation of guaranteed profits.[23] Instead, as proposed by Lessard and Paddock (1980), the value of a project is the value of the components that are contractual, non-contractual and those that are like options, and hence the value

$$= \int_{t=0}^{\infty} e^{-rt}(p - w^*)dt - I + R(\Delta) \tag{14}$$

SIMULATIONS TO DETERMINE THE SENSITIVITY OF OPERATIONAL FLEXIBILITY

This section is divided into two subsections. In the first a sensitivity analysis is conducted to determine the impact of various variables on the value of operational flexibility. This subsection shows how the investment analysis should be conducted when a foreign investment not only meets increases in demand but also allows the MNE to produce a bulk of total production at the lowest (worldwide) marginal cost. It also shows how an exclusion of the value of flexibility can lead to an incorrect rejection of a foreign project. The second subsection extends this analysis to a related problem. Competing investment opportunities in different countries are compared, including the home country. Assume that these countries are similar in every respect except that the domestic currency equivalent of unit costs and the volatility of cost savings (degree of correlation of the foreign country with the home country) are different. In addition to evaluating the investment location decision this chapter attempt to show how capacity choice decisions might be affected when one recognises that excess capacity is valuable if it is in a foreign location.

Sensitivity analysis

The effects of various parameters on the value of the portfolio of options are simulated to determine how $R(\Delta)$ is affected by changes in the interest rate, cost saving and the volatility of cost saving. Data for the US and Germany are used along with arbitrarily select values for p and r to highlight the value of $R(\Delta)$ under different conditions.[24] To make the illustration more interesting, the data for 1989 are used as Germany has a higher unit cost than the US ($w^* > w^A$). From Table 2, $\sigma_\omega = 1.59$ and assume that this measure of volatility is appropriate as of 1989. This process highlights the tradeoff that MNEs need to consider between experiencing lower costs of production today versus having access to lower costs of production in the future. The reader is referred to Table 3.

In this simple model, $R(\Delta)$ is the value of the extra unit of capacity in the foreign location. As can be seen from the table above, higher interest rates and lower volatility reduce the value of the portfolio of options. If the real interest rate is high, then the present value of future cost saving is low

Table 3. Valuing real flexibility in Germany

Assume that the sunk cost of investment (I) = 80
Assume that the price of output (p) = US$15

	Interest rate r (%) (1)	σ_ω (2)	Wage rate in the US (3)	Wage rate in Germany (4)	Δ = (w^{US} – w^*) (5)	R(Δ) (6)	Simple NPV in Germany = (p – w)/r – I (7)	Adj NPV = (6) + (7) (8)
(1)	6	1.59	10.49	11.27	–0.78	17.95	–17.83	0.12
(2)	6.5	1.59	10.49	11.27	–0.78	16.60	–22.62	–6.02
(3)	7	1.59	10.49	11.27	–0.78	14.76	–26.71	–11.95
(4)	6	1.30	10.49	11.27	–0.78	16.00	–17.83	–1.83
(5)	6	1.40	10.49	11.27	–0.78	17.15	–17.83	–0.68
(6)	6	1.50	10.49	11.27	–0.78	18.22	–17.83	0.39
(7)	6	1.59	9.50	11.27	–1.77	14.47	–17.83	–3.36
(8)	6	1.59	10.50	11.27	–0.77	17.99	–17.83	0.16
(9)	6	1.59	11.50	11.27	0.23	22.37	–17.83	4.54

(rows 1–3, column 6). However, increased volatility in cost saving raises the value of excess capacity (rows 4–6, column 6). Values for σ_ω capture the degree to which domestic wages and the dollar equivalent of foreign wages are positively correlated. The higher the σ_ω the lower the positive correlation, which in turn implies that there is a higher probability that the firm will exercise the option to use the extra unit of capacity in the foreign Δ location. Notice further that in this model, R(Δ) is *strictly increasing* in Δ (rows 7–9, column 6). As the hourly wage in the US (w^{US}) approaches w^* (hourly wage in Germany) there is a higher probability that w^{US} will be greater than w^* and that excess capacity in Germany will be utilised by the firm.

Incorporating this valuation of excess capacity into the NPV analysis could change the final decision of the firm. In a number of instances, a simple NPV analysis would suggest that the investment in Germany was not profitable to domestic and foreign investors. However, on including the value of R(Δ) in the calculations one has the possibility that the investment could be attractive to a firm domiciled in the US (for example, rows 6, 8 and 9).

Applying sensitivity analysis

In a domestic setting, expectations of increased volatility in input prices could lead firms to postpone investment decisions, either of entire plants or of incremental capacity in a plant, as suggested by Pindyck and He (1990). While higher volatility raises the value of the option to wait, it may also increase the value of the option to invest abroad. Therefore, a firm with

Table 4. Summary statistics for wage data (1975–89)

	Germany	Canada	UK	Ireland	France	US
1 Hourly wage in country (US$) in 1987	10.97	9.38	7.85	7.79	6.23	9.91
2 Average hourly wage (US$)	6.94	7.83	5.21	4.73	3.97	8.02
3 $\sigma(w^i_{US})$	2.33	1.92	1.77	1.86	1.35	1.91
4 $\sigma(w^{us} - w^i)$	1.59	0.64	1.18	0.98	1.16	NA

international business could find this situation to be conducive to investing abroad and exploiting the ability to source in the cheapest markets.

Usually, when a firm considers a foreign investment to service a global market it has to decide between a number of sites in different countries. In this section, we compare the value to a US-based MNE, of investments in Germany, Canada, the UK and Ireland in an attempt to show the contribution to firm value of investment sites that have different unit costs (w^i) and different volatilities of cost saving (σ_ω).[25] There is an implicit assumption being made that the average wage is the same in the countries. Table 4 provides summary statistics for the wage data used in these simulations, and from Table 4 the reader will notice that this is not the case. However, it is demonstrated below that this will not affect the comparative results.

For these comparisons, assume that $r = 6\%$, and $p = 15$. For simplicity, first compare the *expected present value* of the cashflows in all locations and hence set $I = 0$. The issue of the cost of investment is addressed later on, as this will *affect the NPV* of the investments. Moreover, this chapter will try to discuss how investment location decisions are affected when the cost of expanding capacity in the US is lower than the cost of installing a new plant in a foreign country.

Tables 5A, B, C, D and E compare the value of investments in the countries mentioned above and the US for the years 1985–9. The difference between an

Table 5A. Comparing investment locations for 1985 (w^{us} = US$9.54)

Price of output (p) = US$15
Nominal interest rate = 6%

		US (invest in 1 unit)	Germany (invest in 2 units)	Canada (invest in 2 units)	UK (invest in 2 units)	Ireland (invest in 2 units)
1	Wage in country (US$)	9.54	6.57	8.29	5.33	5.21
2	σ	1.91	1.59	0.64	1.18	0.98
3	Static PV = (p – w)/r	91.00	140.50	111.83	161.16	163.16
4	R(Δ): value of excess capacity		57.89	27.86	72.70	73.85
5	Adjusted present value	124.11	198.39	139.69	233.87	237.01
6	R(Δ) as a percentage of the adjusted present value = (4)/(5) (%)		29.00	19.90	31.00	31.00

Table 5B. Comparing investment locations for 1986 (w^{us} = US$9.73)

Price of output (p) = US$15
Nominal interest rate = 6%

		US (invest in 1 unit)	Germany (invest in 2 units)	Canada (invest in 2 units)	UK (invest in 2 units)	Ireland (invest in 2 units)
1	Wage in country (US$)	9.73	8.66	8.66	5.85	6.30
2	σ	1.91	1.59	0.64	1.18	0.98
3	Static PV = (p − w)/r	87.83	105.67	105.67	152.50	145.00
4	R(Δ): value of excess capacity		36.00	25.57	67.71	60.52
5	Adjusted present value	105.50	141.67	131.24	220.21	205.52
6	R(Δ) as a percentage of the adjusted present value = (4)/(5) (%)		25.00	19.50	31.00	29.00

Table 5C. Comparing investment locations for 1987 (w^{us} = US$9.91)

Price of output (p) = US$15
Nominal interest rate = 6%

		US (invest in 1 unit)	Germany (invest in 2 units)	Canada (invest in 2 units)	UK (invest in 2 units)	Ireland (invest in 2 units)
1	Wage in country (US$)	9.91	10.97	9.38	7.85	7.79
2	σ	1.91	1.59	0.64	1.18	0.98
3	Static PV = (p − w)/r	84.83	67.17	93.67	119.16	120.17
4	R(Δ): value of excess capacity		17.74	19.41	43.47	42.57
5	Adjusted present value = (3) + (4)	118.69	84.91	113.08	162.63	162.74
6	R(Δ) as a percentage of the adjusted present value = (4)/(5) (%)		21.00	17.00	27.00	26.00

Table 5D. Comparing investment locations for 1988 (w^{us} = US$10.19)

Price of output (p) = US$15
Nominal interest rate = 6%

		US (invest in 1 unit)	Germany (invest in 2 units)	Canada (invest in 2 units)	UK (invest in 2 units)	Ireland (invest in 2 units)
1	Wage in country (US$)	10.19	10.20	10.77	8.15	7.30
2	σ	1.91	1.59	0.64	1.18	0.98
3	Static PV = (p − w)/r	80.17	80.00	70.50	114.17	128.33
4	R(Δ): value of excess capacity		24.75	10.27	42.68	52.35
5	Adjusted present value = (3) + (4)	114.60	104.75	80.77	156.85	180.68
6	R(Δ) as a percentage of the adjusted present value = (4)/(5) (%)		24.00	13.00	27.00	29.00

Table 5E. Comparing investment locations for 1988 (w^{us} = US$10.49)

Price of output (p) = US$15
Nominal interest rate = 6%

		US (invest in 1 unit)	Germany (invest in 2 units)	Canada (invest in 2 units)	UK (invest in 2 units)	Ireland (invest in 2 units)
1	Wage in country (US$)	10.49	11.27	11.69	7.88	7.91
2	σ	1.91	1.59	0.64	1.18	0.98
3	Static PV = (p − w)/r	75.17	62.17	55.17	118.67	118.17
4	R(Δ): value of excess capacity		18.01	8.14	49.14	47.68
5	Adjusted present value = (3) + (4)	110.22	80.18	63.30	167.81	165.85
6	R(Δ) as a percentage of the adjusted present value = (4)/(5) (%)		22.00	13.00	29.00	29.00

investment in the US and one abroad is that the foreign investment provides two units of capacity, while the investment in the US (essentially) increases total capacity by only one unit. It is clear from Tables 5A–E that the lowest wage country is also the country with the highest adjusted present values (APV). (In Tables 5A–E, excess capacity = 25% of total capacity.)

Two interesting conclusions can be derived from comparing (i) Germany to Canada and (ii) Ireland to the UK. Comparing the attractiveness of the investments in Germany and Canada (See Table 5B) in 1986, when the hourly wages (in dollars) in the two countries are the same, it is clear that the higher volatility in Germany (1.59 as opposed to 0.64 in Canada) makes the German opportunity more attractive. This result follows because German hourly wages (in dollars) are less strongly correlated with US hourly wages than Canadian hourly wages (in dollars). Therefore, investing in Germany provides greater diversification benefits to a US-based MNE than investing in Canada, and will be more valuable especially when the German dollar costs are less than or equal to Canadian costs.

Comparing Ireland and the UK for the year 1987, once again one derives interesting results. While the hourly wage in Ireland (US$7.79) is less than the hourly wage in the UK (US$7.85), the higher volatility of cost-saving of the UK investment leads to a situation where the investment in the UK has a marginally lower adjusted PV (US$162.63) than the Irish investment (US$162.74). This would indicate that the higher costs of production in any one location *may not be a sufficient reason for the disqualification* of that location, if there are benefits to be captured from diversifying the sourcing of inputs. Moreover, except for 1988, the adjusted present values of producing in Ireland and the UK are extremely close to one another (possibly because of their relatively similar macroeconomic policies). These two countries present identical investment opportunities (other things equal), so in deciding between the two countries one may want to take into con-

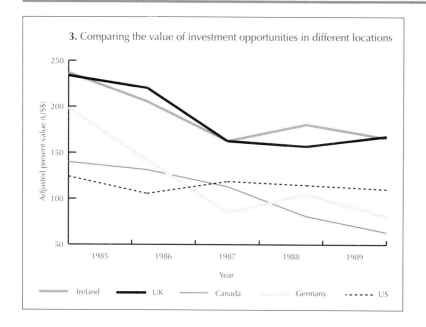

3. Comparing the value of investment opportunities in different locations

Ireland — UK — Canada — Germany ----- US

sideration the fact that the average dollar-equivalent wage in Ireland is lower than the average dollar-equivalent wage in the UK.

The previous analysis suggests that MNEs should diversify across currency areas, rather than within currency areas (Germany versus Canada), and further may be relatively indifferent between countries in the same currency area (Ireland and UK), but the chapter has not compared investing abroad to expanding capacity in the US. As Figure 3 and Tables 5A–E demonstrate, in 1985 and 1986, US-based MNEs might have been willing to pay substantially more to invest in Germany, Ireland and the UK rather than expanding capacity at home. For example, in 1985, if the sunk cost of expanding capacity in the US = US$100 (adjusted NPV = US$24.11), a US-based MNE would have found an investment in Germany to be more attractive if the cost of investing in Germany was less than US$174 (adjusted NPV = US$24.39 if I = US$174) and it would have found investing in excess capacity in the UK and Ireland to be more attractive if the sunk cost of investing in these countries was less than US$200 (adjusted NPV being approximately US$33).[26] However, the subsequent depreciation of the dollar has led to a sharp increase in the cost of producing in Germany (in dollars) in the last few years, and hence US-based firms will be willing to pay more to invest in *only* the UK and Ireland.[27]

One last observation can be made from these tables. Although excess capacity = 25% of total capacity in all locations, the value of excess capacity as a proportion of the adjusted PV varies across the countries. Including the value of flexibility is more important for projects where the measure of σ is high (low degree of correlation with the US), indicating that the company is investing in a diversified input-sourcing programme. The value of operational flexibility (the value of excess capacity) is more significant for projects in Germany and the UK for US-domiciled MNEs than it may be for projects in Canada. This result follows because of the high correlation between wages in Canada and the US, and hence maintaining excess capacity in Canada may be suboptimal.

It is clear from these comparisons that if the present cost of producing in country B is higher than the present cost of producing in C, the firm is going to invest in B only if $\sigma_\omega(w^A - w^B)$ is significantly higher than $\sigma_\omega(w^A - w^C)$. Therefore, while there is some value to holding excess capacity when firms have operational flexibility, management will invest in a relatively high-cost country only if the benefits to diversification of production promise significant cost saving in the future. Furthermore, for US-based MNEs, maintaining excess capacity in Europe may be more attractive than maintaining excess capacity in Canada, and firms may be willing to pay more to invest in these countries than to expand capacity in the US.

EXTENSIONS OF OPERATION FLEXIBILITY

The caveats to the model presented above can be divided into two categories: those that are specific to the mathematical techniques employed and those that relate to the business environment assumed.

The portfolio of options will take on different values if one assume different stochastic processes.[28] In addition, if one is extremely rigid with the selection of the boundary conditions they may be forced to solve for $R(\Delta)$ numerically. In defence of the methodology used, the model is designed to capture the basic notion of using (and valuing) real options in the valuation of certain projects and hence the allowance for some flexibility in how those options are *best valued*.

The business environment could be altered to test the generality of the model. The most restrictive assumption in this specification was that capacity expansion is *lumpy*. This need not be the case and hence raises a few issues for discussion. In the previous section it was demonstrated how adding the extra cost of investing in excess capacity to the adjusted NPV of the foreign investment would affect the final decision. This implies that there is a trade-off between holding excess capacity (and gaining the option to switch) and expanding capacity in existing locations to meet demand. Firms need to question whether maintaining excess capacity is justified by the value of the portfolio of options. Most firms never attain full capacity utilisation and if this is the case then maintaining that excess capacity in a foreign location may be preferred to maintaining excess capacity in another local plant, especially when inputs are immobile.[29]

The next assumption that is suspect is that demand was chosen to be three units and was not expected to change thereafter. This assumption can be modified to one where demand is allowed to rise to four units at some time period T in the future. Now the options will have value from today until time period T, and then will have no value. Additional extensions to this approach could stem from assuming that demand too is stochastic. Two variations are possible:

❑ a perfectly competitive environment where the price of output is sto-chastic and the firm has to decide how much to supply the market at that price (for example, in the chemical industry); and
❑ a monopolist facing a stochastic world demand curve.

These two situations present a setting where choosing *optimal capacity* becomes a key decision, in addition to decisions on the *location* and *timing* of the investment.

It was also assumed that production could be switched costlessly from one plant to another. With an extremely long horizon, and very low switching costs, one might find that further into the horizon, the expected switching cost could approach zero.[30] Alternatively, one could assume that there is some fixed switching cost "s" that must be incurred to switch from country A to B or vice-versa. This would reduce the value of the options, and would affect the optimal exercise rule that was used in the model.

A related assumption that begs scrutiny was that production could be switched from one country to another the moment the firm realises that the wage rate in one country is higher than the wage rate in the other. On occa-sion, the company will be restrained from doing so by wage contracts and other factors. This delay greatly reduces the value of the options, because by the time the firm is ready to exercise the option to switch production, the option might not be in the money or as valuable.[31]

Two other assumptions that are worthy of discussion are that factors of production (inputs) are immobile and that no tariffs or taxes exist. Essentially, one market imperfection (immobility) is used and all others are assumed away. As long as a situation exists where the markets for the input in the two countries are separated by some exogenous condition (such as tariffs or different tax policies), valuing these options may prove to be a fruitful exercise.

Other issues that were not explicitly addressed by the assumptions may need to be examined. It was implicitly assumed that managers in each of the locations would be compensated by enlightened management in the parent company, who would recognise their efforts to maximise the global optimum. Issues relating to management compensation may make the task of shifting capacity utilisation a little more difficult than modelled in this chapter. It may be appropriate to extend the model to include some of the above to obtain more realistic values for the options. The tradeoff is that one may need more complex mathematical techniques and then closed-form solutions are not guaranteed. Finally, this model is designed to be illustrative rather than specific and hence a relatively simple methodology was chosen to value flexibility.

IMPLICATIONS AND CONCLUSIONS

On a macro-policy level, countries that wish to encourage investment, either from domestic or foreign investors, could extract the message that *stability* is desirable. The models suggest that increased volatility in factor markets and/or exchange rates increases the value of the option to post-pone investment or else invest abroad.[32] Recent attempts by the European Union to integrate labour markets and align exchange rates will reduce the cost differentials between producing in any two member countries. Therefore, firms that have manufacturing facilities dispersed around Europe may find that the value of excess capacity may be greatly diminished. On the other hand, firms positioned to treat the European market as one market may reap the economies of scale of producing in one location. Here optimal decision making will depend on the definition of markets that will be truly independent so as to provide a cost differential.

There is an additional implication for the correct valuation of MNEs by stock markets. Present wisdom indicates that the value of the firm is the present discounted value of all future cashflows, but this analysis suggests that the value of intangibles, like flexibility, should be included.[33] Are MNEs consistently undervalued by capital markets because transactors do not incorporate the value of flexibility? This is an empirical question that is beyond the scope of this chapter, but it could provide additional avenues for research.

Multinational enterprises, or firms considering multinationality, should recognise that investments in more than one country or in different business environments are valuable when cost conditions are changing, because of the flexibility that these investments create for the entire multinational system. This chapter demonstrated how excess capacity should be valued when MNEs can shift capacity utilisation to the most favourable cost location. The value of the flexibility depends critically on the volatility (degree of correlation of the host and home country) of input markets and exchange rates. The greater the volatility (lower the degree of correlation) in these areas, the greater the value of being multinational. Finally, the chapter showed how static NPV rules should be modified and that, for US-domiciled MNEs, maintaining excess capacity in Europe is more valuable than maintaining excess capacity in Canada. Moreover, under certain conditions, US-based MNEs might be willing to pay more to invest in excess capacity abroad than to expand capacity in the US.

APPENDIX A – DATA FOR TABLES 1 AND 2

These data are taken from the *Yearbook of Labor Statistics*. Hourly wages in manufacturing = earnings per hour, which is pre-tax and includes overtime, but does not include employer contributions for social security etc.

Hourly wages in manufacturing – local currency

Year	Canada	France	Germany	Ireland	Mexico	Spain	UK	US
1990	14.30		20.07	5.33	3848.00		5.38	10.84
1989	13.54	36.70	19.10	5.10	3220.00	780.00	4.92	10.49
1988	12.84	35.35	18.33	4.90	2215.00	735.00	4.54	10.19
1987	12.24	34.35	17.53	4.70	1213.00	678.00	4.23	9.91
1986	11.95	33.28	16.80	4.50	327.00	620.00	3.96	9.73
1985	11.59	31.56	16.20	4.20	314.00	564.00	3.71	9.54
1984	11.16	28.86	15.49	3.90	235.00	514.00	3.43	9.19
1983	10.59	26.70	15.14	3.52	149.00	457.00	3.21	8.83
1982	10.25	23.97	14.64	3.17	101.00	399.00	2.98	8.49
1981	9.17	20.72	13.92	2.77	63.00	346.00	2.93	7.99
1980	8.19	18.46	13.18	2.32	39.02	285.00	2.66	7.27
1979	7.44	16.04	12.36	2.01	31.88	242.00	2.28	6.70
1978	6.84	14.20	11.73	1.70	28.16	198.00	1.95	6.17
1977	6.38	12.58	11.14	1.47	25.56	155.00	1.69	5.68
1976	5.76	11.11	10.35	1.26	22.16	135.97	1.56	5.22
1975	5.06	9.82	9.69	1.10	15.44	104.73	1.40	4.83
1974	4.37	8.39	8.94	0.83	13.80	78.82	1.12	4.42
1973	3.85	7.05	8.03	0.69	10.64	62.48	0.93	4.09
1972	3.54	5.82	7.24	0.56	8.68	52.2	0.82	3.82
1971	3.28	5.18	6.66	0.49	7.94	44.81	0.72	3.57
1970	3.01	4.66	5.96	0.42	7.32	39.47	0.64	3.36
1969	2.79	4.21	5.28	0.36	6.82	34.69	0.56	3.19
1968	2.58	3.79	4.79		6.33	31.16		3.01
Average	7.86	17.85	12.29	2.51	517.77	298.06	2.53	6.81
SD	3.90	11.61	4.66	1.75	1080.60	254.42	1.50	2.71

End of year exchange rate (LC/US$)

Year	Canada	France	Germany	Ireland	Mexico	Spain	UK
1989	1.16	5.79	1.70	0.64	2637.00	109.70	0.62
1988	1.20	6.13	1.80	0.67	2263.00	113.60	0.56
1987	1.30	5.51	1.60	0.60	2198.50	108.85	0.54
1986	1.38	6.43	1.94	0.71	923.00	131.88	0.68
1985	1.40	7.56	2.47	0.81	369.40	154.30	0.70
1984	1.32	9.70	3.17	1.02	191.88	174.85	0.88
1983	1.25	8.51	2.79	0.90	144.37	156.63	0.71
1982	1.23	6.66	2.35	0.71	95.00	124.80	0.62
1981	1.18	5.73	2.26	0.64	25.98	97.55	0.53
1980	1.18	4.54	1.96	0.53	23.07	79.22	0.42
1979	1.17	4.02	1.72	0.43	22.82	66.04	0.45
1978	1.19	4.24	1.85	0.50	22.72	70.43	0.50
1977	1.09	4.62	2.07	0.51	22.66	80.09	0.51
1976	1.00	4.93	2.35	0.58	19.98	68.24	0.59
1975	1.01	4.44	2.60	0.49	12.50	59.54	0.50
Average	1.20	5.92	2.17	0.65	598.12	106.38	0.58
SD	0.12	1.65	0.45	0.16	948.70	36.49	0.12

APPENDIX B – DETERMINING THE VALUE OF R(Δ) AND N(Δ)

$$d\Delta = \sigma_\omega dz \qquad \text{(B1)}$$

where $dz = \varepsilon(t)(dt)^{1/2}$ is the increment on standard Brownian motion. $\varepsilon(t)$ has zero mean and unit standard deviation. $E[dz] = 0$ and $E[(dz)^2] = dt$. σ_ω is the instantaneous standard deviation.

If the firm expands capacity in country A then its costs in every period are $(x + d)w^A$ as long as the unit labour cost is below p. If w^A exceeds p, the firm may want to shut down, unless it is trying to protect market share. However, if the firm invests in country B to complement its original investment in A, then costs are equal to $\min[xw^A + dw^*, dw^A + xw^*]$. Therefore, a simple NPV analysis to evaluate the investment in B that assumed that the plant in B would produce only one unit of output would underestimate the true value of the foreign investment. A static NPV analysis might assume that the extra unit of capacity will be left unused at all times, given insufficient demand, whereas the approach presented below takes into account the benefit of maintaining that extra unit of capacity when unit costs in one environment are more volatile than they are in another.

If one assumes that shutdown is costless and that the firm will not produce output in A when the wage rate in A exceeds the price of output, one can find the value of flexibility.

Define

$$b = p - w^* \qquad \text{(B2)}$$

Define

$$w^A = w^* + \Delta \qquad \text{(B3)}$$

This implies that

$$p - w^A = b - \Delta \qquad \text{(B4)}$$

Now the cashflows generated by a national firm

$$= (x + d)(p - w^A)^+ \qquad \text{(B5)}$$

where one defines

$$(p - w^A)^+ = \max[p - w^A, 0] \qquad \text{(B6)}$$

For simplicity assume that $x = 2$ and $d = 1$.

Therefore, if the firm expands capacity at home, the cashflows generated by a national firm in every period (ignoring time subscripts)

$$= 3(p - w^A)^+ = 3(b - \Delta)^+ = (x + d)(b - \Delta)^+ \qquad \text{(B7a)}$$

since expanding capacity at home will generate additional cashflows

$$= (b - \Delta)^+ \quad \text{in every period} \quad (= d(b - \Delta)^+) \qquad \text{(B7b)}$$

On the other hand, the cashflows generated by a MNE in every period (ignoring time subscripts)

$$\begin{aligned} &= (p - w^A)^+ + b + p - \min(w^A, w^*) &\text{(B8a)} \\ &= (b - \Delta)^+ + b + p - (w^* + \min(\Delta, 0)) &\text{(B8b)} \\ &= 2b + (b - \Delta)^+ - \min(\Delta, 0) &\text{(B8c)} \\ &= 2b + (b - \Delta)^+ + \max(-\Delta, 0) &\text{(B8d)} \\ &= 2b + (b - \Delta)^+ + (-\Delta)^+ &\text{(B9)} \end{aligned}$$

Alternatively

$$= xb + d(b - \Delta)^+ + (x - d)(-\Delta)^+$$

Notice, though, that the incremental cashflows of the foreign project = cashflows provided by a MNE less the cashflows that existing investments in the home country will provide. From (B7a), (B7b) and (B9), incremental cashflows

$$\begin{aligned} &= 2b + (b - \Delta)^+ + (-\Delta)^+ - 2(b - \Delta)^+ &\text{(B10a)} \\ &= 2b - (b - \Delta)^+ + (-\Delta)^+ &\text{(B10b)} \end{aligned}$$

Alternatively

$$= xb - (x - d)(b - \Delta)^+ + (x - d)(-\Delta)^+$$

Equation (B10b) will be crucial for our calculation of operational flexibility. The expected value of the MNE is the expected discounted value of future cashflows. Therefore define $M(\Delta)$ = value of the MNE. From (B9)

$$M(\Delta) = E_t \left[\int_{t=0}^{\infty} e^{-rt} \left| 2b + (b - \Delta_t)^+ + (-\Delta_t)^+ \right| dt \Big| \Delta_0 = \Delta \right] \qquad \text{(B11)}$$

Define

$$N(b, \Delta) = E_t \left[\int_{t=0}^{\infty} e^{-rt} \left| (b - \Delta)^+ \right| dt \Big| \Delta_0 = \Delta \right] \qquad \text{(B12)}$$

or

$$N(b, \Delta) = \max_{j=0/1} E_t\left[\int_{t=0}^{\infty} e^{-rt} j(b - \Delta_t)|dt|\Delta_0 = \Delta\right]$$

Given that Δ follows the stochastic process specified in (B1), the Bellman equation for the value of the portfolio of options $N(b, \Delta)$ is

$$rN = \max_{j=0/1}\left\{j(b - \Delta) + \frac{1}{dt} E_t\, dN\right\} \qquad \textbf{(B13)}$$

By Itô's lemma

$$dN = N'd\Delta + \tfrac{1}{2} N'' (d\Delta)^2 \qquad \textbf{(B14)}$$

where the prime denotes the derivative with respect to $(b - \Delta)$. Substituting for $d\Delta$,

$$dN = \sigma_\omega N'dz + \tfrac{1}{2}\, \sigma_\omega^2 N''dt \qquad \textbf{(B15)}$$

Plugging (B15) into (B13),

$$rN = \max_{j=0/1}\{j(b - \Delta) + \tfrac{1}{2}\sigma_\omega^2 N''\} \qquad \textbf{(B16)}$$

Maximising with respect to j: set $j = 1$ if $(b - \Delta) > 0$ (produce the unit of output) and set $j = 0$ (do not produce the unit of output) otherwise.

One needs to solve

$$\tfrac{1}{2}\, \sigma_\omega^2 N'' - rN + j(b - \Delta) = 0$$

subject to the following conditions:

$$N(\infty) = 0 \qquad \textbf{(B18a)}$$

$$\frac{\lim N}{\Delta \to -\infty} = \frac{b - \Delta}{r} \qquad \textbf{(B18b)}$$

$$N(\Delta = b^+) = N(\Delta = b^-) \qquad \textbf{(B19a)}$$

$$N'(\Delta = b^+) = N'(\Delta = b^-) \qquad \textbf{(B19b)}$$

where the prime denotes the derivative with respect to $b - \Delta$.

Condition (B18b) states that when $\Delta = -\infty$, wages at home are substantially below wages abroad, and the firm will earn $p - w^A$ in every period. (B18a) is included because as w^A becomes very large, the probability that the firm produces output at home goes to zero. (B19a) and (B19b) are the smoothness and continuity conditions. Therefore

$$N(b, \Delta) = a_1 e^{(-b + \Delta)g} + \frac{b - \Delta}{r} \qquad \text{when } \Delta < b \qquad \textbf{(B20a)}$$

$$= a_2 e^{(b - \Delta)g} \qquad \text{when } \Delta > b \qquad \textbf{(B20b)}$$

where $g^2 = 2r/\sigma_\omega^2$, and e is the base for the natural logarithm.
From the continuity conditions one finds that

$$a_1 = a_2 = \frac{1}{2rg} \qquad \textbf{(B21)}$$

$$N'(\Delta = 0^+) = N'(\Delta = 0^-) \Rightarrow -gae^{-\Delta g} + \frac{1}{r} = gae^{\Delta g} \Rightarrow 2ag = \frac{1}{r} \text{ which is solved for a.}$$

$$N(b, \Delta) = \frac{1}{2rg} e^{(-b + \Delta)g} + \frac{b - \Delta}{r} \qquad \text{when } \Delta < b \qquad \textbf{(B22a)}$$

$$= \frac{1}{2rg} e^{(b - \Delta)g} \qquad \text{when } \Delta > b \qquad \textbf{(B22b)}$$

Define $N(\Delta) =$ expected value of a unit of capacity in the home country. From (B7b) and (B12), $N(\Delta) = N(b, \Delta)$, which is given by (B22a) and (B22b).

A brief explanation of (B22a) and (B22b) is in order. Let us examine (B22a) first. When $\Delta < b$, this implies that $p > w^A$ and the firm is producing output at home. If the wage in A were never to change the present value of all future earnings $= b - \Delta/r$. However, should the wage in A rise above p, the firm will shut down and the value of this option $= (1/2rg)e^{(-b + \Delta)g}$.

Equation (B22b) states that if the wage in A is higher than p, the firm is not producing output but has the option to produce the additional unit of output when the wage rate in A falls. The value of the option to restart production $= (1/2rg)e^{(b - \Delta)g}$.

One can conclude from (B7a) that the expected value of the national firm is $= 3N(\Delta) = (x + d)N(\Delta)$.

What is

$$E_t \left[\int_{t=0}^{\infty} e^{-rt} (\Delta)^+ |dt| \Delta_0 = \Delta \right]? \qquad \textbf{(B23)}$$

This is nothing but $N(b, \Delta)$, where $b = 0$.

Under the usual boundary, smoothness and continuity conditions, it can be shown from the work above that

$$N(0, \Delta) = \frac{1}{2rg} e^{(\Delta)g} + \frac{-\Delta}{r} \qquad \text{when } \Delta < 0 \qquad \textbf{(B24a)}$$

$$= \frac{1}{2rg} e^{(-\Delta)g} \qquad \text{when } \Delta > 0 \qquad \textbf{(B24b)}$$

From (B11), define M(Δ) = Expected value of the MNE, and

$$M(\Delta) = E_t\left[\int_{t=0}^{\infty} e^{-rt}\left|2b + (b - \Delta_t)^+ + (-\Delta_t)^+\right|dt\Big|\Delta_0 = \Delta\right]$$

$$= \frac{2b}{r} + N(b, \Delta) + N(0, \Delta)$$

Using the results derived in (B22a), (B22b), (B24a) and (B24b) one can show that

$$M(\Delta) = \frac{2b}{r} + \frac{1}{2rg}e^{(-b+\Delta)g} + \frac{b - \Delta}{r} + \frac{1}{2rg}e^{(\Delta)g} + \frac{-\Delta}{r} \quad \text{when } \Delta < 0 \qquad \textbf{(B25a)}$$

$$= \frac{2b}{r} + \frac{1}{2rg}e^{(-b+\Delta)g} + \frac{b - \Delta}{r} + \frac{1}{2rg}e^{(-\Delta)g} \quad \text{when } 0 \le \Delta \le b \quad \textbf{(B25b)}$$

$$= \frac{2b}{r} + \frac{1}{2rg}e^{(b-\Delta)g} + \frac{1}{2rg}e^{(-\Delta)g} \quad \text{when } \Delta \ge b \qquad \textbf{(B25c)}$$

These can be rewritten as

$$= \frac{b}{r} + \frac{1}{2rg}e^{(-b+\Delta)g} + \frac{2(b - \Delta)}{r} + \frac{1}{2rg}e^{(\Delta)g} \quad \text{when } \Delta < 0 \qquad \textbf{(B25a)}$$

$$= \frac{2b}{r} + \frac{1}{2rg}e^{(-b+\Delta)g} + \frac{b - \Delta}{r} + \frac{1}{2rg}e^{(-\Delta)g} \quad \text{when } 0 \le \Delta \le b \quad \textbf{(B25b)}$$

$$= \frac{2b}{r} + \frac{1}{2rg}e^{(b-\Delta)g} + \frac{1}{2rg}e^{(-\Delta)g} \quad \text{when } \Delta \ge b \qquad \textbf{(B25c)}$$

A brief explanation of what the above equations imply is provided below. Consider (B25a); when $\Delta < 0$, the wage rate in A is less than the wage rate in B, and the firm is producing two units of output at home (= $[2(b - \Delta)]/r$) and one in the foreign location (= b/r), with the option to produce two units abroad if the wage rate at home rises above the wage rate abroad, and the option to not produce at all in A if the wage in A rises above p. For (B25b), consider the region where the wage at home is higher than the wage abroad, but below the price of output. Now, the firm is producing two units in the foreign location, and one at home, but it has the option to switch or shut down production at home. (B25c) examines the case where $w^A > p$, and now the MNE is producing two units of output (= b/r) abroad, but has the option to restart domestic production.

To value flexibility determine the incremental cashflow of the foreign project, and deduct the cashflows from producing one unit of output abroad. This calculation provides the firm with the cashflows that the foreign project would have generated over and above satisfying the increase in demand. From (B10b), the incremental cashflow provided by the foreign project $= 2b - (b - \Delta)^+ + (-\Delta)^+$. Therefore the cashflows associated with flexibility

$$= 2b - (b - \Delta)^+ + (-\Delta)^+ - b \qquad \textbf{(B26)}$$

because b is the guaranteed cashflow produced by the foreign investment from satisfying the unit increase in demand.

Alternatively,

$$= xb - (x - d)(b - \Delta)^+ + (x - d)(-\Delta)^+ - db$$
$$= (x - d)b - (x - d)(b - \Delta)^+ + (x - d)(-\Delta)^+$$

Define $R(\Delta)$ = value of flexibility = expected present value of all cashflows that the foreign project generates through the optimal usage of excess capacity. Then from (B26)

$$R(\Delta) = E_t \left[\int_{t=0}^{\infty} e^{-rt} \left| b - (b - \Delta_t)^+ + (-\Delta_t)^+ \right| dt \middle| \Delta_0 = \Delta \right] \qquad \textbf{(B27)}$$

Once again, with appropriate boundary, smoothness and continuity conditions it can be shown that

$$R(\Delta) = \frac{b}{r} - N(b, \Delta) + N(0, \Delta)$$

$$= \frac{b}{r} - \frac{1}{2rg} e^{(-b+\Delta)g} - \frac{b - \Delta}{r} + \frac{1}{2rg} e^{(\Delta)g} + \frac{-\Delta}{r} \quad \text{when } \Delta < 0 \qquad \textbf{(B28a)}$$

$$= \frac{b}{r} - \frac{1}{2rg} e^{(-b+\Delta)g} - \frac{b - \Delta}{r} + \frac{1}{2rg} e^{(-\Delta)g} \quad \text{when } 0 \le \Delta \le b \qquad \textbf{(B28b)}$$

$$= \frac{b}{r} - \frac{1}{2rg} e^{(b-\Delta)g} + \frac{1}{2rg} e^{(-\Delta)g} \quad \text{when } \Delta \ge b \qquad \textbf{(B28c)}$$

These equations can be reduced to the following

$$= -\frac{1}{2rg} e^{(-b+\Delta)g} + \frac{1}{2rg} e^{(\Delta)g} \quad \text{when } \Delta < 0 \qquad \textbf{(B28a)}$$

$$= \frac{\Delta}{r} - \frac{1}{2rg} e^{(-b+\Delta)g} + \frac{1}{2rg} e^{(-\Delta)g} \quad \text{when } 0 \le \Delta \le b \qquad \textbf{(B28b)}$$

$$= \frac{b}{r} - \frac{1}{2rg} e^{(b-\Delta)g} + \frac{1}{2rg} e^{(-\Delta)g} \quad \text{when } \Delta \ge b \qquad \textbf{(B28c)}$$

The interpretations for (B28a), (B28b) and (B28c) are very similar to those detailed above with respect to equations (B25a), (B25b) and (B25c). From (B28a) it can be concluded that when $\Delta < 0$, the wage rate at home is less than the wage rate in B, and even though the firm is not using the excess capacity abroad, it has the option to do so in the future. However, if w^A should rise above the price of output, the maximum saving afforded by the foreign investment is $= b$ in every period. When $0 \le \Delta \le b$, then the wage in A is above the foreign wage and below p. From (B28b), it can be concluded that if the wage in A were never to change the present value of all cost savings provided by excess capacity abroad $= \Delta/r$. However, if the wage rate in A should fall below the wage rate abroad, the firm will want to switch production back to the home country, and this is a valuable option. In addition, if the wage rate in A rises above p, the maximum cost saving from producing the third unit of output abroad in every period $= b$. Equation (B28c) considers the case where w^A is greater than p and the analysis is similar to that described above for equation (B28b).

APPENDIX C

Suppose it was assumed that the wages in country A and country B were stochastic. How would the valuation of flexibility and that of the MNE be affected?

Define

$$\Delta = (w^A - w^B) \tag{C1}$$

Assume that

$$dw^A = \sigma_A dz \quad \text{and that} \quad dw^B = \sigma_B dz \tag{C2}$$

Then

$$d\Delta = d(w^A - w^B) = \sigma dz \tag{C3}$$

because the difference between two Brownian motions is a Brownian motion, if the joint distribution is Brownian.

Define

$$b_t = p - w^B(t)$$

The cashflows generated by a MNE in every period

$$= (p - w^A)^+ + (p - w^B)^+ + p - \min(w^A, w^B) \tag{C4a}$$
$$= (p - w^A)^+ + (p - w^B)^+ + (p - w^B)^+ - \min(-\Delta_t, 0) \tag{C4b}$$
$$= 2(b_t)^+ + (p - w^A)^+ - \min(-\Delta_t, 0) \tag{C4c}$$

which is clearly different from the assumption made in Appendix B, because b_t is not fixed in every period. This is a difficult model to solve, and it is clear that if one allows wages in country B to be stochastic then this in turn will affect the cashflows associated with flexibility. However, one can treat the value of flexibility derived in Appendix B as a first approximation for the value of flexibility when wages in both countries are stochastic.

APPENDIX D

An interesting extension to the work presented above is to attempt to draw implications for firms about the optimal timing and optimal location of investment. A firm must consider is not only whether to invest today versus investing tomorrow, but also whether to invest at home or abroad.

Pindyck (1991) demonstrates how a firm should value the option to invest when investment is irreversible and Pindyck (1988) presents a methodology for valuing incremental capacity. The critical idea is that when demand is stochastic, the firm has the option in every period to decide whether or not to use a unit of capacity. The firm acquires this portfolio of options when it invests in a unit of capacity. However, the key decision for the firm is the investment decision – the decision whether it should pay a sunk cost to acquire that unit of capacity today or else wait until some future period. From his work he is able to show that in the presence of stochastic demand firms may postpone investment rather than invest today.

The following attempts to show how the option to invest might be valued for a domestic firm when investment is irreversible, marginal costs are stochastic and the price of output is fixed. From Appendix B, the value of expanding capacity at home today $= N(\Delta)$.

$$N(\Delta) = \frac{1}{2rg} e^{-\Delta g} + \frac{\Delta}{r} \qquad \text{when } \Delta > 0 \qquad \textbf{(D1a)}$$

$$= \frac{1}{2rg} e^{\Delta g} \qquad \text{when } \Delta < 0 \qquad \textbf{(D1b)}$$

What is the option to invest?

The firm can either invest today by paying US\$I (a sunk cost) and acquire a project of value $N(\Delta)$, or else wait until some future period.

Let $F(\Delta) = $ option to invest in country A.

$$F(\Delta) = \max E_t[(N_T - I) e^{-rT}] \qquad \textbf{(D2)}$$

where $T = $ time period when the firm decides to make the investment.

The corresponding Bellman equation is

$$rF = \frac{1}{dt} E_t \, dF \qquad \textbf{(D3)}$$

By Itô's Lemma

$$dF = F' d\Delta + \tfrac{1}{2} F''(d\Delta)^2 \qquad \textbf{(D4)}$$

where the prime denotes the derivative with respect to Δ. Substituting for $d\Delta$,

$$dF = \sigma_p F' dz + \tfrac{1}{2}\sigma_p^2 F'' dt \qquad \text{(D5)}$$

Plugging (D5) into (D3), one needs to solve for F

$$rF = \tfrac{1}{2}\sigma_p^2 F'' \qquad \text{(D6)}$$

subject to the following conditions:

$$F(\Delta = -\infty) = 0 \qquad \text{(D7a)}$$
$$F(\hat{\Delta}) = N(\hat{\Delta}) - I \qquad \text{(D7b)}$$
$$F_\Delta(\hat{\Delta}) = N_\Delta(\hat{\Delta}) \qquad \text{(D7c)}$$

where Δ = optimal value for Δ at which you will exercise.
   A solution to the above is

$$F(\Delta) = ne^{\Delta g} \qquad \text{when } \Delta < \hat{\Delta} \qquad \text{(D8a)}$$
$$= N(\hat{\Delta}) - I \qquad \text{when } \Delta > \hat{\Delta} \qquad \text{(D8b)}$$

where

$$n = \frac{1}{2}\left[\frac{\hat{\Delta}}{r} + \frac{1}{gr} - I\right]e^{-\hat{\Delta}g} \qquad \text{(D9)}$$

and $\hat{\Delta}$ is the solution to

$$\left[\frac{\hat{\Delta}}{r} + \frac{1}{gr}e^{-\hat{\Delta}g}\right] = I + \frac{1}{gr} \qquad \text{(D10a)}$$

Rewriting (D10a), $\hat{\Delta}$ is the solution to

$$g\hat{\Delta} + e^{-\hat{\Delta}g} = Irg + 1 \qquad \text{(D10b)}$$

   If one attempts to extend this analysis to an optimal investment timing problem one will find that, although greater volatility makes a unit of capacity more valuable because of the option to shut down, increased volatility also has the characteristic of making the option to wait more valuable. A simple analysis is provided for 1986 with the results provided in Table D1. In 1986, investing abroad would have been preferred to postponing the domestic investment. However, if costs were identical, as the volatility of domestic costs in the US (1.91) is greater than the measure of volatility of cost savings of countries like Germany, Canada, US firms will exercise the option to wait rather than acquire the factory today.[34]

Table D1. Comparing investment locations for 1986 (w^{us} = US$9.73)

Price of output (p) = US$15
Nominal interest rate = 6%

		US – postpone invest.	US – invest today (invest in 1 unit)	Germany (invest in 2 units)	Canada (invest in 2 units)	UK (invest in 2 units)
1	Wage in country (US$)	9.73	9.73	8.66	8.66	5.85
2	σ	1.91	1.91	1.59	0.64	1.18
3	Static PV = (p – w)/r			105.67	105.67	152.50
4	R(Δ): value of excess capacity			36.00	25.57	67.71
5	Adjusted present value		105.50	141.67	131.24	220.21
6	Adjusted net present value (to account for stochastic costs and sunk cost of investment = US$90)	35.69	15.50	51.67	41.24	130.21

It is therefore suggested that management of firms that operate in the global economy, which are considering increases in capacity expansion, be cognisant of not only domestic business conditions but also opportunities that foreign locations provide to increase firm value. As shown in this appendix, embedded options in investments at home and abroad clearly affect *investment timing and location* decisions and hence must be valued carefully.

1   The author is an employee of J.P. Morgan. The views expressed in the paper are primarily theoretical and academic in nature, and do not represent the views of J.P. Morgan or its affiliates. All opinions, theories and errors, as such, are purely those of the author. This paper is a chapter of my PhD thesis (1992). I would like to thank Franco Modigliani, Jean-Luc Vila, Donald Lessard, Louis Wells Jr, Sanjay Muralidhar and Shaila Muralidhar for their helpful comments and assistance with developing these ideas. All errors are my own.
2   Uncertainty exists for individual models, which then translates into uncertainty about aggregate demand.
3   See Kogut (1985).
4   This flexibility is called "mix flexibility".
5   Muralidhar (1992b) demonstrates how MNEs may value the financial flexibility of shifting profits to the most favourable country in the face of tax regime volatility.
6   A similar example would be Zenith's movement of manufacturing operations to Mexico from its operations in Illinois, because of lower labour costs in Mexico.
7   See *Supplement to Corporate Finance*, June 1990, p. 23.
8   Alternatively, one can structure the problem such that the firm is replacing existing capacity and has to decide between expanding capacity in existing locations and investing in capacity in new locations.
9   This is a relatively simple calculation. Call this

$$\text{base NPV (abroad)} = \int_{t=0}^{T} (p - w^*)qe^{-rt}dt - I$$

where p = price, w^* = marginal cost, q = quantity, and I = sunk cost of investment.

10 Local currency equivalent = unit costs abroad * exchange rate.

11 A similar argument is made in Muralidhar (1992b) for financial flexibility.

12 See also Levi (Chapter 15), and Lessard and Shapiro (1983).

13 Pindyck (1988) provides a review of this literature and Brealey and Myers (4th edition), chapter 21, outlines a few situations where options pricing theory is useful for valuing certain aspects of real investments.

14 This type of flexibility had been referred to as "mix flexibility".

15 Once it is shown how to correctly value foreign projects, this result is combined with the results of Pindyck (1988) to discuss the optimal timing of investments. See Appendix D.

16 For example, one could assume that a car manufacturer has to manufacture a fixed number of car engines and is considering distributing manufacturing facilities around the world. I thank Professor Stewart Myers for this example.

17 This assumption will be addressed later in the chapter.

18 This paper ignores modelling all issues arising from exchange rate fluctuations for simplicity, but this is not an egregious assumption. One could consider the home currency equivalent of the foreign unit labour cost = w^*, where $w^* = w^B e$ (e = exchange rate).

19 This definition does not preclude the possibility that wages in country B can fluctuate, but for the sake of simplifying the discussion assume that w^* remains unchanged.

20 Another business climate that one can consider is where the aggregate demand of the firm is split 50–50 between the foreign and home markets. The decision for the firm is whether to invest all its capacity in one location; invest in both countries, but use each facility to satisfy local demand; or invest in both countries and use both factories to ensure the global optimum.

21 In Appendix B the cashflows are expressed in terms of x and d and the results are shown when one substitutes for their values assumed above.

22 If one had chosen to let the maximum cost saving be unbounded, rather than bounded by b, they would have overstated the value of operational flexibility. This is similar to a binomial distribution, and in such a situation

$$R(\Delta) = E_t \left[\int_{t=0}^{\infty} e^{-rt} |(\Delta)^+| \, dt | \Delta_0 = \Delta \right]$$

23 If one wanted to compare the value of a national firm with one that is multinational, they would compare $3N(\Delta)$ (adjusted PV of producing three units at home) to $M(\Delta)$ (where $M(\Delta)$ is the value of a MNE, and this is derived in Appendix C), ignoring the costs of investment. It would be interesting to see the conditions under which being multinational is preferred to being national – the values of Δ, and σ for which this would be true.

24 While the valuation technique in the previous section was based on real rates and real wages, in this analysis nominal variables are used. Values for Germany and the US were selected from Tables 1 and 2.

25 This comparison is a first approximation because it had been assumed in the model that the foreign environment was static. Therefore, to be exact, one must use the measure of volatility that is derived from wages in the US (σ_{us}). However, this is compensated by using the values of σ_ω from Table 2 for each of the countries, rather than using σ_{us} as the measure of volatility for all countries. If σ_{us} were used as the measure of volatility of cost saving for *all* the countries, the comparison would be meaningless, but valuing flexibility would still be possible for the individual countries.

26 The wage in the US = US$9.54; UK = US$5.33; and Ireland = US$5.21.

27 From Table 5E, in 1989, the difference between the adjusted present value of investing in the UK (or Ireland) and the US is US$55. Therefore, a US-based MNE will invest in capacity in the UK and/or Ireland only if the cost of investing abroad is at most US$50 more than expanding capacity in the US.

28 Three processes that present themselves for selection include Brownian motion with drift, mean reverting process and the Poisson process. Each of these captures an interesting facet of

wage rates. For example, Poisson processes are best suited to mimic jumps/discontinuities in w^A, and further these may allow for a comparison between the mean values of the variables. However, with these processes analytical solutions are not guaranteed, and numerical solutions may be necessary. One way to extend this analysis would be to perform Monte Carlo simulations to determine whether the value is derived from the underlying stochastic process or from having operational flexibility.

29 See McRae (1990). Kogut (1985), p. 33 suggests that the loss in economies of scale should be less than the sum of the option to shift production and the cost of holding excess capacity.

30 I would like to thank Professor Stewart Myers for pointing this out to me.

31 Once again Kogut (1985) argues that the value of flexibility depends on the ability of the firm to capitalise on differences in marginal costs when exchange rates fluctuate, and that some measure of industrial relations be included in the valuation.

32 Refer to Appendix D and Pindyck (1988).

33 Refer to Brealey and Myers (1984), chapter 21, for a description of some of the other intangibles that should be included in firm value.

34 In 1985, when the dollar appreciated significantly, US firms might have found it preferable to invest in countries like Germany, the UK and Ireland, rather than waiting to invest at home. On the other hand, in low-wage countries like Mexico or Thailand, the direct cost advantage may clearly offset any benefit to waiting to invest at home. In these low-cost countries, US based MNEs will find it advantageous to invest abroad today, rather than waiting to invest at home.

BIBLIOGRAPHY

Baldwin, C.Y., 1986, "The Capital Factor: Competing for Capital in a Global Environment" in *Competition in Global Industries*, ed. by Michael Porter, Boston, Harvard University Press.

Brealey, R. and S. Myers, 1984, *Principles of Corporate Finance*, 4th edition, New York, McGraw-Hill.

Kogut, B., 1985, "Designing Global Strategies; Profiting from Operational Flexibility", *Sloan Management Review*, Fall, pp. 27–38.

Kogut, B. and N. Kulatilaka, 1991, "Multinational Flexibility, Growth Opportunities and the Theory of Foreign Direct Investment", *Boston University Working Paper*.

Lessard, D., 1978, "Evaluating Foreign Projects: An Adjusted Present Value Approach", in *International Financial Management*, ed. Donald Lessard, Boston, Warren, Gorham & Lamont.

Lessard, D., 1989, "Finance and Global Competition: Exploiting Financial Scope and Coping with Volatile Exchange Rates", in *New Developments in International Finance*, eds. Joel M. Stern and Donald Chew, Oxford, Basil Blackwell.

Lessard, D. and J.L. Paddock, 1980, *Evaluating International Projects: Weighted Average Cost of Capital versus Valuation by Components*, unpublished working paper.

Lessard, D. and A. Shapiro, 1983, "Guidelines for Global Financing Choices", *Midland Corporate Finance Journal*, Winter.

Levi, M., 1990, *International Finance*, 2nd edition, New York, McGraw-Hill.

MacRae, D., 1990, "Managing Corporate Risk", *Supplement to Corporate Finance*, June, p. 23.

Muralidhar, A., 1992b, Valuing the Financial Flexibility of a Multinational Enterprise: An Options Pricing Approach, unpublished PhD thesis, MIT Sloan School of Management.

Myers, S., 1977, "Determinants of Corporate Borrowing", *Journal of Financial Economics*, 5, November, pp. 147–75.

Pindyck, R., 1988, "Irreversible Investment, Capacity Choice and the Value of the Firm", *The American Economic Review*, 78(5), pp. 969–85.

Pindyck, R., 1991, "Irreversibility, Uncertainty and Investment", *Journal of Economic Literature*, 29, September, pp. 1110–48.

Pindyck, R. and H. He, 1990, "Investments in Flexible Production Capacity", unpublished working paper.

Triantis, A.J. and J.E. Hodder, 1990, "Valuing Flexibility as a Complex Option", *The Journal of Finance*, 45(2), June, pp. 549–65.

Trigeorgis, L. and S.P. Mason, 1987, "Valuing Managerial Flexibility", *Midland Corporate Finance Journal*, 5, pp. 14–21.

Vila, J.-L. and B. Tuckman, 1991, "Grandfather Clauses and Optimal Portfolio Revision", *Journal of Risk and Insurance*.

World Currency Monitor Annual (1976–1989), 1990, Bank of America Information Service; Westport CT: Meckler Corporation.

Yearbook of Labor Statistics (various issues), Geneva, International Labor Office Publications.

A Note on Bibliographical Evolution of Real Options

Marco Antônio Guimarães Dias

Petrobras

The origin of the term "real options" can be attributed to Stewart Myers (1977), published four years after the seminal work of Black and Scholes (1973) and Merton (1973). Myers first identified the fact that many corporate real assets can be viewed as call options. Tourinho (1979) was the first to apply option-pricing ideas to value reserves of natural resources. Before the contributions of Black and Scholes and Merton, the most noteworthy literature for the development of real options is the work of Samuelson (1965), which introduces the stochastic calculus in finance and calculates the early exercise of an American option – the "high-contact" condition, (also known as the "smooth-pasting" condition). The environmental literature of Arrow and Fisher (1974) and of Henry (1974a, b), demonstrates how irreversible decisions create an option value.

Literature on real options modelling started to appear in the 1980s. In 1987 the first special issue of a journal dedicated to real options was published in the *Midland Corporate Finance Journal*. Among the most cited real options papers of the 1980s are:

❑ Kester (1984) on growth options; Brennan and Schwartz (1985) on the natural resource valuation of a copper mine;
❑ Mason and Merton (1985) predicting the future of the *contingent claims* analysis for real assets applications;
❑ Titman (1985) on urban land valuation; McDonald and Siegel (1986) on the option to delay;
❑ Majd and Pindyck (1987) on the time to build sequential options; Trigeorgis and Mason (1987) on the value of managerial flexibility;
❑ Paddock and Siegel and Smith (1988) on the valuation of oil reserves;
❑ Kulatilaka and Marks (1988) on the strategic value of flexibility;
❑ Pindyck (1988) on the irreversibility and capacity of choice; Ekern (1988) on petroleum investments cases; and

❏ Dixit (1989) on the entry and exit decisions of a firm and Sick (1989) on a new capital budgeting approach with real options.

In the 1990s, literature on real options became even more widespread. Among the most cited real options papers are:

❏ Triantis and Hodder (1990) on the valuation of complex options;
❏ Ingersoll Jr. and Ross (1992) on the effect of interest rate uncertainty on real options;
❏ Dixit (1992) on investment and hysteresis; Trigeorgis (1993) on multiple real options interactions;
❏ Pindyck (1993) on combining technical and market uncertainties;
❏ Leahy (1993) on revealing the coincidence between the option value threshold of a monopolist firm and the firm-free entry threshold in a purely competitive case; Quigg (1993) on empirical tests of real options;
❏ Kogut and Kulatilaka (1994) on corporate strategic capabilities as a platform of options;
❏ Capozza and Li (1994) on investment intensity and timing to develop urban lands;
❏ Smith and Nau (1995) comparing real options with traditional decision analysis;
❏ Abel and Dixit and Eberly and Pindyck (1996), on the theory of investment under uncertainty;
❏ Schwartz (1997) on comparing different models for commodity price uncertainty; Laughton (1998) on modern asset pricing valuation of flexibility in petroleum field development; and
❏ Moel and Tufano (1999) analysing the bidding rules of a mine concession using real options.

Books specifically dedicated to real options have only recently begun to appear. Useful collections of real options papers have been edited by Lund and Øksendal (1991), Trigeorgis (1995), Micalizzi and Trigeorgis (1999) and Brennan and Trigeorgis (1999). Three textbooks on real options appeared in the 1990s. Dixit and Pindyck (1994), which was written with economists in mind, presents an in-depth analysis of modelling issues. It focuses on continuous-time framework, using the partial differential equation (PDE) approach. The second book, by Trigeorgis (1996), is more financially oriented and concentrates on modelling (in both discrete and continuous time) and the theory of real options. The third book, by Amram and Kulatilaka (1999), is aimed at management level and is the most accessible, and also contains examples of contemporary applications, including internet projects. All three books have great appeal and can be considered complementary readings.

The following papers document empirical industry applications of real options. Recent examples in journals include: Nichols (1994) on the Merck case; Corman (1997) on real options cases in New England Electric, Merck, British Gas, Enron etc; Coy (1999) report real options cases in Hewlett-Packard, Enron, Airbus, Anadarko and Cadence. Examples of papers detailing modelling cases are Kemna's (1993) examination of three cases based on her long consultancy with Shell; Kaslow and Pindyck (1994) examine applications at New England Power Co; Faulkner (1996) on R&D applications at Kodak; Stonier (1999) on the Airbus case, and Micalizzi (1999) on the Schering Plough case amongst others.

What direction will real options literature take in the near future? On a theoretical level, the combination of real options theory with other economic and/or financial theories is very likely, for example, the synthesis of real options with game theory, and with agency theory. In the 1990s some papers appeared which combined game theory with real options – "option-games". These include: Smit and Ankum (1993); Lambrecht and Perraudin (1994, 1996); Grenadier (1996, 1999); and Kulatilaka and Perotti (1997). The application of real options theory combined with agency theory appears in Brennan and Trigeorgis (1999) and in Maeland (1999).

On a more practical level, the use of the Monte Carlo approach to solve complex real options problems is a very recent method. Corporate applications in some cases require complex models, with several sources and several types of uncertainties and options. But this approach has two problems, first it is computationally very intensive, and second it is only a simulation tool (not an optimisational one), and therefore has difficulties in coping with the early exercise features of real options[1]. The first problem is increasingly less relevant as computers continue to grow in capacity. The second problem has recently been solved by optimisation methods linked to the simulation process, which allows for the use of Monte Carlo methods for American type options. Examples of real options applications using Monte Carlo are Cortazar and Schwartz (1998) and Winston (1999). The latter uses genetic algorithms as an optimisation tool. Examples of the Monte Carlo method for American options are Longstaff and Schwartz (1998), Broadie and Glasserman (1997) and Ibáñez and Zapatero (1999).

---

1   In contrast with financial options, the decision rule (earlier exercise threshold of an American option) in general is very important in the real options context, whereas the "greeks" (important for hedging purposes in financial derivatives) play no special role in real options applications.

BIBLIOGRAPHY

Abel, A.B., A.K. Dixit, J.C. Eberly and R.S. Pindyck, 1996, "Options, the Value of Capital, and Investment", *Quarterly Journal of Economics*, August, pp. 753–77.

Amram, M. and N. Kulatilaka, 1999, *Real Options – Managing Strategic Investment in an Uncertain World*, Harvard Business School Press, Harvard, Massachusetts.

Arrow, K.J. and A.C. Fisher, 1974, "Environmental Preservation, Uncertainty, and Irreversibility", *Quarterly Journal of Economics*, 88(1), pp. 312–19.

Black, F. and M. Scholes, 1973, "The Pricing of Options and Corporate Liabilities", *Journal of Political Economy*, (81), pp. 637–59.

Brennan, M.J. and E.S. Schwartz, 1985, "Evaluating Natural Resource Investment", *Journal of Business*, 58(2), pp. 135–57.

Brennan, M.J. and L. Trigeorgis, (eds), 1999, *Project Flexibility, Agency, and Competition – New Developments in the Theory and Applications of Real Options*, Oxford University Press, Oxford.

Broadie, M. and P. Glasserman, 1997, "Pricing American-Style Securities Using Simulation", *Journal of Economic Dynamics and Control*, 21(8-9), pp. 1323–52.

Capozza, D.R. and Y. Li, 1994, "The Intensity and Timing of Investment: The Case of Land", *American Economic Review*, 84(4), pp. 889–904.

Corman, L., 1997, "To Wait or Not To Wait?", *CFO Magazine*, 13(5), pp. 91–4.

Cortazar, G. and E.S. Schwartz, 1998, "Monte Carlo Evaluation Model of an Undeveloped Oil Field", *Journal of Energy Finance & Development*, 3(1), pp. 73–84.

Coy, P., 1999, "Exploiting Uncertainty", *Business Week*, US Ed., June 7, pp. 118–24.

Dixit, A.K., 1989, "Entry and Exit Decisions under Uncertainty", *Journal of Political Economy*, 97(3), pp. 620–38.

Dixit, A.K., 1992, "Investment and Hysteresis", *Journal of Economic Perspectives*, 6(1), pp. 107–32.

Dixit, A.K. and R.S. Pindyck, 1994, *Investment under Uncertainty*, Princeton University Press, Princeton, New Jersey.

Ekern, S., 1988, "An Option Pricing Approach to Evaluating Petroleum Projects", *Energy Economics*, April, pp. 91–9.

Faulkner, T.W., 1996, "Applying 'Options Thinking' to R & D Valuation", *Research Technology Management*, May–June, pp. 50–6.

Grenadier, S.R., 1999, "Information Revelation Through Option Exercise", *The Review of Financial Studies*, 12(1), pp. 95–129.

Grenadier, S.R., 1996, "Strategic Exercise of Options: Development Cascades and Overbuilding in Real Estate Markets", *Journal of Finance*, 51(5), pp. 1653–79.

Henry, C., 1974a, "Investments Decisions under Uncertainty: The Irreversibility Effect", *American Economic Review*, 64(6), pp. 1006–12.

Henry, C., 1974b, "Option Values in the Economics of Irreplaceable Assets", *Review of Economic Studies* (Symposium Issue), pp. 89–104.

Ibáñez, A. and F. Zapatero, 1999, "Monte Carlo Valuation of American Options Through Computation of the Optimal Exercise Frontier", working paper, Instituto Tecnológico Autónomo de México & University of Southern California.

Ingersoll Jr., J.E. and S.A. Ross, 1992, "Waiting to Invest: Investment and Uncertainty", *Journal of Business*, 65(1), pp. 1–29.

Kaslow, T. and R.S. Pindyck, 1994, "Valuing Flexibility in Utility Planning", *The Electricity Journal*, 7, pp. 60–5.

Kemna, A.G.Z., 1993, "Case Studies on Real Options", *Financial Management*, Autumn, pp. 259–70.

Kester, W.C., 1984, "Today's Options for Tomorrow's Growth", *Harvard Business Review*, (62), March–April, pp. 153–60.

Kogut, B. and N. Kulatilaka, 1994, "Options Thinking and Platform Investments: Investing in Opportunity", *California Management Review*, Winter, pp. 52–71.

Kulatilaka, N. and S. Marks, 1988, "The Strategic Value of Flexibility: Reducing the Ability to Compromise", *American Economic Review*, pp. 574–80.

Kulatilaka, N. and E.C. Perotti, 1997, "Strategic Growth Options", *Management Science*, 44(8), pp. 1021–31.

Lambrecht, B. and W. Perraudin, 1996, "Real Options and Pre-emption", working paper, Cambridge University and Birkbeck College, London and CEPR.

Lambrecht, B. and W. Perraudin, 1994, "Option Games", working paper, Cambridge University and CEPR (UK), August.

Laughton, D.G., 1998, "The Management of Flexibility in the Upstream Petroleum Industry", *Energy Journal*, 19(1), pp. 83–114.

Leahy, J.V., 1993, "Investment in Competitive Equilibrium: The Optimality of Myopic Behavior", *Quarterly Journal of Economics*, pp. 1105–33.

Longstaff, F.A. and E.S. Schwartz, 1998, "Valuing American Options By Simulation: A Simple Least-Square Approach", working paper 25–98, UCLA, November.

Lund, D. and B. Øksendal, (eds), 1991, *Stochastic Models and Options Values*, New York: North-Holland.

Maeland, J., 1999, "Valuation of Irreversible Investment and Agency Problems", paper presented at the 3rd Annual International Conference on Real Options, Wassenaar, The Netherlands.

Majd, S. and R.S. Pindyck, 1987, "Time to Build, Option Value, and Investment Decisions", *Journal of Financial Economics*, (18), pp. 7–27.

Mason, S.P. and R.C. Merton, 1985, "The Role of Contingent Claims Analysis in Corporate Finance", *Recent Advances in Corporate Finances*, eds. E. Altman and M. Subrahmanyam, Homewood, IL: Richard D. Irwin, pp. 7–54.

McDonald, R. and D. Siegel, 1986, "The Value of Waiting to Invest", *Quarterly Journal of Economics*, November, pp. 707–27.

Merton, R.C., 1973, "Theory of Rational Option Pricing", *Bell Journal of Economics and Management Science*, (4), pp. 141–83.

Micalizzi, A., 1999, "Timing to Invest and Value of Managerial Flexibility. Schering Plough Case Study", paper presented at the 3rd Annual International Conference on Real Options, The Netherlands.

Micalizzi, A. and L. Trigeorgis, (eds), 1999, *Real Options Applications – Proceedings of the First Milan International Workshop on Real Options*, E.G.E.A., Università Bocconi.

Moel, A. and P. Tufano, 1999, "Bidding for the Antamina Mine: Valuation and Incentives in a Real Options Context", paper presented at the 3rd Annual International Conference on Real Options, Wassenaar, The Netherlands.

Myers, S.C., 1977, "Determinants of Corporate Borrowing", *Journal of Financial Economics*, (5), pp. 147–75.

Nichols, N.A., 1994, "Scientific Management at Merck: An Interview with CFO Judy Lewent", *Harvard Business Review*, January–February, pp. 89–99.

Paddock, J.L., D.R. Siegel and J.L. Smith, 1988, "Option Valuation of Claims on Real Assets: The Case of Offshore Petroleum Leases", *Quarterly Journal of Economics*, August, pp. 479–508.

Pindyck, R.S., 1988, "Irreversible Investment, Capacity Choice, and Value of the Firm", *American Economic Review*, 78(5), pp. 969–85.

Pindyck, R.S., 1993, "Investments of Uncertain Cost", *Journal of Financial Economics*, 34, pp. 53–76.

Quigg, L., 1993, "Empirical Testing of Real Option-Pricing Models", *Journal of Finance*, 48(2), pp. 621–40.

Schwartz, E.S., 1997, "The Stochastic Behavior of Commodity Prices: Implications for Valuation and Hedging", *Journal of Finance*, 52(3), 1997, pp. 923–73.

Sick, G.A., 1989, "Capital Budgeting with Real Options", Salomon Brothers' Monograph Series in Finance & Economics.

Samuelson, P.A., 1965, "Rational Theory of Warrant Price", *Industrial Management Review*, Spring, pp. 13 – 39.

Smit, H.T.J. and L.A. Ankum, 1993, "A Real Options and Game-Theoretic Approach to Corporate Investment Strategy under Competition", *Financial Management*, Autumn, pp. 241–50.

Smith, J.E. and R.F. Nau, 1995, "Valuing Risky Projects: Option Pricing Theory and Decision Analysis", *Management Science*, 14(5), pp. 795–816.

Stonier, J.E., 1999, "What Is an Aircraft Purchase Option Worth? Quantifying Asset Flexibility Created through Manufacturer Lead-Time Reductions and Product Commonality", paper presented at the 3rd Annual International Conference on Real Options, The Netherlands; also appeared in *Handbook of Airline Finance*.

Titman, S., 1985, "Urban Land Prices Under Uncertainty", *American Economic Review*, June, pp. 505–14.

Tourinho, O.A.F., 1979, "The Valuation of Reserves of Natural Resources: An Option Pricing Approach", PhD dissertation, November, University of California, Berkeley.

Triantis, A.J. and J.E. Hodder, 1990, "Valuing Flexibility as a Complex Option", *Journal of Finance*, 45(2), pp. 549–65.

Trigeorgis, L., 1996, Real Options – Managerial Flexibility and Strategy in Resource Allocation, MIT Press, Cambridge, Massachusetts.

Trigeorgis, L., (ed) 1995, *Real Options in Capital Investments: Models, Strategies, and Applications*, Praeger Publisher, Westport, Connecticut.

Trigeorgis, L., 1993, "The Nature of Options Interactions and the Valuation of Investments with Multiple Real Options", *Journal of Financial and Quantitative Analysis*, 28(1), pp. 1–20.

Trigeorgis, L. and S.P. Mason, 1987, "Valuing Managerial Flexibility", *Midland Corporate Finance Journal*, Spring, pp.14–21.

Winston, W.L., 1999, *Decision Making Under Uncertainty – with Risk Optimizer*, Palaside Co., Eds.

Index